almanac of modern terrorism

almanac of modern terrorism

JAY M. SHAFRITZ

E. F. GIBBONS, JR.

GREGORY E.J. SCOTT

Facts On File

New York • Oxford • Sydney

Almanac of Modern Terrorism

Facts On File, Inc.
460 Park Avenue South
New York NY 10016
USA

Facts On File Limited
Collins Street
Oxford OX4 1XJ
United Kingdom

Library of Congress Cataloging-in-Publication Data
Shafritz, Jay M.
    Almanac of modern terrorism / by Jay M. Shafritz, E. F. Gibbons,
Jr., Gregory E. J. Scott.
        p.   cm.
    Includes bibliographical references and index.
    ISBN 0-8160-2123-6
    1. Terrorism—Handbooks, manuals, etc.   I. Gibbons, E. F.
II. Scott, Gregory E. J.   III. Title.
HV6431.S465   1991
909.82—dc20   90-21005

British CIP data available on request from Facts On File.

Facts On File books are available at special discounts when purchased in bulk quantities for businesses, associations, institutions or sales promotions. Please contact the Special Sales Department of our New York office at 212/683-2244 (dial 800/322-8755 except in NY, AK or HI).

Text design by Ron Monteleone
Jacket design by Mary McKenna Ridge
Composition by the Maple-Vail Book Manufacturing Group
Manufactured by R. R. Donnelly & Sons, Inc.
Printed in the United States of America

10 9 8 7 6 5 4 3 2 1

This book is printed on acid-free paper.

CONTENTS

INTRODUCTION

Much of modern terrorism is made possible by the existence of the modern mass media. It is essentially what the 19th-century French writer Paul Brouss first called "propaganda by deed" and what American historian Daniel Boorstin would call a "pseudoevent"—one that could not take place were it not for the potential of media coverage. Thus a major goal of the modern terrorist organization is to commit crimes so despicable that they engender maximum publicity. The crime itself is seldom as important as the attention it gets. U.S. Senator John Glenn was correct when he asserted that "international publicity is the mother's milk of terrorism."

To get publicity for whatever political cause they espouse, terrorists commit acts that are seen by some as heinous, such as murdering and maiming innocent people. Those sympathetic to the terrorists' cause, however, may regard the terrorists as freedom fighters who have been forced to take unfortunate but necessary actions. The problem of definition is universal. Because many governments and other less formal groups use terrorism in their own interests, they will not be bound by clear definitions of what actions constitute terrorism. Yet definitions abound. Beginning in the 1970s, a new intellectual industry has emerged based on producing books and articles, by scholars and journalists alike, on the nature, scope and definition of the face of modern terrorism. All this effort has resulted in no agreement or conclusion.

Into this morass of definitional confusion, we insert this book. We have tried to provide those who deal with terrorism with a ready source of factual and generally accepted information about the subject. The almanac has five sections:

(1) A chronology of the most seminal terrorist incidents and milestones since World War II. A listing of *every* incident worldwide would require thousands of pages, so we limited ourselves to events that we thought readers might expect to find—events that were highly publicized when they occurred. For each word or name printed in small capital letters in the Chronology, an entry containing additional or related information can be found in the section called "Terrorism A to Z." While this Almanac deals with modern terrorism, we started the chronology at the end of World War II in 1945 to better place events in historical perspective.

(2) "Terrorism A to Z," an encyclopedic compilation of individuals, organizations and events popularly associated with terrorism, arranged in alphabetical order. The section contains descriptions and analyses of the world's major terrorist movements as well as their leaders and martyrs. Also included are important historical incidents or theorists that influenced modern terrorism; descriptions of weapons, tactics and key concepts; and expanded accounts of important terrorist events given only brief coverage in the chronology.

(3) A sampling of statements made by various political figures and analysts on terrorism today.

(4) A chronologically organized selection of definitions of terrorism.

(5) A bibliography. While many A-to-Z entries contain bibliographic references, this general bibliography contains the items we most recommend for further reading.

Every effort has been made to maintain objectivity and accuracy. We have been necessarily reliant upon secondary sources. All research was done at university libraries, especially at the University of Pittsburgh, and at federal government agencies. We have interviewed no terrorists. None of the authors has ever met a terrorist or has any desire to do so. We have made liberal use of published research by the U.S. Departments of Defense and State, the Federal Bureau of Investigation and the Central Intelligence Agency. All of this information is available to the public. We had no inside source. We publicly thank the legions of anonymous federal officials who produced so many useful public-domain materials.

DEFINITIONS OF TERRORISM

It is far easier to disparage scholarly (and less-than-scholarly) attempts to define the term terrorism than to embrace any one of the many attempts to do so—or to construct a definition of one's own. A growing number of commentators argue that the failure to reach a clear definition is proof that the term itself is too problematic to use in any truly meaningful context. Christopher Hitchens, in an article in *Harper's* magazine called "Wanton Acts of Usage" (September 1986), argues that no definition or usage of "terrorism" and "terrorist" can avoid being either tautological, vacuous, clichéd or chauvinistic (meaning uncritically patriotic). Hitchens proposes conventional usage of less tainted and more specific terminology to describe perpetrators of the various violent acts that are lumped more or less indiscriminately under the umbrella label of terrorism. In pleading for the acceptance of terms such as guerrilla, kidnapper, hijacker, assassin and anarchist, Hitchens wonders, "How can a word with no meaning and no definition . . . have become the political and media buzzword of the eighties?" Of course, the term does have meaning—both in a historical context, and as a result of its more recent emergence as a "buzzword." The very level of popularity and usage of "terrorism" and "terrorist" makes them the terms with which we must grapple.

It seems to be generally accepted that these terms date back to the 1793–94 rule of the Jacobins in revolutionary France. They used the words to denote their "reign of terror," during which more than 17,000 citizens were officially executed and many thousands more perished under less formal and less official circumstances. Later the words acquired the sting of reprobation, signifying criminal and unacceptable forms of political violence. The recriminatory nature of the terms "terrorism" and "terrorist" has not only survived to the present day, but has been enhanced in recent years as the usage of the terms has increased.

It is unlikely that any definition will ever be generally agreed upon. The U.S. government, which has shown little hesitation to apply the term, has yet to put forth an official definition. Just as the branding of an act as terrorism is a subjective act, a moral judgment grounded in cultural and political mores, so is the act of defining terrorism. All peoples tend to reserve the label "terrorism" for politically motivated violence that they find unacceptable.

Formal efforts to define terrorism often end in exhaustion. However, applying explicit criteria and the clear acknowledgment of value judgments seems to offer the most hopeful and the most honest means of facing the definitional difficulties inherent in any discussion of the term. Thus the U.S. Vice President's Task Force on Combatting Terrorism concluded in 1986 that terrorism is "a phenomenon that is easier to describe than define." One is reminded of Associate Justice Potter Stewart of the U.S. Supreme Court, who sought to deal with the definitional problem posed by pornography by asserting that he could not define it, but knew it when he saw it.

PRE-MODERN TERRORISM

While the terms "terrorism" and "terrorist" apparently only date back to 18th-century France, incidence of what is now popularly labeled "terrorism" undoubtedly stretch far beyond documented political history. Terrorism, in one form or another, has been practiced by discontents of one stripe or another in every society. For instance, a strong strain of regicide and tyrannicide has coursed through political history (although this sort of terrorism has sometimes found widespread approval and justification in Western thought).

Some authors have attempted to draw similar parallels between modern events and historical precedent by citing the 13th-century Islamic Assassins as forerunners of modern terrorists. Their name is derived from the word "hashish," and the Assassins are said to have partaken of the drug before embarking on "blessed" ritual stabbings of political enemies. The Assassins provide a fascinating and convenient historical touchstone for those of us who are all too familiar with "holy" attacks by Islamic extremists. While tracing the antecedents of modern terrorism back to Palestine and Persia is an interesting exercise, such efforts run the risk of reinforcing the perception of terrorism as a phenomenon undertaken largely by crazed fanatics in Middle Eastern hotbeds of political intrigue. This is a misguided perception.

It is to left-wing movements in mid to late 19th-century Russia that we can more accurately trace the roots of modern terrorism. The Russian revolutionary group Norodnaya Volya ("The Will of the People") is in many ways the prototype of many 20th-century movements. In its brief but eventful violent struggle with tsarist authorities in the late 1870s and 1880s, this organization assassinated several government and police officials of the highest rank. After several highly publicized unsuccessful attempts, the group ultimately assassinated Tsar Alexander II himself in 1881, before Russian police forces brought Norodnaya Volya's bloody campaign to a close later that same year.

The violence of Norodnaya Volya was the organized response of intellectual revolutionaries to the autocratic repression of the tsarist regime. Its importance in the history of terrorism, as documented by Walter Laqueur in *Terrorism* (1977) and others, lies chiefly in the group's systematic pursuit of its goals, which were inextricably tied to the rising European expectations of democracy and nationalism. Members of the group have been termed "liberals with bombs," for they yearned for constitutional democracy with guaranteed civil liberties and political rights. Terrorism was considered by Norodnaya Volya to be a cost-effective, humanitarian approach to the Russian political dilemma. Their violence was confined strictly to those whom the group considered to be the foremost culprits of autocracy. The group believed that the social and political upheavals which could be precipitated through well-placed violent strikes would save lives in the long run, for Norodnaya Volya was certain of the inevitability of revolution in Russia.

At the turn of the century a successor organization to Norodnaya Volya, the Social Revolutionary Party, made itself heard in Russian political events. While more avowedly leftist than their predecessors, the Social Revolutionaries also sought to further their agenda through assassinations of high-ranking officials. Through their terrorist arm Boevaya Organisatia ("Fighting Organization") they announced their arrival in 1902 with the assassinations of the minister of the interior and two tsarist governors. In 1904 they were responsible for the assassination of yet another minister of the interior.

The Social Revolutionaries were committed to the necessity of "propaganda by deed," which they considered vastly more effective than propaganda through words. Like Norodnaya Volya, they found their violence to be quite rational and sought to introduce chaos into Russian political life, thinking it would eventually bring down the regime. The examples set by Russian revolutionaries had considerable influence among the political discontent of later years and were a major inspiration for political terrorists in Armenia, the Balkans, India and elsewhere.

The impact of the violent Russian left on the phenomenon of terrorism far exceeded that of the European anarchists of the late 19th and early 20th centuries. While anarchists were responsible for many bombing incidents and a number of important assassinations of political leaders, including U.S. president William McKinley in 1901 and King Umberto of Italy in 1900, these acts were carried out by isolated individuals. Anarchist violence lacked the systematic nature of the violence of the Russian revolutionaries—contrary to the widespread rumors of a well-organized, international anarchist conspiracy.

Organized political terrorism was, however, waged in several nationalist-separatist struggles which began in the late 19th century and extended into the 20th century. The best known to Western readers is the struggle of the Irish Fenians, who staged a campaign of violence against the English in the 1870s and 1880s and then again in the years preceding and during World War I. Armenian activists led attacks against their Turkish oppressors in the last years of the 19th century, only to be brutally repressed and massacred. Macedonians belonging to the Inner Macedonian Revolutionary Organization (IMRO) also carried out strikes against a succession of "occupation" governments.

It is important to note that many of the violently nationalist organizations of the 20th century have not been leftist groups. After World War I, right-wing terrorism became the dominant brand, especially as found in fascist movements in Italy, Germany and Croatia. During the early years of this century, the Black Hundreds, a reactionary Russian group organized by members of the tsar's secret police, was responsible for pogroms and other anti-Semitic atrocities.

Several common threads ran between the nationalist-ethnic terrorism of the left and the right: belief in propaganda by deed; conviction that any change in the political and social status quo would be an improvement; contempt for liberal democracy; and confidence in their historic role as the harbingers of political change.

Systematic terrorism arose in the Middle East in the 1930s and 1940s with the fundamentalist Muslim Brotherhood in Egypt, and Irgun and LEHI battling the British in Palestine. Anti-colonial terrorism also was waged against the British Empire in Cyprus and Aden and against the French in Algeria by the FLN.

MODERN TERRORISM

If political terrorism can be viewed historically, why then do so many contemporary commentators, scholars and political figures decry today's terrorism as a uniquely modern phenomenon, foisted upon Western societies by newly minted fanatics and ideologues whose ruthless tactics threaten the fabric of civilization?

This lack of a historical perspective has several explanations:

- a lack of historical awareness;
- a calculated desire to portray contemporary terrorism as a new phenomenon in order to achieve certain political, social or economic objectives; or
- a reasoned belief that modern terrorism actually is unique.

While this third possibility is at best arguable, there are certain characteristics of contemporary terrorism that stand in marked contrast to earlier instances of political violence. The modern age of terrorism, which is commonly dated from the mid-1960s, is more than simply an extension of historical-

political violence. It can be differentiated from terrorism of the past in several ways:

- modern terrorism is left-wing to a greater degree than ever before;
- the modern print and broadcast media have brought terrorist incidents and actors to the forefront of world events;
- modern communications, transportation, and weapons technology have vastly aided the causes of terrorists and have contributed to the more international nature of modern terrorism;
- nations have become in several instances intimately involved with terrorist organizations, and terrorism has in some cases taken on the character of "war by proxy"; and
- the constitutional principles of the liberal democracies hamper military options for combatting terrorism, as well as surveillance activities, in ways that did not restrain nations of the past.

The generally accepted dating of the "modern age" of terrorism from the 1960s is the result of two seemingly separate events. The first of these was the failure of the European and North American New Left, and the terrorism that ensued when a tiny minority of the failed student movements opted to carry on their revolutionary struggle through violent means. The second was the emergence, or the rekindling, of a number of nationalist/separatist movements in Ireland, Spain, the Middle East and Asia.

In order to better grasp the sweep of terrorism today, it is useful to categorize the groups popularly referred to as terrorist organizations. Many authors have presented such groupings, with varying degrees of success and validity. But every effort to categorize the groups which we call terrorist is problematic, for there are usually no clear lines of demarcation between conventional categories; there has been widespread disagreement among experts on the subject of groupings. We suggest five basic categories:

Nationalist–Separatist groups. These organizations carry on a struggle against what they consider to be foreign occupation of an ethnic and/or national homeland. This includes such groups as the Irish Republican Army; the Basque ETA; the Kurdish People's Party; the Moro National Liberation Front; the various Palestinian nationalist groups such as the Palestine Liberation Organization and the Abu Nidal Organization; and Sikh terrorists attempting to forge an independent state of Khalistan in northern India.

Anarcho–Communist groups. This category includes the violent residue of the 1960s student New Left movements in North America, Europe and Japan, including the Italian Red Brigades, the German Red Army Faction, the Belgian Communist Combatant Cells, the Japanese Red Army, and the Weather Underground in the United States. They seek through acts of terrorism to inspire repressive reactions by the liberal democracies, hoping that the reactions will in turn foment a popular revolution that will destroy the foundations of Western capitalism. The ambitious goal of these groups is the building of a new communist society. Urban guerrilla warfare has often been their modus operandi.

"Traditional" guerrilla groups. This broad category includes insurgencies of both the right and left, struggling to unseat established governments through tactics which many commentators consider terroristic. Latin American groups comprise much of this category and include the M-19 in Columbia, the FMLN in El Salvador, and the Peruvian Sendero Luminoso. The African National Congress and the Nicaraguan contras also have been grouped under this heading.

Right-wing extremism. This category includes both right-wing responses to left-wing activity as well as racist, supremacist violence. The Argentine AAA, the right-wing death squads of El Salvador, the Turkish Grey Wolves, the American Ku Klux Klan, the German Hoffman Sports Group, the Italian Avanguardia Nazionale, and the Israeli Gush Emunim present examples of this widely varied grouping.

Islamic fundamentalist extremism. This category includes the recently emerged Shi'ite fundamentalist organizations such as Hezbollah, Islamic Jihad, and Dawa, as well as the long-standing Muslim Brotherhood.

It is readily apparent that a case may be made for including some groups in different categories, or for constructing other conceptual groupings. For instance, one might argue for the inclusion of Sikh and fundamentalist-Hebrew terrorism with Shi'ite organizations in a grouping of religious-fundamentalist terrorism. However, it would seem that the agendas of the Sikhs and right-wing Hebrew groups such as Gush Emunim are far more nationalistic and political in spirit than is the agenda of the Shi'ites. The Islamic terrorism movement is first and foremost a religious mission and is less concerned with national borders than with the global spread of the faith of Islam. The Shi'ite terrorists consider themselves to be quite literally in a state of war against the non-Shi'ite world, and the unique quality of this resurgence of Islamic violence seems to warrant its own category.

STATE-SPONSORED AND STATE TERRORISM

As noted previously, another distinguishing characteristic of modern terrorism has been the increasing role of national governments in the activities of terrorist organizations. In effect, several nations have found that state sponsorship of shadowy terrorist organizations provides a very effective vehicle for clandestine pursuit of violent state objectives, with minimal expense and a great deal of deniability. Certain nations have employed terrorist organizations to a degree that may be considered war-by-proxy. Syria's utilization of Palestinian organizations such as the Popular Front for the Liberation of Palestine, Iran's influence over Lebanese Shi'ite groups such as Hezbollah, and Libya's sponsorship of the Abu Nidal Organization and other groups are perhaps the foremost examples of this troubling phenomenon. Government-supported terrorism, while rare, was not unknown before the present day. For example, suspected international involvement in the 1934 assassinations of both King Alexander I of Greece and French Foreign Minister Jean-Louis Barthou in Marseilles spurred a League of Nations conference on terrorism. Nonetheless, despite such historical precedent, prevalent state sponsorship of extra-national terrorist organizations is primarily a modern phenomenon.

In discussions of state-sponsored terrorism, however, caution must be urged. Sponsorship is not control, and inspiration is not sponsorship. All too frequently, widely recognized authorities on terrorism have depicted indirect and often tenuous relationships between nations and terrorist organizations as direct, hierarchical linkages. In the early 1980s, a flurry of writings appeared which characterized the Soviet Union as the control center of an intricate network of left-wing terrorist organizations that took their marching orders from Moscow. Not only did these books become instantly accepted into the "mainstream" of the literature of terrorism, but these ill-conceived schematics of Soviet terrorism took firm root in the highest reaches of the Reagan admin-

istration. It is no more reasonable to draw direct links between, for instance, Euroterrorist groups such as the Red Army Faction and the Kremlin, than it is reasonable to connect the actions of Hebrew fundamentalist terrorists in the West Bank with the U.S. Government.

Similarly, terrorism "experts" have often claimed that Teheran controls Hezbollah. While the revolutionary Shi'ite government of Iran holds substantial sway with the group and has provided it with resources of various kinds, Iran's role with Hezbollah has primarily been as inspiration to a fiercely independent entity. Indeed, it is difficult to ascertain whether anyone truly controls Hezbollah, which is a distinctly non-Western, unstructured conglomeration of violent extremists.

State terrorism, as differentiated from state-sponsored terrorism, is terrorism actually perpetrated by a recognized nation against its own citizens. In may respects, it may be a misnomer to use the word terrorism to describe the terror of the state, which may take the form of repression, torture, murder and even genocide. Comparing the terrorism of small groups with the terrorism of national security organizations is a classic case of comparing apples and oranges. Some writers have simply opted not to use the term "state terrorism" in reference to the terror of the state. However, a persuasive case may be made for its usage: If the actions of nations are excluded from discussions and writings on terrorism, then by far the largest component of the world's illicit and immoral political violence is arbitrarily ignored. In recent years, the boundaries between state terror and the terrorism of small groups has become increasingly blurred. This is especially true in the case of Latin American regimes which have been implicated in the terrorist activities of right-wing death squads.

While the terms have at times been used interchangeably, we will use state-sponsored terrorism to refer to the direct sponsorship of extra-national terrorist organizations by established nations, and state terrorism to refer to the terrorist actions of a nation itself.

CONCLUSION

In offering a resource book for those who seek information about an amorphous but seemingly omnipresent topic, we can only offer what some may consider frivolous advice (especially under a subheading entitled Conclusion): be cautious in your conclusions. The conventional wisdom regarding terrorism is not to be taken at face value. Even instances of violence which have been universally decried as terrorist acts by government, the media, and the general public often warrant careful scrutiny. For instance, was the bombing of the U.S. Marine barracks in Beirut in 1983 by a Shi'ite suicide bomber a terrorist act? That question has never truly been raised in a popular dialogue in the United States. Many readers are undoubtedly shocked to even consider such a question, for it tugs at our collective, national and patriotic heart-strings.

Yet, upon closer examination, the basis for the question becomes more understandable. Were not the U.S. Marines viewed (not without reason) by Shi'ite forces as a foreign military presence intervening in a bitterly fought civil war, and on the side of the Maronite Christian enemy? Had not the USS *New Jersey* shelled the Muslim civilian quarter of West Beirut? Could not the bombing of the Marine barracks be viewed as an act of war, rather than a terrorist act? The Shi'ites had openly declared war in Leba-

non, and it is difficult to substantiate a position that denies that the United States had interjected its Marines into the front line of a war. The only truly debatable question is whether the Marines were combatants in that war, or whether they were indeed "peacekeepers"—though finding the peace which was to be kept seems a daunting task at best. The Shi'ites, obviously and not surprisingly, saw the U.S. Marine barracks as the headquarters of a heavily armed, foreign enemy force and as an overt symbol of Western interference in their political, cultural and religious affairs.

After examining the evidence, a reader may very well find that his or her view of the barracks bombing as a terrorist act is secure. This exercise, of course, is simply meant to emphasize the subjective nature of the topic of terrorism—and the pitfalls that beset any topic so subjective. The perils of muddled or partisan thinking about terrorism often have consequences as dire in both the domestic and international political arenas as actual acts of terrorism themselves.

The scourge of terrorism is not to be denied, for it poses a real if generally overstated threat to the fabric of Western democratic society. But its menace also lies in overreaction to the threat. The label of "terrorism" is more and more commonly used as a battle cry to pursue state policies of force euphemistically referred to as counterterrorism. We need to maintain clarity of thought and honesty of objectives when dealing with the specter of terrorism, if we are not to compromise and even irreversibly mar the great principles which we profess to be protecting from the brutal tactics of terrorists. After all, we do not want the cure to be worse than the disease.

Part I

chronology of terrorism: 1946–90

1946

January 7
Germany. NAZI sympathizers murdered two U.S. occupation officials in Passau, in the U.S. Zone.

July 22
Palestine. IRGUN, the Jewish terrorist organization led by Menachem BEGIN, blew up the King David Hotel in Jerusalem, killing 91 people. The crime was ostensibly directed at British government offices in the hotel. However, in addition to 28 British deaths, 17 Jews and 46 other non-British innocents were killed. The hotel had been warned of the attack shortly beforehand but had not taken the threat seriously.

1947

February 10
Italy. British General R.W.M. De Winten was shot to death by a female Italian nationalist seeking revenge for the ceding of the city of Pola, and other Italian territory east of Trieste, to Yugoslavia as part of the postwar settlement.

July 30
Palestine. Jewish terrorists murdered two British soldiers and then booby-trapped their bodies. Many incidents of this type took place in an attempt to pressure the British government into turning over its Palestinian Mandate to the Jewish settlers.

December 25
Sweden. An Italian FASCIST stabbed to death Alberto Bellardi Ricci, an Italian diplomat.

1948

January 30
India. Mohandas K. Gandhi (known as Mahatma Gandhi), the Indian nationalist and advocate of nonviolence, was murdered by a Hindu militant enraged by his willingness to accept the partition of the Indian subcontinent and his tolerance of India's Muslim minority. Gandhi was but one of an estimated 750,000 Indians who were killed in the sectarian violence that racked the former British territory between the end of World War II and the creation, in 1948, of the independent nations of India and Pakistan.

April 9
Palestine. At the Arab village of DEIR YASSIN (near Jerusalem, in what was then the Arab portion of Palestine as alotted by the UN in 1947) two Jewish terrorist organizations, Lehi and IRGUN, slaughtered more than two hundred Arab men, women and children. This and other terrorist attacks were among the factors that ultimately drove many Palestinian Arabs out of the region that comprises present-day ISRAEL.

September 17
Israel. Count Folke BERNADOTTE of Sweden and French Colonel André Serot were murdered in Jerusalem by three members of the infamous STERN GANG of Jewish terrorists. The Count was killed because of his role as United Nations mediator between Israel and the Arabs.

December 28
Egypt. Prime Minister of Egypt Mahmoud Fahmy el-Nokrashy Pasha was assassinated by a member of the MUSLIM BROTHERHOOD, an extremist group angered by Egypt's inability to prevail in its war with Israel.

1949

February 13
Egypt. The leader of the ultra-nationalist MUSLIM BROTHERHOOD, SHEIKH HASSAN AL-BANNA, was assassinated in Cairo.

December 3
Malaysia. The British colonial governor, Duncan Stewart, was mortally wounded by Malay nationalists. He died of his wounds a week later.

1950

November 1
United States. Puerto Rican nationalists engaged in a gun battle with security personnel outside Blair House, across the street from the White House, during a failed attempt to assassinate President Harry S. Truman.

1951

March 20
Philippines. John Hardie, an American citizen, and his wife were murdered at their farm outside Manila by the HUKS.

July 20
Trans-Jordan. While visiting the tomb of his father, King ABDULLAH I of Jordan was shot and killed by a lone Palestinian gunman.

October 25
Philippines. The HUKS killed two Americans near Olongapo.

1952

December 5
Tunisia. RED HAND, the terrorist organization sponsored by pro-French colonists in North Africa, assassinated Farhat Hached, a leader of the Tunisian Labor Federation.

1954

March 1
United States. Four Puerto Rican nationalists seated in the visitor's gallery of the House of Representatives opened fire on the Congressmen in the chamber. Five Representatives were wounded in the attack and all four terrorists were captured alive by security personnel.

1955

August 20
Algeria. The FLN, already one of the most bloodthirsty of terrorist groups, began the wholesale slaughter of Europeans in North Africa. On this date the FLN carried out the Philippeville massacre, in which they murdered and then mutilated 37 men, women and children.

1956

March 15
Algeria. The OAS burst into a social center, removed six men, and shot them outside the building.

October 21–22
Algeria. Saadi Yacef's network of FLN assassins murdered 49 people over a two-day period.

1958

November 28
Cyprus. Cypriot nationalists killed two British soldiers outside an off-duty club in Nicosia.

1959

August 31
Spain. On this date, which happens to be the feast day of the Basque Saint Ignatius of Loyola, the "Basque Fatherland and Liberty" movement (ETA) was founded by a group of Basque separatists.

1960

March 20
South Africa. Police killed 69 blacks, among them many women and children, when they opened fire on civil rights demonstrators. The attack became known as the SHARPE-VILLE INCIDENT, after the township in which it took place, and led to the abandonment of the policy of nonviolence by the AFRICAN NATIONAL CONGRESS.

October 8
Algeria. An FLN terrorist threw a hand grenade into a crowded sidewalk cafe, killing one person and injuring 16, including five French soldiers.

1961

September 18
Rhodesia. A mysterious plane crash took the life of Dag Hammarskjold, the Swedish-born secretary general of the United Nations. Hammarskjold was on his way to mediate in talks between warring factions in the Congo.

1962

January 25
France. The homes of 14 well known Frenchmen were bombed by the OAS. There were no casualties.

1963

November 27
Venezuela. FALN kidnapped a U.S. Army military attaché and demanded that 70 political prisoners be released as ransom. The government released the prisoners and the American was let go.

1964

September 10
Uruguay. The home of the Brazilian ambassador was bombed by the TUPAMAROS.

1965

May 6
Uruguay. The TUPAMAROS group bombed the offices of two American businesses.

1966

October
United States. Huey Newton and Bobby Seale, black militants, formed the BLACK PANTHERS.

1967

February 27
Ethiopia. The Mobil petroleum terminal in Aseb in the province of Eritrea was heavily damaged by an ERITREAN LIBERATION FRONT attack.

October 12
Greece. A British European Airways plane carrying 66 people exploded in midair over the sea near the island of Rhodes. No group claimed responsibility.

1968

July 28
Italy. Three members of the POPULAR FRONT FOR THE LIBERATION OF PALESTINE-GENERAL COMMAND (PFLP-GC) hijacked an Israeli EL AL airline flight en route from Rome to Tel Aviv, forcing it to land at Dar al-Bayda Airport in Algiers. Once in Algeria, the terrorists released the 23 non-Israelis from among their 48 hostages. Not until Septem-

ber 1 were the remaining hostages released in exchange for 16 Arabs held in Israeli jails.

August 28

Guatemala. U.S. Ambassador to Guatemala John Gordon Mein was shot and killed on a Guatemala City street by members of the Rebel Armed Forces (FAR), a faction of the GUATEMALAN NATIONAL REVOLUTIONARY UNITY group.

October 10

Brazil. A U.S. Army captain was assassinated by two gunmen in Sao Paulo.

November 22

Israel. A car bomb exploded in the Jewish sector of Jerusalem, killing 12 people.

December 26

Greece. One passenger was killed when two Palestinians, brandishing hand grenades and pistols, attacked an EL AL jetliner at the Athens airport.

December 28

Lebanon. Israeli commandos attacked the Beirut International Airport, destroying 13 commercial airliners belonging to three Arab carriers.

1969

February 18

Switzerland. PFLP-GC terrorists firing machine guns wounded six passengers and crew members of an EL AL jet as it prepared to take off from Zurich.

May 30

Israel. The POPULAR FRONT FOR THE LIBERATION OF PALESTINE (PFLP) blew up a section of the Aramco Trans-Arabian pipeline in the Golan Heights.

June 20

Uruguay. TUPAMAROS guerrillas claimed responsibility for an arson fire which de-

stroyed the Montevideo offices of General Motors Corporation.

July 18

United Kingdom. Marks and Spencer, a Jewish-owned London department store, was bombed by Palestinian terrorists.

July 29

Italy. TWA Flight 840, en route from Rome to Tel Aviv, was hijacked by two members of the POPULAR FRONT FOR THE LIBERATION OF PALESTINE who ordered the plane flown to Damascus, where it was later destroyed. Although the hijackers released the passengers unharmed, Syria detained six Israelis. They were held until December 5, when the International Red Cross facilitated their release in exchange for 13 Syrians and 58 Eygptians held in Israeli prisons.

August 29

Syria. Once again, a TWA jetliner was hijacked and diverted to Damascus, this time by the PFLP-GC. After evacuating the passengers and crew, the terrorists used explosives to destroy the aircraft.

September 4

Brazil. The U.S. Ambassador to Brazil, Charles Elbrick, was abducted in Rio de Janeiro. The ambassador was freed after authorities met the terrorists' demand for the release of 15 prisoners being held in Mexican jails.

October

Argentina. During the month, bomb attacks were directed against a number of U.S. multinational corporations, including Pepsi-Cola, IBM and General Electric.

November 4

Brazil. CARLOS MARIGHELLA, an urban guerrilla leader, was killed during a gun battle with police in San Paulo.

December 12

Italy. Sixteen people were killed and more than 90 injured when a bomb was detonated in the National Bank of Agriculture in Milan.

December 17

Guatemala. Right-wing politician David Guerra Guzman was assassinated, in Guatemala City, by leftist gunmen.

1970

February 10

West Germany. The Munich Airport was the site of a hand grenade attack by members of the Executive Committee for the Liberation of Palestine (ECLP) in which one passenger was killed. One terrorist was wounded and three more were captured.

February 21

Switzerland. All 47 people aboard were killed when Swissair Flight 330 exploded in midair and crashed shortly after takeoff from Geneva. AHMED JABRIL's terror organization, the POPULAR FRONT FOR THE LIBERATION OF PALESTINE-GENERAL COMMAND, claimed responsibility for the destruction of the Tel Aviv-bound plane.

March

Ethiopia. The ERITREAN LIBERATION FRONT abducted five members of a National Geographic Society expedition. No demands were ever made and the captives were released two and a half weeks later, unharmed.

March 31

Japan. Nine members of the JAPANESE RED ARMY, led by Kozo Okamoto, hijacked a Japan Air Lines flight en route from Tokyo to Kukuoka. They demanded to be flown to P'yongyang, capital of North Korea.

March 31

Guatemala. West Germany's ambassador to Guatemala, Count Karl von Spreti, was kidnapped from his home in the capital. He was found dead of a gunshot wound to the head on April 4, 1970.

April 12

Uruguay. Police intelligence director Hector Moran Charquero was killed by TUPAMAROS gunmen.

May 29

Argentina. Former provisional president of Argentina, Pedro Eugenio Aramburo, was kidnapped by leftist guerrillas, who announced his execution on July 1, 1970.

June 10

Jordan. U.S. embassy attaché Army Major Robert P. Perry was murdered at his Amman home by PALESTINE LIBERATION ORGANIZATION (PLO) assassins.

June 24

Canada. One woman employee was killed when the FRONT DE LIBERATION DU QUEBEC (FLQ) exploded a bomb at the Defense Ministry in Ottawa.

July 21

Bolivia. Members of EJERCITO DE LIBERACION NACIONAL (ELN) abducted two West German engineers. Their demand that the government release a number of imprisoned guerrillas was met, and the hostages were freed on July 23.

July 22

Lebanon. An Olympic Airways flight was hijacked by five members of the POPULAR STRUGGLE FRONT as it flew from Beirut to Athens. After lengthy negotiations involving the International Red Cross, the incident was ended on August 12 with the release of seven Palestinians held in Greek jails.

July 31

Uruguay. TUPAMAROS guerrillas seized American official Daniel A. Mitrione and Aloisio Gomide, a Brazilian diplomat. Mitrione was found dead on August 10. Gomide was released in February of the following year after his family met a ransom demand.

August 7

Uruguay. Once again TUPAMAROS kidnapped an American official. After more than 200 days in captivity, during which he suffered a heart attack, the prisoner was released.

September 6

Jordan. Four commercial airliners were hijacked in midair with two being diverted to DAWSON'S FIELD, a World War II British airstrip outside Amman. The third plane landed in Cairo, Egypt, where the hijackers destroyed it on the runway. The seizing of the fourth plane, an El Al jet, was prevented by plainclothes Israeli security guards on board the aircraft. On September 9, a fifth plane was hijacked and joined the first two at Dawson's Field, bringing the total number of hostage air travelers at the field to more than 400. Their hijacker-captors were members of the POPULAR FRONT FOR THE LIBERATION OF PALESTINE (PFLP). The hostage drama dragged on for nearly three weeks before authorities, in negotiations with the PFLP, agreed to release eight Palestinians held in Western jails.

October 5

Canada. Britain's trade commissioner for Quebec, James Cross, was kidnapped by the FRONT DE LIBERATION DU QUEBEC (FLQ), which demanded both money and a prisoner release as ransom. Government officials refused and the terrorists freed Cross on December 3 in exchange for passage to Cuba.

October 10

Canada. FLQ members kidnapped and killed Pierre LaPorte, Quebec's Minister of Labour, reportedly in retaliation for the Canadian government's refusal to meet the demands of the James Cross kidnappers.

December 1

Spain. Eugene Beihl, West German honorary consul, was kidnapped by ETA (Basque Fatherland and Liberty) in a successful attempt to prevent the execution of six Basque separatists by the Franco government.

1971

January 8

Uruguay. The eight-month ordeal of British Ambassador to Uruguay Geoffrey Jackson began when he was kidnapped by TUPAMAROS terrorists. Though the Uruguayan government officially refused to comply with the kidnappers demand for the release of 150 prisoners, Jackson was freed after 106 prisoners "escaped" custody.

January 30

India. Two members of the KASHMIRI LIBERATION FRONT hijacked an Indian Airlines flight to Lahore, Pakistan. The Indian government refused the terrorists' demand for the release of 36 prisoners and the hijackers proceeded with the destruction of the aircraft, injuring themselves in the process.

March 14

Netherlands. One million dollars in damages was caused when five members of AL-FATAH blew up fuel tanks at the Rotterdam docks.

March 1

United States. The U.S. Senate Office Building received heavy damage to one of its wings when a bomb planted by the WEATHER UNDERGROUND exploded inside.

July 20
Italy. Al-FATAH terrorists attacked the office of Alia (Royal Jordanian Airlines) in Rome.

July 24
Egypt. Al-FATAH attacked an Alia plane at the Cairo airport.

September 16
Lebanon. An attempt was made to hijack an Alia plane flying between Beirut and Cairo by a lone al-FATAH terrorist armed with a hand grenade. He was disarmed by a Jordanian security officer aboard the aircraft.

October 20
United States. Members of the Soviet delegation to the United Nations, while in their New York apartment, were fired on by riflemen of the JEWISH DEFENSE LEAGUE (JDL).

November 28
Egypt. Jordanian Prime Minister Wasfi el-Tal was assassinated in Cairo by a team of BLACK SEPTEMBER gunmen.

December 4
Northern Ireland. The ULSTER VOLUNTEER FORCE claimed responsibility for a bomb which killed 15 people in a Belfast pub.

December 15
United Kingdom. BLACK SEPTEMBER ambushed and wounded Jordan's ambassador to the United Kingdom, Zaid Rifai, as he drove through London.

1972

January 27
United States. Two New York City police officers were murdered by members of the radical BLACK LIBERATION ARMY.

January 30
Northern Ireland. Thirteen Catholic demonstrators died in the city of Londonderry when British troops fired on a group of protesters. The incident became known as BLOODY SUNDAY.

February 2
Ireland. Angry demonstrators, marching to protest the BLOODY SUNDAY killings, burned down the United Kingdom's embassy in Dublin.

February 6
West Germany. Gunmen from the terrorist group BLACK SEPTEMBER killed five Jordanian workers it claimed were actually Israeli spies.

February 22
India. A Lufthansa 747 en route from New Delhi to Athens, Greece was hijacked by five Palestinians, who diverted the plane to Aden, South Yemen. There the aircraft's crew was held hostage until the West German government paid a $5 million ransom. The hijackers then surrendered to South Yemeni authorities, who, after a payment of $1 million from the ransom monies, released them.

February 22
West Germany. An Esso Oil facility was attacked by members of BLACK SEPTEMBER.

March
United Kingdom. The London residence of King Hussein of Jordan was attacked by a team of BLACK SEPTEMBER terrorists.

May 8
Israel. Four members of BLACK SEPTEMBER hijacked a Sabena airliner, holding it on the ground at Tel Aviv's Lod Airport. The terrorists had hoped to trade their hostages for 317 FEDAYEEN (Arab commandos) being held in Israeli jails, but the Israelis recap-

tured the plane by force. During the brief gun battle two of the hijackers, as well as one of the passengers, were killed.

May 11

West Germany. The RED ARMY FACTION carried out six separate bombing attacks aimed at U.S. Army personnel and a West German Supreme Court justice.

May 30

Israel. Once again the Lod Airport was the scene of terrorist violence as three members of the JAPANESE RED ARMY, operating on behalf of the POPULAR FRONT FOR THE LIBERATION OF PALESTINE, carried out a machine gun attack inside the passenger terminal. The three killers responsible for what became known as the LOD AIRPORT MASSACRE murdered 25 people and wounded 76 others before two of the terrorists died and the third was captured.

June 15

Argentina. An Austral Airlines jet was hijacked by six members of the Ejercito Revolucionario de Pueblo (ERP) who had escaped from Rawson Prison (Argentina). They took the plane to Santiago, Chile where they were granted asylum by Chilean President Salvador Allende.

July 8

Lebanon. Israeli operatives assassinated Ghassan Kanafani, one of the leaders of the POPULAR FRONT FOR THE LIBERATION OF PALESTINE, in reprisal for the LOD AIRPORT MASSACRE of May 30.

July 21

Northern Ireland. The infamous Bloody Friday during which the PROVISIONAL WING OF THE IRISH REPUBLICAN ARMY triggered 22 bombings in the Belfast area that combined to kill 11 and wound more than 100.

September 5

West Germany. The 1972 Summer Olympic Games became the site of what was later known as the MUNICH MASSACRE. Eight BLACK SEPTEMBER terrorists attacked the dormitory of Israeli athletes. Before the lengthy crisis was over, 11 Israeli athletes and coaches had been killed. Though five of the eight BLACK SEPTEMBER terrorists were killed, the three others, who were captured, were freed a few weeks later by the West German authorities as part of the ransom for a Lufthansa hijacking that took place on October 29th.

September 15

Sweden. An SAS airliner was hijacked by Croatian terrorists, who exchanged their hostages for six other Croatians being held in Swedish prisons. The terrorists then ordered the plane flown to Spain, where they surrendered to authorities.

September

Netherlands. During the month BLACK SEPTEMBER terrorists sent letter bombs from Amsterdam to Israel and Israeli missions in Paris, Geneva, Montreal, Vienna, Ottawa, Brussels, Kinshasa, Buenos Aires, Phnom Penh, and Washington, D.C.

October 29

Lebanon. BLACK SEPTEMBER terrorists hijacked a West German Lufthansa flight en route from Beirut to Ankara, Turkey in order to secure the release of the three surviving members of the MUNICH MASSACRE assault team. They were successful, and the hijackers and Munich killers were reunited in Libya, where they were given a hero's reception.

November 8

Ethiopia. Seven students, members of the ERITREAN LIBERATION FRONT (ELF), hijacked an Ethiopian passenger plane en route to Paris. They had hoped to secure the release of jailed ELF comrades, but security guards on board the plane opened fire on the terrorists while the aircraft was still in flight.

Six of the seven hijackers were killed, but not before the plane was seriously damaged by a grenade detonated by one of them. The aircraft was landed safely in Addis Ababa with no fatalities, and only nine injuries, among the plane's 100 passengers.

December
Thailand.   The Israeli Embassy in Bangkok was seized by BLACK SEPTEMBER terrorists, who held six employees hostage for 19 hours before releasing them.

1973

January 26
Spain.   Israeli intelligence officer Baruch Cohen was murdered on a Madrid street by a BLACK SEPTEMBER assassin.

March 1
Sudan.   Eight BLACK SEPTEMBER guerrillas seized the Saudi Arabian Embassy in the capital city of Khartoum during a diplomatic reception. The terrorists demanded the release of the sole surviving terrorist from the LOD AIRPORT MASSACRE (1972), RED ARMY FACTION leaders imprisoned in West Germany, SIRHAN SIRHAN, and others. Their demands were refused, whereupon they murdered American Ambassador Claude Noel, American chargé d'affaires George Curtis Moore and Belgian chargé d'affaires Guy Eid.

March 29
Ireland.   Irish authorities seized the cargo vessel CLAUDIA off the coast of the Republic. On board were found four members of the PROVISIONAL WING OF THE IRISH REPUBLICAN ARMY and a huge quantity of arms and munitions that the PIRA had obtained from LIBYA.

July 20
Libya.   Three hijackers from the POPULAR FRONT FOR THE LIBERATION OF PALESTINE and one from the JAPANESE RED ARMY seized a Japanese airliner en route from Amsterdam to Tokyo. After taking it to Libya, the terrorists destroyed the plane.

August 5
Greece.   Two terrorists from the ARAB NATIONALIST YOUTH ORGANIZATION FOR THE LIBERATION OF PALESTINE (ANYOLP) ambushed a group of TWA passengers as they disembarked from their Tel Aviv flight. Five people were killed and 55 others were wounded.

September
United Kingdom.   During the month the PROVISIONAL WING OF THE IRISH REPUBLICAN ARMY conducted an extensive bombing campaign against targets in the London area.

September 5
Italy.   Police arrested five members of the BLACK SEPTEMBER group and seized two SAM-7 antiaircraft missiles before the terrorists had an opportunity to use the rockets against an EL AL plane as they had planned.

September 28
Austria.   Two Palestinian SA'IQA terrorists attacked a train carrying Soviet Jewish émigrés and took five hostages. They demanded that Austria close its facilities for receiving Jews emigrating from Russia.

November 25
Lebanon.   A KLM 747 in flight from Beirut to New Delhi was hijacked by three members of the ARAB NATIONALIST YOUTH ORGANIZATION FOR THE LIBERATION OF PALESTINE. The hijackers made a series of landings throughout the Mediterranean region before surrendering to police in Dubai. They released their prisoners in exchange for safe passage.

December 17
Italy.   Five Palestinians, members of ARAB NATIONALIST YOUTH ORGANIZATION FOR THE

LIBERATION OF PALESTINE, murdered 33 Pan Am passengers as their plane sat on the ground at Rome's Leonardo da Vinci Airport. The terrorists then hijacked a Lufthansa jet to Kuwait, where they surrendered and were turned over to the PLO.

December 20

Spain. Basque terrorists from ETA assassinated the Spanish Premier, Luis CARRERO BLANCO, in Madrid by detonating a bomb planted beneath his automobile.

December 21

United Kingdom. The IRA bombed the London Hilton Hotel, causing damage but no injuries.

December 31

United Kingdom. The infamous terrorist CARLOS attempted to murder British millionaire Teddy Zeiff, the Jewish owner of the fashionable London store Marks & Spencer. Zeiff was wounded, but he escaped further injury when his assailant's gun malfunctioned.

1974

January 31

Singapore. Members of the JAPANESE RED ARMY and the POPULAR FRONT FOR THE LIBERATION OF PALESTINE jointly attacked Shell Oil's storage facilities and later kidnapped five people, whom they exchanged for safe passage to South Yemen.

February 3

United Kingdom. The PROVISIONAL WING OF THE IRISH REPUBLICAN ARMY bombed a bus carrying British soldiers and their families. Twelve people were killed: nine soldiers, one woman and two children.

February 5

United States. Patricia Hearst was kidnapped by members of the SYMBIONESE LIBERATION ARMY.

March 3

Lebanon. A British Airways flight to London carrying 102 passengers was hijacked by two members of the ARAB NATIONAL YOUTH ORGANIZATION FOR THE LIBERATION OF PALESTINE. The plane landed in Amsterdam; crew and passengers were released, but the aircraft was destroyed by the terrorists.

March 26

Ethiopia. Members of the ERITREAN LIBERATION FRONT abducted the passengers and crew of a private American helicopter. The group held their captives until June 1974.

April 11

Israel. Members of the POPULAR FRONT FOR THE LIBERATION OF PALESTINE-GENERAL COMMAND attacked the Israeli town of QIRYAT SHEMONA killing 18 villagers and wounding 16 others. The attack was intended to secure the release of 100 Palestinians being held in Israeli jails, but Israeli troops assaulted the apartment complex where the three terrorists had barricaded themselves and killed them all.

April

Italy. Public Prosecutor Mario Sossi was held for 35 days in a "people's prison" by members of the RED BRIGADES. He was released in exchange for eight "political" prisoners.

April 13

Philippines. The NEW PEOPLE'S ARMY murdered three U.S. Navy personnel near the Subic Bay Naval Base. Killed were Commander Leland Dobler, Captain J.T. Mitchell, and Lieutenant Charles Jeffries.

May 15

Israel. Gunmen of the DEMOCRATIC FRONT FOR THE LIBERATION OF PALESTINE seized a school building and more than 100 students and teachers in the village of Ma'alot. During a gun battle with Israeli forces attempting to retake the school, 27 of the children died in what has come to be known as the MA'ALOT MASSACRE.

May 17
United States. Six members of the SYMBIONESE LIBERATION ARMY were killed in a shoot-out with Los Angeles police.

June 17
United Kingdom. The PROVISIONAL WING OF THE IRISH REPUBLICAN ARMY bombed the Tower of London while it was crowded with tourists, killing one and injuring more than 40.

June 19
Argentina. A series of explosions rocked British and American commercial targets.

June 24
Israel. Three members of al-FATAH landed by small boat just south of the Israeli town of Nahariyya, where they killed three villagers, a woman and her two children, before being killed by Israeli troops.

August 4
Italy. A bomb exploded aboard an Italian train bound for Munich from Bologna killing 12 people and wounding four dozen others. The Italian fascist group BLACK ORDER claimed responsibility.

September 7
Greece. Eighty-eight people were killed when a TWA airliner exploded in midair after departing the Athens airport. The ARAB NATIONALIST YOUTH ORGANIZATION FOR THE LIBERATION OF PALESTINE is believed to have been responsible.

September 13
Netherlands. Three members of the JAPANESE RED ARMY seized the French Embassy in The Hague and demanded the release of another JRA member being held by authorities. The four were then provided a plane which took them to SYRIA.

September 13
Spain. The ETA bombed a crowded Madrid cafe frequented by police personnel who worked in the nearby national police headquarters building. Twelve people were killed in the blast and more than 80 were wounded.

October 6
United States. The first of a series of attacks by the FALN (Fuerzas Armadas de Liberacion Nacional), the Puerto Rican separatist organization, took place. Five banks in New York City were bombed.

November 9
West Germany. The RED ARMY FACTION murdered West German Supreme Court president Guenther Drenkman in his Bonn home.

November 21
United Kingdom. The PROVISIONAL WING OF THE IRISH REPUBLICAN ARMY bombed two Birmingham pubs, killing 21 and wounding nearly 200.

November 22
Dubai. Four members of the ARAB NATIONALIST YOUTH ORGANIZATION FOR THE LIBERATION OF PALESTINE climbed over the airport fence and hijacked a British Airways flight bound for Singapore. The hijackers ordered the plane to Libya, and then to Tunis, demanding the release of Palestinian terrorists held in Egypt and the Netherlands. Before surrendering to Tunisian authorities on November 25 they murdered a passenger and injured two crew members. They were turned over to the PLO.

1975

January 24
United States.   A bomb planted by the FALN (Fuerzas Armadas de Liberacion Nacional) exploded inside the crowded Fraunces Tavern, a historic landmark and restaurant in the Wall Street district of New York City. Four patrons were killed and another 60 were wounded.

January 25
Lebanon.   The ARMENIAN SECRET ARMY FOR THE LIBERATION OF ARMENIA (ASALA) bombed the Beirut headquarters of the World Council of Churches because of that group's role in helping Armenians to emigrate to other countries.

January 29
United States.   The U.S. State Department headquarters in Washington, D.C. received extensive damage from a bomb planted by the WEATHER UNDERGROUND.

February 25
Argentina.   John P. Egan, the U.S. honorary consul in the city of Cordoba, was kidnapped by MONTENEROS terrorists. He was found murdered two days later.

February 27
West Germany.   Peter Lorenz, a leading West German politician, was kidnapped and held by members of the RED ARMY FACTION who were seeking the release of imprisoned terrorists. He was freed when his captors' demands were met and five RAF members were released from prison.

March 1
Iraq.   A domestic Iraqi Airways flight was hijacked by Kurdish nationalists and taken to Teheran, Iran. Iraqi security guards on board the flight engaged in a gun battle with the terrorists, which led to their sur-

render to Iranian authorities. On April 7 Iran executed the hijackers by firing squad.

April 7
Philippines.   Three members of the MORO LIBERATION FRONT (MLF) hijacked a domestic Philippine Airlines flight. The plane's 70 passengers were released in Manila, but the ship's crew and an airline executive were retained as hostages to guarantee the terrorists' safe passage to Libya. On April 13, after arriving in Libya, the terrorists freed their hostages and surrendered to the Libyan government, which granted them asylum.

April 17
Cambodia.   The KHMER ROUGE reign of terror was launched in Phnom Penh. On this date the terrorist regime began the forced ruralization of Cambodia's "corrupt" urban populations, literally driving them out of the cities with a systematic terror campaign.

May 21
Philippines.   In a repeat of the group's April 7 hijacking, members of MLF again seized a Philippine Airlines plane and demanded it be flown to Libya. This time, however, a gunfight with Filipino troops ensued and three of the six hijackers, as well as 10 passengers, died. The other three hijackers were captured and later executed.

July 14
Ethiopia.   Two United States citizens were abducted by the ERITREAN LIBERATION FRONT and held until May 1976. It is believed a private ransom was paid for their release.

August 4
Malaysia.   Terrorists of the JAPANESE RED ARMY (JRA) took over the U.S. Consulate and the Swedish Embassy in Kuala Lumpur. The terrorists threatened to blow up the buildings and kill their 52 hostages if

their demand for the release of seven JRA prisoners in Japan was not met. Although the Japanese government was prepared to release the seven, only five were willing to go. They, and the Malaysian group, were flown to Tripoli, Libya.

August 23

Egypt. Three terrorists, claiming to be members of the Abu al-Nasir Movement, hijacked an Egypt Air 737 flying from Cairo to Luxor. They demanded the release of five Libyans in Egyptian jails. The hijackers ordered the plane to Libya, but during a refueling stop in Luxor Egyptian troops stormed the plane and captured the hijackers. No passengers were injured.

September 2

Northern Ireland. Gunmen from the PRO-VISIONAL WING OF THE IRISH REPUBLICAN ARMY shot and killed six Protestants in South Armagh.

September 15

Spain. BLACK SEPTEMBER terrorists occupied the Egyptian Embassy in Madrid. They seized six diplomats, whom they threatened to kill unless Egypt withdrew from its peace talks with Israel and condemned the interim agreements already reached at those Geneva, Switzerland meetings. The gang took the hostages to Algiers, where they were released.

October 6

Colombia. The ELN (Ejercito de Liberacion Nacional) assassinated Ramon Arthur Rincon Quinones, Inspector General of the Colombian Army.

October 22

Austria. The JUSTICE COMMANDOS OF THE ARMENIAN GENOCIDE (JCAG) assassinated Danis Tunaligil, the Turkish Ambassador to Austria, in Vienna.

October 24

France. The JCAG killed Turkey's Ambassador to France, Ismail Erez, on a Paris street, as he sat in his automobile.

November 27

United Kingdom. The PROVISIONAL WING OF THE IRISH REPUBLICAN ARMY murdered Ross McWhirter, coeditor of the *Guinness Book of Records,* in front of his London home. McWhirter is believed to have been killed because of his outspoken opposition to terrorism and his offers of cash rewards for information that led to the capture of terrorists.

December 23

Greece. Athens CIA station chief, Richard Welch, was murdered by members of REVOLUTIONARY ORGANIZATION 17 NOVEMBER.

December 29

United States. The suburban Chicago home of a Yugoslavian consular official was damaged by a bomb planted by Serbian nationalists of the organization Freedom for the Serbian Fatherland.

1976

January 4

Northern Ireland. Five Catholics were murdered in two separate attacks by Protestant gunmen.

January 5

Northern Ireland. Ten Protestants were removed from a bus in Armagh by the PROVISIONAL WING OF THE IRISH REPUBLICAN ARMY and were executed at the roadside.

January 21

Colombia. The ELN bombed the Spanish Embassy in Bogota.

May 23

Netherlands. MOLLUCCAN terrorists seized a school and a passenger train in two separate but coordinated incidents. The Molluccans sought to put pressure on the Dutch government to assist them in securing their independence from Indonesia, a former Dutch colony. After four days the seige at the school ended quietly, but it was not until 22 days later that the hostage ordeal on board the train came to a violent end as Dutch Marines stormed the train. Six of the terrorists died in the assault, as did two of the hostage passengers.

June 18

Argentina. ERP (Ejercito Revolucionario de Pueblo) is believed to have been responsible for the murder of General Cesareo Cardoza, chief of the Federal Police, who died when a bomb planted beneath his bed was detonated.

June 27

Uganda. Seven operatives of the POPULAR FRONT FOR THE LIBERATION OF PALESTINE and the RED ARMY FACTION hijacked an Air France flight en route from Tel Aviv to Paris, diverting the plane to Entebbe airfield in Uganda. The hijackers demanded the release of 53 terrorists in French, Swiss, Kenyan and Israeli jails. While they held their 240 prisoners at the airport they received the support of Uganda's president, IDI AMIN. On July 1 a planeload of Israeli commandos landed at the airport and in a near flawless assault known as the ENTEBBE RAID rescued the great majority of the passengers. The seven terrorists and a score of Uganda soldiers were killed in the process.

July 21

Ireland. The British ambassador to Ireland, Christopher Ewart-Biggs, died when a land mine detonated as he drove through the countryside near Dublin. The death of Ewart-Biggs, who had been appointed ambassador barely three weeks earlier, was believed to be the work of the PROVISIONAL WING OF THE IRISH REPUBLICAN ARMY.

August 11

Turkey. Four EL AL passengers were killed and another 20 were injured in the Istanbul airport terminal by gunmen from the POPULAR FRONT FOR THE LIBERATION OF PALESTINE.

September 10

United States. Six Croatian nationalists hijacked a TWA 727 as it flew from New York to Chicago, redirecting it first to Newfoundland, then to Iceland, and finally, to Paris. After authorities complied with the hijackers' demands that a communiqué be published in major newspapers and that propaganda leaflets be dropped over Montreal, London and Paris, the terrorists directed police to a bomb contained in a subway locker in New York's Grand Central Station. The bomb exploded, killing one policeman and badly injuring others, when they attempted to deactivate it. French authorities turned the terrorists over to the United States for prosecution.

September 21

United States. The Foreign Minister of Chile, ORLANDO LETELIER, was assassinated in Washington, D.C. by agents of the Chilean secret police, DINA.

October 4

Spain. A senior advisor to King Juan Carlos was machine gunned in front of his San Sebastian home by terrorists of the ETA/M, the militant faction of the Basque Fatherland and Liberty group.

November 29

Italy. The leftist terror group PRIMIA LINEA attacked the Turin factory of the Fiat Automobile Company.

1977

January 11
France. French authorities released ABU DAOUD, despite pleas for extradition by the West German government, which sought to try him for the 1972 MUNICH MASSACRE.

February 6
Rhodesia. Seven Catholic missionaries were killed by guerrillas near Salisbury.

February
Colombia. This month marked the beginning of a three-year hostage ordeal for an American Peace Corp volunteer kidnapped by members of FARC (Fuerzas Armadas Revolucionarias de Colombia). The volunteer was finally released after the payment of a $250,000 ransom.

March 4
Japan. The office of the Federation of Economic Organizations was seized by four terrorists.

March 9
United States. Three buildings in Washington, D.C. were seized by Hanafi Muslim gunmen, who took a total of 134 people hostage. After two days the group surrendered to authorities.

April 7
West Germany. The RED ARMY FACTION murdered West German Federal Prosecutor Siegfried Buback as he rode in his automobile. Buback had had a hand in the conviction of other RAF members.

May 17
Spain. GRAPO (the Grupo de Resistencia Antifascista, Primera de Octubre) bombed the U.S. Cultural Center in Madrid on the day that U.S. vice president Walter Mondale arrived for a visit.

June 9
Italy. The Turkish ambassador to the Vatican, Taha Carim, was assassinated by members of the JUSTICE COMMANDOS OF THE ARMENIAN GENOCIDE.

July 31
West Germany. One of Germany's most prominent bankers, Juergen Pronto, was killed in his home by members of the RED ARMY FACTION.

August 3
United States. The Puerto Rican separatist group FALN set off bombs in two New York City office buildings; one bystander was killed.

August 8
Lebanon. Six al-FATAH dissidents hijacked a Kuwaiti airliner en route from Beirut to Kuwait and demanded the release of 300 prisoners in Arab jails. The hijackers freed their hostages in Kuwait in exchange for safe passage to South Yemen; however, they redirected their flight to Syria, where five of the terrorists overpowered their leader and surrendered to Syrian authorities.

September 5
West Germany. The RED ARMY FACTION kidnapped German businessman Hans-Martin Schleyer, killing his driver and three bodyguards in the process. The RAF demanded that 11 imprisoned members of the gang be freed. The POPULAR FRONT FOR THE LIBERATION OF PALESTINE became involved when it hijacked a Lufthansa airliner in a supporting attack, taking the plane to Mogadishu, Somalia. After West German commandos rescued the Lufthansa passengers on October 18, many of the 11 RAF prisoners committed suicide in their cells, and Schleyer was murdered for revenge.

September 12

South Africa. Imprisoned black activist Steven B. BIKO died as the result of severe beatings while in police custody.

September 28

India. The JAPANESE RED ARMY hijacked a Japan Air Lines flight, directing it to Dacca, Bangladesh. The terrorists demanded a $6 million ransom and the release of nine Japanese prisoners. The Japanese government met the demands and the hostages were released in stages as the hijacked plane traveled from Dacca to Kuwait, then to Syria, and finally to Algiers, where the terrorists surrendered.

October 13

Spain. Four terrorists from the POPULAR FRONT FOR THE LIBERATION OF PALESTINE hijacked a Lufthansa plane in support of the earlier RED ARMY FACTION kidnapping of Hans-Martin Schleyer in West Germany. After a number of stops throughout the Middle East, and the murder of the pilot, the plane ended up in Mogadishu, Somalia on October 17. The next day West German GSG-9 commandos stormed the plane, rescuing the captives and killing three of the four terrorists. The failure of this hijacking led to the prison suicides of a number of RAF leaders the hostage taking had been designed to free.

December 4

Malaysia. A hijacked Malaysian airliner crashed as it prepared to land in Singapore. It was reported that the unidentified terrorists apparently shot the plane's pilot and copilot.

1978

January 4

United Kingdom. The ABU NIDAL Organization (ANO) began its campaign against the moderate wing of the PLO by murdering Said Hammami, an associate of Yasir ARAFAT.

February 17

Northern Ireland. The PROVISIONAL WING OF THE IRISH REPUBLICAN ARMY killed 12 and wounded more than 20 in the bombing of the La Mon Restaurant.

February 18

Cyprus. Yussef al-Sabai, leader of the Afro-Asian People's Solidarity Organization, was murdered by two of ABU NIDAL's gunmen. In order to make their escape from Cyprus the killers seized 30 hostages, 12 of whom they traded for safe passage to the airport at Larnaca. At the airport the terrorists swapped seven additional hostages for a Cypriot airliner in which they then took off for LIBYA. The terrorists were unable, however to secure asylum in Libya or anywhere else in the region. In the early morning hours of February 19 the plane landed in Djibouti, where it refueled before returning to Larnaca. That evening 100 Egyptian commandos landed at the Larnaca airport intending to recapture the aircraft; Cypriot National Guardsmen unexpectedly opened fire on the commandos, however, killing 15. The incident finally ended when the terrorists surrendered to Cypriot authorities. Cyprus tried the two men and sentenced them to death but later commuted their sentences.

March 16

Italy. The former Italian prime minister and president of the Christian Democratic Party, ALDO MORO, was kidnapped by RED BRIGADES terrorists. When the Italian government refused to give in to the terrorists' demands for the release of 13 of their imprisoned comrades, Moro was murdered. On May 9 his body was found in the trunk of a car parked on a Rome street.

April 11

Israel. Eleven al-FATAH guerrillas landed by sea outside the port city of Haifa and promptly hijacked a passing bus in an attempt to reach Tel Aviv. The bus was intercepted outside Tel Aviv and a gun battle ensued in which 25 passengers and nine of the terrorists died.

July 28

United Kingdom. BLACK SEPTEMBER terrorists attempted to assassinate the Iraqi ambassador to the United Kingdom.

August 2

Pakistan. Al-FATAH assassins attempted to kill the Iraqi consul in Karachi.

August 20

United Kingdom. An EL AL flight crew was attacked outside their London hotel; one female flight attendant was killed.

September 12

Colombia. M-19 terrorists murdered the former minister of the interior, Rafael Pardo Buelvas.

October

Turkey. The ARMENIAN SECRET ARMY FOR THE LIBERATION OF ARMENIA exploded two bombs in Istanbul, killing one and injuring four.

1979

January 3

Spain. Basque separatists murdered General Constantine Ortin Gill in Madrid.

February 12

Rhodesia. Guerrillas from the Zimbabue African People's Union (ZAPU) used a Soviet-made antiaircraft missile to shoot down an Air Rhodesia plane on a domestic flight. All 59 persons aboard the civilian airliner died.

February 14

Afghanistan. The United States ambassador to Afghanistan, Adolph Dubs, was kidnapped and murdered by Muslim terrorists.

March 5

Spain. GRAPO assassins killed semi-retired General Agustin Munoz Vazquez in Madrid to protest Spain's entry into NATO.

March 22

Netherlands. The British Ambassador, Sir Richard Sykes, was gunned down in front of his home in The Hague by terrorists of the PROVISIONAL WING OF THE IRISH REPUBLICAN ARMY. Ambassador Sykes had formerly been the British ambassador to Dublin.

March 30

United Kingdom. Airey Neave, the Conservative Party's spokesman on Northern Ireland, died when a bomb destroyed his car as he left the House of Commons garage in central London. The IRISH NATIONAL LIBERATION ARMY claimed responsibility.

May 1

France. A bomb exploded at the Paris offices of the National Council of French Employers. This was the first violent act claimed by ACTION DIRECTE.

May 26

United States. A gang of KU KLUX KLAN members violently broke up a civil rights march in Decatur, Alabama. Two civil rights workers and two Klansmen died before police restored order.

May 30

El Salvador. Members of FPL (Fuerzas Popular de Liberacion) killed Hugo Wey, the Swiss chargé d'affaires during what was apparently a botched kidnapping.

June 20

United States. A Serbian nationalist, demanding the release of a Serbian priest in a

Chicago jail, hijacked an American Airlines flight traveling from New York to Chicago. Both the hijacker and the priest were members of Freedom of the Serbian Fatherland (SEPO) and, along with four other members of that group, had already been convicted of the December 1975 bombing of the Chicago home of an assistant to the Yugoslavian consul. Although the priest was not released, the hijacker freed all 127 passengers and five of the plane's eight crew members at Chicago's O'Hare airport. The hijacker then directed the remaining crewmen to fly him back to New York, where he transferred to a larger airliner, which transported him to Ireland. Upon his arrival at the airport in Shannon, Ireland on June 21 he surrendered to the Irish authorities, who immediately returned him to the United States.

June 25

Belgium. NATO's Supreme Allied Commander, General Alexander Haig, narrowly escaped death when a bomb set by members of the RED ARMY FACTION exploded in front of the car in which he was traveling.

June/July

Spain. ETA-PM, the political–military wing of the Basque Fatherland and Liberty group, conducted a month-long "tourist war" along the Spanish seaside resorts. Fourteen bombs exploded during the period, injuring only two but causing extensive property damage.

July

France. During the month the JUSTICE COMMANDOS OF THE ARMENIAN GENOCIDE bombed a number of Turkish targets in Paris, including the offices of the Turkish airline, the Turkish tourist bureau and the Turkish labor attaché.

August 27

Ireland. The PROVISIONAL WING OF THE IRISH REPUBLICAN ARMY killed Louis, Earl MOUNTBATTEN, and two others, including the Earl's grandson, when they detonated a bomb hidden aboard the party's fishing boat.

August 27

Northern Ireland. The PROVISIONAL WING OF THE IRISH REPUBLICAN ARMY murdered 19 people, mostly British soldiers, when it executed a double bombing near Warrenpoint.

September 7

Lebanon. An Alitalia jetliner flying from Teheran to Rome was hijacked by three SHI'ITE Muslims protesting the 1978 disappearance of Imam Musa al-SADR. They demanded to be flown to the conference of nonaligned nations taking place in Havana, Cuba. The Cuban government agreed on the condition that the hostages be freed in Rome before the plane proceeded to Havana. Foul weather prevented the Rome landing and instead the plane was diverted to Teheran, where the hijackers surrendered.

September 21

Italy. Carlo Ghiglieno, a senior executive of Fiat, the Italian automobile company, was murdered by terrorists of the RED BRIGADES.

November 3

United States. Five members of a U.S. Communist group were killed by the KU KLUX KLAN in Greensboro, North Carolina during an anti-Klan rally and march. The victims became known as the GREENSBORO FIVE.

November 4

Iran. At the instigation of the Ayatollah KHOMEINI the REVOLUTIONARY GUARDS stormed the U.S. Embassy in Teheran, taking 53 American personnel hostage. The so-called IRANIAN HOSTAGE CRISIS dragged on for 444 days before the Americans were released on January 20, 1981.

November 20
Saudi Arabia. SUNNI Muslim fundamentalists seized the GRAND MOSQUE in the holy city of Mecca and held it for five days before an all-out assault by Saudi military and police ejected them in a bloody battle. More than 100 people were killed.

December 2
Puerto Rico. Members of MACHETEROS, a Puerto Rican separatist group, killed two sailors in an attack on a U.S. Navy bus.

1980

March 24
Honduras. Terrorists belonging to the CINCHONEROS POPULAR LIBERATION MOVEMENT hijacked a Honduran 737 and forced it to fly to Managua, Nicaragua in an effort to gain the freedom of 15 Salvadoran leftists being held in Honduran jails. Negotiations fell through, however, and the five hijackers took the plane to Panama where they surrendered.

March 24
El Salvador. The Roman Catholic Archbishop of El Savador, Oscar ROMERO y Galdames, was assassinated in his San Salvador church as he celebrated mass.

March 28
Indonesia. Five members of a previously unknown group, "Komando Jihad," hijacked an Indonesian airliner and diverted it to Penangy, Indonesia. They were seeking the release of 20 prisoners jailed in Indonesia. On March 31, as two passengers, a Briton and an American, escaped from the plane, Indonesian government forces stormed the aircraft. The gun battle resulted

in the death of the pilot, one commando and four of the terrorists.

March 30
France. ACTION DIRECTE bombed and completely destroyed a police station in Toulouse.

April 30–May 5
United Kingdom. From April 30 until May 5, six anti-KHOMEINI Iranian-Arab terrorists held as many as 26 hostages in the Iranian Embassy in London. The British government refused to negotiate with the members of the "Democratic Revolutionary Front for the Liberation of Arabistan," who sought to bring attention to the plight of the Arab minority in revolutionary IRAN. The siege ended on May 5 when British commandos of the 22nd Special Air Service Regiment (SAS) executed a bold daylight assault, retaking the embassy and killing five of the terrorists in the process. Though two of the hostages died, the rescue operation was considered a great success, proving the utility of specially trained commandos as COUNTERTERRORISM forces.

May
Portugal. A new European terrorist organization emerged in Portugal, launching a series of deadly attacks during the month. FP-25, a radical left-wing group, in separate incidents murdered a Portuguese businessman; attempted to kidnap the Minister of Labor, murdering a security guard in the process; and bombed the Royal Club in Lisbon and the British Airways office in Oporto.

July 7
Italy. The GUARDIANS OF THE ISLAMIC REVOLUTION claimed responsibility for explosions at the Rome headquarters of the Snia-Technit Corporation.

July 15
Chile. Four MIR gunmen armed with machine guns murdered Lieutenant General

Roger Vergara Campos, the director of the Chilean Army Intelligence School, and his chauffeur.

July 22

United States. Ali Akbar Tabatabai, the former Iranian press attaché at Iran's Washington embassy during the reign of the Shah and a prominent anti-KHOMEINI exile, was murdered by David Blelefield (also known as Daoud Salahuddin).

July 31

United States. The pro-KHOMEINI group the MOSLEM STUDENTS ORGANIZATION was believed to be behind the attempted murder of Iranian exile Shah Rais. The lone gunman, believed to be the same one who killed Ali Akbar Tabatabai on July 22, succeeded only in slightly wounding a bodyguard.

August 2

Italy. Eighty-four people died and scores more were injured by a bomb planted in the Bologna railway station. Responsibility for the attack was claimed by an obscure right-wing terrorist group, the Armed Revolutionary Nuclei (NAR).

September 2

Spain. GRAPO assassins gunned down General Enrique Briz Armengol in Barcelona.

September 26

Yugoslavia. Three armed Croatians hijacked a Yugoslav aircraft carrying more than 100 passengers and directed the flight to Tel Aviv. The plane was denied landing permission in Israel, however, and instead landed in Larnaca, Cyprus. The terrorists' plan collapsed when their hostages, faking a fire aboard the plane, escaped to safety. Subsequently, the hijackers surrendered to authorities.

October 5

United States. The JUSTICE COMMANDOS OF THE ARMENIAN GENOCIDE claimed responsi-

bility for two bombings aimed at Turkish interests in the United States. In New York City no one was hurt when a car bomb exploded outside the Turkish Center in Manhattan. One person was injured by a bomb planted near the residence of the Turkish Consul in Los Angeles.

October 13

Turkey. A Turkish domestic flight was hijacked by five armed men who demanded that the plane first be flown to Teheran, Iran, then on to Jidda, Saudi Arabia. However, as the plane was being refueled for the journey at Diyarbakir, Turkey, it was stormed by government troops. Four of the terrorists were captured alive, though one passenger was killed and another 13 were wounded.

December 4

El Salvador. Four American women, three of whom were Roman Catholic nuns, were found shot and strangled on the outskirts of San Salvador. They are believed to have been the victims of a right-wing DEATH SQUAD of the Salvadoran army.

December 7

Venezuela. Heavily armed members of BANDERA ROJA simultaneously hijacked three planes, assembling them at the airfield at Barranquilla, Colombia. They demanded, but did not secure, the release of seven political prisoners and a ransom of $10 million in cash. Instead, the aircraft were flown to Havana, Cuba, where the hijackers were taken into custody.

December 15

Colombia. In an effort to disrupt the Latin American summit taking place in Colombia, 12 M-19 terrorists hijacked a domestic Colombian airliner and flew it around the region, releasing some of their passenger hostages at each of five stops they made before proceeding to Havana, Cuba.

December 17

Australia. Armenian terrorists are believed to have been responsible for the murder of Sarik Ariyak, a Turkish diplomat. Ariyak and his bodyguard were gunned down on a Sydney street.

December 31

Kenya. Sixteen people attending a New Year's party died and more than 80 were injured when a terrorist bomb exploded inside Nairobi's Norfolk Hotel. The device was so powerful that it did millions of dollars of damage to the historic structure. On January 8, 1981, the POPULAR FRONT FOR THE LIBERATION OF PALESTINE announced that it had carried out the attack.

1981

January 3

El Salvador. Two Americans and a Salvadoran involved in land redistribution projects were killed by members of a right-wing DEATH SQUAD.

January 21

Northern Ireland. Sir Norman Stronge, a prominent Protestant politician, and his son James were shot and killed in the family's South Armagh castle, after which the castle itself was destroyed with explosives.

February 5

Spain. ETA/M murdered the chief engineer of a Bilboa nuclear power plant.

March 2

Pakistan. Three members of a splinter group of the PAKISTAN LIBERATION ARMY hijacked a Pakistan International Airlines plane and demanded the release of jailed Pakistani student protesters. The plane was directed to fly to Kabul, Afghanistan; while there the terrorists murdered a Pakistani diplomat who had been among the passengers. On March 8 the aircraft went on to Damascus, Syria, where the hijackers were joined by 54 Pakistani prisoners released in accordance with the hijackers' demands. The incident ended when the terrorists surrendered to Syrian police. On November 30, 1981 seven Western nations, upset by what they regarded as Afghan complicity in the diplomat's murder, suspended all air traffic with Afghanistan, citing both the Hague Convention and the BONN DECLARATION as their legal justification.

March 4

France. The ARMENIAN SECRET ARMY FOR THE LIBERATION OF ARMENIA assassinated the Turkish Labor attaché, Tecelli Ari, and the consul for Religious Affairs, Resat Morali, in Paris.

March 7

Colombia. A private U.S. citizen, Chester Allen Bitterman, was murdered by his M-19 captors.

May 4

Spain. Brigadier General Andres Gonzalez de Suso was murdered in Madrid by GRAPO terrorists.

May 9

United Kingdom. The PROVISIONAL WING OF THE IRISH REPUBLICAN ARMY detonated a bomb at a North Sea oil facility while Queen Elizabeth II was visiting the facility. There were no injuries and the incident occurred some distance away from the Queen's party.

May 11

West Germany. The REVOLUTIONARY CELLS (RZ) claimed responsibility for the murder of the economics minister for the Lander of Hesse, Heinz Herbert Karry. Karry was shot to death in his home, though a later RZ message claimed their original intention had been only to disable him by shooting him in the legs.

May 13

Italy. Turkish-born international terrorist Mehet Ali AGCA attempted to assassinate Pope John Paul II. The pope was seriously wounded, having been shot twice, but recovered fully.

June 1

Belgium. Naim Khader, a senior PLO official, was assassinated in Brussels.

July 6

Italy. RED BRIGADES terrorists murdered Giuseppe Talierico, an Italian businessman they had kidnapped two months earlier.

August 31

West Germany. A car bomb detonated by the RED ARMY FACTION injured 18 Americans and two West Germans at the U.S. Air Force base in Ramstein.

September 4

Lebanon. French Ambassador to Lebanon Louis Delamare was shot to death by terrorists of the Lebanese Red Brigades, an Iranian-backed group.

September 15

West Germany. The RED ARMY FACTION (RAF) attempted to kill the commanding general of U.S. forces in Europe, U.S. Army General Frederick Kroesen. The RAF fired two RPG-7 grenades at the general's car as he and his wife rode along the highway near Heidelberg. One grenade did strike the car, causing minor injuries to the Kroesens.

October 6

Egypt. Anwar al-SADAT, President of Egypt, was assassinated as he sat in the reviewing stand observing a military parade. Members of a terrorist group—probably TANZIM AL-JIHAD—sprang from the back of a passing parade vehicle and assaulted the presidential party with automatic weapons and gre-

nades, killing eight others in addition to Sadat.

October 9

Italy. Majid Abu Shrar, a PLO leader, died in a bomb blast that destroyed his Rome hotel room.

October 10

United Kingdom. Two people were killed and another 40 were wounded when a nail bomb planted by the PROVISIONAL WING OF THE IRISH REPUBLICAN ARMY exploded in the midst of a group of British troops returning from a ceremony in central London.

October 20

United States. The Revolutionary Armed Task Force attempted the unsuccessful holdup of an armored car outside Nyack, New York. Two policemen and one of the vehicle's security guards died in the shootout. Arrested and turned over to the FEDERAL BUREAU OF INVESTIGATION was KATHY BOUDIN, a member of the 1960s terrorist organization WEATHER UNDERGROUND, who had eluded police for more than a decade.

November

France. An ACTION DIRECTE bombing spree during the month hit a variety of civilian targets, including a Rolls Royce automobile dealership, a toy store, a clothing store and an exclusive restaurant.

November 14

Northern Ireland. The Rev. Robert J. Bardford was shot to death in Belfast. Bradford, a Methodist minister and Member of Parliament, was a vehement opponent of the IRISH REPUBLICAN ARMY, whose Provisional Wing claimed responsibility for the murder.

November 28

Syria. The MUSLIM BROTHERHOOD killed 64 people in a Damascus bombing as part of the general campaign against the Syrian government of President Hafez al-ASSAD.

December 17
Italy. U.S. Army Gen. James Lee Dozier was kidnapped by members of the RED BRIGADES from his Verona home. Dozier commanded NATO's Southern Europe Ground Forces based in Verona. Forty-two days later Italian COUNTERTERRORISM forces freed Dozier in a spectacularly successful raid on the terrorists' hideout.

1982

January 18
France. American military attaché Lt. Col. Charles R. Ray was murdered outside his home by terrorists belonging to the Lebanese Christian group FARL.

January 27
Colombia. Seven members of M-19 hijacked a Colombian airliner and directed it to the city of Calí. The plane was disabled, however, when it struck a truck blocking the runway. The terrorists then threatened to blow up the aircraft, with passengers on board, if a replacement plane was not provided. Authorities supplied an executive jet which took the hijackers to Havana, Cuba.

January 28
United States. Turkey's consul general, Kemal Arikan, died at the hands of the JUSTICE COMMANDOS OF THE ARMENIAN GENOCIDE.

February 2
Syria. President Hafez al-ASSAD lashed out at the SUNNI Muslim opponents of his secular regime in a predawn attack on the Syrian city of HAMAH. The city served as the operational base of the MUSLIM BROTHERHOOD, a terrorist guerrilla organization dedicated to the overthrow of the Damascus government. It has been estimated that the

fighting and destruction in Hamah resulted in as many as 25,000 deaths among a population of 180,000.

February 24
Lebanon. Twelve SHI'ITE gunmen, led by HAMZA akl Hamieh, attacked Kuwait Airways flight 561 after it had landed in Beirut. The terrorists forced the passengers and crew to reboard the plane and held them hostage in a vain effort to ascertain the whereabouts of the spiritual leader Iman Musa al-SADR, who had disappeared while on a visit to Libya. The gunmen ultimately were forced to exchange their prisoners for safe conduct to Syria.

February 26
Tanzania. Four armed members of the REVOLUTIONARY YOUTH MOVEMENT OF TANZANIA, accompanied by their families, hijacked an Air Tanzania flight, forcing it to make stops in Kenya, Saudi Arabia, Greece, and finally the United Kingdom, where they surrendered to authorities. They had unsuccessfully sought to force the resignation of Tanzanian President Julius Nyerere.

March 28
Guatemala. Leftist terrorists assassinated Bendicto Santos, a senior police official.

April 3
France. A female assassin dispatched by FARL shot and killed Israeli diplomat Ya'acov Bar Simantov in Paris.

April 22
France. In Paris, a bomb exploded near the offices of Al-Watan al-Arabi, an Arab-language pro-Iraqi newspaper. The bombing coincided with the opening of the trial of two associates of the terrorist CARLOS. Although no group claimed responsibility, the French government believed the bombers were linked to SYRIA and, as a result, expelled two Syrian diplomats and withdrew

the French ambassador in Damascus in protest.

April 28
Honduras. Four members of the FRP-LZ (Lorenzo Zelaya Popular Revolutionary Forces) hijacked a domestic flight belonging to the Honduran Air Service and held it on a Honduran airstrip. The terrorists originally demanded a ransom of $1 million and the release of 32 political prisoners, but they eventually reduced their demand to $100,000. The hostage crisis came to an abrupt end on May 1, when 10 of the passengers, among them eight Americans, escaped via the plane's emergency exit. The hijackers then released the remaining 11 passengers in exchange for passage to Cuba.

April
Honduras. FRP-LZ terrorists waged a campaign of violence against the Tegucigalpa diplomatic community, attacking the American, Chilean, Peruvian, and Argentine embassies in that city.

May 12
Guatemala. The Brazilian Embassy in Guatemala City was seized by 13 members of the January 31 Popular Front and nine hostages were taken, including the ambassador. The group was protesting the rule of Guatemala's military junta. The Mexican government stepped in to end the crisis by offering political asylum to the terrorists in exchange for the safe release of all hostages.

May 24
Lebanon. A female employee of the French Embassy in Beirut was killed, as were 12 bystanders, when her car was destroyed by a bomb just outside the embassy compound.

June 1
West Germany. The German terrorist group REVOLUTIONARY CELLS initiated a bombing campaign against American military and business targets in the Federal Republic of Germany. The attacks, which began with a bombing outside U.S. Army headquarters in Frankfurt, were linked to the upcoming visit of U.S. President Ronald Reagan.

June 3
United Kingdom. Israel's ambassador to the Court of St. James', Shlomo ARGOV, was seriously injured in London as the result of a BLACK JUNE assassination attempt. The attack, orchestrated by ABU NIDAL, became part of the justification for Israel's invasion of Lebanon a few days later.

June 17
Italy. The ABU NIDAL Organization murdered PLO representative Kamal Hussein in Rome.

July 19
Lebanon. David Dodge, acting president of the American University of Beirut, was kidnapped. He was released on July 21, 1983.

July 20
United Kingdom. The PROVISIONAL WING OF THE IRISH REPUBLICAN ARMY killed 11 people in two separate bomb attacks at popular central London sites. The first bomb exploded in Hyde Park as members of the Royal Household Cavalry participated in the ceremonial changing of the guard at Buckingham Palace. The second bomb exploded two hours later during a band concert in Regent's Park.

July 23
France. A senior member of the PLO, Fadel el-Dani, was killed near his Paris home.

July 31
West Germany. A bomb exploded in the EL AL area of Munich's airport, injuring several people. The bomb is thought to have

detonated prematurely, having been intended to destroy an El Al plane in flight. Responsibility for the attack was claimed by the Justice for Palestine Organization.

August

France. ACTION DIRECTE conducted attacks on Israeli and Jewish targets in and around Paris.

August 4

El Salvador. FMLN guerrillas murdered the mayor of San Lorenzo, Romiro Ponce.

August 7

Turkey. Seven people were killed and more than 70 injured when an Armenian terrorist set off a hand grenade and sprayed machinegun fire at Ankara'a Esenboga Airport. A subgroup of the ARMENIAN SECRET ARMY FOR THE LIBERATION OF ARMENIA calling itself the "Martyr Kharmian Hayrik Suicide Squad" claimed responsibility.

August 9

France. Terrorists attacked a crowded Jewish restaurant in Paris with grenades and automatic weapons during lunch hour. The same terrorists, ABU NIDAL operatives, then proceeded to attack the crowd in front of a nearby synagogue. In all, six people died during the attacks and 27 others were wounded. Although ACTION DIRECTE claimed responsibility for the carnage, French authorities uncovered evidence that suggests the involvement of ABU NIDAL'S BLACK JUNE.

August 17

Mozambique. A letter bomb killed the South African political activist and AFRICAN NATIONAL CONGRESS member Ruth First.

August 21

France. A bomb planted by FARL terrorists beneath the car of an American Embassy employee exploded as members of a bomb disposal team attempted to disarm it. One of the technicians working on the device was killed and two others were injured.

August 27

Canada. While driving to his office in Ottawa, Turkish military attaché Col. Atilla Altikat was attacked and killed by gunmen from the JUSTICE COMMANDOS OF THE ARMENIAN GENOCIDE.

September 6

Switzerland. The Polish Embassy in Berne was seized by a small group of armed men demanding the lifting of martial law in Poland, freedom for Polish political prisoners, and the closure of Polish labor camps. Swiss police staged a successful hostage rescue operation on September 9 and arrested the gunmen.

September 14

Lebanon. The newly elected president of Lebanon, Bashir Gemayel, was killed when a bomb destroyed his Beirut headquarters. His assassin was Habib Tanios CHARTOUNY, a member of the SYRIAN SOCIAL NATIONALIST PARTY.

September 16

Lebanon. CHRISTIAN PHALANGISTS allied with the Israeli occupation force began a two-day massacre of unarmed Palestinian refugees in the SABRA AND SHATILA camps outside Beirut. The Red Cross estimated the death toll at 800 to 1,000.

September 17

Honduras. Members of the CINCHONEROS POPULAR LIBERATION MOVEMENT, a leftist guerrila organization, killed one person and took 105 hostages at an economic conference held at the Chamber of Commerce Building in San Pedro Sula. The terrorists' demands included the release of nine prisoners held in Honduran jails and the expulsion of foreign military advisors. When their demands were not met they agreed to exchange their hostages for safe passage out of the country. They received asylum in Cuba.

September 28

Lebanon. Approximately 30 armed men ambushed and killed Abu Walid along the highway between the towns of Baalbek and Rayak in northern Lebanon. Walid had been one of the PLO's principal military commanders; his murder has been alternately blamed on Syria and Israel.

October

Spain. Over the course of the month nearly two dozen bombs exploded at banks throughout the Basque provinces.

October 9

Italy. The ABU NIDAL Organization is believed to have been responsible for the attack on worshippers exiting a Rome synagogue.

November 4

Spain. Two ETA terrorists, mounted on a motorcycle, gunned down General Victor Lago Roman of the Spanish Army, in Madrid.

December 6

Northern Ireland. A popular bar in Ballykelly, frequented by members of British security forces, was bombed by the IRISH NATIONAL LIBERATION ARMY. Seventeen people were killed, including 11 soldiers.

1983

January–November

West Germany. The REVOLUTIONARY CELLS carried out a series of 19 bombings during this period targeted primarily against government facilities.

April 10

Portugal. ABU NIDAL'S BLACK JUNE group murdered PLO moderate Issam Sartawi at a convention of the Socialist International.

April 18

Lebanon. Forty-nine people died and 120 were injured by a suicide truck bombing of the U.S. Embassy in Beirut. The operation was claimed by ISLAMIC JIHAD.

July 15

France. The Orly Airport ticket counter of the Turkish airline was bombed by the ARMENIAN SECRET ARMY FOR THE LIBERATION OF ARMENIA. Seven bystanders died; another 60 were wounded.

July 27

Portugal. The Turkish Embassy in Lisbon was seized by the ARMENIAN REVOLUTIONARY ARMY. The five terrorists blew up the building, killing themselves and two of their hostages.

August 21

Philippines. The exiled leader of the political opposition to President Ferdinand Marcos, Benigno AQUINO Jr. was assassinated at Manila Airport only minutes after he had reentered the country. Though security forces on the scene alleged that Aquino had been shot by Rolando Galman, who was himself gunned down at the same moment, the complicity of the Marcos regime immediately became evident.

September 16

United States. The Puerto Rican terrorist group MACHETEROS struck the West Hartford, Connecticut, terminal of the Wells Fargo Company, escaping with $7.2 million, making it one of the largest robberies in U.S. history.

October 9

Burma. Nineteen people were killed when suspected North Korean agents staged the bombing of a delegation of South Korean dignitaries on an official visit to Rangoon. South Korean President Chun Doo Hwan narrowly escaped the bombing when he arrived late at the bombing site.

October 10

El Salvador. Four prominent left-wing politicians were murdered by the Maximiliano Hernandez Martinez Anti-Communist Brigade, a right-wing DEATH SQUAD.

October 23

Lebanon. Two hundred forty-one American servicemen died when a suicide truck bomb was driven into the U.S. Marine barracks in Beirut. ISLAMIC JIHAD claimed responsibility. The U.S. Department of Defense appointed a special panel, which became known as the LONG COMMISSION, to investigate the tragedy. Islamic Jihad conducted a nearly identical attack on the French military barracks in Beirut, killing 56 soldiers.

November 23

Colombia. Dr. Jamie Betancur Cuartes, brother of Colombian President Belisario Betancur, was kidnapped and held for 15 days by members of ELN. He was finally released after the intercession of Cuban leader Fidel CASTRO.

November–December

Portugal. Over a six-week period the FP-25 group detonated a number of bombs in and around Lisbon, apparently to protest government labor policies.

November 6

United States. The Senate wing of the United States Capitol Building was bombed by members of the ARMED RESISTANCE UNIT, a radical left-wing organization. The attack was launched to protest the U.S. invasion of Grenada.

November 15

Greece. Members of the REVOLUTIONARY ORGANIZATION 17 NOVEMBER murdered U.S. Navy Capt. George Tsantes in Athens.

December

Spain. During the month IRAULTZA terrorists bombed the offices of IBM in Vitoria, 3M in Bilboa, and NCR and Coca-Cola in San Sebastian.

December 12

Kuwait. Both the U.S. and French Embassies were struck by bombing attacks conducted by al-DAWA, a radical Shi'ite Muslim group.

December 17

United Kingdom. Five people were killed and 90 wounded when a car bomb exploded in the midst of a crowd of Christmas shoppers in front of Harrod's department store in London. The PROVISIONAL WING OF THE IRISH REPUBLICAN ARMY was responsible.

December 31

United States. A series of FALN bombs exploded in New York City, damaging police headquarters, the FEDERAL BUREAU OF INVESTIGATION offices, and a federal courthouse.

1984

January 18

Lebanon. Malcolm H. Kerr, an American citizen and president of the American University in Beirut, was killed by ISLAMIC JIHAD gunmen.

January 29

Spain. ETA/M murdered retired Spanish military leader Lt. Gen. Guillermo Quintana Lacaci.

February 3

United Kingdom. The KASHMIR LIBERATION ARMY kidnapped Indian diplomat Ravindra Mhartre in an attempt to secure the release of a condemned associate imprisoned in New Delhi. The Indian government rebuffed the terrorists' demands and on

February 5 Mhartre's captors killed him; six days later the Indians executed their Kashmiri prisoner.

February 7
France. An exiled Iranian leader, General Gholam Ali Oveisi, was murdered by an unidentified assailant. The Iranian regime of Ayatollah KHOMEINI is suspected.

February 8
France. The Arab Revolutionary Brigade, an offshoot of the ABU NIDAL Organization, gunned down Khalifa Ahmed Abdel Aziz al-Mubarak, Ambassador of the United Arab Emirates.

February 10
Lebanon. Frank Regier, professor at the American University in Beirut, was abducted by HEZBOLLAH.

February 14
Italy. Leamon Hunt, an American diplomat and Director General of the Multinational Peacekeeping Force in the Sinai, was assassinated by FARL terrorists.

March 16
Lebanon. William Buckley, the Beirut station chief of the CENTRAL INTELLIGENCE AGENCY, was kidnapped by ISLAMIC JIHAD. Although Buckley's body was never found, authorities believe that he died in October 1986 after being tortured by his captors. Islamic Jihad claimed, at that time, that they had "executed" their prisoner as revenge for the Israeli air raid on the Tunis headquarters of the PLO.

March 19
United States. The UNITED FREEDOM FRONT bombed an IBM facility outside New York City.

March 28
Greece. The ABU NIDAL Organization murdered British diplomat Kenneth Whitty in Athens.

April 5
United States. The U.S.-based RED GUERRILLA RESISTANCE bombed the New York City offices of Israeli Aircraft Industries.

April 17
United Kingdom. A female London police constable was shot and killed outside the Libyan Embassy in St. James' Square by a gunman inside the diplomatic mission. After a prolonged siege the embassy was surrendered to police and diplomatic relations between the United Kingdom and Libya were severed.

May
Spain. During the month GRAPO bombed Spanish government offices in Madrid, Barcelona and other cities.

May 3
Cyprus. Two SA'IQA gunmen killed Hanna Moqbell, an opponent of Yasir ARAFAT.

May 8
Lebanon. The Reverend Benjamin Weir was kidnapped in Beirut by SHI'ITE extremists from HEZBOLLAH. Weir was released in September 1985.

May 26
Mozambique. RENAMO murdered three Portuguese citizens and kidnapped a fourth.

June 5–6
India. Indian government troops assaulted the Sikh extremist stronghold, the GOLDEN TEMPLE OF AMRISTAR. Among the hundreds killed was Sikh leader Jarnail Singh BHINDRANWALE.

June 18
United States. Controversial Denver radio talk-show host Alan BERG was murdered by members of the neo-Nazi white supremacist group the ORDER.

July 14
Pakistan. Pakistani police arrested eight Iranians suspected of planning attacks against Pan Am and Saudi airlines.

July 31
West Germany. ISLAMIC JIHAD terrorists hijacked an Air France jetliner and diverted it to Iran.

July–August
Spain. GRAPO exploded a series of 15 bombs in several Spanish cities. Although there were no casualties, property damage was extensive, particularly at the French Consulate and offices of General Motors and a French banking firm.

August
Chile. The MANUEL RODRIGUEZ PATRIOTIC FRONT conducted a bombing campaign throughout central Chile during the month. American business interests were the predominant targets.

September 20
Lebanon. The U.S. Embassy annex in East Beirut was severely damaged by a truck bomber from ISLAMIC JIHAD. Twenty-three people were killed, including two Americans, and at least 60 were injured.

September 27
United States. A Union Carbide office complex was bombed by the UNITED FREEDOM FRONT to protest that company's interests in South Africa.

October
Belgium. During the month members of the COMMUNIST COMBATANT CELLS bombed the Brussels headquarters of Litton Data Systems, the M.A.N. Corporation, Honeywell-Bull, and the Belgian Liberal Party Research Center.

October 12
United Kingdom. The PROVISIONAL WING OF THE IRISH REPUBLICAN ARMY narrowly

missed in an attempt to assassinate British Prime Minister Margaret Thatcher when they bombed a Brighton hotel in which members of the government were staying. As it was, the BRIGHTON BOMBING killed Sir Anthony Barry, MP and injured a number of other cabinet officals and senior Conservative party leaders.

October 29
Poland. Eleven days after his disappearance, the body of Polish activist Reverend Jerzy Popieluszko was found floating in the Wloclawek reservoir. Three officers of the Polish secret police were eventually tried and convicted for the crime.

October 31
India. Prime Minister Indira GANDHI was assassinated by two of her own bodyguards. Both men were Sikhs, and the attack was a reprisal for India's bloody assault on the Sikh shrine, the GOLDEN TEMPLE OF AMRISTAR.

November 17
United Kingdom. The radical animal rights terrorists of the group known as the ANIMAL LIBERATION FRONT caused a panic when they announced they had poisoned candy bars produced by the Mars candy company. As a result, millions of Mars chocolate bars had to be removed from store shelves and destroyed.

November 18
Austria. Members of the ARMENIAN REVOLUTIONARY ARMY assassinated Turkish United Nations employee Evner Ergun.

November 27
India. The British High Commissioner in Bombay, Percy Morris, was murdered by members of the ABU NIDAL Organization.

November 1984–January 1985
Philippines. The communist NEW PEOPLE'S ARMY murdered the mayors of Za-

boanga City and Santa Ana, the deputy mayor of Lapuyan, and the police chief of Nueva Ecija.

December 3
Iran. Radical SHI'ITES of ISLAMIC JIHAD hijacked a Kuwaiti airliner to Iran. The terrorists murdered two Americans, representatives of the U.S. Agency for International Development, before "surrendering" to Iranian authorities.

December 11
Belgium and West Germany. The first in a series of bomb attacks destroyed a portion of a NATO fuel pipeline near Verviers, Belgium. The bombings continued throughout the month and appeared to be a coordinated effort of a number of terrorist organizations including the RED ARMY FACTION, COMMUNIST COMBATANT CELLS, REVOLUTIONARY CELLS, and ACTION DIRECTE.

December 25
United States. Anti-abortion activists simultaneously bombed three abortion clinics in Pensacola, Florida.

1985

January 8
Lebanon. Father Martin Jenco, a U.S. citizen living in Beirut, was kidnapped by ISLAMIC JIHAD. He was released in July 1986.

January
El Salvador. During the month, leftist gunmen murdered three prominent Salvadoran right-wing politicians.

January 25
France. French General Rene Auduran was murdered by ACTION DIRECTE terrorists apparently acting in concert with the West German terror group RED ARMY FACTION.

February
Colombia. Throughout the month the Medellin area was rocked by bomb blasts caused by the RICARDO FRANCO FRONT.

February 1
West Germany. The RED ARMY FACTION gunned down German industrialist Ernst Zimmerman near his Munich home.

February 23
United States. As bomb was detonated near a New York City Police Department precinct house by the U.S.-based terror group the RED GUERRILLA RESISTANCE.

March 7
El Salvador. Terrorists from FMLN assassinated Salvadoran army spokesman Lieutenant Colonel Ricardo Aristides Cienfuegos.

March 16
Lebanon. Terry A. Anderson, an American and the chief Middle East correspondent of the Associated Press, was kidnapped by ISLAMIC JIHAD. At this writing, Anderson remains imprisoned, the longest serving of the Western hostages taken in Lebanon.

March 23
El Salvador. The founder of the right-wing paramilitary organization ORDEN, General Jose Alberto Medrano, was killed by members of the FMLN.

March 25
Lebanon. The ABU NIDAL Organization, under the cover name "Revolutionary Association of Socialist Muslims," kidnapped British journalist Alex Collett. Collett is believed to have been hung by his terrorist captors in April 1986, but his body has not been found.

March 26
Peru. Gerardo Veracruz Berrocal, mayor of Pampa Cangallo, was murdered by SENDERO LUMINOSO terrorists.

March 27
Italy. The Italian RED BRIGADES killed Professor Ezio Tarantelli, president of the Institute of Economic Studies, Rome University.

April 21
Israel. Israeli defense forces sunk the coastal freighter *Atavarius*, killing 20 al-FATAH guerrillas attempting INFILTRATION from the sea.

May 22
Lebanon. French citizens Jean-Paul Kauffmann and Michel Seurat were abducted by SHI'ITE terrorists. Seurat was later murdered by his captors.

May 28
Lebanon. U.S. citizen David Jacobsen was kidnapped in Beirut by ISLAMIC JIHAD. He was released in November 1986.

June 9
Lebanon. The acting Dean of Agriculture at the American University in Beirut, Thomas M. Sutherland, a U.S. citizen was taken hostage by ISLAMIC JIHAD terrorists. Dr. Sutherland is still being held.

June 14
Greece. TWA's Rome-bound flight 847 was hijacked by HEZBOLLAH terrorists, who directed the plane, carrying 145 mostly American passengers, to Beirut. At Beirut the plane was refueled and flown to Algiers, then back again to Beirut. On the second stop at Beirut the two hijackers murdered U.S. Navy diver Robert Dean STETHEM, whom they had already beaten severely. The plane flew again to Algiers, where it picked up a third terrorist, then once again to Beirut. During the various stops terrorists released a number of the passengers, eventually whittling the hostage count down to 39. The crisis ended finally on June 30 with the release of the remaining captives. The terrorists were never prosecuted.

June 23
Ireland. An Air India flight, a Boeing 747 with 329 people on board, disappeared en route from Toronto, Canada to London. The wreckage found in the sea off the Irish coast indicated the aircraft had been destroyed in flight by a huge explosion. The Dashmesh Regiment, a Sikh group, and the KASHMIR LIBERATION ARMY each claimed responsibility for the crime.

July
Sweden, Denmark and the Netherlands. Nearly identical aluminum-dust bombs destroyed the Copenhagen and Stockholm offices of Northwest Airlines, the Amsterdam office of EL AL, and a Copenhagen synagogue. In 1989 Swedish authorities arrested four Arab men: Mohammed ABU TALB; Imandi Chaban; and two brothers, Mahmoud and Mustafa al-Moghrabi, for the crimes. It was this unrelated arrest that later led police officials to link Abu Talb to the December 1988 bombing of PAN AM 103.

July 10
New Zealand. The Greenpeace ship "RAINBOW WARRIOR" was blown up in Auckland. One Greenpeace activist died in the blast. Two French espionage agents were later charged with the crime.

July 24
Turkey. SHI'ITE killers shot and killed a Jordanian diplomat, Zaid J. Sati, in Ankara.

July 29
Spain. Vice Admiral Fausto Escrigas Estrada, Spain's Director of Defense Policy, was shot and killed by ETA/M in Madrid.

August 8
West Germany. The RED ARMY FACTION detonated a car bomb at the Rhein-Main Air Base, killing two and injuring 17. The terrorists had killed an off-duty American serviceman the previous night and used his military identification to gain access to the base.

August 20
India. SIKH terrorists attacked the New Delhi home of Gurdial Saini, president of India's powerful Congress Party. Saini was wounded and one of his guests was killed. Elsewhere, in the Punjab on the same day Sikhs also murdered Harchand Singh Longowal, a prominent Sikh moderate.

September 4
India. A leading member of the Congress Party, Arjun Dass, was assassinated by SIKH extremists.

September 25
Cyprus. Al-FATAH terrorists seized three Israelis in Larnaca. When their demands were not met, the terrorists murdered their captives. They had hoped to trade the Israelis for 20 Palestinians in Israeli jails.

September 30
Lebanon. For the first time Soviets were kidnapped during Lebanon's hostage-taking spree. Though one hostage was killed, the other three were quickly released by their captors from the ISLAMIC LIBERATION ORGANIZATION.

October 7
Mediterranean. The cruise ship ACHILLE LAURO was hijacked by POPULAR LIBERATION FRONT terrorists. During the hostage crisis the terrorists brutally murdered the wheelchair-bound and elderly American passenger Leon Klinghoffer.

October 11
United States. Alex Odeh, director of the American-Arab Anti-Discrimination League, died when a bomb planted by the JEWISH DEFENSE LEAGUE destroyed his Los Angeles office.

October 25
Mozambique. Two Jesuit priests were kidnapped by RENAMO terrorists, who later murdered the men.

November 6
Colombia. M-19, the Colombian terrorist organization, seized Bogota's Palace of Justice, taking almost 500 hostages, including justices of the Supreme Court and the Council of State. The following day security forces launched a full-scale attack to retake the building and rescue the hostages. All of the nearly 20 terrorists died in the battle, as did 11 Colombian soldiers, 11 Supreme Court justices and 50 other hostages.

November 23
Malta. Four members of the ABU NIDAL Organization, operating as the previously unknown "Egyptian Liberation Organization," hijacked an Egyptair jet carrying 98 people as it flew from Athens to Cairo. The flight was forced to land at Luqa, Malta after a brief gun battle between the terrorists and an on-board security guard. Once on the ground, 13 women were allowed to leave the plane. Then, in an effort to force the Maltese to refuel the craft, the killers began slowly shooting their hostages one by one. On November 24, an Egyptian commando force recaptured the plane, but not before 57 people—passengers, terrorists and commandos—died in a gun battle and ensuing fire on board the plane.

November 25
West Germany. An Iranian terrorist is believed to have been responsible for a bomb-

ing at a U.S. military shopping center in Frankfurt.

December
France. A series of HEZBOLLAH bombings rocked Paris. The group claimed the attacks were on behalf of the "Committee in Solidarity with Arab Political Prisoners."

December 23
South Africa. The AFRICAN NATIONAL CONGRESS detonated a bomb at a Durban shopping center, killing five people and wounding 48.

December 27
Italy and Austria. Terrorist killers of the renegade ABU NIDAL Organization slaughtered 18 holiday travelers in the Rome and Vienna airports in coordinated attacks.

1986

January 2
Guatemala. The chief of Guatemala's secret police, Ignacio Gonzalez Palacios, was shot as he drove through Guatemala City.

January–May
Lebanon. The ARMENIAN SECRET ARMY FOR THE LIBERATION OF ARMENIA went on a five-month-long rampage during which the group was responsible for one kidnapping, nine assassinations, numerous injuries and substantial property damage. The target of this aggression was the membership of the right-wing Armenian Dashnag Party.

January–October
West Germany. A concerted bombing campaign, aimed at both business and public institutions, was conducted by the REVOLUTIONARY CELLS group during this period.

February 6
Spain. Vice Admiral Cristobol Colon de Caraval y Maroto and his chauffeur were killed in a grenade attack by ETA/M.

February 22
Italy. Two women and a man, RED BRIGADES terrorists, attempted to murder Antonio da Empoli, economic advisor to Prime Minister Bettino Craxi. Da Empoli was slightly wounded, but his bodyguard killed one female terrorist and wounded the other. The male terrorist escaped.

February 28
Sweden. Olaf Palme, Prime Minister of Sweden, was assassinated as he and his wife left a Stockholm movie theater. Originally there was speculation that the KURDISH WORKER'S PARTY was involved, but Swedish police eventually arrested a Swede. He was released in 1989 because of irregularities in the evidence against him. At this writing the murder remains a mystery.

March 2
West Bank. The recently appointed Arab mayor of Nablus in the occupied territories, Zafir al-Masri, a moderate, was murdered by Arab extremists.

March 8
Lebanon. Four members of a French television news team were abducted by HEZBOLLAH.

April 2
Greece. A TWA airliner was rocked by a midair bomb explosion as it approached the Athens airport. The plane was able to land safely despite a hole in the fuselage, but the blast killed four passengers. Authorities linked one of the passengers to terrorism sponsor Syria.

April 5
West Germany. Three people were killed, two of whom were American servicemen, and more than 200 were injured when an explosion ripped through the crowded LA BELLE DISCO in West Berlin. The U.S. government's investigation linked the incident

to Libya and on April 15 the U.S. Air Force conducted a retaliatory raid on two Libyan cities.

April 11
Lebanon. Brian Keenan of Ireland was kidnapped by the Iranian-backed SHI'ITE terrorists of the REVOLUTIONARY JUSTICE ORGANIZATION.

April 17
Lebanon. British citizen John McCarthy was taken hostage by a group calling itself the "Revolutionary Commando Cells."

April 17
United Kingdom. Another airliner disaster was averted when EL AL security personnel discovered a bomb in the luggage of an Irish woman. The woman, who was pregnant, had apparently been duped into carrying the bag by her Jordanian boyfriend. The investigation led back to Syria and Libya.

April 28
Lebanon. The ISLAM LIBERATION ORGANIZATION, also known as HEZBOLLAH, kidnapped two Greek Cypriots in Beirut.

May 3
Sri Lanka. An Air Lanka airliner was destroyed by the LIBERATION TIGERS OF TAMIL EELAM. Seventeen people were killed in the bomb blast.

May 5
Peru. Left-wing guerrillas, probably from SENDERO LUMINOSO, assassinated Rear Admiral Carlos Ponce de Leon Canessa.

May 7
Sri Lanka. A bomb exploded in the capital city of Colombo, killing 14 and wounding more than 100.

May 14
Indonesia. The ANTI-IMPERIALIST INTERNATIONAL BRIGADE claimed responsibility for a car bombing outside the Canadian Embassy in Jakarta.

May–June.
The Netherlands and Indonesia. Authorities implicated terrorists from the JAPANESE RED ARMY in separate investigations half a world apart. Yu KIKUMURA was apprehended at Amsterdam's Schiphol Airport carrying a bomb in his luggage. Tsutomu Shirosaki was identified from fingerprints left in a hotel room from which mortars had been fired at both the U.S. and Japanese embassies in Jakarta.

June
Spain. The northern city of Bilboa was hit by several IRAULTZA bombing attacks during the month.

June 18
Peru. Between 150 and 200 SENDERO LUMINOSO guerrillas being held in a Peruvian jail outside Lima were killed when they rioted in the prison.

June 26
Peru. SENDERO LUMINOSO bombed a train carrying visitors to the Inca ruins at Machu Picchu. Eight tourists were killed and 40 were injured.

July 14
Spain. ETA/M killed 10 Civil Guard cadets with a truck bomb; 56 other people were wounded.

July
Sri Lanka. During a three-day period the LIBERATION TIGERS OF TAMIL EELAM killed more than 100 people in bombing attacks.

August 8
Saudi Arabia. Saudi authorities intercepted 113 Muslim pilgrims from IRAN as they entered the country to visit Mecca. The Saudis confiscated more than 50 kilos of plastic explosives.

August 10

India. The SIKH organization DAL KHALSA claimed responsibility for the assassination of General A.S. Vaidya, the leader of the Indian Army's attack on the GOLDEN TEMPLE OF AMRISTAR.

September 1

India. SIKH assassins killed R.P. Gaind, a Punjabi judge.

September 5

Pakistan. Twenty people died when terrorists from the ABU NIDAL Organization opened fire on a group of passengers aboard a Pan Am plane at Karachi airport. The killers had been thwarted in their attempt to hijack the aircraft.

September 6

Turkey. Two members of the ABU NIDAL Organization attacked an Istanbul synagogue, killing 21 people. The terrorists committed suicide.

September 9

Lebanon. The director of a private school in Beirut, Frank Herbert Reed, was taken hostage by a group identified as the "Arab Revolutionary Cells." Reed was released in 1990.

September 12

Lebanon. Joseph James Cicippio, an American employee of the American University in Beirut, was kidnapped by the radical Iranian-sponsored SHI'ITE group the REVOLUTIONARY JUSTICE ORGANIZATION.

September 17

France. A FARL terrorist murdered five people and injured dozens more when he threw a bomb into a crowded Paris shop.

September

Portugal. The "Armed Revolutionary Organization," apparently a cover name for FP-25, conducted a bombing campaign against coastal tourist sites in Portugal.

October

Greece. Both the REVOLUTIONARY ORGANIZATION 17 NOVEMBER and the ELA claimed responsibility for a series of bomb attacks focused on Greek government tax offices.

October 10

West Germany. The head of the political department at West Germany's Foreign Ministry was murdered by terrorists from the RED ARMY FACTION.

October 21

Lebanon. The REVOLUTIONARY JUSTICE ORGANIZATION abducted U.S. citizen Edward Austin Tracy.

October 25

Spain. The Spanish military governor of Guipuzcoa, a Basque province, was killed by ETA/M. General Rafael Garrido Gil, his wife and son all perished when a bomb exploded atop the automobile in which they were traveling.

October 25

India. SIKH terrorists continued their assassination campaign against India's ruling Congress Party by murdering Onkar Chandh, the party's leader.

November

Colombia. The ELN was particularly active during the month, killing a Colombian soldier in an ambush, bombing a gold mining dredge in the Nechi River, attacking an oil camp, and kidnapping two people.

November 17

France. Renault president George Besse was murdered by ACTION DIRECTE gunmen near his Paris residence.

December 15

France. ACTION DIRECTE attempted to assassinate Justice Minister Alain Peyrefitte.

December

Peru. MRTA and MIR merged their organizations and conducted numerous anti-U.S. bombings during the month.

December 25

Saudi Arabia. Iranian-sponsored terrorists attempted to hijack an Iraqi airliner en route from Baghdad to Amman, Jordan. The aircraft crashed in Saudi Arabia, killing 62 of the 107 people on board, including two of the four hijackers.

1987

January–June

Colombia. In the first six months of 1987 the ELN continued to target Colombia's oil production facilities. During this period, ELN seems to have displaced M-19 as the senior partner in the National Guerrilla Coordinator.

January 20

Lebanon. In two separate incidents, SHI'ITE extremists thought to be connected with HEZBOLLAH abducted West Germany businessmen Rudolf Cordes and Alfred Schmidt. Schmidt was released in September 1987, Cordes in September 1988.

January 20

Lebanon. Terry Waite, the personal emissary of the Archbishop of Canterbury, was abducted while on one of his numerous missions to the Middle East to seek the release of Western hostages. The Anglican Church envoy is believed to be a prisoner of ISLAMIC JIHAD.

January 24

Lebanon. A Palestinian offshoot of ISLAMIC JIHAD, calling itself "Islamic Holy War for the Liberation of Palestine," seized three Americans: Jesse Turner, a mathematics professor at Beirut University College; Alann

Steen, a professor of journalism; and Robert Polhill, an assistant professor of business. Polhill was released in April 1990.

February 21

France. French police arrested the four top leaders of the terrorist group ACTION DIRECTE in a farmhouse near the city of Orleans. The arrests greatly decreased the organization's operational capacity.

February–March

Chile. The MANUEL RODRIGUEZ PATRIOTIC FRONT destroyed pylons and towers carrying electrical power on a number of occasions. At various times during the two-month period sections of Santiago, Valparaiso, and Vina del Mar were blacked out.

February

Peru. During the month SENDERO LUMINOSO bombers hit seven Lima banks.

March 18

Djibouti. A bomb exploded inside the crowded Cafe Historil, a bistro known to be frequented by Europeans, killing five Frenchmen, three West Germans, and three of the local populace; another 50 people were injured. The bomber, a Palestinian, was arrested a short time later. His motive may have been to avenge recent Libyan defeats at the hands of the French in the Chad war.

March 20

Italy. Two terrorists, mounted on a motorcycle, shot and killed Italian Air Force General Licio Giogieri as he was being driven to his home. At the time of his death, Giorgieri was director general of armaments in the aerospace sector of the Italian Defense Ministry.

March 23

West Germany. A large car bomb exploded outside an officers' club at the British Army base at Rheindahlen, injuring more than 30 people. The PROVISIONAL WING OF THE IRISH REPUBLICAN ARMY claimed responsibility. Ironically, most of those hurt were West Germany military personnel and their spouses, and not the targeted British.

March
Peru.   During the month MRTA introduced a new modus operandi focusing on propagandizing. They took over a radio station, invaded a church, and occupied a private manufacturing concern, all for the purpose of delivering revolutionary speeches.

March
Japan.   CHUKAKU-HA launched a series of bombing attacks intended to terrorize construction companies involved in the expansion of Narita Airport.

April 24
Greece.   A remote-control bomb was detonated as a busload of American military personnel passed near its hidden location. Sixteen servicemen were injured. The REVOLUTIONARY ORGANIZATION 17 NOVEMBER immediately claimed responsibility.

April
Sri Lanka.   The LIBERATION TIGERS OF TAMIL EELAM went on a bloody rampage against the Singhalese populace during the month, blowing up four passenger buses and the central bus station in Colombo. In all, more than 200 people were killed.

May 25
Puerto Rico.   A group calling itself the GUERRILLA FORCES FOR LIBERATION claimed responsibility for the placement of eight crude pipebombs at seven locations on the island. Only four of the devices actually exploded, causing minor damage.

June 9
Italy.   A series of terrorist incidents took place in Rome, apparently timed to coincide with the Economic Conference of the seven Western industrial powers, who were meeting in Vienna. Outside the U.S. Embassy, a car bomb exploded; inside the compound, two rocket-like devices landed, and a similar missile struck the grounds of the British Embassy. Some of these projectiles failed to detonate, and those that did explode caused only minor damage. The ANTI-IMPERIALIST INTERNATIONAL BRIGADE, believed to be a group associated with, if not an element of, the JAPANESE RED ARMY, claimed responsibility for the attacks.

June 17
Lebanon.   "The Organization for the Defense of Free People," another alias of the Iranian-sponsored terrorists of HEZBOLLAH, kidnapped American journalist Charles Glass. Glass apparently escaped from his captors on August 17.

July 14
Pakistan.   Authorities believe that coordinated bombings at two locations within a crowded Karachi shopping district were STATE-SPONSORED TERRORISM. The U.S. Department of State has attributed the attacks to WAD, the Afghan secret police organization. The attacks were apparently intended to dampen Pakistani support for the Afghan resistance.

July 24
Central African Republic.   An Air Afrique flight that had originated in Bangui was hijacked by a single terrorist. The plane landed in Geneva, where the hijacker murdered a French passenger. The hijacker demanded that imprisoned HEZBOLLAH terrorists be released. The incident ended when a group of passengers disarmed the hijacker.

August 8
Honduras.   Twelve people, among them six Americans, were injured in Comayuga when a pipe bomb exploded outside a pop-

ular Chinese restaurant frequented by U.S. servicemen from the nearby Palmerola Air Base.

August 10
Greece. The REVOLUTIONARY ORGANIZATION 17 NOVEMBER struck a busload of U.S. servicemen. The bomb blast injured 10 Air Force personnel from the Hellenikon Air Base.

August 10
Switzerland. In Geneva, a former Iranian Air Force pilot who had defected earlier in the year was shot by two unknown assailants.

September 15
Cyprus. PLO guerrillas murdered three vacationing Israelis as they sat aboard a pleasure boat in Larnaca harbor.

September–October
Peru. SENDERO LUMINOSO detonated car bombs near the Congress building, causing a partial blackout in Lima. Also during the period, the group slaughtered 40 civilians in two villages in Tocache province and assassinated APRA party leader Nelson Pozo.

October 1
Tunisia. The Israeli Air Force struck the PLO's Tunis headquarters in an air attack that destroyed the building and killed 65 people, many of whom were innocent bystanders.

October 2
United Kingdom. An anti-KHOMEINI activist and his son were murdered in their London home by a group calling itself the "Guardians of the Islamic Revolution and Soldiers of Iman Khomeini."

October 26
Philippines. In separate incidents, two U.S. military personnel and a Filipino business-

man were murdered by assassination teams known as SPARROW SQUADS dispatched by the NEW PEOPLE'S ARMY.

October 30
France. The EKSUND, a merchant vessel, was seized off the coast of Brittany. The ship contained more than 150 tons of munitions, including surface-to-air missiles. Among the crew were five members of the PROVISIONAL WING OF THE IRISH REPUBLICAN ARMY; the weapons originated in Libya.

November 8
Northern Ireland. A ceremony in the town of ENNISKILLEN honoring Britain's war dead was bombed by the PROVISIONAL WING OF THE IRISH REPUBLICAN ARMY. Eleven people died and another 60 were wounded.

November 25
Zimbabwe. Sixteen people, including six children, living and working on a Bulawayo farm operated by Pentecostal missionaries were brutally murdered by 20 machete-wielding terrorists. The attack was believed to have been racially motivated. All but one of the victims was white and the assailants are thought to have been members of the black guerrilla organization ZAPU.

November 29
Burma. STATE SPONSORED TERRORISM claimed the lives of 115 passengers and crew of (South) Korean Airlines flight 858. The aircraft was destroyed by an explosive device secreted on the plane by two North Korean agents who had hoped to spoil the following summer's Seoul Olympic Games. The two terrorists, a man and a woman who had disembarked at the plane's last stop, were apprehended by authorities. Both attempted suicide, but only the man succeeded. The woman, Kim Hyun Hee, confessed to the crime and implicated the North Korean government.

November

Colombia. In separate attacks conducted throughout the month, ELN murdered 17 Colombian policemen and four soldiers.

December 11.

Spain. Eleven people died and more than 40 were wounded when ETA bombed an apartment complex in Zaragosa housing Spanish Civil Guard members. Among the dead were four children.

December 8

West Bank and the Gaza Strip. The date marks the beginning of the INTIFADA, the often violent unrest in the Israeli-occupied territories.

December 26

Spain. A bar in Barcelona run by the American USO (United Services Organization) was struck by two Catalan separatist groups, the CATALAN RED ARMY and TERRA LLIURE. The hand grenade attack killed one American serviceman and injured nine others.

1988

January 12

Zimbabwe. A remote-control car bomb, planted by ex-Rhodesian security force members, exploded outside a home owned by the AFRICAN NATIONAL CONGRESS. The only casualty of the blast was the Zambian accomplice of the three terrorists.

January 18

Japan. The construction site at Tokyo's Narita Airport, a favorite target of Japanese leftists, was struck by five homemade rockets. The projectiles fell short of their apparent target, a passenger terminal. CHUKAKU-HA claimed responsibility for the attack.

January 21

Greece. An American officer of the Drug Enforcement Agency was the target of a failed REVOLUTIONARY ORGANIZATION 17 NOVEMBER assassination attempt.

February 17

Lebanon. U.S. Marine Corps Lt. Col. William R. HIGGINS, commander of the United Nations Truce Supervisory Observer Group in that country, was kidnapped by HEZBOLLAH terrorists using the name ORGANIZATION OF THE OPPRESSED ON EARTH. Lt. Col. Higgins was murdered by his captors in July 1989.

February 20

Senegal. Authorities arrested three men at Dakar Airport for possession of explosives and weapons. One of the potential terrorists was a Senegalese national. The other two men were from Libya.

March 7

Israel. Al-FATAH terrorists killed six people on board a passenger bus.

March 11

Sri Lanka. Sinhalese terrorists killed 17 Tamils, ostensibly in retaliation for a terrorist attack by the LIBERATION TIGERS OF TAMIL EELAM that had claimed 39 Sinhalese lives.

March 23

Colombia. The U.S. Embassy in Bogota was struck by a rocket fired by M-19 terrorists. There were no casualties and only minor property damage resulted.

March 25

India. Crew members of Italian air carrier Alitalia were the target of an attack by a lone terrorist dispatched by the ABU NIDAL Organization. The assault, which wounded a pilot, came as the flight personnel rode in a bus at Bombay airport.

April 5

Kuwait. The Iranian-supported terrorists of HEZBOLLAH hijacked Kuwait Airways flight 422 as it traveled from Bangkok, Thailand to Kuwait. The hostage crisis, initiated in a vain effort to compel the Kuwaiti government to release 17 SHI'ITE terrorists from prison, dragged on for more than two weeks. During that time the plane traveled to Iran and Cyprus. The hijackers murdered two of their Kuwaiti captives but their demands were not met.

April 12

United States. Yu KIKUMURA, a JAPANESE RED ARMY member, was arrested at a New Jersey Turnpike rest area. Kikumura's car contained three powerful bombs along with other explosives gear. It is believed that he intended to bomb some site frequented by U.S. military personnel in retaliation for the U.S. air raid on Libya in April 1986.

April 14

Italy. A car bomb detonated outside a Naples USO club, killing a U.S. Navy enlisted woman and four other people. Responsibility for the attack, which took place just one day short of the second anniversary of the U.S. air raid on Libya, was claimed by the JAPANESE RED ARMY front group "The Organization of the Jihad Brigades."

April 14

Colombia. M-19 terrorists bombed the office of the U.S. Information Service in Medellin.

April 15

Spain. Another bombing, apparently linked to the anniversary of the Libyan raid, took place at the U.S. Air Force communications center in Humosa.

April 16

Italy. The COMMUNIST COMBATANT PARTY, an Italian terrorist organization linked to the RED BRIGADES, assassinated Italian Senator Roberto Ruffilli, a member of the ruling Christian Democratic Party, in his home.

April 16

Peru. Another United States Information Service bi-national center was attacked, this time in Lima. MRTA claimed responsibility.

April 16

Tunisia. A hit team, believed to have been dispatched by Israel, killed al-FATAH deputy commander Khalil al-WAZIR. Al-Wazir was known by the nom de guerre Abu Jihad.

April 19

Costa Rica. Another U.S. Information Service bi-national center became the target of a terrorist attack. Several people were injured in the San Jose offices.

April 28

Greece. Hagop HAGOPIAN, leader of the ARMENIAN SECRET ARMY FOR THE LIBERATION OF ARMENIA, was shot to death outside his Athens home, apparently by members of his own terrorist group.

May 1

Netherlands. In two coordinated attacks terrorists from the PROVISIONAL WING OF THE IRISH REPUBLICAN ARMY (PIRA) struck at British servicemen. Three Royal Air Force airmen were shot, one fatally, by PIRA gunmen as they left a bar in the Dutch town of Roermond. In Nieuw Bergen a car bomb killed two other RAF personnel.

May 10

India. Indian authorities believe the JAPANESE RED ARMY was responsible for the bombing of the New Delhi offices of Citibank. The attack killed one person and injured 13.

May 11

Cyrpus. A suicide car bomber killed two people and wounded 17 when he detonated his device outside Israel's Nicosia embassy building. The ABU NIDAL Organization claimed the attack was in retaliation for the shooting of Khalil al-WAZIR.

May 15
Sudan. The Acropole Hotel and the British Sudan Club in Khartoum were simultaneously attacked by ABU NIDAL Organization terrorists. Grenades and automatic weapons fire killed eight and wounded 21.

June 9
Peru. The U.S. ambassador's residence was the target of a MRTA mortar attack. The terrorists fired three rounds without effect.

June 13
Peru. Two contract employees of the U.S. Agency for International Development were ambushed and murdered by terrorists from the SENDERO LUMINOSO group.

June 28
Greece. The U.S. Defense attaché at the Athens embassy, Captain William Nordeen, was killed by a car bomb set by REVOLUTIONARY ORGANIZATION 17 NOVEMBER.

July 11
Greece. The cruise ship CITY OF POROS was the scene of an attack by ABU NIDAL Organization terrorists that killed nine people and injured 100. A second bomb, possibly intended to explode after the ship docked, instead detonated prematurely in an automobile, parked near the dock, killing the two suspected terrorist occupants.

July 13
West Germany. Nine members of the British Army's Royal Engineer Corps were injured when a bomb planted by the PROVISIONAL WING OF THE IRISH REPUBLICAN ARMY detonated outside their barracks in Duisberg.

July 17
Honduras. CINCHONERO terrorists claimed responsibility for an attack in San Pedro Sula that injured a number of American servicemen.

August 8
Bolivia. A bomb exploded as the motorcade carrying American Secretary of State George Shultz passed along a stretch of highway outside the Bolivian capital of La Paz. Neither the secretary nor any member of his party was hurt. The "Simon Bolivar Commando" group is believed to have been responsible for the attack.

August 20
Northern Ireland. The IRISH REPUBLICAN ARMY bombed a British Army bus in County Tyrone, killing eight of the soldiers on board.

September 7
Italy. The RED BRIGADES were dealt a serious blow when 21 suspected members were arrested by Rome police.

September 11
Haiti. Nine people died and 77 were wounded when soldiers and members of the TONTON MACOUTE burst into a religious service in the St. Jean Bosco Church in Port-au-Prince. The attack reportedly was engineered by Col. Frank Romain, mayor of the city and close associate of the president, Henri Namphy, and it appeared to be aimed at the parish's chief priest, Jean-Bertrand Aristide, a prominent member of the regime's political opposition. The incident and others like it that took place during the following days led to the ouster of Namphy by Gen. Prosper Avril on September 17.

September 11
Japan. Police preempted a possible CHUKAKU-HA terrorist attack when they raided the group's hideout and weapons cache in

a warehouse outside Niigata City. Seized in the raid were a large quantity of explosives and a number of mortars.

September 20

West Germany. The International Monetary Fund/World Bank Conference in West Berlin was the scene of a failed RED ARMY FACTION assassination attempt, aimed at a member of West Germany's Foreign Ministry.

October 21

Turkey. A Saudi official was assassinated in Ankara by members of the ISLAMIC JIHAD IN HEJAZ.

October 26

West Germany. Hafez Dalkimoni, Marwan Khreesat, Hashim Abassi, Mohammed al-Moghrabi and 12 others were arrested when West German police raided Abassi's apartment in the village of Nuess. Many of those arrested were known to be associated with the POPULAR FRONT FOR THE LIBERATION OF PALESTINE-GENERAL COMMAND. A search of the apartment turned up a quantity of Semtex (a type of plastic explosive) and an explosive device, concealed in a cassette player, activated by a barometric switch of the type which terrorists used to destroy airliners in flight. The West German police quickly released all their prisoners except Dalkimoni and one other man, citing insufficient evidence. They also failed to uncover additional bombs on the premises and in Khreesat's car parked outside. Investigators now believe that the bomb which destroyed PAN AM 103 on December 21, 1989 was missed in that search. After the Pan Am disaster West German officials were persuaded to search Abassi's apartment again; this time they discovered three more similar bombs, one of which exploded and killed the West German bomb expert trying to open it.

November 1

El Salvador. FMLN guerrillas attacked the National Guard headquarters in San Salvador and assaulted a prison facility.

November 5

El Salvador. A rocket, believed to have been fired by FMLN terrorists, struck the Sheraton Hotel in San Salvador. There were no injuries.

November 11

United States. An incident of ANIMAL RIGHTS TERRORISM was averted when a woman was arrested as she planted a bomb outside a Connecticut company's offices. The firm uses dogs in its medical testing procedures.

November 17

Lebanon. Peter Winkler, a Swiss official of the International Red Cross, was kidnapped by three gunmen who stopped his car outside the city of Sidon. He was released unharmed on December 17, 1988. Although no group ever claimed responsibility for the abduction, a Swiss government official indicated that Yasir ARAFAT had played a role in obtaining Winkler's release.

November 28

Northern Ireland. The only victims of an IRISH REPUBLICAN ARMY bomb that had been intended for ROYAL ULSTER CONSTABULARY personnel were a Catholic man and his 13-year-old granddaughter.

December 5

Peru. Four rural development workers, two Frenchmen and two Peruvians, were murdered by SENDERO LUMINOSO terrorists.

December 13

Zambia. A car bomb killed two people and wounded 13 in Livingstone. Zambian authorities blamed the South African government.

December 21

United Kingdom. PAN AM 103 exploded in midair as it flew over Scotland, killing all 259 people on board. On the ground an additional 11 people perished when a huge section of the shattered aircraft crashed into a row of houses in the village of Lockerbie. The giant 747, bound for New York from London, had been destroyed by a bomb concealed inside a radio-cassette player, probably loaded aboard in Frankfurt, West Germany. Though no one has yet been charged with the crime, evidence points to the POPULAR FRONT FOR THE LIBERATION OF PALESTINE-GENERAL COMMAND, the terrorist organization led by Ahmed JABRIL. Investigators now suspect that Mohammed ABU TALB, a Jabril lieutenant, recently imprisoned in Sweden for bombing attacks against the offices of Northwest Airlines in 1985–86, may have played a role in getting the bomb aboard Pan Am 103.

1989

January 10

Greece. REVOLUTIONARY ORGANIZATION 17 NOVEMBER assassinated public prosecutor Costas Androulidakis in Athens.

January 18

Greece. Public prosecutor Panayotis Tarasouleas was murdered by REVOLUTIONARY ORGANIZATION 17 NOVEMBER terrorists.

January 23

Greece. Gunmen mounted on a motorcycle killed public prosecutor Anastassios Bernardos outside his Athens home. The terrorist group REVOLUTIONARY ORGANIZATION 1 MAY claimed responsibility.

January 23

Argentina. The TABLADA army base was seized by leftist guerrillas under the command of Enrique GORRIARIAN MERLO.

January 25

Honduras. The CINCHONEROS POPULAR LIBERATION MOVEMENT killed former army chief General Gustavo Alvarez Martinez.

February 12

Northern Ireland. Prominent Roman Catholic lawyer Pat Finucane was shot and killed in the kitchen of his home, where he was eating a meal with his family, by members of the ULSTER FREEDOM FIGHTERS.

February 14

United Kingdom. Indian-born British novelist Salman RUSHDIE went into hiding after the Ayatollah Ruhollah KHOMEINI called on Muslims to kill the author of *Satanic Verses*, a book that is considered blasphemous by Islamic fundamentalists. Mr. Rushdie emerged from hiding in December 1990.

February 28

United States. Two California bookstores were bombed during the night to protest their sale of the Salman RUSHDIE novel *Satanic Verses*.

March 7

Northern Ireland. Three Protestant men were murdered in Coagh by IRISH REPUBLICAN ARMY gunmen.

March 10

United States. A pipe bomb exploded in the van driven by the wife of U.S. Navy Capt. Will C. Rogers. Mrs. Rogers escaped unhurt. The attack was believed to be in retaliation for the downing of an Iranian civil airliner in the Persian Gulf in July 1988 by the USS *Vincennes*, the navy cruiser commanded by Captain Rogers.

April

Sri Lanka. Bombing campaigns carried out by the JVP, TAMILS and other militant groups killed more than 100 people during the month.

April 3
United States. Members of the ANIMAL LIBERATION FRONT broke into a research facility of the University of Arizona and freed more than 1,200 rabbits, mice, frogs, and other test animals. They then set fire to the building housing the laboratories and to the school's administration building.

April 17
West Germany. A police officer died when the explosive device he was attempting to disarm detonated. The bomb had been hidden in a radio-cassette player similar to the one used to destroy PAN AM 103 over Lockerbie, Scotland, in December 1988. The device had been seized in a raid on a hideout of the POPULAR FRONT FOR THE LIBERATION OF PALESTINE-GENERAL COMMAND near Dusseldorf.

April 19
El Salvador. A previously unheard-of terrorist group, the "Gerardo Barrios Civic Forces," claimed responsibility for a car bomb that took the life of Salvadoran Attorney General Roberto Garcia Alvarado.

April 21
Philippines. Communist terrorists of the NEW PEOPLE'S ARMY murdered U.S. military advisor Lieutenant Colonel James N. Rowe in Manila.

May 1
South Africa. Dr. David Webster, an anti-APARTHEID activist, was murdered. Later in the year, South African police arrested Ferdi Barnard, an ex-narcotics detective recently paroled from prison for killing a police suspect, and charged him with the crime. Barnard was believed to be linked to an organization systematically assassinating liberal activists.

May 7
Peru. SENDERO LUMINOSO terrorists killed two Peruvian congressmen.

May 12
Lebanon. A hitherto unknown terrorist group, the "Cells of Armed Struggle," kidnapped Jack Mann, a 75-year-old British citizen.

June 9
El Salvador. The FMLN is believed to be responsible for the death of Jose Antonio Rodriguez Porth, Minister of the Presidency.

July 31
Lebanon. The ORGANIZATION OF THE OPPRESSED ON EARTH delivered a gruesome videotape to the Beirut offices of a Western news agency. The tape showed the lifeless body of American Marine Lieutenant Colonel William R. Higgins swinging by the neck at the end of a rope. The murderers claimed the hanging of Lt. Col. Higgins was in retaliation for the kidnapping by ISRAEL, on July 27, of HEZBOLLAH leader Sheikh Abdel Karim Obeid.

August 18
Colombia. Senator Luis Carlos Galan, a leading presidential candidate, was assassinated by MEDELLIN CARTEL gunmen as he delivered a campaign speech.

September 12
Namibia. Dr. Anton Lubowski, a member of the SWAPO leadership, was murdered, allegedly by Donald Acheson, a man police believe had ties to an assassination ring that had been attempting to eliminate leftist politicians.

September 19
Niger. All 171 people aboard French airline UTA's flight from Brazzaville, Congo to Paris died when the aircraft exploded in

midair shortly after takeoff from an intermediate stop in Chad. ISLAMIC JIHAD terrorists took credit for the bombing, linking it to Israel's kidnapping of Sheikh Abdel Karim Obeid.

November 11

El Salvador. A massive offensive by more than 1,000 FMLN guerrillas was launched against the capital city of San Salvador. Large areas of the city were occupied by the terrorists before an army counterattack finally drove them out of the city four days later.

November 16

El Salvador. Six Roman Catholic priests and two women employees were dragged from their beds at Jose Simeon Canas University of Central America and executed by a right-wing DEATH SQUAD. The government later charged nine Salvadoran military personnel with the crime.

November 18

Northern Ireland. Three British soldiers were killed while on patrol in the Mourne Mountains, County Down; a fourth soldier was wounded. The victims were riding in an armored vehicle when it struck a landmine, planted by the IRISH REPUBLICAN ARMY. On the same day in Colchester, England, another bomb, planted under the driver's seat of an automobile, critically injured an off-duty soldier and his wife.

November 20

Spain. Two fascist gunmen attacked seven members of the Spanish parliamentary delegation of Herri Batasuna, the political arm of ETA, as they ate in a Madrid restaurant. One of the members of the delegation, Josu Muguruza, was killed.

November 22

Lebanon. Just 17 days after his election the Christian president of Lebanon, Rene Moawad, was assassinated. Mr. Moawad

and 23 others died when a powerful bomb exploded as his motorcade passed through the streets of Beirut. Narrowly escaping death in the same blast were the two other principal members of the new Lebanese government, Prime Minister Selim al-Hoss and Speaker of the Parliament Hussein al-Husseini. The three, a Christian, a SUNNI Muslim, and a SHI'ITE Muslim respectively, had been elected as part of a national unity government designed to bind together a Lebanese nation torn apart by more than 14 years of ethnically and religiously motivated civil war. Though no group stepped forward to claim responsibility for the killings, it was widely suspected to have been the work of followers of the Maronite Christian leader General Michel Aoun. Aoun has claimed to be the rightful leader of Lebanon since his "appointment" as interim prime minister in 1988 by outgoing president Amin Gemayel.

November 27

Colombia. The EXTRADITABLES, the terrorist arm of the notorious MEDELLIN CARTEL, planted a bomb aboard a domestic Avianca Airlines Boeing 727 flight, destroying the plane in midair and killing all 107 people on board. The group claimed the aircraft had been bombed to kill five police informants they said were among the passengers.

November 28

El Salvador. Leftist gunmen murdered Jose Francisco Guerrero, personal secretary of El Salvador's president, as he stepped out of a San Salvador restaurant.

November 30

West Germany. A remote-controlled bomb killed Alfred Herrhausen, the head of the Deutsche Bank, as his chauffeur-driven automobile passed through the Frankfurt suburb of Bad Homburg. Responsibility was immediately claimed by the RED ARMY FACTION.

December 5

Israel. An army patrol killed five Palestinian gunmen attempting the INFILTRATION of Israel via the Sinai desert border with Egypt. The heavily armed guerrillas carried with them automatic weapons and more than 50 hand grenades.

December 6

Colombia. More than 50 people were killed and 250 injured when a truck bomb exploded in front of the headquarters of the Colombian police. The massive bomb, estimated to contain more than 1,000 pounds of dynamite, was detonated by the EXTRADITABLES, a group of NARCO-TERRORISTS.

December 7

Northern Ireland. A 500-pound car bomb exploded in a shopping center in Lisburn. The IRISH REPUBLICAN ARMY claimed credit for the attack that injured 19 people.

December 8

India. The daughter of interior Minister Mufti Mohammad Sayeed was kidnapped by Kashmiri separatists. She was released five days later after the Indian government freed five separatists from custody.

December 11

France. Corsican separatists destroyed 40 holiday homes, owned by mainland French, under construction on the island.

December 13

Italy. An Italian court dismissed charges of armed insurrection against 168 members of the notorious RED BRIGADES terrorist organization on the grounds that the group had never seriously threatened the security of the state.

December 15

Colombia. The Bogota government scored its first major victory in its war with the MEDELLIN CARTEL when Colombian troops and police cornered and killed the cocaine trafficker Jose Gonzalo RODRIGUEZ GACHA. Rodriguez Gacha, his son Freddy, and 15 of their gunmen died in a shootout with authorities near the city of Cartagena.

December 16

United States. A series of apparently racially motivated mail bomb attacks aimed at individuals associated with civil rights cases heard by the U. S. Court of Appeals for the 11th Circuit began with a parcel bomb that killed Judge Robert S. Vance at his home in Birmingham, Alabama. A second bomb two days later killed civil rights attorney Robert Robinson at his Savannah, Georgia law office. Third and fourth bombs were discovered and disarmed at the headquarters of the 11th Circuit in Atlanta, Georgia and at the offices of the NAACP in Jacksonville, Florida. A previously unknown group, "Americans for a Competent Federal Judiciary System," claimed responsibility for the attacks.

December 16

Panama. Soldiers in Panamanian strongman Manuel Antonio NORIEGA's Defense Forces shot and killed an unarmed American Marine, Lieutenant Robert Paz. The previous day General Noriega had declared his country to be in a state of war with the United States.

December 20

Panama. U. S. President George Bush dispatched American combat forces to PANAMA to protect U.S. citizens and the Panama Canal and to seize the Panamanian leader, Manuel Antonio NORIEGA. Noriega had been indicted by an American grand jury in Miami, Florida on drug charges the previous year. Though Noriega initially elluded the U.S. forces, four days later he sought refuge in the Vatican's Panama City embassy. (See January 3, 1990 below.)

December 28

Spain. Terrorists from the OCTOBER 1 ANTI-FASCIST RESISTANCE murdered two Civil Guardsmen as they stood sentry duty in front of a government building in the city of Gijon.

1990

January 2

Northern Ireland. The IRISH REPUBLICAN ARMY detonated a car bomb that killed a Belfast taxi driver, who they claimed was a member of the Protestant ULSTER FREEDOM FIGHTERS.

January 3

Panama. Manuel Antonio NORIEGA, who had been hiding within the Vatican's Panama City embassy, surrendered to American authorities and was immediately extradited to the United States to face charges stemming from alleged NARCO-TERRORIST activities.

January 6

Philippines. Javier Hizon, mayor of the town of Mexico, was killed by the Communist NEW PEOPLE'S ARMY.

January 7

Colombia. The NARCO-TERRORISTS of the MEDELLIN CARTEL kidnapped more than 20 wealthy Colombians during the month's first week. The terrorists, who call themselves the EXTRADITABLES, have used the kidnappings to undermine support for the government's drug war.

January 8

Japan. The JAPANESE RED ARMY simultaneously attacked residences of Japan's royal family in Kyoto and Tokyo, using homemade rockets.

January 9

Peru. The nation's former defense minister, General Lopez Albujar, was killed by machinegun fire as he drove his car in a Lima suburb. SENDERO LUMINOSO is believed responsible.

January 12

Guatemala. El Salvadoran leftist Hector Oqueli Colindres was kidnapped in Guatemala City. His body was found the following day; he had been shot in the head.

January 12

Peru. SENDERO LUMINOSO stopped a bus carrying more than 70 people and removed two French tourists, who they then brutally murdered.

January 12

Sri Lanka. George Thambiraja, leader of the India-backed Tamil National Army, was assassinated by the LIBERATION TIGERS OF TAMIL EELAM.

January 17

Papua New Guinea. Between 70 and 100 rebels on the island of Bougainville assaulted the island's jail in an attempt to free other rebels held there. Six people were killed while another 11 were injured in the attack.

January 29

Peru. SENDERO LUMINOSO terrorists murdered the deputy mayor of the village of Ahuac.

January 31

Peru. Fifteen SENDERO LUMINOSO guerrillas sneaked into the town of San Juan de Iscos and dragged the deputy mayor from his house and shot him, leaving for the authorities a note that read: "This is how the new starvers of the people die."

February 4

Egypt. A previously unheard-of group, the "Organization for the Defense of the Oppressed of Egypt's Prisons,'' attacked a tour bus carrying a group of Israelis. Eight people were killed and another 17 were wounded.

February 7
Northern Ireland. Short Brothers, an Ulster aircraft manufacturer, was bombed by the PROVISIONAL WING OF THE IRISH REPUBLICAN ARMY.

February 10
India. Srinagar, capital of Jammu and Kashmir state, was rocked by eight bombs believed to have been planted by terrorists of the JAMMU-KASHMIR LIBERATION FRONT.

February 21
South Africa. It was revealed by a Johannesburg newspaper that Defense Minister Magnus A. Malan had been aware since at least 1987 of the activities of police DEATH SQUADS. More than 75 political assassinations and disappearances had been blamed on such death squads since 1977. It was unclear whether Malan had acted on his knowledge.

February 25
Nicaragua. In free elections the SANDINISTA government of Daniel Ortega was defeated by UNO, the democratic party of Violeta Chamorro, bringing an end to that nation's STATE-SPONSORED TERRORISM.

February 25
Sri Lanka. A group of men, one wearing a police uniform, dragged Richard de Zoysa, a popular Sri Lankan television news anchor, from his home during the early morning hours. De Zoysa's body, which the DEATH SQUAD had dumped at sea, was found the following day.

March 2
Peru. Peasant farmers from the highland town of Cochas, armed only with sickles and machetes, ambushed a band of SEN-DERO LUMINOSO guerrillas and captured nine, whom they promptly beheaded. Just three days earlier another group of peasants from nearby Comos had captured and decapitated four members of the terrorist organization.

March 7
Turkey. Cetin Emec, a prominent journalist, was gunned down by members of a previously unknown Islamic group.

March 8
Colombia. After 16 years of terror more than 1,000 members of M-19 surrendered their weapons to authorities. The group's leader, Carlos Pizarro Leon-Gomez, renounced violence and became a candidate for the Colombian presidency. Mr. Pizarro was assassinated on April 26, 1990.

March 9
Colombia. ELN reportedly launched a ''Don't Vote'' campaign aimed at disrupting the country's May 27 national elections. The terrorists threatened to cut off the fingers of those who dared to vote.

March 17
United States. The offices of the Drug Enforcement Agency at Fort Myers, Florida were destroyed by a firebomb planted by NARCO-TERRORISTS.

March 21
Chile. Gen. Gustavo Leigh, former commander of the Chilean Air Force, and a business associate Enrique Ruiz were seriously wounded by gunmen from the MANUEL RODRIGUEZ PATRIOTIC FRONT. Leigh had been linked to DEATH SQUAD violence during the reign of Chilean dictator Augusto Pinochet.

March 21
Hungary. The Hungarian National Airline, Malev, began refusing to fly Jewish

émigrés to Israel after receiving threats from ISLAMIC JIHAD.

March 22
Colombia. Left-wing presidential candidate Bernardo Jaramillo was killed at Bogota airport by a 16-year-old gunman who had been hired for $600. Reports have linked NARCO-TERRORISTS to the killing.

March 24
Czechoslovakia. President Vaclav Havel disclosed that his nation's former Communist regime had sold more than 1,000 metric tons of SEMTEX explosives to Libya, enough to supply terrorists for the next 100 years.

March 27
Lebanon. William Robinson, an American living in Rashaya Foukhar, a village inside the Israeli security zone in southern Lebanon, was killed by three gunmen of the Lebanese National Resistance Front. Robinson was believed to be working to assist Jewish settlers to move into this Arab community.

March 28
Peru. Lima was struck by terrorist bombings for the fourth consecutive night. SENDERO LUMINOSO was blamed.

March 28
United Kingdom. British police arrested five people at Heathrow airport as they attempted to smuggle nuclear weapons components to Iraq.

March 29
Philippines. The NEW PEOPLE'S ARMY murdered a lone soldier outside Manila.

March 31
Colombia. NARCO-TERRORISTS entered the Medellin offices of Colombia's second largest newspaper, *El Espectador*, and killed the circulation manager. The attack was appar-

ently in fullfilment of a threat against the paper made by the EXTRADITABLES.

April 6
Peru. Twenty-four people from the village of Alto Pauralli were murdered by SENDERO LUMINOSO terrorists.

April 9
Northern Ireland. Four soldiers of the largely Protestant ULSTER DEFENSE REGIMENT were killed when the armored vehicle in which they were riding was destroyed by a bomb that had been hidden beneath the road. The explosive device had been planted by members of the IRISH REPUBLICAN ARMY.

April 12
Peru. SENDERO LUMINOSO terrorists killed 50 villagers in Sonomoro.

April 19
India. A bomb placed aboard a passenger bus exploded as the vehicle traveled along a highway near the northern India city of Pathankot. Thirteen people died and 42 were wounded. SIKH terrorists are believed to have been responsible.

April 22
Lebanon. American hostage Robert Polhill was released in Beirut by his captors, the group ISLAMIC HOLY WAR FOR THE LIBERATION OF PALESTINE. Polhill had been kidnapped along with Jesse Turner and Alann Steen on January 24, 1987. The other two men remain the prisoners of this Iran-backed terrorist group.

April 23
Spain. A letter bomb campaign launched by ETA injured a prison official and a staff member for the 1992 Seville World's Fair in separate incidents.

April 26
Colombia. Carlos Pizarro Leon-Gomez, a left-wing Colombian presidential candidate

and the former leader of the recently disbanded M-19 guerrilla organization, was assassinated aboard a civilian airliner while the plane was in flight. The lone gunman had hid in the plane's restroom until 10 minutes after takeoff, when he emerged firing a machine gun. Pizarro's bodyguards killed the attacker. Responsibility for the attack was claimed by the EXTRADITABLES. Pizarro was the third presidential candidate to be assassinated since August 18, 1989.

April

Ecuador. Members of a Colombian guerrilla group, the PEOPLE'S LIBERATION ARMY, kidnapped American Scott Heimdal. Heimdal was later released unharmed after the citizens of his hometown, Peoria, Illinois, raised $60,000 ransom.

April 29

Northern Ireland. A customs outpost at Newry was damaged by a bomb planted by the IRISH REPUBLICAN ARMY. The IRA also claimed responsibility for two bombs discovered along the road near Castlewan and a third in a housing project in Dungannon. None of the bombs caused any casualties.

April 30

Lebanon. HEZBOLLAH released American hostage Frank Herbert Reed, whom they had held since September 1986.

May 5

United States. The FBI rounded up a group of Colombians in the employ of the MEDELLIN CARTEL leader Pablo ESCOBAR who were in Florida attempting to arrange the purchase of 24 Stinger anti-aircraft missiles stolen from the American military. The NARCO-TERRORISTS were reportedly willing to pay $5–6 million for the weapons, which would be capable of shooting down even the largest airliners.

May 14

Philippines. Two American airmen were shot and killed as they waited for a taxi just outside the gates of the U. S. Air Force's Clark Air Base. The communist NEW PEOPLE'S ARMY is thought to be responsible.

May 14

United Kingdom. The London office of the Directorate of Army Education was the scene of a bomb blast that injured several civilian employees but killed no one. The IRISH REPUBLICAN ARMY took credit for planting the bomb, which had been hidden in a flower bed near the building's front entrance.

May 15

United States. The presidential commission charged with investigating the December 21, 1988 bombing of PAN AM 103 recommended that the United States consider military strikes against "known terrorist enclaves."

May 16

United Kingdom. One British soldier was killed and a second was wounded when their van exploded near an army recruiting depot.

May 21

India. A leading Islamic figure, the Mirwaiz of Kashmir, Maulvi Mohammed Farooq, was assassinated by three men who entered his office and shot him 15 times at close range. Farooq was a leader of the Kashmiri separatist movement for many years. His supporters have variously blamed Hindu fundamentalists and the Indian army for the killing.

May 21

Israel. A lone Jewish gunman murdered seven Palestinians during a shooting spree in the GAZA STRIP. The attack by the emo-

tionally disturbed young man ignited another round of rioting in the occupied territories and gave new life to the INTIFADA.

May 21
Colombia. Senator Federico Estrada Velez
and his two bodyguards were murdered in
Medellin. Drug traffickers had also kidnapped the senator in April but at that time
had released him unharmed.

May 24
Colombia. Eleven people died and 25 more
were wounded when a car bomb exploded
in front of Medellin's Inter-Continental Hotel. NARCO-TERRORISTS in the employ of drug
trafficker Pablo ESCOBAR are presumed to
have been responsible.

May 24
United States. Two members of Earth First,
a radical environmentalist group, were injured when a bomb placed under the front
seat of their automobile exploded. Police
officials believed the bomb was intended for
use in disrupting the logging operations of
companies cutting down redwood trees in
northern California. The two occupants of
the car insisted that they in fact were victims
of a bomb planted by lumber interests. On
July 17, Alameda County prosecutors announced they would not charge the two
with transporting the bomb.

May 28
Israel. ISLAMIC HOLY WAR FOR THE LIBER-
ATION OF PALESTINE terrorists detonated a
bomb on a busy Jerusalem street, killing
one passerby and injuring nine others.

May 28
Netherlands. The IRISH REPUBLICAN ARMY
"mistakenly" murdered two Australian
tourists whom the terrorists had believed to
be British soldiers.

May 30
Israel. Government troops intercepted two
small speedboats as they attempted a sea-
borne assault on the Israeli coast. The boats
carried PALESTINE LIBERATION FRONT guerrillas. Five terrorists were captured near shore
outside Ga'ash, while seven more were
seized on the beach near Nitzanim. In addition, four other members of the Nitzanim
team were killed in a brief gunfight with
Israeli soldiers. Israeli spokesmen claimed
the attack had been sponsored and logistically supported by Libya.

June 1
United Kingdom. Three British soldiers
were shot and wounded, one fatally, by two
IRISH REPUBLICAN ARMY gunmen as the
troops waited for a train at the Lichfield
station.

June 1
West Germany. A British army major was
shot and killed as he arrived at his Dortmund home.

June 8
United Kingdom. A veteranarian employed by the government's Chemical Defence Establishment escaped injury when
her automobile was destroyed by a bomb
planted by ANIMAL RIGHTS activists.

June 9
United Kingdom. Seventeen civilians were
injured when a bomb exploded in a barracks
hall of the Honorable Artillery Company.
The hall, which is located in central London, had been rented for a birthday party.

June 10
Greece. Terrorists armed with a bazooka
destroyed the Athens offices of Procter &
Gamble, an American firm. There were no
injuries.

June 10
United Kingdom. A 13-month-old baby was seriously injured by a car bomb set by ANIMAL RIGHTS terrorists. The target had been a medical researcher from Bristol University.

June 11
Sri Lanka. Terrorists from the LIBERATION TIGERS OF TAMIL EELAM overran 10 police staions on the island and kidnapped 600 police officers. It is believed they may have murdered as many as 117 of their prisoners.

June 13
Colombia. Police killed drug trafficker and NARCO-TERRORIST Juan Jairo Arias Tascoon in a shootout. Arias was considered the fifth most important figure in the MEDELLIN CARTEL and the mastermind of the 10-month-long campaign of terror bombings carried out by the EXTRADITABLES.

June 13
Philippines. An American Peace Corp worker, Timothy Swanson, was kidnapped by the communist NEW PEOPLE'S ARMY.

June 25
United Kingdom. The IRISH REPUBLICAN ARMY bombed London's fashionable Carlton Club, injuring seven persons. The club is frequented by members of Britain's ruling Conservative Party.

June 28
Colombia. The EXTRADITABLES are suspected of planting a car bomb which exploded outside a Medellin police station, killing 14 people and wounding 30 more.

June 30
Israel. Israeli authorities reported that as of the end of June the INTIFADA uprising had resulted in 725 Palestinians being killed by government troops and another 228 dying at the hands of other Palestinians. During the same period 47 Jews had been killed.

June 30
East Germany. During the final two weeks of June, East German authorities rounded up 10 terrorists of the RED ARMY FACTION (RAF) who were living in this former communist state. The newly elected democratic government of the German Democratic Republic learned of the whereabouts of the terrorists from the files of the secret police organization known as Stasi. Stasi's Division XXII, the "anti-terrorism" directorate, as well as many high communist officials including former head of state Eric Honecker, are suspected of having given aid and asylum to RAF fugitives.

June 30–July 4
South Africa. During a five-day period, right-wing terrorists of the group the WHITE WOLVES exploded four bombs in and around the city of Johannesburg. The targets included the liberal Afrikaans newspaper, *Vyre Weekblad;* the homes of two Johannesburg politicians; and a Jewish synagogue. There were no injuries in any of the attacks.

July
Eastern Europe. Newly elected non-Communist governments in East Germany, Czechoslovakia, and Hungary began releasing information gleaned from the files of their respected secret police agencies. The news releases linked those agencies to various well-known terrorists, including the RED ARMY FACTION and the infamous CARLOS, and some of their most spectacular crimes. The East German Stasi apparently assisted agents of Libya in the preparations for the bombing of the LA BELLE DISCO in West Berlin.

July 6
United Kingdom. Police defused a bomb planted in London's Regent Park by the ANIMAL LIBERATION FRONT.

July 9
Peru. Forty-eight members of MRTA escaped from Cantogrande, Lima's maximum security prison, by tunnelling more than 250 yards beneath the prison's walls. Among those who escaped was Victor Polay Campos, the leader of Peru's second largest leftist guerrilla organization.

July 11
India. Sikh extremists gunned down Balwant Singh, his two bodyguards and driver as they drove through the Punjab provincial capital of Chandigarh. Mr. Singh was a former minister in the provincial government.

July 13
Philippines. The "Reform the Armed Forces Movement" took credit for six bomb blasts that rocked the Philippine capital during the early morning hours. The bombs, which caused only minor damage and no injuries, were targeted against major tourist hotels and financial district buildings.

July 14
Sri Lanka. The LIBERATION TIGERS OF TAMIL EALAM were believed responsible for the murders of 35 Muslims near the city of Kalmunai. The victims were dragged from passenger buses stopped by the terrorists.

July 16
India. A prominent Indian Oil Corporation executive, his son and their driver were kidnapped by members of the United Liberation Front of Assam.

July 20
United Kingdom. The London stock exchange was damaged by an IRISH REPUBLICAN ARMY bomb; there were no injuries.

Advance warning of the blast, telephoned by the IRA to the Reuters news agency offices in London, allowed police and fire officials to evacuate the building before the bomb detonated.

July 24
Northern Ireland. A 1,000-pound bomb planted under the Killyea Road, outside the city of Armagh, detonated and killed four people in passing autos. Three members of the ROYAL ULSTER CONSTABULARY, riding in an unmarked police vehicle, died, as did a Roman Catholic nun driving in a second car.

July 27
France. The French government released from prison ANIS NACCACHE and four of his accomplices, all of whom were immediately flown to Iran. The five had been convicted 10 years earlier of attempting to assassinate former Iranian Prime Minister Shahpur Bakhtiar and sentenced to life in prison. Although the French government denied it, it was widely believed that the release was a belated repayment to Iran, which had facilitated the 1988 release of all six French hostages held in Lebanon.

July 27
West Germany. Hans Neusal, the German government's leading anti-terrorist officer, was slightly injured by a bomb that detonated as his car passed nearby. The RED ARMY FACTION claimed responsibility.

July 28
Israel. A pipe bomb exploded on a crowded Tel Aviv beach, killing a Canadian tourist and injuring 18 other persons.

July 30
United Kingdom. Conservative MP and former cabinet official in the Thatcher government Ian Gow was killed by an IRISH REPUBLICAN ARMY bomb planted beneath

the seat of his automobile. Mr. Gow had been one of the IRA's staunchest critics.

July 31
South Africa. South Africa's Defense Force announced it was disbanding its Civil Cooperation Bureau, a clandestine army detachment linked to DEATH SQUAD activities in that country.

August 1
Bulgaria. The new government of Bulgaria offered to open the files of its state-run arms-exporting company, Kintex, to Western police agencies investigating terrorism. Kintex is believed to have been a major supplier of arms to Libya and other terrorist sponsors and groups.

August 2
El Salvador. FMLN gunmen broke into the homes of two families in the village of Sosoman and murdered a total of 11 persons, including four children.

August 2
Philippines. American Peace Corps volunteer, Timothy Swanson, and a Japanese aid worker, Fumio Mizuno, were released by their NEW PEOPLE'S ARMY captors. The two had been kidnapped in separate incidents two months previously.

August 6
United Kingdom. A bomb was discovered and diffused in the driveway of the former home of Lord Armstrong of Ilminster. Ilminster, now retired, had been the chief security adviser to then Prime Minister Margaret Thatcher.

August 9
Lebanon. Swiss Red Cross worker Emanuel Christen was released by his captors. Christen and another Swiss Red Cross worker, Elio Erriquez, were kidnapped on October 6, 1989 by members of the previously unknown group the "Palestinian Revolutionary Squads."

August 11
Colombia. The number two man in the MEDELLIN CARTEL, Gustavo de Jesus Gaviria, was killed in a gun battle with police. Gaviria is believed to have been in charge of the NARCO-TERRORISM activities of the cartel.

August 13
Lebanon. Elio Erriquez, a Swiss Red Cross worker, was released by his "Palestinian Revolutionary Squads" captors.

August 14
Peru. Terrorists of SENDERO LUMINOSO crashed a bomb-laden car into the presidential palace in Lima. Although the building was damaged, newly elected president Alberto Fujimori escaped injury. About the same time, also in Lima, other Shining Path guerrillas killed two police officers in a dynamite attack on a police station.

August 15
India. India's Independence Day was marred by two fatal bombings carried out by Sikh terrorists. Five people were killed in a temple near Delhi while another six perished when a bomb exploded aboard a bus in the Punjab province.

August 24
Lebanon. The only Irish hostage, Brian Keenan, was released by his "Islamic Dawn" captors. The government of Iran was apparently instrumental in obtaining the release.

September 3
Iraq. GEORGE HABASH, leader of the POPULAR FRONT FOR THE LIBERATION OF PALESTINE, became the latest terrorist leader to move his headquarters to the Iraqi capital of Baghdad in a gesture of solidarity with President Saddam Hussein. Terrorists ABU

NIDAL and ABU ABBAS as well as PALESTINE LIBERATION ORGANIZATION leader YASIR ARAFAT had earlier moved to Baghdad and declared their support for Hussein, and thus raised the specter of a new wave of Middle Eastern terrorism, in his confrontation with the United States and a coalition of other countries that opposed his annexation of Kuwait.

September 6

Brazil. AMNESTY INTERNATIONAL accused Brazilian police officials of operating DEATH SQUADS that targeted that nations homeless children. Another group, the Brazilian Institute for Social and Economic Analysis, claimed to know of 457 poor, urban children killed in a "clean the streets" campaign.

September 16

Northern Ireland. A Royal Ulster Constabulary officer was kidnapped and believed executed by the IRISH REPUBLICAN ARMY.

September 17

Spain. Six persons were injured in a series of three nearly simultaneous bomb blasts in Madrid. The terrorist group GRAPO was responsible for the attacks which damaged the Madrid stock exchange, the Constitutional Court, and the offices of the Economics Ministry.

September 18

United Kingdom. Sir Peter Terry and his wife were wounded by IRISH REPUBLICAN ARMY gunmen who attacked them in their home. Sir Peter had been the governor of Gibraltar in March 1988 when a British SAS detachment ambushed and killed an IRA team believed to be in Gibraltar to conduct terrorist activities.

September 19

Colombia. Francisco Santos Calderon, the anti-drug cartel editor of *El Tiempo*, was kidnapped outside his Bogota office. Mr.

Santos' driver was murdered by the kidnappers who are believed to be in the employ of the EXTRADITABLES, Colombia's narco-terrorists.

September 26

Greece. Pavlos Bakoyannis, a conservative member of the Greek parliament, was shot and killed as he arrived at his Athens office. The assassin, who escaped, left behind a note claiming responsibility for the murder in the name of REVOLUTIONARY ORGANIZATION 17 NOVEMBER.

September 26

Philippines. Terrorists staged two incidents designed to coincide with the arrival in Manila of United States Vice President J. Danforth Quayle. Two Americans employed by Ford Aerospace were murdered by six gunmen who sprayed the men's car with automatic weapons fire just outside a U.S. Air Force base while a captain of Philippine President Corazon Aquino's presidential guard was shot and killed in Manila.

September 28

United Kingdom. An IRISH REPUBLICAN ARMY bomb was discovered and defused by police just moments before the commencement of a conference sponsored by the Research Institute for the Study of Conflict and Terrorism. The powerful bomb, fashioned from 4 pounds of SEMTEX, was concealed in the speaker's podium.

October 3

South Africa. The residence of United States Ambassador to South Africa William Swing was slightly damaged by a bomb. There were no injuries. Although no group claimed responsibility, the bomb was similar in design to those often used by South Africa's white supremacist terrorists.

October 6

Turkey. Bahriye Ucok, a theology professor and outspoken critic of the Islamic fundamentalist movement, was killed by a package bomb at her Ankara home. A previously unheard of group, "Islamic Movement," claimed responsibility.

October 9

India. Forty-seven passengers died when People's War Group terrorists set fire to a railroad coach after having first bolted shut the compartment's exit doors.

October 10

Colombia. Two managers of the anti-drug newspaper *El Espectador* were gunned down by narco-terrorists outside the paper's Medellin offices.

October 11

Spain. Three persons died and 46 others were injured when an explosion ripped through a discotheque in the northern province of Galicia. Responsibility for the bombing was claimed by the Guerrilla Army of the Free Galician People.

October 12

Egypt. Rifaat al-Mahgoub, speaker of the Egyptian parliament, died when his car was sprayed with machine-gun fire as it traveled along a Cairo street. Although no group took responsibility, Egyptian officials speculated that the attack may have been ordered by Iraq in retaliation for Egypt's opposition to the Iraqi annexation of Kuwait.

October 17

Colombia. Gunmen mounted on motorcycles shot and killed High Court Justice Hector Jimenez Rodriguez in Medellin. The narco-terrorist group the EXTRADITABLES claimed responsibility.

October 18

Colombia. Diego Vargas Escobar, a Medellin radio journalist, was murdered by narco-terrorists.

October 19

United States. Three members of the white supremacist ARYAN NATIONS were convicted of conspiring to bomb a Seattle, Washington disco frequented by gays.

October 21

Lebanon. Dany Chamoun, leader of one of Lebanon's Christian factions and son of a former president of that nation, was murdered, along with his wife and two of his children, in their Beirut home. The gunmen, whose affiliation is not known, gained access to the house by posing as soldiers.

October 21

Israel. A Palestinian Muslim fundamentalist stabbed and killed three people in a Jewish section of Jerusalem.

October 22

Peru. Three SENDERO LUMINOSO gunmen killed a television reporter in the doorway of his home in the northern city of Huaraz.

October 23

France. Iranian extremists are suspected to have been behind the murder of Cyrus Elahi, a leader of the Iranian exile community.

October 24

Northern Ireland. The IRISH REPUBLICAN ARMY conducted three "hostage bombings" against three different British Army installations in the northern counties. In each case the IRA forced a man they considered to be a British collaborator to drive a car bomb onto a British base in a suicide attack. The bombers' families were held hostage to ensure compliance. The bombing in Londonderry killed five soldiers and the bomber while injuring 26; in Newry one soldier was killed and the bomber, who had attempted to shout a warning, escaped with his life; in the third attempt, this time in Tyrone, the bomb driver escaped when the bomb failed to detonate.

November 2
Japan. One police officer was killed and five were injured when two bombs were detonated in a Tokyo police barracks.

November 4
Chile. Eight people, including three United States Navy sailors, were injured when a bomb exploded in a crowded seaside restaurant.

November 7
Burma. AMNESTY INTERNATIONAL reported that a "secret state of terror" had descended over Burma. The group charged that the Burmese military regime was responsible for the torture and disappearance of hundreds of citizens opposed to the government.

November 7
India. Nine passengers on a Punjab bus were killed by Sikh extremists.

November 12
Colombia. FARC killed five children who were riding to a youth meeting in a police car.

November 15
India. Sikh militants murdered 10 people in the Dabwali town park.

November 17
Chile. Fourteen ounces of dynamite, concealed within a softball bat, exploded during a United States vs. Chile softball game, killing one person and wounding five others. In a call to a Santiago radio station, an unidentified man claimed responsibility for the bombing in the name of the PALESTINE LIBERATION ORGANIZATION. The Tunis headquarters of the PLO denied the claim.

November 20
India. Sikh terrorists gunned down 28 shoppers in a crowded market in the city of Amristar. Thirteen of the victims, mostly Hindus, died of their wounds.

November 22
India. Thirteen persons were killed and a dozen more were wounded when Sikh gunmen opened fire on a passenger bus in Punjab province.

November 23
Northern Ireland. IRISH REPUBLICAN ARMY terrorists forced a kidnapped man to drive a truck carrying a 3,500-pound bomb to a British Army checkpoint near Annaghmartin. The man escaped harm when the bomb failed to detonate.

November 24
Israel. An Egyptian border guard slipped over the Israeli border from his frontier post and opened fire on vehicles passing by on a nearby highway. Four Israelis were killed before their attacker fled back into Egypt, where he was apprehended by Egyptian authorities. In Amman, Jordan a group calling itself "Islamic Holy War of Jerusalem" claimed responsibility for the shootings.

November 24
Lebanon. In a sucide attack a young women laden with explosives rushed two Israeli soldiers patrolling near the Israeli border. The bomb blast killed the girl and slightly wounded the two Israelis. The SYRIAN SOCIALIST NATIONAL PARTY claimed responsibility.

December 3
Northern Ireland. In a tragic case of mistaken identity the IRISH REPUBLICAN ARMY gunned down a young bakery worker they mistook for a member of the security forces.

December 5

Bolivia. Jorge Lonsdale, the president of the Bolivian subsidiary of Coca-Cola, who was kidnapped on June 11, 1990, was killed during a shootout between his captors and Bolivian police. Mr. Lonsdale's abductors belonged to the little known "Nestor Paz Zamora Committee."

December 8

Spain. Six policemen were killed when a bomb concealed in a parked car was detonated as their van passed alongside. The Basque separatist group ETA is believed to have been responsible.

December 12

Colombia. Seven policemen died when the bus they were riding in was bombed by FARC terrorists near Medellin.

December 14

Israel. Two Palestinians of the "Islamic Resistance Movement" stabbed to death three Israeli factory workers in Jaffa.

December 17

Greece. The Athens offices of the European Community were the target of a rocket attack by the REVOLUTIONARY ORGANIZATION 17 NOVEMBER. There were no injuries.

December 19

Kuwait. AMNESTY INTERNATIONAL reported that Iraq had been engaged in STATE-SPONSORED TERRORISM against the citizens of Kuwait since the August 2, 1990 invasion of that country. Another human rights group, Middle East Watch, claimed more than 1,000 Kuwatis had been murdered. The Amnesty report chronicled incidents of torture, summary execution and the murder of more than 300 premature Kuwaiti babies taken from their hospital incubators and left on the hospital floors to die.

December 24

United Kingdom. Novelist Salman RUSHDIE announced that he would not permit the paperback publication of his controversial book *Satanic Verses* and that he now recanted the passages in the book Muslims had found to be blasphemous. Mr. Rushdie, who had first emerged from hiding on December 5, said he hoped that the government of Iran would accept his apology and lift the death sentence it had imposed. However, the following day the Iranian newspaper *Abrar* rejected the author's plea and claimed the Ayatollah KHOMEINI's death sentence still stood.

December 28

Israel. Three Arab residents of the occupied West Bank were wounded when the car in which they were riding was fired upon by snipers. A right-wing Jewish extremist group, the Zionist Avengers, claimed credit for the attack.

Part II

---

terrorism
a to z

A

AAA (ARGENTINE ANTI-COMMUNIST ALLIANCE)

Also known as "Triple A." A right-wing Argentine DEATH SQUAD that had strong ties to the military junta that ruled Argentina from 1976 to 1983. This paramilitary organization played a major role in Argentina's DIRTY WAR, in which liberals, leftists, Jews, and members of the intelligentsia of the nation were kidnapped, tortured, and, in many cases, murdered. Many thousands simply disappeared without a trace (*see* DISAPPEARED).

The AAA was assembled by Argentina's minister for social welfare, Jose Lopez Rega, purportedly to combat violent left-wing guerrillas, especially the ERP and MONTENEROS organizations. AAA terror, however, was soon directed not only against leftist terrorists but against large numbers of the general population. AAA actions were sanctioned, at least implicitly, by the government, which made no arrests of AAA terrorists; indeed, government funds were funneled to the group through the social welfare ministry. Many members of the policy and military forces were active in the death squads.

References: John Simpson and Jana Bennett, *The Disappeared* (London: Robson Books, 1985); Richard Gillespie, *Soldiers of Peron:*
Argentina's Monteneros (Oxford: Oxford University Press, 1982).

ABDALLAH, GEORGES IBRAHIM

Also known as Salah al-Masri or Abdul-ader Saadi. Leader of the Lebanese left-wing terrorist group FARL (Lebanese Armed Revolutionary Faction). Abdallah was arrested by French police in 1984, and in July 1986 he was sentenced by a French court to a four-year prison term. His followers, attempting to obtain his release, were responsible for a wave of bombings in Paris in September 1986. In 1987 French authorities sentenced Abdallah to a life term in a French prison; there he remains.

ABDULLAH I, IBN HUSSEIN (1881–1951)

First King of Jordan, assassinated as he entered the al-Aqsa Mosque by a Palestinian in Jerusalem on July 20, 1951. Considered by many Arab political hard-liners to be a collaborator with the Israelis and the British, Abdullah made many enemies in the Arab world by annexing the West Bank of the Jordan River into the Hashemite Kingdom of Jordan after the 1948 war with Israel. Although no conspiracy was ever uncovered, it is doubtful that the assassin, a young tailor with a criminal record, acted alone. Abdullah I was the grandfather of the current ruler of Jordan, King Hussein, who was present at the time of the assassination.

References: Mary C. Wilson, *King Abdullah, Britain, and the Making of Jordan* (London: Cambridge University Press, 1988); Avi Shlaim, *Collusion Across the Jordan: King Abdullah, The Zionist Movement and the Partition of Palestine* (New York: Columbia University Press, 1988).

ABORTION CLINICS

These medical facilities, where women may seek the termination of unwanted pregnancies, have long been the focus of criticism by the right wing in American politics, the right wing in Western democracies, as well as many Central and Latin American nations. Abortion clinics have in recent years emerged as the objects of arson and bombings by the more militant members of the American "Right-to-Life" movement. According to the FBI, more than 60 such attacks have taken place during the 1980s. The FBI has been criticized for refusing to classify attacks on abortion clinics as terrorist acts, arguing that the attacks have not been found to be part of an organized movement. Critics of the FBI policy find the refusal to be politically motivated and reflective of the anti-abortion stance of recent Republican administrations.

Reference: David C. Nice, "Abortion Clinic Bombings as Political Violence," *American Journal of Political Violence* 32 (February 1988).

ABU ABBAS

Also known as Abul Abbas and Mohammed Abbas. Head of the PALESTINE LIBERATION FRONT (PLF) and member of the Executive Committee of the PALESTINE LIBERATION OR-GANIZATION (PLO). Born in Haifa, which became part of Israel one year after his birth, Abbas grew up in Palestinian refugee camps in Syria and attended the University of Damascus. He joined the POPULAR FRONT FOR THE LIBERATION OF PALESTINE (PFLP) during the 1960s and followed Ahmed JABRIL when he instituted his more radical splinter group, the pro-Syrian PFLP-GENERAL COMMAND. Abbas formed his own group, the PLF, out of dissatisfaction with Syrian involvement in the Lebanese civil war of the mid-1970s.

Although not one of the four actual hijackers of the ACHILLE LAURO, Abbas was the mastermind of the October 1985 siege of the Italian cruise liner, during which an elderly, wheelchair-bound Jewish American, LEON KLINGHOFFER, was murdered and thrown overboard. Abbas negotiated the surrender of the hijackers to Egyptian authorities after the ship was refused port in Syria. American fighter jets intercepted the Egyptian airliner transporting Abbas and his fellow conspirators to Tunisia and forced the plane to land in Sicily. Italian authorities took Abbas and his men into custody, but despite repeated U.S. pleas for extradition, Abbas was released by the Italian police on October 12, 1985. Abbas' release strained U.S.–Italian relations and prompted the resignation of Italy's minister of defense. In the summer of 1986 Abbas was convicted in absentia by an Italian court for his role in the hijacking and was sentenced to life imprisonment. In a November 1988 interview with the *New York Times*, Abbas, who was attending a conference of the PALESTINIAN NATIONAL COUNCIL in Algiers, joked openly about the death of Klinghoffer, suggesting that "maybe he was trying to swim for it." The NBC television network telecast an interview with Abbas in May 1986, raising the ire of the U.S. State Department, as well as many in the media, who considered the interview, conducted under Abbas' restrictions of secrecy, to be irresponsible journalism.

Abbas has nurtured a reputation for brutality. Operations which he has masterminded include a 1979 raid on an Israeli party in which a four-year-old girl was killed by bashing her head on a rock. Abbas is also well known for his creative (though often flawed) methods of attack, including unsuccessful 1981 raids into Israel in hot air balloons and hang gliders. He is known to travel with an Iraqi passport, and Iraq is thought to be the primary state sponsor of Abbas and the PLF. Abbas has proven to be an occasional embarrassment to the PLO, but he has also been a long-standing if unpredictable ally of Yasir ARAFAT. In 1985, *Newsweek* quoted a PLO official as calling Abbas "a would-be Palestinian Rambo, big on brawn with some cunning. The problem is he has no brains."

References: "Hijacker, at Algiers Meeting, Dismisses Cruise Ship Killing," *New York Times* (November 14, 1988); George C. Church, "A Would-Be Palestinian Rambo," *Newsweek* (October 18, 1985).

ABU AMAR

The nom de guerre (pseudonym) of Yasir ARAFAT. The name Abu Amar is derived from the Arabic "to build."

ABU DAOUD

The nom de guerre of Mohammed Daoud Oudeh, a founder of BLACK SEPTEMBER, one of the most violent of Palestinian terrorist groups. Among the acts ascribed to him and his organization are the assassination of Jordanian Prime Minister Wasfi al-TAL in Cairo on November 28, 1971; the MUNICH MASSACRE of Israeli athletes at the 1972 Olympic Games; and the assassination of U.S. Am-

bassador Claude Noel and the Belgian chargé d'affaires at the Saudi Arabian Embassy in Khartoum on March 1, 1973. He was arrested in Paris in 1977 on an Interpol warrant, issued by West German police, as a suspect in the Munich Olympics episode. A Parisian court refused to honor Israel's request for extradition, however, and ordered him released. West German and Israeli authorities and many members of the Western press were highly critical of Daoud's release, and questions were raised about France's commitment to international antiterrorist efforts. In August 1981 Daoud was himself the victim of an assassination attempt while in Warsaw, Poland. He was wounded by gunmen thought to be members of the Abu Nidal Organization or the Israeli secret service, Mossad.

Reference: Sandra E. Rapoport, "Abu Daoud and the Law," *Commentary* (March 1977).

ABU GHARBIYAH, BAHJAT

See POPULAR STRUGGLE FRONT.

ABU IBRAHIM

See UMARI, MOHAMMED AL-.

ABU IYAD

See KHALEF, SALEH.

ABU JIHAD

See WAZIR, KHALIL AL-.

ABU MUSA

The nom de guerre of a former al-FATAH lieutenant who led the 1983 Syrian-backed mutiny against Yasir ARAFAT. Born Said Musa

Murgahra near Jerusalem, Musa was widely considered to be one of al-Fatah's most militarily distinguished members, and he became one of the most vocal members of the NATIONAL SALVATION FRONT.

Reference: Adam M. Garfinkle, "Sources of the Al-Fatah Mutiny," *Orbis* 27 (Summer 1983).

ABU NIDAL

"Father of the Struggle." The nom de guerre of Sabri al-Banna, one of the foremost contemporary organizers of terror. Abu Nidal was born in Jaffa, Palestine to a well-to-do family, which lost its fortune following the creation of the state of Israel in 1948. He was later educated at the American University in Beirut, and he joined al-FATAH after the Six Day War in 1967. He served as a representative of the Palestine Liberation Organization in Baghdad in the early 1970s, but disenchantment with Yasir Arafat's policies led him to form his own organization in 1974, the FATAH REVOLUTIONARY COUNCIL (FRC). Iraq, anxious to support an organization that could counterbalance the influence of their Ba'thist rival, Syria, and that would take a more militant stance than Arafat's Fatah within the PLO, aided in the creation of the Abu Nidal group. Since then, great antipathy has existed between Arafat and Abu Nidal, and between their respective organizations. A PLO tribunal has imposed a death sentence on Abu Nidal in absentia, while the FRC has attempted to assassinate Arafat on several occasions. Abu Nidal's operatives have been successful in their attacks on other PLO officials: PLO representatives in Paris and London, among others, have fallen to FRC assassins.

Groups under Abu Nidal's direction have included BLACK JUNE (used against Jordanian targets) and the REVOLUTIONARY OR-GANIZATION OF SOCIALIST MUSLIMS (used against British targets). The U.S. State Department now encompasses these related groups under the umbrella classification of the "Abu Nidal Organization" (ANO). Also known as the Arab Revolutionary Council, this organization has been responsible for terrorist activities in at least 20 nations. Among the more than 90 attacks of which it is accused are the slayings of travelers in the Rome and Vienna airports in December 1985 and the assassination attempt against the Israeli ambassador to Great Britain, Shlomo ARGOV, on June 3, 1982. The ISTANBUL SYNAGOGUE MASSACRE on September 6, 1986 is widely thought to have been an ANO operation. In July 1988, Abu Nidal operatives were responsible for the attack on the Greek cruise ship CITY OF POROS. Syria, Iraq, and Libya have been conspicuous past supporters of the Abu Nidal Organization, both financially and logistically. Iraq, seeking to improve its international image, expelled Abu Nidal in 1983. He is thought to have lived in Libya since 1984, though reports in 1989 asserted that Libyan strongman Muammar Qaddafi had cut off supplies of money and weapons to the Abu Nidal Organization and other terrorist groups. International pressure, especially from the United States and Great Britain, is credited with prompting Syria's June 1987 expulsion of the ANO from Syrian soil. Today, the Abu Nidal Organization is probably based in the Bekaa Valley and in several Palestinian refugee camps in Lebanon. The group is believed to be responsible for the kidnapping of two Oxfam relief workers in that country in March 1988. The U.S. Department of State has called the ANO the "most active and brutal international terrorist group operating today." A report in *Newsweek* (December 11, 1989) quoted CIA Director William Webster, answering a question about Abu Nidal: "I can tell you a lot about him, but I don't know whether any of it is true."

References: Judith Miller, "Who Is Abu Nidal?," *New York Times Magazine* (January 4, 1987); "Syrian Support for International Terrorism: 1983–86," U.S. State Department Special Report no. 157 (Washington, D.C.: Bureau of Public Affairs, 1986); Yossi Melman, *The Master Terrorist: The True Story of Abu Nidal* (New York: Avon, 1986).

ABU NIDAL ORGANIZATION (ANO)

See ABU NIDAL.

ABU SALIM, SALIM

See POPULAR FRONT FOR THE LIBERATION OF PALESTINE–SPECIAL COMMAND.

ABU SHARIF, BASSAM

Once a leading member of POPULAR FRONT FOR THE LIBERATION OF PALESTINE (PFLP) and a participant in the 1970 DAWSON'S FIELD hijackings which contributed to the BLACK SEPTEMBER clash with Jordanian forces. An Israeli letter bomb severely injured Abu Sharif in 1972 and contributed to his own and his organization's reassessment of the tactics of terrorism as "counterproductive." He split with the PFLP leadership and joined al-FATAH. He became a spokesman for the PLO and Yasir ARAFAT and a major figure in the moderate faction within the PLO.

ABU TALB, MOHAMMED

Terrorist of AHMED JABRIL'S POPULAR FRONT FOR THE LIBERATION OF PALESTINE-GENERAL COMMAND, now serving a life sentence in Sweden for terrorist bombings in Stockholm and elsewhere. Abu Talb has been impli-

cated as a suspect by investigators looking into the December 21, 1988 bombing of PAN AM 103.

ABU ZA'IM

Former top PLO operative who was expelled from al-FATAH in April 1986 for organizing opposition to Yasir ARAFAT. He is considered by some to be an emerging rival to Arafat's dominance of the PLO, and his "Reformatory Movement," which is prepared to support less violent efforts toward a Palestinian solution, enjoys the enthusiastic support of the Jordanian government.

Abu Za'im was born in Beit Soreek, near Jerusalem; the date of his birth is uncertain. He left the Jordanian army in 1968 to become head of military intelligence for al-Fatah. It has been speculated that Abu Za'im engineered the flawed attempt to seize the GRAND MOSQUE in Mecca in 1979. In 1981 he staged the successful Beirut abduction and ransoming of Nasser al-Said, who is considered to be a leading opponent of the Saudi ruling family and its domination of the political process in Saudi Arabia. For turning al-Said over to the Saudi authorities, Abu Za'im was paid an estimated $3 million.

Reference: Norman Frankel, "Abu Za'im—Alternative to Yasir Arafat," *Terrorism* 11, no. 2 (1988).

ACHILLE LAURO

The Italian cruise liner hijacked by four members of the PALESTINE LIBERATION FRONT (PLF) on October 7, 1985. During the siege, an elderly Jewish American, Leon Klinghoffer, was murdered and his body, still in the wheelchair to which he was confined, was thrown overboard. Italian authorities responded to the hijacking by successfully requesting that Syria, Cyprus, and Tunisia deny port to the hijacked vessel and by making arrangements with the Egyptian government to facilitate the release of the ship in exchange for the hijackers' freedom.

The U.S. government, dissatisfied with Egypt's refusal to hold the hijackers upon release of the vessel and aware that ABU ABBAS (leader of the PLF) was to accompany the hijackers on their bartered flight to freedom, staged a daring midair interception of the Egyptian airliner carrying the four terrorists and their leader. U.S. fighter planes forced the jet to land at a NATO air field at Signolla, Sicily, on Italian soil. A potentially explosive situation ensued there, as the U.S. DELTA FORCE, a special unit under orders to capture the terrorists, faced off against Italian carabinieri, who knew nothing of the Americans' instructions. The standoff was defused only upon direct orders from the White House, and the five PLF members entered Italian custody. Thereupon President Ronald Reagan, during a news conference on October 11, 1985, told the world: "These young Americans [the U.S. forces that captured in midair a planeload of terrorists] sent a message to terrorists everywhere. The message: You can run but you can't hide."

The Italian and Egyptian governments were infuriated by the American interdiction. International tension was only exacerbated by the decision of an Italian magistrate to release Abu Abbas on grounds of insufficient evidence, despite American pleas for his extradition; he subsequently fled the country, in possession of an Iraqi diplomatic passport. A wealth of evidence citing Abbas as the mastermind of the hijacking surfaced soon thereafter, and an Italian court later convicted him in absentia. The four hijackers are all serving long prison terms in Italian prisons.

Renamed and revamped, the former *Achille Lauro* is now operating around-the-world cruises.

References: Malvina Halberstam, "Terrorism in the High Seas: The *Achille Lauro*, Piracy, and the IMD Convention on Maritime Safety," *American Journal of International Law* 82 (April 1988); Joseph LaPalombara, "The Achille Lauro Affair: A Note on Italy and the United States," *Yale Review* 75 (October 1986); Stephen Segaller, "The Achille Lauro Episode," in *Invisible Armies: Terrorism into the 1990s* (London: Michael Joseph, 1986).

ACTION DIRECTE (AD)

"Direct Action." A French Marxist group formed in 1979 to combat "international imperialism and capitalism." AD has a history of bombings, arson, robberies, and assassinations against French, U.S., Israeli/Jewish, and NATO targets. It is believed to have evolved from French radical groups of the 1970s, including the Revolutionary International Action Group (GARI) and the Armed Nuclei for Popular Autonomy (NAPAP). These groups occasionally resorted to terrorist tactics but never demonstrated the organizational sophistication and operational capability displayed by the AD.

The group first emerged in May 1979 with an attack on the Paris office of the National Council of French Employers. In March 1980 AD bombed and destroyed a Toulouse police station and in May of that year injured eight in a bombing at Orly Airport in Paris. Bombings against banks, businesses, and other targets identified with capitalist interests dominated AD terrorism until 1985. In August 1985 AD claimed joint responsibility with the RED ARMY FACTION for a bombing at the U.S. Air Force base at Rhein–Main, West Germany, in which two American servicemen were killed. The two groups, possibly together with the COMMUNIST COMBATANT CELLS, have formed an ANTI-IMPERIALIST ARMED FRONT (AIAF). This front called for the formation of an "international proletarian urban combat organization" to combat the "Americanization of Europe" and in January 1985 murdered French General Rene Audran. AD is also believed to have had past associations with the Italian RED BRIGADES, the Basque separatists ETA, the IRISH NATIONAL LIBERATION ARMY, and several militant Palestinian groups. In November 1986 the group assassinated Georges Besse, chairman of the automobile manufacturer Renault.

AD comprises a domestic and an international wing. The U.S. Department of State considers the latter, based in Paris and reportedly Belgium, to be "more dangerous and indiscriminate." It is thought to be led by Jean-Marc Rouillan. The international wing has a highly decentralized mode of organization, in which specific terrorist acts are planned and conducted by CELLS operating in relative isolation. AD has financed its operation primarily through bank robberies and has used a wide variety of weapons and explosives in its attacks. In 1986 and 1987 many of the organization's leaders were arrested, including Rouillan. AD, believed to have been severely crippled by this and other police successes, has not conducted an attack since that time.

References: "The Nice Folks From the Farm," *The Economist* 302 (February 28, 1987); Bonnie J. Cordes, "Action Directe Comes of Age," *TVI Journal* 5, no. 1 (1985).

ACTION FRONT FOR NATIONAL SOCIALISTS

A West German neo-NAZI organization, and a violent offshoot of the right-wing National Democratic Party. The Action Front was formed during the 1970s and is responsible for some of the West German right-wing extremist violence of the 1980s, much of which is racially-motivated vandalism. The Action Front is strongly nationalistic and stands in violent opposition to immigrants, Jews and leftists.

ACTION–REACTION

A phenomenon often used to explain behavior during crises, which implies that each side responds to the behavior of others with pre-planned moves. Thus, the sequence of actions as a crisis unfolds may not necessarily be directed by long-term goals or underlying motivation. The best example remains the events leading up to World War I. The initial response to the 1914 assassination of Archduke Ferdinand of Austria set off a chain reaction: mobilization by Russia sparked mobilization by Germany, which in turn led to mobilization by others. In each case participants were reacting almost automatically, rather than moving as a result of a deliberate decision. The Israeli–Palestinian conflict is a contemporary case study in the action–reaction phenomenon and the seesaw of aggression between Israel and the INTIFADA is a particularly acute example of it.

Reference: John D. Elliot, "Action and Reaction: West Germany and the Baader-Meinhof Guerrillas," *Strategic Review* 4 (Winter 1976).

ACTIVE MEASURES

Operations by the Soviet Union designed to influence policies of other nations, which are distinct from normal diplomacy and traditional espionage. Active measures include the use of communist parties and front organizations abroad; the dissemination of false rumors (i.e., disinformation); forgery of documents; manipulation of the press; and personal and economic blackmail. The KGB (the Soviet intelligence agency) has primary responsibility for developing and implementing active measures. Examples of active measures directed against the United States are campaigns "sponsored" by local communist parties to have U.S. military bases removed in Greece and in Spain, and KGB support and encouragement of Palestinian terrorist actions against targets in Western European democracies.

References: John J. Dziak, "Soviet 'Active Measures,' " *Problems of Communism* 33 (November–December 1984); Nils H. Wessel, "Arms Control and 'Active Measures,' " *Orbis* 27 (Spring 1983); Lawrence S. Eagleburger, "Unacceptable Intervention: Soviet Active Measures," *NATO Review* 31 (April 1983).

AFGHANISTAN

Cited by the U.S. Department of State as having been in the forefront of STATE-SPONSORED TERRORISM during the height of power of the Soviet-installed regime. The Afghan Communists, through their KGB-affiliated Ministry of State Security (WAD), directed a massive domestic campaign of violent repression. WAD is the successor to KHAD, the Bureau of State Security, the infamous Afghan secret police force. An estimated 35,000 people disappeared and many others were subjected to atrocities, including torture, barbarous imprisonment, and murder, in the years following the Soviet-inspired coup of April 1978. WAD, like its predecessor KHAD, has recruited, trained, supplied, funded and directed Pakistani anti-government terrorists. WAD, usually through paid Pakistani Operatives, has perpetrated

bombings, assassinations and attacks on public utilities in neighboring Pakistan.

When the Democratic Republic of Afghanistan, a Marxist regime installed by the Soviets during a 1978 coup, was unable to deal with an insurgency and the Afghan army began to collapse, the Soviet Union intervened. On the night of December 24, 1979, large numbers of Soviet airborne forces began to land in the capital of Kabul. Soviet troop strength in Afghanistan would grow to over 120,000. But the Soviets and the puppet regime they maintained were unable to make good the Soviet conquest. Afghan freedom fighters, or mujahidin, forced the Soviets to begin a military withdrawal in May 1988, which was completed in February 1989. In initial response to the invasion, the United States canceled its participation in the 1980 Moscow Olympics and embargoed shipments of American wheat to the Soviet Union. In addition to providing extensive humanitarian aid to Afghan refugees in Pakistan, the United States gave extensive clandestine military assistance to the Afghan resistance, including hundreds of Tennessee mules for mountain transport and stinger antiaircraft missiles. The man-portable stingers transformed the military situation by allowing the Afghan guerrillas to shoot down many hundreds of Soviet aircraft. This is one of the few instances in which a small tactical weapon has had strategic significance. On January 27, 1989, the *New York Times* quoted an anonymous aide to the Soviet Union's Communist Party's Central committee offering this analysis: "It's a defeat, no question about it. We had your experience in Vietnam right before our eyes, and we still went in like fools."

References: Rosanne Klass, ed., *Afghanistan: The Great Game Revisited* (New York: Freedom House, 1987); Barnett R. Rubin and Jeri Laber, *A Nation is Dying: Afghanistan*

Under the Soviets, 1979–87 (Evanston, Ill.: Northwestern University Press, 1988); "A Brutal Force Batters a Country," *Insight* 4 (December 5, 1988); Gerard Chaliand, *Report from Afghanistan* (Baltimore: Penguin, 1982).

AFRICAN NATIONAL CONGRESS (ANC)

Based in Zambia, the ANC is the primary South African anti-apartheid organization and the oldest liberation movement in the world. The ANC's lineage may be traced to 1912; its forebear was the South African Native National Congress. Though chiefly a political and guerrilla organization, acting ANC president Oliver Tambo proposed in 1986 to escalate unrest and violent opposition against the South African regime, and the ANC has recently launched repeated attacks on government officials, transportation and security targets and civilians.

The ANC was an organization dedicated to passive and nonviolent resistance for much of its history. Chief Albert Luthuli, a longtime ANC leader, was awarded the Nobel Peace Prize in 1960. Following the SHARPEVILLE INCIDENT on March 20, 1960, when South African police killed 69 blacks (including a number of women and children), ANC executives Tambo and Nelson MANDELA began to support more forceful measures, including industrial sabotage, through a new military operations wing, the Umkhonto We Sizwe. The organization has been outlawed in South Africa since 1961. ANC guerrilla attacks historically avoided possible civilian casualties, but since beginning in 1983 the organization's activities became far less discriminate. The drastic initiatives of recent years may be seen as the acts of an ANC frustrated by the futility of less violent actions.

In the summer of 1988 the ANC drew heavy criticism from its international supporters for its attacks on sporting events, fast-food restaurants, and shopping centers. The ANC leaders were quick to blame the attacks on "impassioned" young insurgents. Such questionable tactics prompted the U.S. Department of Defense to include the ANC in its 1988 listing of world terrorist groups. This inclusion prompted heated reaction from the group's supporters, as well as from the U.S. Department of State, which does not classify the ANC as a terrorist organization.

The ANC receives financial support from a number of African countries, as well as from governments and private contributors in the West. Military supplies are provided by the Soviet Union and by Soviet-bloc nations. The ANC maintains more than 20 international offices that serve as bases for rallying political support. ANC guerrillas are known to operate in many nations of Southern Africa, including Angola, Lesotho, Mozambique and Botswana.

Mandela, in prison from 1962 to 1990, retains the title of ANC president. He is the most enduring and internationally recognized symbol of the anti-apartheid movement. ANC leaders have often been the targets of assassins. Joe Gqabi, a representative in Zimbabwe, was gunned down on July 31, 1981, and Dulcie SEPTEMBER, the Paris representative of the ANC, was shot and killed at her office on March 29, 1988. The South African government is believed to be responsible for the shootings. In a reversal of policy, however, the South African government in 1990 released Mandela from prison and made the ANC a legal opposition party.

References: Heidi Holland, *The Struggle: A History of the African National Congress* (New York: George Braziller, 1990); Stephen M. Davis, *Apartheid's Rebel's: Inside South Africa's Hidden War* (New Haven, Conn.: Yale

University Press, 1987); Mary Benson, *Nelson Mandela: The Man and the Movement* (New York: W.W. Norton, 1986).

AGCA, MEHMET ALI

Would-be assassin of Pope John Paul II, whose unsuccessful attempt on the Pontiff's life took place in St. Peter's Square in Rome on May 13, 1981. As a member of the radical right-wing Turkish organization GREY WOLVES, Agca was convicted of the 1979 murder of a liberal Istanbul newspaper editor, but he escaped from Turkish prison in November 1979. After his arrest in Rome, Agca attempted to implicate the Bulgarian Secret Service and the KGB in the plot to kill the Pope. He was sentenced to life in prison by the Rome Assize Court after a spectacular trial during which he maintained that he was Jesus Christ—a claim that undermined the credibility of his accusations against the Bulgarians and the Soviets. Although the Italian Courts acquitted the Bulgarians named by Agca as co-conspirators due to a lack of substantive evidence, the presiding magistrates proclaimed that they had evidence that Agca had not acted alone. Many Western authorities support the theory of KGB or Bulgarian government complicity, but the question remains a debated issue. The notion of KGB implication remains wholly unsubstantiated.

References: Paul Henze, *The Plot to Kill the Pope* (New York: Scribner's, 1985); Claire Sterling, "Unraveling the Riddle," in *Terrorism: How the West Can Win*, edited by Benjamin Netanyahu (New York: Farrar, Straus, Giroux, 1986).

AHMED, ABDUL RAHIM

Leader of the Iraqi-backed Palestinian movement, the ARAB LIBERATION FRONT (ALF). Ahmed is a virulent critic of the peace initiatives of PLO chairman Yasir Arafat.

AHMED JABRIL

See JABRIL, AHMED.

AIIC

See ANTI-IMPERIALIST INTERNATIONAL BRIGADE.

AKALI DAL

The primary SIKH political party, which supports a Sikh state independent of India.

AL-ASIFA

See FATAH, AL-.

ALEXANDER I (1888–1934)

King of Yugoslavia, assassinated in Marseilles on October 9, 1934. Louis Barthou, the French foreign minister, was also killed when Vlada Cherizemsky, a Bulgarian in the employ of the Croatian separatist leader Ante PAVELIC, boarded the king's open parade car and opened fire with an automatic weapon. (During World War II the Germans made Pavelic [1889–1959] head of a puppet Croat state after the Axis conquest of the Balkans in 1941. After the war Pavelic fled to safety in Argentina.) The League of Nations responded to the incident by convening two international conventions to combat political terrorism.

Reference: Allen Roberts, *The Turning Point: The Assassination of Louis Barthou and King Alexander I of Yugoslavia* (New York: St. Martin's Press, 1970).

ALEXANDER II (1818–81)

Tsar of Russia from 1855 to 1881, assassinated by members of NORODNAYA VOLYA on March 13, 1881. Although Tsar Alexander introduced a host of political reforms to the Russian Empire, his efforts were judged to be insufficient by many members of an increasing vocal and active intelligentsia. The government answered their protests with police repression, which helped to inspire the formation of the secret society known as Norodnaya Volya ("Will of the People"). The Tsar's response was to increase the use of the force by the secret police against the terror campaign. He also exiled close to 150,000 political prisoners to Siberia between 1863 and 1874. This period can be characterized as the beginning of the political violence process that assisted the Bolsheviks to rise to power at the turn of the century.

ALFARO VIVE, CARAJO (AVC)

Spanish, "Alfaro Lives, Damn It!". An Ecuadorian urban terrorist organization that first surfaced in August 1983. Founded in the late 1970s, the group was named for Eloy Alfaro, an early 20th-century leader of rebellion against the government of Ecuador. AVC is dedicated to the removal of "oligarchic and imperialistic" institutions in Ecuador, though it denies any Marxist philosophy. It is primarily an urban organization, and its members are thought to number approximately 200–300. During 1986 AVC carried out a number of bank robberies, kidnappings and minor bombings. Many of the group's terrorist activities have been efforts to gain publicity, and AVC tries to utilize the news media and its own pamphlets to spread its message. Financing for group operations comes primarily from bank robberies. In 1986 and 1987 AVC suffered serious setbacks from government security forces, including the arrest of its leaders. Since that time, the group has conducted little terrorist activity.

AVC has reportedly received support from the Cuban government and is also thought to have had ties to Libya and Nicaragua. The group has received support from Colombia's M-19 and cooperated with that group in the 1985 kidnapping of an Ecuadorian banker. M-19 appears to have greatly influenced AVC activities, and indeed AVC's initial terrorist operation, the theft of Alfaro's swords, mirrored M-19's first public act. AVC has also reportedly collaborated with Peru's MRTA (Tupac Amaru Revolutionary Movement).

AVC is also known as Fuerzas Armadas Populares Eloy Alfaro.

Reference: Robert Thomas Baratta, "Political Violence in Ecuador and the AVC," *Terrorism* 10 (1987).

ALIANZA APOSTOLICA ANTI-COMMUNISTA (AAA)

Spanish, "Anti-Communist Apostolic Alliance" a radical, right-wing Spanish guerrilla organization dedicated to the violent opposition of separatism, socialism and communism. AAA has generally directed its terrorism against Spanish left-wing groups and individuals whom it considered to be threats to the AAA's values of traditionalism and authoritarianism. In January 1977, AAA members murdered five socialist attorneys in Madrid. The group's activities ceased in the 1980s.

AMAL

Arabic, "Hope." One of the two primary SHI'ITE Muslim militia organizations in Lebanon, the other being HEZBOLLAH. Amal was founded in the mid-1970s by Imam Musa al-SADR as the military wing of "The Movement of the Disinherited." Amal was conceived to gain a more equitable share of power for the Shi'ites in their struggle with the Maronite Christians and SUNNI Muslims, who have dominated the Lebanese state since independence from France in 1943. Amal is often considered to be the proxy army of Syria, its primary source of supply and most important ally.

Imam Musa al-Sadr is believed to have been killed on a trip to Libya in 1978. Leadership of Amal was taken over by Nabih BERRI, a lawyer whose policies, moderate in comparison with those of other Shi'ite leaders, have at times caused dissension within the organization. Berri's willingness to consider nonviolent approaches to the Lebanese struggle led to much intra-militia strife in 1982 and led the militia commander Hussein MASAWI to form his group, the extremist ISLAMIC AMAL.

Amal has had violent confrontations with Palestinian groups (whom it charges have brought the wrath of Israel to bear on Amal), including the Amal–PLO "War of the Camps." More than 3,000 died as Amal and PLO guerrillas battled in Beirut and Southern Lebanon from 1985 until December 1988, when they signed a 1988 peace pact that stated the combatants' intent to focus their efforts against their common enemy, Israel. Amal and fellow Shi'ites in Hezbollah faced off in 1988 and 1989 in violent battles for power among the 1,000,000 Shi'ites of West Beirut and Southern Lebanon. Syrian military assistance permitted Amal to maintain its superior tactical position in Southern Lebanon, but Syria's direct involvement in the militia battles strained Iranian–Syrian relations. Amal lost much of its dominance in Beirut to Hezbollah. The two groups signed a formal truce on January 30, 1989,

but fierce battles continued to flare up between the militias.

See also SADR, IMAM MUSA AL-.

References: A. G. Norton, *Amal and the Shia* (Austin: University of Texas Press, 1987); A. G. Norton, "Changing Actors and Leadership Among the Shi'ites of Lebanon," *Annals of the American Academy of Political and Social Science* 482 (November 1985).

AMIN, IDI

Former president of Uganda who took power during a 1971 military coup and ruled with an unusually severe degree of terror. In June 1976 he aided the hijackers of Air France Flight 139 by allowing them to divert the plane to Uganda's Entebbe airfield. This led to the dramatic rescue of the hostage passengers, most of whom were Jewish, by the Israeli military. In 1977 the heads of 33 British Commonwealth nations condemned his regime. Amin was deposed by a Tanzanian invasion in 1979 and escaped to Saudi Arabia, where he was given refuge.

See also ENTEBBE RAID.

References: Mahmood Mamdani, *Imperialism and Fascism in Uganda* (Trenton, N.J.: Africa World Press, 1984); Richard H. Ullman, "Human Rights and Economic Power: The United States versus Idi Amin," *Foreign Affairs* 56 (April 1978); David Gwyn, *Idi Amin: Death-Light of Africa* (Boston: Little, Brown and Co., 1977).

AMNESTY

The act of "forgetfulness" by a government for crimes committed by a group of people. Amnesty commonly is granted after a civil war to help reunite a country. For example, after the American Civil War Pres. Andrew Johnson granted amnesty to all Confederate soldiers. An amnesty is usually granted to a group to "forget" political offenses. (A pardon, on the other hand, is usually applied to individuals for criminal acts.) President Jimmy Carter granted amnesty to all Vietnam draft evaders (but not to military deserters) in 1977. Uruguay granted amnesty to both the anti-government TUPA-MAROS and to members of the Uruguayan Armed Forces to help heal the wounds which the left-wing insurgency of the 1960s and 1970s, and the military response to the guerrillas, had inflicted on the nation.

AMNESTY INTERNATIONAL

A worldwide organization dedicated to gaining the release of political and religious prisoners by publicizing their plights and by organizing letter writing and other campaigns to free individuals and groups. Since its founding in 1961, Amnesty International has been especially concerned with and effective in exposing government-sanctioned programs of torture. In 1972 Amnesty International was awarded the Nobel Peace Prize for its efforts.

Reference: Egon Larsen, *A Flame in Barbed Wire: The Story of Amnesty International* (New York: Norton, 1979).

ANANDA MARG

"The Path of Eternal Bliss." The Ananda Marg is a mystical, quasi-political, Indian Hindu group founded in 1955 by Prabhat Ranjan Sarkar. Its members worship Kali, the Hindu God of Destruction. The Ananda Marg was responsible for the assassination of Narayan Mishra, India's minister of railways, in January 1975. In March of that year, the group failed in its attempt to murder the Chief Justice of India in a grenade attack. The Ananda Marg was among the

groups banned by the government on July 4, 1975 for "creating conditions of violence and chaos in the country." The ban was lifted in 1977. In 1977 and 1978 the Ananda Marg instigated anti-Indian bombings in Australia, including the bombing of the Sydney Hilton hotel during a conference of Asian and Pacific Commonwealth heads of government. Two people died in the Hilton blast. Seventeen Ananda Marg members were killed by an angry mob in Calcutta on April 30, 1982, after rumors linked the group to a rash of kidnappings that had swept the city.

ANARCHISM

The belief that government and its administrative institutions are intrinsically evil, and that they should be abolished (typically by violence) so that they may be replaced by new arrangements not "corrupted" by exploitive and oppressive governments. The term is derived from the ancient Greek "anarkhia," meaning "non-rule." Anarchism as an organized movement, which emerged during the late 19th century in the Russian Empire, was influenced to a large extent by the writings and exhortations of Mikhail BAKUNIN, who espoused the violent overthrow of all societal institutions. The alleged rationale of anarchist terrorist attacks can be attributed to the theory of "propaganda by deed," a term coined by the 19th-century French writer Paul Brouss to describe individual acts of terror and violence presented as revolutionary statements of purpose.

References: Paul Avrich, *Anarchist Portraits* (Princeton, N.J.: Princeton University Press, 1988); Wolfgang L. Mommsen and Gerhard Hirschfeld, eds., *Social Protest, Violence, and Terror in Nineteenth- and Twentieth-Century Europe* (New York: St. Martin's Press, 1982); Robert Goehlert, "Anarchism:

A Bibliography of Articles, 1900–1975," *Political Theory* 4 (1976).

ANARCHY

A social context in which legitimate political authority does not exist; the absence of formal legal order. The international system of sovereign states is often referred to as anarchic because, even though international organizations, alliances and understandings exist, sovereign states do not recognize any greater authority than their own. This view is reflected by Hedley Bull in the title of his analysis of international relationships, *The Anarchical Society* (London: Macmillan, 1977).

ANGLO-IRISH AGREEMENT

The 1985 agreements between the Republic of Ireland and the United Kingdom, which offered a partial solution to the violent religious and political conflict in Northern Ireland. It provides for limited participation by the Republic of Ireland in the governing of the six counties of Ulster province, which makes up Northern Ireland. Northern Ireland is ruled by the United Kingdom directly. In addition, the agreement gives increased rights to the Roman Catholics living in Northern Ireland. A temporary solution at best, the agreement does not have the support of either of Northern Ireland's religious factions. The Protestant majority, which makes up nearly two-thirds of Northern Ireland's population, opposes the idea of the predominantly Roman Catholic Republic of Ireland having any formal voice in Northern Ireland's government, while Roman Catholics in Northern Ireland reject any solution short of a fully united Ireland.

Reference: Michael Connolly and John Loughlin, "Reflections on the Anglo-Irish Agreement," *Government and Opposition* 21 (Spring 1986).

ANGRY BRIGADE

A radical British left-wing organization active in the late 1960s and early 1970s. From 1968 until 1971 the group was responsible for 27 bombings. Other activities included bank robberies and machine gun attacks on British public buildings. The group has been described as the British equivalent of the German Baader-Meinhof Gang. The Angry Brigade collapsed in 1972 following the arrest and imprisonment of its leaders.

Reference: Gordon Carr, *The Angry Brigade: The Cause and the Case* (London: Gollanz, 1975).

ANIMAL LIBERATION FRONT (ALF)

Radical animal rights organization, active in the United States and Great Britain, that stands in violent opposition to the use of animals as foodstuffs or as subjects of scientific research. Founded by Englishman Ronnie Lee in 1978, the ALF has an active membership numbering in the thousands. The group has staged violent terrorist attacks on slaughterhouses and research facilities and advocates break-ins to "liberate" captive animals.

The British ALF's best-known operation was the 1984 lacing of Mars candy bars with rat poison in Southampton, England, in protest of the candy maker's use of monkeys in tooth decay research. Mars bars were pulled from shop shelves throughout Britain, resulting in a serious financial setback for the manufacturer.

In Spring of 1987, the American ALF was believed to be responsible for the arson fire that destroyed a livestock disease laboratory under construction at the Davis campus of the University of California. Damage from the fire was estimated at $3.5 million. ALF activists also have conducted many acts of protest vandalism, such as the splashing of blood on walls and doors. ALF violence has increased in recent years, despite the many complaints of less radical members of the growing worldwide animal rights movement that terrorist acts impede the progress of the cause.

References: Katherine Bishop, "Animal Rights Battle Gaining Ground," *New York Times* (January 12, 1989); Susan Sperling, *Animal Liberators: Research and Morality* (Berkeley: University of California Press, 1988); G. Davidson Smith, "Political Violence in Animal Liberation," *Contemporary Review* 247 (1985); Terry Mulgannon, "The Animal Liberation Front," *TVI Journal* 5 (Spring 1985).

ANIMAL RIGHTS MILITIA (ARM)

A British splinter group of the ANIMAL LIBERATION FRONT. The ARM has launched violent terrorist attacks against researchers whose work involves experiments upon laboratory animals, and against research facilities.

ANIMAL RIGHTS TERRORISM

Starting in the mid-1970s, an increasingly vocal animal rights movement has spawned a number of individuals and groups that support the use of violence and intimidation to further their cause. Organizations such as the ANIMAL LIBERATION FRONT and the ANIMAL RIGHTS MILITIA have directed campaigns of terror against medical researchers, meat processing companies, the fur industry and corporations that use animal subjects in product research. The basis of the animal rights movement is the belief that animals, like humans, have inalienable rights that must be protected. Most members of animal rights groups support nonviolent approaches to their cause, and several of the larger organizations, such as the Fund for Animals, have issued statements deploring the terroristic acts of their more militant animal rights groups.

ANTI-COMMUNIST SECRET ARMY

A Guatemalan far-right death squad and terrorist organization. In 1988, it was speculated that this group was responsible for the bombing of Soviet Tass press offices in Guatemala City.

ANTI-IMPERIALIST ARMED FRONT (AIAF)

A defunct Western European alliance of left-wing terrorist groups, banded together to form a common front against NATO targets. The AIAF was founded in the early 1980s by the French ACTION DIRECTE (AD) and the West German RED ARMY FACTION (RAF).

ANTI-IMPERIALIST INTERNATIONAL BRIGADE (AIIB)

A left-wing terrorist group suspected of being a front for the JAPANESE RED ARMY. In 1986 and 1987 terrorists claiming to represent the AIIB carried out a series of rocket and mortar assaults against U.S. embassies in Jakarta, Rome and Madrid. The AIIB also claimed responsibility for several other minor bombing incidents in Rome against U.S. and British diplomatic targets in 1987.

APARTHEID

Afrikaans, "separate development." The term apartheid refers to the South African government's policy of racial segregation formally adopted in 1948. Apartheid classifies all South Africans into one of four racial groups: white, black, colored, or Asian. A person's political and economic rights follow from this classification. White supremacy is maintained by laws limiting the political participation and economic advancement of the other racial groups. Apartheid has been formally denounced by the United Nations in various resolutions; the 1966 resolution (2202/XXI) calls it a "crime against humanity." Since 1962 the U.N. General Assembly has also repeatedly called for economic and diplomatic sanctions against South Africa. Today many nations have imposed such sanctions to encourage the dismantling of apartheid, but to seemingly little effect, and although the government of South Africa has repeatedly made public expressions of intent to enact drastic change in its racial policies, reforms have so far been limited.

References: Heribert Adam and Kogila Moodley, *South Africa Without Apartheid* (Berkeley: University of California Press, 1986); Pauline H. Baker, "Facing Up to Apartheid," *Foreign Policy* 64 (Fall 1986); Paul Rich, "Insurgency, Terrorism, and the Apartheid System in South Africa," *Political Studies* 32 (March 1984).

APRIL 19TH MOVEMENT

See M-19.

AQUINO, BENIGNO S., JR. (1932–83)

Popular Filipino opposition leader, often called "Ninoy," who was assassinated by agents of the Marcos regime as he returned from exile on August 21, 1983 at Manila International Airport. He was shot by Ro-

lando Galman, who was in turn killed by security force officers. The military attempted to portray Galman as a member of the Communist Party and the NEW PEOPLE'S ARMY (NPA), but the evidence pointed to an assassination planned and carried out by the Filipino military, with the direct involvement of General Fabian Ver, the Armed Forces Chief of Staff. The assassination proved to be a turning point in U.S.–Filipino relations and in the political history of the Philippines. Ninoy Aquino's widow, Corazon Aquino, subsequently ran for the presidency of the Philippines. After an election rife with fraud, Marcos announced his own reelection; however, Mrs. Aquino assumed her rightful position as president after a popular uprising forced the discredited Marcos to flee the country. Mrs. Aquino's government brought to light clear evidence that the Marcos regime had engineered and covered up Ninoy Aquino's assassination. In November 1988 investigators unearthed the remains of two women killed by the military during the attempted cover-up.

References: Stanley Karnow, *In Our Image: America's Empire in the Phillipines* (New York: Random House, 1988); Sandra Burton, *Impossible Dream: The Marcoses, the Aquinos, and the Unfinished Revolution* (New York: Warner, 1988); Benigno S. Aquino, Jr., *Testament From a Prison Cell* (Manila: B. S. Aquino, Jr. Foundation, 1984).

ARAB LIBERATION FRONT (ALF)

Founded in April 1969 by Iraq in response to its perceptions that Syria exercised undue influence in Palestinian organizations. The ALF represents Iraqi Ba'thist interests in Lebanon, where the group has been involved in clashes with the AMAL militia. The group operates on the periphery of the PAL-

ESTINE LIBERATION ORGANIZATION (PLO) but is not a major voice within that body. It helped form the REJECTIONIST FRONT in the mid-1970s. ALF actions have generally consisted of armed raids into Israeli territory.

ARAB NATIONALIST YOUTH ORGANIZATION FOR THE LIBERATION OF PALESTINE (ANYOLP)

A defunct radical Palestinian organization that broke away from the POPULAR FRONT FOR THE LIBERATION OF PALESTINE (PFLP) in 1972 and immediately pursued an agenda of violent attacks and hijackings. Its attack on an Israeli diplomat in Cyprus in April 1973 triggered an Israeli raid on Beirut, which resulted in the deaths of several members of the PLO leadership.

ARAB ORGANIZATION OF 15 MAY

See MAY 15 GROUP.

ARAB RADICALS

An amorphous term pervasive in the literature of terrorism, often used in vastly differing contexts and fashions. The most clearly articulated definition of the term has been presented by Professor Adeed Dawisha: "the term (Arab) radical characterizes the ideas and actions of groups that work to overthrow an established political order; of countries and regimes that aim to undermine the political authority and legitimacy of other states and regimes; and of states seeking to modify or change existing power relationships in an international system." The leaders of these states or organizations are motivated by nationalistic or Islamic ideology, which they hope to use to enhance the Arab's position in the international sys-

tem. Such a perspective leads Dawisha to cite the states of Libya, Syria, South Yemen, Algeria and Iraq and the organizations of the Palestine Liberation Organization, Hezbollah, Islamic Jihad, Amal, Dawa and the Muslim Brotherhood (and its offshoots) as the Arab radicals.

Reference: Adeed Dawisha, *The Arab Radicals* (New York: Council on Foreign Relations, 1986).

ARAB REVOLUTION

Pseudonym of the POPULAR FRONT FOR THE LIBERATION OF PALESTINE.

ARAB REVOLUTIONARY BRIGADES

A cover used by the ABU NIDAL Organization.

ARAB REVOLUTIONARY COUNCIL

A cover used by the ABU NIDAL Organization.

ARAFAT, YASIR

Chairman of the PALESTINE LIBERATION ORGANIZATION (PLO) and leader of the largest of its constituent organizations, al-FATAH. Born in Jerusalem in 1929, the son of a successful merchant family, Arafat graduated from the University of Cairo as a civil engineer. During his years at the university he began to study guerrilla tactics. He was one of the founding members of al-Fatah in the mid-1950s and became well known as the organizer of Fatah raids into Israeli territory in the mid-1960s. Al-Fatah became one of the component Palestinian groups that in 1964 formed the Palestine Liberation Organization.

In 1969 Arafat and his organization ascended to leadership roles in a PLO greatly humbled by its defeat in the Arab–Israeli Six Day War in 1967. He stated then, as he has continued to state, that the PLO is the "sole, legitimate representative of the Palestinian people." In November 1974 Arafat addressed the U.N. General Assembly, becoming the first non-government representative to be accorded such an opportunity. He has been criticized by many Palestinian activists in the 1980s, and by the Syrian government, as being too "moderate." In 1982 he was forced to flee to Tunisia as a result of the Israeli invasion of Lebanon. He returned to Southern Lebanon in 1983 but was forced to flee again when rebel PLO forces rose in mutiny against him. He regrouped his loyal troops in Northern Lebanon, but he soon found himself surrounded by the rebels. Mediation by Syria and Saudi Arabia contributed to a U.N.-sponsored escort of Arafat and his forces to a safe haven in Tunisia and North Yemen.

After this setback Arafat adopted a new strategy. The INTIFADA, a campaign of civil disobedience begun by Palestinians in the Israeli-occupied territories in December 1987, had helped to build sympathy for Palestinians, while the response of the Israeli army somewhat weakened support for Israel, especially in the United States and Western Europe. During December 1988 Arafat made a series of statements, before the U.N. General Assembly and elsewhere, through which he gradually made more explicit his willingness to accept U.N. RESOLUTION 242 and RESOLUTION 338, and to renounce terrorism. These were preconditions the United States insisted had to be met before any meaningful dialogue could begin between the United States and the PLO. The promised discussion began in Tunis shortly thereafter.

Arafat's sudden willingness to negotiate a settlement to the Palestinian question bears testament to his diplomatic skill and the political pragmatism that have characterized his long-running leadership of the Arab cause. Still, many of the more hard-line members of the Palestinian movement, such as the REJECTIONIST FRONT groups, have been angered by Arafat's apparent readiness to compromise; and recent terrorist acts by these groups can be seen as attempts to disrupt Arafat's initiative. The leftist factions within the PLO have accepted Arafat's "Peace Initiative," acting as the loyal opposition. These factions are the Popular Front for the Liberation of Palestine, the Democratic Front for the Liberation of Palestine, and the Palestine Liberation Front.

References: Alan Hart, *Arafat: A Political Biography* (Bloomington: Indiana University Press, 1988); Marie Colvin, "The Ambiguous Yasir Arafat," *New York Times Magazine* (December 18, 1988); Shaul Mishal, *The PLO Under Arafat: Between Gun and Olive Branch* (New York: Yale University Press, 1986); Alan Hart, *Arafat: Terrorist or Peacemaker?* (London: Sidgwick and Jackson, 1984); Janet and John Wallach, *Arafat: In the Eyes of the Beholder* (New York: Carol Publishing Group, 1990).

ARENA

"Republican National Alliance" (in Spanish: Alianza Republicana Nacional). A right-wing political party that has been responsible for assassinations and many other forms of political violence in the troubled Central American country of El Salvador. The party was founded in 1982 by a coalition of wealthy businessmen and right-wing politicians. ARENA, which has been linked to paramilitary activity, is led by Roberto D'Aubisson, who lost a bid for president in a 1984 election that many experts insist was engineered by the United States to ensure victory for the more moderate Christian Democratic candidate, Jose Napoleon Duarte. D'Aubissson stands accused of direct involvement in the rampant DEATH SQUAD activity in El Salvador, as do many members of ARENA. In March 1989 ARENA candidate Alfredo Christiani emerged victorious in the Salvadoran presidential election. He professed to represent a party that is more moderate and practical than its earlier incarnation.

Reference: Neil C. Livingstone, "Death Squads," *World Affairs* 146 (Winter 1983–84).

ARGENTINA

During the years of military rule from March 1976 to December 1983, the Argentine military and right-wing DEATH SQUADS directed an era of state terror cynically known as the "Process of National Reorganization." This period is better known as the DIRTY WAR in which perhaps 20,000 citizens, including many women and children, "DISAPPEARED." Many of the disappeared were incarcerated for long periods of time before being tortured and killed at the hands of the military or the paramilitary death squads.

The dirty war was the right wing's response to the pervasive Argentine left-wing guerrilla violence of the late 1960s and early and mid-1970s. The dirty war, however, was directed not only against the violent left, but against moderates and liberals, Jews, and other perceived or potential opponents of the right-wing regime. When the democratic government of Raul Alfonsin ascended to power in December 1983, President Alfonsin appointed the National commission on Disappeared Person (CODEP) to uncover the fates of the thousands of disappeared. CODEP's report, issued in September 1984, documented a level of state repression that may be the most glaring example of state terrorism in a Western nation since Nazi Germany.

References: Donald C. Hodges, *Argentina, 1943–1987: The National Revolution and Resistance* (Albuquerque: University of New Mexico Press, 1988); John Simpson and Jana Bennett, *The Disappeared* (London: Robson Books, 1985); "The Argentine Military Junta's Final Report on the War Against Subversion and Terrorism, April 1983," *Terrorism* 7 (1984); Amnesty International, *Political Killings by Governments: Argentina* (London: Amnesty International, 1983); Jacobo Timerman, *Prisoner Without a Name, Cell Without a Number* (New York: Knopf, 1981).

ARGOV, SHLOMO

Israeli Ambassador to the United Kingdom who was severely wounded on June 3, 1982 in an assassination attempt by BLACK JUNE, a radical Palestinian group led by ABU NIDAL. The attack helped prompt Israeli Prime Minister Menachem BEGIN to launch the 1982 invasion of Lebanon in an attempt to drive the PLO out of that country. The PLO denied any complicity in the Argov incident. Three Arabs, including the nephew of Abu Nidal, were arrested by London police after the shooting; in March 1983 three were sentenced to prison terms ranging from 30 to 35 years.

ARM

See ANIMAL RIGHTS MILITIA.

ARMED RESISTANCE UNIT (ARU)

A U.S. left-wing organization thought to be connected with or a cover name for the UNITED FREEDOM FRONT. The ARU claimed responsibility for the November 6, 1983 bombing of the U.S. Capitol building. The group later stated that the bombing was in protest of the invasion of Grenada and U.S. involvement in Lebanon.

ARMENIAN LIBERATION ARMY (ALA)

A violent guerrilla organization dedicated to achieving Armenian autonomy. The group bombed several Turkish targets in Western Europe in the late 1970s. It has faded from view in recent years.

See also ARMENIAN TERRORISM.

ARMENIAN REVOLUTIONARY ARMY (ARA)

An Armenian nationalist organization that first surfaced in 1983 to claim credit for the murder of two Turkish diplomats in Brussels in July 1983 (an act also claimed by the ARMENIAN SECRET ARMY FOR THE LIBERATION OF ARMENIA). On July 27, 1983 five ARA members died in an attack on the Turkish Embassy in Lisbon. The group is thought to be a splinter group or a cover name of the JUSTICE COMMANDOS OF THE ARMENIAN GENOCIDE (JCAG).

ARMENIAN SECRET ARMY FOR THE LIBERATION OF ARMENIA (ASALA)

Founded in Beirut in 1975, ASALA is a Marxist-Leninist group that seeks revenge for Ottoman Turkey's alleged annihilation of an estimated 1.5 million Armenians in 1915 and calls for an end to the Turkish government's discrimination against ethnic Armenians. ASALA's ultimate goal is the establishment of an independent Armenian state in the historical Armenian homeland of eastern Turkey, northern Iran, northern Iraq, and the Armenian Soviet Socialist republic of the Soviet Union. ASALA is decidedly pro-Soviet and regards the Armenian Soviet Socialist Republic as a "liberated nation." It is also violently anti-NATO because of Turkey's membership in NATO and is anti-Zionist.

ASALA is composed primarily of Lebanese of Armenian descent. It has directed its terrorist violence mainly against Turkish institutions and diplomats in Western Europe. France and Switzerland, which incurred the wrath of ASALA by arresting Armenians traveling with forged passports in 1980 and 1981, were subjected to bombings and attacks until they made concessions that included the release of jailed Armenian terrorists.

In 1982 the group was forced from Southern Lebanon, along with the Palestinian guerrillas, during the Israeli invasion. In August 1982 an ASALA operative carried out a suicide attack at the Ankara airport, and in July 1983 the group bombed Orly airport in Paris, killing seven people. This incident created great dissension within the group and caused ASALA to split into two groups: ASALA-RM (Revolutionary Movement), which found "blind" terrorism to be injurious to the Armenian cause, and ASALA-M (Militant), which continues to support unrestricted violence against Turkish and "imperialist" targets. ASALA-RM is led by Monte Melkonian. The leader of ASALA-M, Hagop Hagopian, was killed in March 1988. Terrorist incidents have declined since the split, although ASALA is suspected of participating in the Paris bombing campaign of September 1986, and is known to have attacked the French Embassy in Lebanon in October 1987. Today the ASALA continues to receive much of its funding and training from radical Palestinian organizations.

References: George S. Harris, *Turkey: Coping with Crisis* (Boulder, Colo.: Westview Press, 1985); Anat Kurz and Ariel Merari, *ASALA: Irrational Terror or Political Tool?* (Boulder, Colo.: Westview Press, 1985).

ARMENIAN TERRORISM

Several of the world's most violent terrorist organizations and campaigns have been launched in the name of Armenian nationalism. Armenian terrorism is a relatively recent phenomenon, having emerged in 1975. Its perpetrators, while varying in some specific aims and motivations, generally seek autonomy for the Armenian people and revenge for the deaths of an estimated 1.5 million members of the minority Christian community at the hands of the Ottoman Turks in 1915, in what has come to be known as the Armenian Genocide.

Much of Armenian terrorism is directed against members of the Turkish government, especially Turkish diplomats at international posts. The present-day Turkish government both disputes the factual basis of the genocide and denies any responsibility for the actions of the Ottomans. Armenian radicals refuse to dismiss what they claim is the historical case and the present reality of a scattered people without an autonomous homeland. In January 1988 the Turkish government announced its intention to open the Ottoman archives, in an effort to disprove the claims of government-directed genocide. Turkish officials have conceded that 300,000 perished during the forcible relocation of the Armenian population during wartime.

Members of Armenian terrorist organizations have repeatedly stated that they have resorted to violence only after the complete failure of 60 years of seeking a peaceful settlement. The two principal terrorist organizations are the ARMENIAN SECRET ARMY FOR THE LIBERATION OF ARMENIA (ASALA) and the JUSTICE COMMANDOS OF THE ARMENIAN GENOCIDE (JCAG), although in recent years the ARMENIAN REVOLUTIONARY ARMY (ARA) has emerged as a new and dangerous group.

References: Michael Gunter, "Cycles of Terrorism: The Question of Contemporary Turkish Counterterror and Harassment against the Armenians," *Journal of Political Science* 14 (Spring 1986); Bonnie Cordes, "Armenian Terrorism in America," *TVI Journal* 5 (Summer 1984); Michael M. Gunter, "The Armenian Terrorist Campaign against Turkey," *Orbis* 27 (Summer 1983); Paul Wilkinson, "Armenian Terrorism" *World Today* 19 (September 1983); Martha N. Kessler, *Syria: Fragile Mosaic of Power* (Washington, D.C.: National Defense University Press, 1987); Moshe Ma'oz and Avner Yaniv, *Syria under Assad: Domestic Constraints and Regional Risks* (New York: St. Martin's Press, 1986).

AROCENA, EDUARDO

See OMEGA 7.

ARYAN NATIONS

A loose organization of U.S. radical right-wing groups that share a common bond of racism and anti-Semitism. These groups include the KU KLUX KLAN and the ORDER, a NEO-NAZI organization founded in 1983. The Aryan Nations organization was founded by Richard Girnt Butler in 1974. It serves as coordinator for its constituent organizations, which maintain contact through a computer-network bulletin board described as a "pro-American, pro-White, anti-Communist network of true believers who serve the one and only God—Jesus, the Christ. . . ." Butler and his organization have been active recruiters of imprisoned convicts. The Aryan Nations support the creation of a sovereign white state in the northwest United States. The group alleges that the United States is controlled by a Jewish cabal, which it terms the "Zionist Occupation Government" of the United States, or "ZOG."

References: James Coates, *Armed and Dangerous* (New York: Noonday, 1987); Ciaran O. Maolain, *The Radical Right* (Harlow, U.K.: Longman, 1987).

ASSAD, HAFEZ AL-

President of SYRIA. Assad became president on November 13, 1970, when as Minister of Defense he seized power from Salah Jadid, who had himself assumed control of the country in 1966 with Assad's assistance. Born on October 6, 1930 in northeastern Syria, Assad is a member of Syria's ethnic and religious minority group the Alawites. The overwhelming majority of Syrians are SUNNI Muslims. Despite their minority status, Alawites have a disproportionate hold on power in both the Syrian government and the ruling Ba'th Party. Assad, though considered to be a radical Arab leader, has constructed a secular government and consequently has been confronted domestically by violent opposition from Islamic fundamentalists. Chief among Syrian opposition forces has been the MUSLIM BROTHERHOOD. Assad demonstrated his ruthlessness in February 1982 when he directed Syrian military forces under the command of his brother Rifaat to crush the Brotherhood and its stronghold in the city of HAMAH. An estimated 25,000 of Hamah's citizens perished during several weeks of carnage and destruction. Assad has also exported terrorist violence beyond his own country's borders and Syria is considered to be one of the principal nations involved in STATE-SPONSORED TERRORISM.

Reference: Patrick Seale, *Asad of Syria: The Struggle for the Middle East* (Berkeley: University of California Press, 1989).

ASSASSINATION

Deliberate murder, especially of a politically prominent person for political motives. The term assassin came into usage with a group of Isma'ili Shi'ite Muslims in the 13th-14th centuries. Their main goal was to murder Christian Crusaders, Sunni Muslim leaders, and other political rivals, and they purportedly used hashish in preparation for their deadly attacks. "Assassin" is a corruption of the word "hashish."

Assassination is a time-honored if not honorable way of removing people from public office. Julius Caesar was assassinated in 44 B.C. U.S. presidents James Garfield, Abraham Lincoln, William McKinley and John F. Kennedy were assassinated, and presidents Andrew Jackson, Theodore Roosevelt, Franklin Roosevelt, Harry Truman, Gerald Ford and Ronald Reagan all narrowly escaped death in various assassination attempts. The events leading to the start of World War I were put into motion by the assassination of Archduke Franz Ferdinand of Austria in 1914. Many of the major figures of the 20th century have died at the hands of assassins. To the extent that the political objectives of the assassins are achieved by a given murder, the assassins can be said to have won. For example, the assassination of the president of Egypt, Anwar al-SADAT, in 1981 has certainly had a chilling effect on peace efforts in the Middle East.

While some governments actively sponsor assassinations, it is illegal for the United States to do so. Executive order 12333, signed by Ronald Reagan in 1981, states: "No person employed by or acting on behalf of the

United States government shall engage in, or conspire to engage in, assassination." However, this did not stop the Reagan administration from bombing the home of Libya's Muammar al-Qaddafi in 1986 in the expectation that he would be killed.

References: H.A.A. Cooper, *On Assassination* (Boulder, Colo.: Paladin Press, 1984); Bernard Lewis, *The Assassins: A Radical Sect in Islam* (New York: Oxford University Press, 1968).

ATA (ANTI-TERRORISM ASSISTANCE)

The U.S. State Department's anti-terrorist program, which provides assistance to foreign governments upon request. ATA includes training for border guards and customs officials and improvements in airport security measures. More than 40 foreign governments have taken advantage of the program.

ATTENTAT CLAUSE

That part of an extradition treaty or law which holds that the murder of a head of state (or family member of a head of state) shall not be considered a political crime for purposes of extradition. As mere criminal or civil defendants, the suspected perpetrators of such crimes are extraditable. Not all nations agree with this practice, however; some feel that violence against rulers is a classic act of political protest. Because Belgium first enacted the attenat clause in 1856, it is sometimes called the "Belgium Clause."

AVANGUARDIA NAZIONALE (AN)

Italian, "National Vanguard." An Italian right-wing terrorist organization founded by fascist Stefano DELLE CHIAIE in 1959. In the 1960s the group established a working relationship with other European right-wing terrorist organizations in a loosely-knit organization dubbed the "Black Orchestra." On December 7, 1970 the AN attempted to take control of the Italian government by coup d'état. The group's most infamous incident was its reported involvement in the bombing of the Bologna train station in August 1980, in which more than 80 people were killed. AN is now thought to be defunct.

AVC

See ALFARO VIVE, CARAJO.

AYATOLLAH

A title of respect in both Arabic and Farsi (meaning "giving divine signs") accorded to the most respected teachers and scholars by Islamic Shi'ites. Ruholla KHOMEINI, as the Ayatollah Khomeini, inspired and led the Iranian revolution of 1979 until his death in 1989.

AZANIAN AFRICAN PEOPLE'S ORGANIZATION (AZAPO)

A splinter group of the AFRICAN NATIONAL CONGRESS (ANC) founded in May 1978. AZAPO is a radical group with a blacks-only membership policy and has found a following in the black townships of South Africa.

B

BAADER, ANDREAS (1943–77)

West German terrorist who co-founded the RED ARMY FACTION (Rote Armee Fraktion), often called the Baader-Meinhof Gang. Baader was a radical leftist, active in the student unrest of the late 1960s. His first terrorist attack was the bombing, with Gudrun ENSSLIN, of a Frankfurt department store in 1968, an act for which he was jailed. He escaped with the aid of Ensslin and Ulrike MEINHOF on May 14, 1970. They fled to the Middle East where they trained with fellow West German terrorists in camps operated by the POPULAR FRONT FOR THE LIBERATION OF PALESTINE (PFLP). Baader and his accomplices returned to West Germany and unleashed a series of terroristic episodes, including bombings, abductions and assassinations. Baader, Meinhof, Ensslin, and several other RAF members were arrested in 1972. Their colleagues made several desperate attempts to force authorities to release the imprisoned Baader and his accomplices, including the hijacking in October 1977 of a Lufthansa airliner. The attempt failed when the hostages were rescued at Mogadishu by West German commandos. On October 18, 1977, in reaction to this incident, Baader, Ensslin, and another jailed RAF member committed suicide in their prison cells.

References: Stephan Aust, *The Baader-Meinhof Group* (London: Bodley Head, 1987); John Bradshaw, "The Dream of Terror," *Esquire* 90 (July 18, 1978); Jillian Becker, *Hitler's Children: The Baader-Meinhof Terrorist Gang* (Philadelphia: Lippincott, 1978); Melvin J. Lasky, "Ulrike and Andreas," *New York Times Magazine* 14 (May 11, 1975).

BAADER-MEINHOF GANG

See RED ARMY FACTION.

BAKUNIN, MIKHAIL (1814–76)

Russian revolutionary and theorist, considered to be one of the founders of anarchism. Together with Sergei NECHAEV, he wrote *The Catechism of a Revolutionary*, which preached the virtues of anarchism and the professional revolutionary. The writings and philosophy of Bakunin were a major influence on Lenin and the Bolsheviks, and his influence is still apparent today in terrorist organizations such as the West German RED ARMY FACTION and the Italian RED BRIGADES.

References: Richard B. Saltman, *The Social and Political Thought of Michael Bakunin* (Westport, Conn.: Greenwood, 1983); Sam Dolgoff, ed., *Bakunin on Anarchy* (New York: Knopf, 1972); Eugene Pyziur, *The Doctrine* *of Anarchy of Michael Bakunin* (Chicago: Henry Regnery, 1968).

BAND OF MERCY

A radical animal rights organization active in the United States during the late 1980s.

BANDERA ROJA (GBR)

Spanish, "Red Flag." A Marxist/Leninist Venezuelan guerrilla organization. The group, a splinter group of MIR, was founded in 1969. Bandera Roja is dedicated to the "dictatorship of the proletariat in Venezuela by means of an armed struggle" and has rejected the assimilation of left-wing elements into legitimate Venezuelan politics. The armed wing of the GBR is called the "Frente Americo Silvio." In 1972, in a joint operation with the MIR, the group kidnapped Carlos Dominguez Chavez, a prominent industrialist, and received $1 million in ransom. In 1975 the Bandera Roja began an organized campaign of abduction of businessmen for ransom. Sporadic operations such as ambushes of military vehicles and temporary takeovers of small towns occurred throughout 1976 and 1977. Arrests of top leaders curtailed operations during the late 1970s. In December 1980 members of the group hijacked three domestic airline flights for ransom.

The group apparently has been unable to secure any outside sponsorship and probably relies on ransoms as well as raids on small towns as means of support. Bandera Roja has had contact with the Colombian guerrilla groups M-19 and ELN. In recent years the Bandera Roja guerrilla front has been dormant, and the group's activities have been limited to political activism and organization.

BANNA, HASSAN AL- (1903–49)

Founder of the MUSLIM BROTHERHOOD, an organization dedicated to returning Egypt to fundamental Islamic values with a government based on the Koran and the Hadith, the basis of the Islamic Sunna or religious doctrine. Al-Banna was considered to be a charismatic leader, and the early success of the Brotherhood is attributed to his personal popularity. He was assassinated on February 12, 1949 by agents of the Egyptian government, who held his organization responsible for the assassination of Prime Minister Nokrashi Pasha and a number of other high government officials.

Reference: Richard P. Mitchell, *The Society of the Muslim Brothers* (London: Oxford University Press, 1969).

BANNA, SABRI AL-

See ABU NIDAL.

BASQUE FATHERLAND AND LIBERTY

See ETA.

BASQUE TERRORISM

Radical Basque separatists have carried on a campaign of violence in the hope of achieving independence for their ethnic homeland in northern Spain. The fascist regime of General Francisco Franco inadvertently stoked the nationalist fervor of a fiercely independent but repressed people who were intent on maintaining their cultural and linguistic identity. The Basque nationalist organization ETA (Euzkadi ta Askatasuna; "Basque Fatherland and Liberty"), founded in 1959, began in 1968 a series of anti-Spanish terrorist acts that continue today. In 1980 the four Basque provinces were granted regional political autonomy by the Spanish government. Such measures did not appease the Basque terrorists, however, and they appear to be ready to settle for nothing less than total Basque sovereignty.

References: Joseba Zulaika, *Basque Violence: Metaphor and Sacrement* (Reno: University of Nevada Press, 1988); Robert P. Clark, *The Basque Insurgents* (Madison: University of Wisconsin Press, 1984); Walther L. Bernecker, "Nationist Violence and Terror in the Spanish Border Provinces," in Wolfgang L. Mommsen and Gerhard Hirschfeld, eds., *Social Protest, Violence, and Terror in Nineteenth- and Twentieth-Century Europe* (New York: St. Martin's Press, 1982).

BEGIN, MENACHEM

The Polish-born (in 1913) former prime minister of Israel (1977–83) and leader of the IRGUN terrorist organization, which was active in the 1940s and was considered to be the most dangerous of the Jewish terrorist groups. Much of Irgun's violence was calculated to make the preservation of Britain's Palestine mandate too costly. Irgun, under Begin's direction, was responsible for the bombing of the KING DAVID HOTEL in Jerusalem in July 1946 and the massacre at the Palestinian village of DEIR YASSIN in April 1948. He founded the right-wing Herut party and served in the Knesset (the Israeli Parliament) as a leader of the opposition (1948–67). He was a member of a national unity government (1967–70) and became prime minister as head of the right-wing coalition led by the Likud party in 1977. He opened negotiations with Egyptian president Anwar Sadat in 1977 when Sadat accepted his invitation to visit Jerusalem and begin a peace process between Israel and Egypt. U.S. president Jimmy Carter helped to mediate the Camp David Accords, which resulted in the 1979 Egypt-Israeli peace treaty for which Begin shared with Sadat the 1978 Nobel Peace Prize. Begin's policy was to increase the number of Israeli settlements on the West Bank. But his invasion of Lebanon in 1982 to attack Palestinian guerrillas resulted in an unpopular drawn-out war, which provoked unprecedented anti-government demonstrations. This and the death of his wife influenced his decision to retire from public life in 1983.

References: Amos Perlmuter, *The Life and Times of Menachem Begin* (Garden City, N.J.: Doubleday, 1987); J. Bowyer Bell, *Terror Out of Zion: Irgun Zvai Leumi, LEHI and the Palestine Underground, 1929–1949* (New York: St. Martin's Press, 1976); David Rosenthal, "Menachem Begin: From Oppositionist to Prime Minister", *Jewish Frontier,* (August 1977); Lenni Brenner, *The Iron Wall: Zionist Revisionism from Jabotinsky to Shamir* (London: Zed Books, 1984).

BERG, ALAN

Controversial Jewish radio announcer and talk-show host in Denver, Colorado, who was murdered on June 18, 1984 by members of the radical right-wing and anti-Semitic group the ORDER. Four members of the Order were arrested and charged with violating Berg's civil rights (because that was a stronger legal case than murder). David Lane and Bruce Pierce were convicted on November 17, 1987 and sentenced to prison terms of 150 years each. The other two members were found not guilty.

BERNADOTTE, COUNT FOLKE (1895–1948)

Swedish count and U.N. mediator for Palestine who was assassinated on September

17, 1948 in Jerusalem by LEHI, also known as the STERN GANG. Bernadotte was targeted by the militant Zionist organization for trying to consider the interests of all parties in Palestine. The newly-emergent state of Israel failed to formally identify the Count's assassins, though evidence was available to do so, in an effort not to provoke a confrontation with Lehi.

References: Cary David Stanger, "A Haunting Legacy: The Assassination of Count Bernadotte," *The Middle East Journal* 42 (Spring 1988); J. Bowyer Bell, *Terror Out of Zion: Irgun Zvai Leumi, LEHI and the Palestine Underground, 1929–1949* (New York: St. Martin's Press, 1977).

BERRI, NABIH

Leader of AMAL, one of the two primary SHI'ITE militia in Lebanon. Berri joined the political movement of Imam Musa al-SADR in 1974 and emerged as head of Amal following the imam's disappearance in 1978. He vaulted into world headlines as the mediator of the TWA FLIGHT 847 hijacking crisis in June 1985, which established him as one of the foremost power brokers in Lebanon. Berri has been a member of the Lebanese national unity governments, holding various portfolios. A former lawyer born in Sierra Leone and a one-time resident of the United States, Berri is considered to be a moderate leader in comparison with his contemporaries in Lebanese organizations such as HEZBOLLAH. Berri's initial willingness to accept U.S. mediation in Lebanon and his acceptance of a seat on the Lebanese National Salvation Council (alongside Amal's right-wing Christian opponents) caused major rifts in the Shi'ite leadership. He in many ways typifies the older generation of Lebanese Shi'ites, who pose a stark contrast to the far more radical and fundamentalist younger generation of Shi'ite activists, exemplified by ISLAMIC AMAL and Hezbollah.

References: R. Norton, *Harakat Amal and the Political Mobilization of the Shia of Lebanon* (Austin: University of Texas Press, 1987); Robin Wright, *Sacred Rage* (New York: Simon and Schuster, 1985).

BHINDRANWALE, SANT JARNAIL SINGH (1947–84)

Militant Sikh religious and political leader who organized and inspired a wave of Sikh violence and terrorism in India in the early 1980s. Bhindranwale used the GOLDEN TEMPLE OF AMRITSAR as his base of terrorist operations, which led the Indian government to mount its massive assault on the Sikh shrine in June 1984. He and hundreds of his followers were killed during the assault, which had far-reaching implications for the government of Indira GANDHI. Bhindranwale's death at the Golden Temple elevated him to the level of martyr in the eyes of many Sikhs.

Reference: James Manor, "Collective Conflict in India," *Conflict Studies* 212 (1988).

BIKO, STEVEN (1946–77)

South African black opposition leader and head of the Black Consciousness Movement who was killed in September 1977 after prolonged interrogation and beatings by the South African security police. Biko emerged as a martyr of the South African anti-apartheid movement, and his widely-publicized death became a symbol of the international anti-apartheid movement. A major motion picture, "Cry Freedom," based on Donald Woods' *Biko* (New York: Paddington Books, 1979), received wide attention in the West.

Reference: Steven Biko, *Black Consciousness in South Africa* (New York: Vintage, 1979).

BLACK BRIGADES

A group of radical SHI'ITE extremists active in Kuwait and Iraq. In July 1985 the group attacked a restaurant in Kuwait.

BLACK HUNDREDS

Russian mobs incited by the tsar's secret police to conduct POGROMS against Jews in the late 19th and early 20th centuries.

BLACK JUNE

Terrorist organization founded by ABU NIDAL. Black June was named for the month in 1976 in which Syrian troops went to the aid of Lebanese Christians and helped them to win a temporary victory in the country's civil war. The Syrian intervention, on behalf of the Maronite Christian militia known as the Phalange, prevented the country's leftist forces from challenging Maronite dominance of the political process, and it also succeeded in reducing PLO influence within Lebanon. One of the results of the Syrian intervention was the massacre of Palestinian civilians in a refugee camp at Tal al-Za'tar in June 1976.

Black June stood in violent opposition to the PLO's diplomatic and political approaches to the Palestinian question, and in 1979 Black June assassinated three European PLO representatives. In 1982 members shot and critically wounded Shlomo ARGOV, the Israeli ambassador to Great Britain. This assassination attempt proved to be the catalyst for the ensuing Israeli invasion of Lebanon.

Reference: Michael Hudson, "The Palestinian Factor in the Lebanese Civil War," *The Middle East Journal* 32 (Summer 1978).

BLACK LIBERATION ARMY (BLA)

The most violent of the militant U.S. black organizations that arose from the student and social unrest of the late 1960s and early 1970s. From 1971 until 1973 the BLA was responsible for eight killings. Many BLA actions were directed against members of the law enforcement community. BLA violence subsided after a massive FBI investigation led to the arrests of many of the group's leading members.

References: David Edgar, "A Crime to Disagree," *New Statesman* 104 (July 23, 1982); R. Daley, *Target Blue* (New York: Delacorte Press, 1973).

BLACKLIST

A listing of individuals or organizations that are banned, boycotted or disapproved. Blacklists generally carry no legal authority, although they have been issued by governments in an effort to silence or preclude opposition. Blacklists are not necessarily associated with terrorism, although all blacklists are designed to intimidate. Most are clandestine. Artists, writers and performers are frequently associated with blacklisting and have been the victims of blacklists in political environments as diverse as the United States during the McCarthy era and Argentina during the DIRTY WAR. The Argentine blacklists were an integral component of the state-sponsored terrorism and death squads during the rule of the military regime (1979–83). Blacklisted people often were unable to pursue their careers, and many went into exile. Ignored blacklists brought the wrath of the military or of death squads such as the AAA. Blacklists, in Argentina and elsewhere, have usually been tools of the right wing in its opposition to the political left.

BLACK ORDER

A right-wing Italian terrorist organization, with ties to MSI, the Italian Social Movement, a fascist political party. The group stands in violent opposition to Italy's present form of government, parliamentary democracy. The Black Order has been implicated in the rash of neo-fascist terrorist attacks that occurred in Italy during the 1970s. The group is considered to be a suspect in the bombing on August 2, 1980 of the crowded Bologna railway station, in which more than 80 people died and more than 200 were injured.

See also FASCISM.

BLACK PANTHERS

An American "black power" organization founded by Huey NEWTON and Bobby SEALE in October 1966, in Oakland, California. This group, formally the "Black Panther Party," was the best-known and most notorious of the militant black organizations that formed out of the student and social unrest of the 1960s. Finding the nonviolent measures of the civil rights movement to be inadequate, the Panthers supported the armed revolt of repressed blacks against repressive American institutions. The assassination of Dr. Martin Luther King Jr. seemed to mark a turning point for the group, for then its emphasis moved to the revolutionary left, and it looked to communist regimes for support. In the late 1960s and early 1970s, U.S. law enforcement officers waged a full-scale assault on the Black Panthers, with the FBI leading the offensive. The Panthers were unable to recover from these blows and ceased to exist as a significant force.

See also CLEAVER, ELDRIDGE.

References: Ward Churchill, *Agents of Repression: The FBI's Secret War Against the Black Panther Party and the American Indian Movement* (Boston: South End Press, 1988); Bobby Seale, *A Lonely Rage* (New York: Times Books, 1978); G. Louis Heath (ed.), *Off the Pigs: The History and Literature of the Black Panther Party* (Metuchen, N.J.: Scarecrow Press, 1976).

BLACK SEPTEMBER

Terrorist group born out of and named after the month in 1970 in which the Jordanian army fought and expelled from Jordan al-FATAH and other Palestinian guerrilla groups. The group has been led by cofounder ABU DAOUD, who has defined it as an "avenging" organization. In 1971 members assassinated Wasfi al-TAL, the Prime Minister of Jordan, whom Black September held primarily responsible for the expulsion of the Palestinian guerrillas. In September 1972 the group abducted members of the Israeli Olympic team; this incident became known as the MUNICH MASSACRE after 11 athletes and five terrorists were killed during an attempted rescue. Many experts have considered Black September to be a clandestine wing of al-Fatah and the PLO, set up to allow the mainstream organizations to remain blameless for terrorist acts. Many members of the group have been assimilated into what is now referred to as the ABU NIDAL organization.

References: Serge Groussard, *The Blood of Israel: The Massacre of the Israeli Athletes, The Olympics 1972* (New York: Morrow, 1975); Christopher Dobson, *Black September: Its Short and Violent History* (New York: Macmillan,

1974); J. B. Wolf, "Black September: Militant Palestinians," *Current History* (January 1973).

BLACK TERRORISM

1. Terrorism of the far right, or fascist terrorism. Like terrorism of the left, or "red" terrorism, black terrorism often seeks to undermine existing political systems. Black terrorism has often found an ally in police, military, or security forces of repressive regimes. Latin American DEATH SQUADS are examples of this phenomenon. Liberals, leftists, and religious minorities (especially Jews) are frequent targets of black terrorism.

See also NAZI, AAA, AVANGUARDIA NAZIONALE.

2. Terrorism committed by U.S. black (Afro-American) militants. Black terrorism was a more common phenomenon in the United States from the mid-1960s until the mid-1970s.

See also BLACK PANTHERS, UNITED FREEDOM FRONT.

BLOODY FRIDAY

On Friday, July 21, 1972, the PROVISIONAL WING OF THE IRISH REPUBLICAN ARMY carried out 22 separate bomb attacks in and around Belfast, Northern Ireland. In total, 11 people were killed and 130 wounded. Almost all the victims were civilians.

BLOODY SUNDAY

1. Sunday, January 30, 1972, when 13 Catholic demonstrators were shot and killed by a British Army unit in Londonderry, Northern Ireland. The incident led to violent IRA reprisals, including an arson attack on the British embassy in Dublin and the shooting of 13 British soldiers. Bloody Sunday and its aftermath contributed to the imposition of direct rule by the British government.

2. Sunday, January 9, 1905, when troops of the tsarist government of the Russian Empire opened fire on unarmed demonstrators in St. Petersburg. Hundreds of men, women and children were killed. More than any other single event, Bloody Sunday united the Russian people against the autocratic rule of the tsar.

BOKASSA, JEAN-BEDEL (1921–   )

Self-styled emperor of the Central African Republic, whose reign was characterized by excesses of all kinds, including terroristic repression of his people and cannibalism. Bokassa, a former captain in the French army, ruled autocratically for more than 13 years before being overthrown by a French-backed coup in 1979. While in exile, he was sentenced to death for his crimes against the nation.

Reference: Alex Shoumatoff, *African Madness* (New York: Knopf, 1988).

BOLIVIA

South American nation that experienced violent state repression and terrorism by right-wing death squads during the period of military rule from July 1980 to September 1982. Attacks were frequently directed against leftists and opponents of the regime, especially members of the Marxist party MIR. Many Bolivians disappeared during military rule, and after the restoration of civilian rule many unmarked common graves were discovered. Members of the military and officials in government intelligence and security agencies were implicated in the right-wing terror. In November 1982 the civilian government passed a law that disbanded and abolished state security agencies, "since these groups . . . have committed a series of acts and actions denigrating to the human condition by lending themselves to the service of instruments of repression and torture."

See also DISAPPEARED.

Reference: Amnesty International, *Amnesty International Report 1983: Bolivia* (London: Amnesty International, 1983).

BOLSHEVIKS

Russian, "majority party." The Marxist revolutionary party of Vladimir Ilyich LENIN and Leon TROTSKY. The Bolsheviks seized power in Russia in the November Revolution of 1917 and used terror as a means of consolidating power and fending off numerous counterrevolutionary threats. The Bolsheviks neutralized their political opposition through mass arrests and suppression of rival parties. Through the CHEKA secret police unit, a wave of "red terror" was unleashed that did not even begin to abate until after the death of Joseph Stalin in 1953.

See also GREAT TERROR.

References: Abbot Gleason *et al*, eds., *Bolshevik Culture: Experiment and Order in the Russian Revolution* (Bloomington: Indiana University Press, 1985); Edward Hallett Carr, *The Bolshevik Revolution: 1917–1923* (Hardmondworth, U.K.: Penguin, 1966).

BONN DECLARATION (1978)

The Joint Statement on International Terrorism of July 17, 1978, issued by the Summit Seven powers (Italy, France, West Germany, the United Kingdom, Canada, the United States and Japan) at a meeting in Bonn in 1978, which declared the intention of the heads of state of the major Western

powers to "intensify their joint efforts to combat international terrorism." The agreement specified that nations which do not cooperate in the "extradition and prosecution of those that have hijacked an aircraft" would be subject to an aviation boycott by the signatory parties to the Declaration.

BOUDIN, KATHY

Daughter of the civil rights attorney Leonard Boudin, she received a degree in Russian literature from Bryn Mawr College, after which she spent a year in the Soviet Union. Not long after returning from the Soviet Union she joined the terrorist WEATHER UNDERGROUND. She quickly became a principal figure in the left-wing radical group and spent more than a decade on the FBI's "most wanted list." She had disappeared in March 1970 after an explosion destroyed the Weathermen's Manhattan bomb factory. She reemerged in October 1981 when she participated in the robbery of a Brinks armored car outside Nyack, New York. During the crime one of the vehicle's guards and two police officers were killed. Boudin was arrested on October 21, 1981. In 1984 she was convicted and received a sentence of from 20 years to life. She told the court that she participated in the crime because of her commitment to the black liberation struggle and its underground movement.

BRIGATE ROSSE

See RED BRIGADES.

BRIGHTON BOMBING

The bombing of the Grand Hotel in Brighton, England on October 12, 1984 during the annual conference of the Conservative Party. Prime Minister Margaret Thatcher was unhurt, but five people died from wounds received from the blast and the subsequent collapse of the rooms surrounding the sixth-floor bathroom in which the device was detonated. Several other members of the government, including Cabinet Member Norman Tebbit and his wife, were badly injured. The PROVISIONAL WING OF THE IRISH REPUBLICAN ARMY, which was responsible for the bombing, later expressed its regret that Mrs. Thatcher had escaped injury. Patrick Joseph Magee, a resident of Belfast, was convicted of the bombing in 1986.

References: David North, "Tracking the Terrorists," *McLeans* 97 (October 29, 1984); Harry Anderson, "The Iron Lady's Brush with Death," *Newsweek* 104 (October 22, 1984).

BUREAU 210

The intelligence organization of the Iranian revolution, which fosters and sponsors Islamic revolutionary groups in many countries.

C

C-4

A member of the composition-C family of plastic explosives, which have as their active ingredient the compound cyclotrimethylene trinitramine. C-4 is very malleable, having the consistency of soft putty, and may be readily shaped into forms that will elude X-ray detection. It is difficult to detect even with advanced technologies such as chromotography and mass spectrometers. The explosive is used by the U.S. armed forces and is a popular choice of terrorist bombers. Libyan strongman Muammar QADDAFI obtained an estimated 20 tons of C-4 in his dealings with former CIA agent Edwin WILSON, and portions of the Libyan stockpile have been used in deadly terrorist attacks around the globe. Compare to SEMTEX.

See PAN AM 103.

CALN

See PUERTO RICAN TERRORISM.

CAMUS, ALBERT (1913–60)

French writer and philosopher, winner of the 1957 Nobel Prize for literature. Camus wrote several influential essays on the nature of rebellion and the role of terrorism in political revolutions. Camus spoke of the admirable and morally correct sacrifice of one's life in an act of violence directed against a repressive entity, but he condemned mass revolutionary terror.

References: Albert Camus, *Neither Victims Nor Executioners* (Chicago: World Without War Publications, 1972); Fred H. Willhoite, *Beyond Nihilism: Albert Camus's Contribution to Political Thought* (Baton Rouge: Louisiana State Press, 1968); Albert Camus, *The Rebel* (New York: Vintage, 1956).

CARIBBEAN REVOLUTIONARY ALLIANCE

A left-wing organization that claimed responsibility for the bombing on March 14, 1985 of a crowded restaurant on the Caribbean island of Guadeloupe. One person died and 11 were injured.

CARLOS

Alias of Ilyich Ramirez Sanchez, the Venezuelan-born international terrorist popularly known as "Carlos the Jackal." Carlos, among the best known of modern terrorists, has been associated with many terrorist organizations, most notably the POPULAR FRONT FOR THE LIBERATION OF PALESTINE (PFLP), which recruited him in the late 1960s. After education in Moscow and training with the PLO, he eventually became one of the leaders of an alleged terrorist international network which included the JAPANESE RED ARMY, the Basque ETA, the Italian RED BRIGADES, and the RED ARMY FACTION. He reportedly provided logistical support and direction for many of these groups' Western European operations in the 1970s, and he is thought to have had direct ties to KGB and Cuban agents. Carlos was responsible for a long and varied line of terrorist episodes around the globe in coordination with the PFLP, including the shooting of Teddy Sieff, a British corporate executive, in 1973; the Paris bombings of three pro-Israeli newspapers in 1974; and the attempted destruction of an El Al airliner at Orly airport in Paris in 1975. Two of Carlos' men were killed in the 1976 Israeli raid on ENTEBBE. In December 1975 Carlos led the PFLP group that seized the oil ministers of 11 nations during the OPEC SIEGE in Vienna, Austria. Although there have been several reports in recent years that Carlos is no longer alive, such reports must presently be regarded as speculation.

References: Max Holland and Kai Bird, "Colombia: The Carlos Connection," *Nation* 240 (June 22, 1985); Claire Sterling, *The Terror Network* (New York: Holt, Rinehart, and Winston, 1981); Christopher Dobson and Ronald Payne, *The Carlos Complex: A Study in Terror* (New York: G. P. Putnam's Sons, 1977); Colin Smith, *Carlos: Portrait of a Terrorist* (New York: Holt, Rinehart, and Winston, 1976).

CARRERO BLANCO, LUIS

Prime minister of Spain who was assassinated on December 20, 1973 by four members of the Basque separatist organization ETA. A bomb was planted in the street over which Carrero Blanco's car traveled; the explosion was so powerful that the automobile was said to have been thrown more than 50 feet in the air. The assassination dealt a forceful blow to right-wing Spanish Francoists; Carrero Blanco, as Francisco Franco's most trusted political aide and his appointed successor, had been envisioned by both adherents and critics of Franco's policies as the natural standard-bearer of the right after Franco's death.

Reference: J. Agirre, *Operation Ogro: The Execution of Admiral Luis Carrero Blanco*, translated by Barbara Probst Solomon (New York: Quadrangle/New York Times Book Co., 1975).

CARTER, JAMES EARL ("JIMMY")

President of the United States from 1977 to 1981. The IRANIAN HOSTAGE CRISIS was a major frustration for President Carter and cast a dark shadow over his tenure in the White House. The seeming paralysis of the U.S. government that ensued from the November 4, 1979 seizure of the U.S. Embassy in Tehran and its 52 occupants was a serious blow to the Carter administration and to the president's hopes for reelection. Carter's initial response to the crisis was to impose an economic boycott and sever diplomatic relations. On April 24, 1980 the president approved, over the objections of his secretary of state, an ill-fated military rescue attempt, in which eight servicemen died. Cyrus Vance, the Secretary of state, resigned in protest and the domestic situation grew worse. Carter was defeated in the presidential election in November 1980 by Ronald Reagan. On January 20, 1981, Reagan's inauguration day, Iran released the hostages.

The Carter Administration was instrumental in investigating the state terror of

Argentina's DIRTY WAR, and pressured the Argentine government to curb its abuses of human rights. Its policy of making human rights a cornerstone of U.S. foreign policy was considered exemplary by some and naive by others.

References: Gaddis Smith, *Morality, Reason, and Power: American Diplomacy in the Carter Years* (New York: Hill and Wang, 1986); Hamilton Jordan, *Crisis: The Last Year of the Carter Presidency* (New York: Putnam, 1982); Jimmy Carter, *Keeping Faith: Memoirs of a President* (New York: Bantam, 1982).

CASTRO, FIDEL

The revolutionary leader of CUBA, Castro rose to power in 1959 after he, his brother, and Che GUEVARA led a successful guerrilla campaign that toppled the corrupt dictatorship of Juan Batista. Castro has been a primary sponsor of revolutionary movements in Latin America, such as ERP in Argentina. None of these groups has been able to duplicate the success of Castro's revolution. The CIA, unsettled by Castro's alliance with the Soviets and his attempts to export his revolution, made several attempts on his life during the 1960s (including poisoning his famous cigars), as documented in the reports of the CHURCH COMMITTEE. Even in the days of *perestroika* and *glasnost*, Castro, now the longest reigning Communist dictator, remains an unrepentant Marxist.

References: Wayne S. Smith, *The Closest of Enemies* (New York: W. W. Norton, 1987); R. A. Hudson, "Castro's America Department: Systemizing Insurgencies in Latin America," *Terrorism* 9 (1987); Peter G. Bourne, *Fidel: A Biography of Fidel Castro* (New York: Dodd, Mead, 1986); Tad Szulc, *Fidel: A Critical Portrait* (New York: Morrow, 1986).

CELL

An insular subdivision of a compartmentalized terrorist or guerrilla organization, comprised of perhaps three to five people, designed to function more or less independently so as to reduce the risk of damage to the overarching organization in the event of INFILTRATION, discovery or arrest. In a cellular structure, communication and interaction between cells is discouraged, in the interest of protecting the integrity of the cell system; similarly, the identity of contacts within the organization is ideally revealed to only one member of each cell.

Reference: H. Edward Price, Jr. "The Strategy and Tactics of Revolutionary Terrorism," *Comparative Studies in Society and History* 19 (January 1977).

CENTRAL AMERICAN REVOLUTIONARY WORKER'S PARTY (PRTC)

Marxist/Leninist group formed in 1976 as a regional insurgency organization, of which the El Salvador group is the largest and the most important. PRTC joined the El Salvador guerrilla umbrella group FMLN (Frente Farabundo Marti de Liberacion Nacional) in 1980 and, although it is the smallest of the FMLN organizations, it has been responsible for some of the most violent acts committed by the coalition. An urban component of the PRTC, called the Mardoqueo Cruz Urban Commando Detachment, was created in 1984. This subgroup carried out several terrorist attacks against U.S. Marines and businessmen in San Salvador in June 1985. Since that time, government countermeasures have badly damaged the PRTC, which is estimated to be several hundred members strong. The group also has branches in Costa Rica, Honduras, Guatemala, and Nicaragua. Its members have received training in Cuba and Nicaragua.

CENTRAL INTELLIGENCE AGENCY (CIA)

The U.S. federal agency established in 1947 to coordinate the various intelligence activities of the United States. Accordingly, the CIA correlates and evaluates intelligence relating to national security and collects, produces, and disseminates foreign intelligence and counterintelligence. The CIA also has intelligence responsibilities for foreign aspects of drug trafficking, and it carries on special activities as approved by the president. The CIA has often been at the forefront of anti-terrorist intelligence operations; however, some of its covert operations have at times supported activities that have been deemed illegal. These issues were addressed by the U.S. Senate's CHURCH COMMITTEE report, issued in 1976. CIA activity of which the Senate committee was critical include organizing or supporting attempts to overthrow established foreign governments in Guatemala (1954), Iran (1953) and Indonesia (1958). The CIA was implicated in the overthrow of the Allende government in Chile in 1973, including financing of rightwing Chilean terrorist organizations and support of a violent military coup. The committee report also cited several CIA plots to assassinate foreign leaders and the CIA's involvement with instruments of state terrorism such as the Iranian secret police organization SAVAK.

References: Rhodri Jeffreys-Jones, *The CIA and American Democracy* (New Haven: Yale University Press, 1989); Bob Woodward, *Veil: The Secret Wars of the CIA 1981–87* (New York: Simon & Schuster, 1987); John Ranelagh, *The Agency: The Rise and Decline of the CIA* (New York: Simon & Schuster, 1986).

CHARTOUNY, HABIB TANIOS

The assassin of Bashir Gemayel, president-elect of Lebanon. Chartouny, a member of the SYRIAN SOCIAL NATIONALIST PARTY, planted the bomb in Gemayel's quarters and detonated the device on September 14, 1982. This assassination further rocked an already unstable nation and helped to spark the atrocities committed against Palestinian refugees in camps at SABRA AND SHATILA. The motive for the assassination is still debated.

Reference: Jonathan Randal, *Going All the Way: Christian Warlords, Israeli Adventures, and the War in Lebanon* (New York: Viking Press, 1983).

CHEKA

The acronym and popular term for the Bolshevik security police responsible for systematic purges and acts of terror during the early years of the Soviet Union. Many hundreds of Russians were killed in the CHEKA's attempts to ferret out members of the Social Revolutionary Party following that group's attempted assassination of V.I. LENIN in 1918. CHEKA was later succeeded by the KGB.

Reference: George Legget, *The CHEKA: Lenin's Political Police* (New York: Oxford University Press, 1987).

CHILDREN, THE

The name commonly applied to organized, militant young blacks in the black townships of South Africa. The Children have, through violent means, effectively ended indirect white rule in these sprawling urban ghettos. They enforce boycotts and strikes with vengeance and have killed many fellow blacks whom they deem to be accomplices of the Pretoria regime.

CHILE

The government of Augusto Pinochet, after its accession to power following the September 1973 coup, was responsible for widespread torture of political detainees, for the expulsion without trial of political opponents and for the disappearances of suspected enemies of the regime. Amnesty International estimates that 650 people were taken to secret detention and torture centers or were killed. The government was implicated in the operations of paramilitary right-wing death squads, especially through its brutal intelligence service DINA, which was dissolved in 1978, only to be reborn again as CNI, the Central Nacional de Informaciones. DINA operatives were involved in the 1976 assassination of former Allende government official Orlando LETELIER in Washington, D.C. The Letelier incident sparked an extradition controversy between the United States and Chile, as the Chilean regime refused to cooperate with the Reagan administration's request for the extradition of the Chilean officials accused of complicity in the assassination.

References: Amnesty International, *Chile Briefing* (London: Amnesty International, 1988); Amnesty International, *Chile: Evidence of Torture* (London: Amnesty International, 1987).

CHRISTIAN PATRIOTS DEFENDER LEAGUE (CPDL)

A U.S. right-wing terrorist organization with a radical Christian and white-supremacist ideology. CPDL member Richard Wayne Snell was sentenced to life imprisonment for the June 1984 murder of an Arkansas state trooper and for the November 1983 killing of a pawnshop proprietor during a theft of loot and weapons.

CHRISTIAN PHALANGE

The Christian militia of Lebanon known in Arabic as al-Kata'ib, formed in the 1930s in reaction to perceptions of growing Muslim influence and power in Lebanon. The Phalange represents the traditional land-owning and commercial sector of the country, through which Christians have held a disproportionate share of political power. The Phalange has been an integral participant in the Lebanese civil wars and internal conflicts and has battled the PALESTINE LIBERATION ORGANIZATION and Muslim militias AMAL and HEZBOLLAH. The Phalange have received the support of Israel and the United States. The Phalangists were responsible for the massacres at SABRA AND SHATILA refugee camps in 1982.

References: Michael W. Suleiman, *Political Parties in Lebanon: The Challenge of a Fragmented Political Culture* (Ithaca, N.Y.: Cornell University Press, 1967); John P. Entellis, *Pluralism and Party Transformation in Lebanon: Al-Kata'ib, 1936–1970* (Leiden: E. J. Brill, 1974).

CHUKAKU-HA

Japanese, "Nucleus" or "Middle-Core Faction." An ultra-leftist Japanese group that is the largest militant organization in Japan, with an estimated 3,000 members. It is dedicated to the abolition of the monarchy and the constitutional democracy and the severing of U.S.–Japanese ties. The Chukaku-Ha is a splinter group of the Kakumaru-Ha, which was the foremost organizer of the Japanese New Left until 1983. At issue between the two factions was whether to develop the philosophy of the New Left, or to instigate a mass struggle. Chukaku-Ha opted to develop the mass struggle. The Japanese New Left is a radical left-wing political movement composed of 23 separate factions and numbering perhaps 35,000, including sympathizers.

While Chukaku-Ha is primarily a radical political group, it also has a small, dangerous, covert action wing, the "Kansai Revolutionary Army." Most of Chukahu-Ha's activities involve public demonstrations, but the group also has made occasional forays into terrorist violence, including attacks against the Japanese transportation system as well as U.S. military and diplomatic targets. Its attacks are geared to cause property damage rather than human injury. The operational and tactical skills of the group are imaginative and include the use of timed incendiary devices, flamethrowers, and mortar-like launchers often referred to as "rockets." In November 1985 members of the group staged a massive assault on the Japanese National Railway in an anti-privatization protest, in which facilities were firebombed and communication lines severed, paralyzing Japan's rail transit system. In September 1988 the group exploded time bombs in the automobiles of three judges who were hearing the cases of Chukaku-Ha members accused of the 1985 railway attack. In recent years the organization has violently opposed the construction of the New Tokyo International Airport at Narita, and in 1987 and 1988 they staged a number of bombings and rocket attacks directed against construction sites and firms involved in the airport construction.

Chukaku-Ha members are a very secretive group, and contacts with outsiders are severely restricted. Funds for the group are generated from contributions solicited from the general membership to support the estimated 200 dedicated activists who have no other source of income.

CHURCH COMMITTEE

Official name: U.S. Senate Select Committee to Study Governmental Operations with Regard to Intelligence. The committee, chaired by Senator Frank Church of Idaho, was established in 1974 to investigate allegations that the CIA had played a major role in destabilizing the leftist government of Salvador Allende in Chile and had helped to foster the overthrow of the legally elected government, which had then been replaced by a military regime. The committee found the allegations to be valid and delved into a far-reaching investigation of the U.S. intelligence community, where it uncovered numerous instances of illegal and ethically questionable activity. Other illegal covert actions included assassination plots against foreign political figures and involvement with state terrorist organizations. The FBI's COIN-TELPRO (Counterintelligence Program) was found to have operated outside its mandate as it mounted illegal intelligence-gathering programs and disinformation campaigns against domestic dissidents and civil rights groups.

CINCHONEROS POPULAR LIBERATION MOVEMENT

In Spanish, "Cinchonero Movimiento Popular de Liberacion" (MPL), the armed wing of the Honduran People's Revolutionary Union (URP), which is one of many splinter groups of the Honduran Communist Party. The Cinchoneros, formed in 1980, are named for the Honduran peasant leader Serapio "Cinchonero" Romero, who was executed in 1865 for refusing to pay tax to the Roman Catholic Church. The group was one of the two most active Honduran terrorist organizations in the early 1980s, the other being the LORENZO ZELAYA POPULAR REVOLUTIONARY FORCES. Cinchonero terrorist activities have consisted mostly of bombings in San Pedro Sula and Tegucigalpa. The group has funded its operations primarily through kidnappings of businessmen and bank robberies. The group may also have received support from Cuba and Nicaragua. A series of arrests of key Cinchonero operatives in early 1984 curtailed the group's operations. In the latter part of the decade the organization seemed to be regrouping for future operations, and it has recently exploded bombs in the capital to revive public awareness of the group's existence.

CITY OF POROS

A Greek passenger liner hijacked on July 11, 1988 by members of the ABU NIDAL Organization while on a day cruise. The terrorists killed nine people on board and injured more than 100 others. A second terror attack, apparently intended to take place after the wounded vessel docked, went awry when a car bomb near the dock detonated prematurely, killing the vehicle's two occupants.

CLARA ELIZABETH RAMIREZ FRONT (CERF)

In Spanish, "Frente Clara Elizabeth Ramirez." A Salvadoran urban terrorist group. The CERF shares the revolutionary ideology of other leftist groups in El Salvador but operates independently. It is a splinter group of the Popular Liberation Forces (FPL) and takes its name from the FPL's designation for its metropolitan San Salvador front. The CERF's high-visibility and inflammatory attacks have drawn denunciations and rejec-

tion from the FPL and other members of the Farabundo Marti National Liberation Front (FMLN). The group, thought to have only 10 to 20 members, specializes in assassinations. It was most active in 1983–85 and was probably responsible for the assassination in May 1983 of the deputy commander of the U.S. Military Advisory Group in San Salvador. In March 1985, CERF assassins shot and killed the top spokesperson for the Salvadoran Armed Forces. The group has also staged attacks on the U.S. and Honduran embassies. The CERF has been relatively quiet since massive Salvadoran counterterrorist operations in 1985, which resulted in the arrest or defection of many of its leaders.

CLAUDIA

Ship carrying several tons of arms and ammunition from Libya to Ireland that was seized by Irish authorities on March 29, 1973. The *Claudia*'s cargo was destined for the PROVISIONAL WING OF THE IRISH REPUBLICAN ARMY (PIRA) and included huge quantities of explosives, revolvers, Kalashnikov rifles and ammunition. Four members of PIRA were convicted of arms smuggling for their roles in the foiled operation.

CLEAVER, ELDRIDGE

A leader of the BLACK PANTHER movement in the United States and one of the leading black militants of the 1960s. Cleaver was arrested in 1968 and while released on bail fled to Cuba and then Algeria, where he set up a Black Panthers party office. He represented the most violently militant faction of the Panthers. In the early 1970s Cleaver unsuccessfully attempted to integrate his black-power faction with Middle Eastern and African radical groups. In 1975 Cleaver reported to the U.S., abandoned his militancy, became a "born again" Christian and a political conservative; and had (in 1979) criminal charges against him dropped. Nevertheless his 1968 best-seller, *Soul on Ice* remains a classic statement of black alienation in American society.

References: Eldridge Cleaver, *Soul On Fire* (Waco, Tex.: Ward Books, 1978); Lee Lockwood, *Conversation With Eldridge Cleaver* (New York: McGraw-Hill, 1970).

CODEP

Spanish acronym for the Argentine "National Commission on Disappeared Persons." CODEP was established by the democratic, civilian government of Raul Alfonsin to investigate the state terrorism of the military regime that had ruled Argentina from March 1976 until December 1983. The report of CODEP, issued on September 21, 1984, was unable to account for 8,960 people who disappeared in the Argentine DIRTY WAR. The CODEP report extends over 50,000 pages and documents a system of terror that included 340 clandestine jails and a regimen of torture, rape and murder. An English summary of the report may be found in John Simpson and Jana Bennet's *The Disappeared* (London: Robson Books, 1985). *Nunca Mas: The Report of the Argentine National Commission on the Disappeared* (New York: Farrar Straus Giroux, 1986) provides a more detailed summary and an English translation of the report.

See ARGENTINA, AAA, DISAPPEARED.

COINTELPRO

The FBI's Counterintelligence Program, which collected intelligence and attempted to disrupt the activities of "subversive" individuals and organizations in the United States. An investigation of the program by the CHURCH COMMITTEE in 1974 found numerous ethically questionable and illegal activities during the 1960s and early 1970s. Outspoken critics of the U.S. government such as Dr. Martin Luther King Jr. had been subjected to illegal surveillance and disinformation campaigns, as had been hundreds of other liberal and left-wing individuals and groups. The Church Committee noted the failure of COINTELPRO to distinguish between terrorist groups and civil rights organizations espousing nonviolence.

Reference: Nelson Blackstock, *COINTELPRO: The FBI's Secret War on Political Freedom* (New York: Vintage, 1976).

COMMANDO OPERATIONS

A British term for raids conducted by specially trained forces against objectives in enemy territory. Both terrorist groups and the counterinsurgency forces that oppose them employ commando operations.

Reference: Bruce Hoffman, "Commando Warfare and Small Raiding Parties as Part of a Counterterrorist Military Policy," *Conflict* 7, 1 (1987).

COMMUNIST COMBATANT CELLS (CCC)

"Cellules Communistes Combattantes." A left-wing terrorist organization founded in Belgium in 1984 and headquartered in Brussels. The CCC literally exploded onto the European terrorism stage with a series of bombings that began in October 1984. Its activities ceased in December 1985 with the apprehension by police of its leader and three other militants. While the police campaign appears to have eliminated the CCC threat, it is possible that the CCC has only halted operations temporarily.

The origins of this Marxist-Leninist group appear to lie in the Belgian political dissent of the 1980s over defense, economic, ethnic, and environmental policies. Impatience with the government's inability to resolve these problems and the belief that terrorism would mobilize leftist opponents of the government and precipitate its downfall helped lead radical leftists to form the CCC.

Prior to the CCC's emergence, Belgium had not experienced any indigenous terrorist threat. Throughout the 1970s, however, Belgium was a refuge for European terrorists fleeing their own countries. The alleged founder and now imprisoned leader of the CCC, Pierre Carrette, a long-time militant in ultra-left political circles, had contacts with terrorists from the French group AC-TION DIRECTE (AD) and the West German RED ARMY FACTION (RAF) prior to the emergence of the CCC in October 1984.

The CCC is believed to have joined with the RAF and AD in the formation of the ANTI-IMPERIALIST ARMED FRONT to conduct attacks in protest of the "Americanization of Europe" and to frustrate increased military cooperation among members of NATO. Although the current existence of such an umbrella organization is in doubt, the CCC shares common ideological goals with both the RAF and the AD.

The CCC relied upon bombings as its sole mode of attack during its period of activity. The only fatalites for which it was responsible were the deaths of two firemen during a bombing attack in May 1985.

COMMUNIST COMBATANT PARTY

An Italian terrorist organization with ties to the RED BRIGADES. On April 16, 1988, members of the group assassinated Christian Democratic Party senator Roberto Ruffilli. In September 1988 Italian police arrested 21 members of the group, including the suspected assassins of Ruffilli.

CONCENTRATION CAMPS

A prison system used by a nation to detain or exterminate political dissidents, members of ethnic or religious minority groups, or other individuals deemed dangerous or undesirable by the regime. Concentration camps were an integral part of the NAZI repression and extermination of Jews, Gypsies, Poles, Communists, homosexuals, and others during World War II. It is estimated that more than six million Jews alone were killed in the Nazi concentration camps, most in poison gas chambers. Many others died as a result of the inhumane conditions in the camps and from maltreatment. Concentration camps have been used as forced-labor camps: the Soviet system of GULAGS has been categorized in this way.

See HOLOCAUST.

References: Anton Gill, *The Journey Back From Hell* (New York: Morrow, 1988); Robert H. Abzug, *Inside the Vicious Heart* (New York: Oxford University Press, 1985); Terrence Des Pres, *The Survivor: An Anatomy of Life in the Death Camps* (New York: Oxford University Press, 1976).

CONSTRUCTIVE ENGAGEMENT

A diplomatic phrase for maintaining political and economic ties with regimes with whom a nation has many disagreements in the hope that the continuation of ties will gradually lead to changes in objectionable policies and practices. It has often been used to describe the policies of the United States toward South Africa. In September 1985, in response to bipartisan congressional pressure, President Ronald Reagan modified the constructive engagement policy and by executive order imposed limited economic sanctions on South Africa. The order prohibited American banks from making loans to most agencies of the South African government and urged American corporations engaged in business in South Africa to comply with the SULLIVAN PRINCIPLES.

References: Michael Clough, "Beyond Constructive Engagement," *Foreign Policy* 61 (Winter 1985); Sanford J. Ungar and Peter Vale, "South Africa: Why Constructive Engagement Failed," *Foreign Affairs* 64 (Winter 1985–86); Robert A. Manning, "Constructive Engagement Round Two," *Africa Report* 30 (January–February 1985).

CONTRAS

The popular term for the counterrevolutionary army, established and financed by the U.S. government, which sought to overthrow the Marxist-Leninist Sandinista regime in NICARAGUA. The contras were armed and led by many former members of the Nicaraguan National Guard, which had been maintained by Pres. Anastasio Somoza Debayle, the right-wing dictator who was deposed by the Sandinistas in 1979. Once in power, the Sandinistas established a one-party system that did not allow other opposition forces to challenge them within the political process, hence popular support for the Sandinistas declined. The Guardsmen who had fled the country after the revolution organized an armed resistance movement—the contras—which operated out of jungle bases just over the border in Honduras.

The contras' cause was greatly aided by the election of Ronald Reagan as president of the United States in 1980. Reagan called the contras "freedom fighters" and said that they "[were] the moral equal of our Founding Fathers and the brave men and women of the French Resistance." Reagan approved a covert aid program by the CIA in December 1981. During the first Reagan administration the CIA poured millions of dollars of financial aid, medical supplies and arms into the contra coffers. However, the contras failed to score any significant military successes, and as the seamier details of the CIA's involvement leaked out, Congressional support for the contras weakened. In 1985 and 1986 contra funding was limited to non-lethal humanitarian aid. Although the administration was successful in the latter part of 1986 in securing another $100 million aid package, the exposure of the IRAN-CONTRA AFFAIR in 1986 all but destroyed Congressional support for Reagan's "freedom fighters."

In the summer of 1989 Central American leaders reached an agreement that called for the disarming of the guerrillas, for free and open Nicaraguan elections, and for a general amnesty for contras who wished to return home. The administration of U.S. president George Bush endeavored to keep enough non-lethal American aid flowing to the contras to sustain them and in their Honduran base camps as an insurance policy until after the Nicaraguan elections promised for 1990. The Sandinistas lost the elections, and Violeta Chamorro became the new president of Nicaragua. Currently, the contras are being disbanded and resettled with the help of the Organization of American States and the United States.

References: Gary Prevost, "The 'Contra' War in Nicaragua," *Conflict Quarterly* 7 (Summer 1987); Bob Woodward, *Veil: The Secret Wars of the CIA 1981–87* (New York: Simon & Schuster, 1987); Brent Hardt, "The Reagan Administration's Battle for Contra Aid," *Fletcher Forum* 10 (Summer 1986); Reed Brody, *Contra Terror in Nicaragua* (Boston: South End Press, 1985); Christopher Dickey,

With the Contras: A Reporter in the Wilds of Nicaragua (New York: Simon & Schuster, 1985).

COUNTERINSURGENCY

Those military, paramilitary, political, economic, psychological and civic actions taken by a government to defeat revolutionaries in a guerrilla war. The basic tactics are (a) to gain intelligence that allows for the identification and destruction of insurgent sanctuaries; and (b) to convince the civilian population to trust the government enough to report guerrilla whereabouts. The classic work on the subject is Robert Thompson, *Defeating Communist Insurgency* (London: Chatto & Windus, 1966).

Reference: D. Michael Shafer, *Deadly Paradigms: The Failure of U.S. Counterinsurgency Policy* (Princeton: Princeton University Press, 1988).

COUNTERTERRORISM

Efforts to prevent and, if necessary, to punish terrorist acts in the expectation that retaliation will discourage further terrorism. Counterterrorist policy relies heavily upon intelligence gathering and analysis and is most successful when terrorist actions are prevented. It includes a wide variety of economic, political, social, psychological and military approaches. COUNTERINSURGENCY and LOW-INTENSITY WARFARE are among the military means employed as counterterrorist weapons against guerrilla forces. Paramilitary options have often been utilized, especially by Latin American nations. History has shown, however, that counterterrorism can be very difficult in a democratic society that attempts to uphold traditional civil freedoms while attacking a terrorist threat.

References: Neil C. Livingstone and Terrell E. Arnold, eds., *Beyond the Iran-Contra Crisis: The Shape of U.S. Anti-Terrorism Policy in the Post-Reagan Era* (Lexington, Mass.: Lexington Books, 1988); Michael T. Klare and Peter Kornbluh, eds., *Low-Intensity Warfare: Counterinsurgency, Proinsurgency, and Antiterrorism in the Eighties* (New York: Pantheon, 1988); David C. Martin and John L. Walcott, *Best Laids Plans: The Inside Story of America's War Against Terrorism* (New York: Harper & Row, 1988); Christopher C. Joyner, "In Search of Anti-Terrorism Policy: Lessons from the Reagan Era," *Terrorism* 11, no. 1 (1988).

COUP D'ÉTAT

French, "a stroke or sharp blow to the state." A sudden and often violent change in the leadership of a government by force brought about by those who already held some form of power (either military or political). A coup d'état differs from a revolution in that revolution is usually brought about by those who are not presently in power, and revolution implies a major change in the social structure or political order. Coups d'état typically take place during periods of social instability and political uncertainty, and a coup usually is the work of right-wing elements determined to impose a social discipline and political order that is felt to be missing. A coup need not be a major military undertaking. Typically, small units take over government buildings, communications and media facilities, and transportation hubs and capture or kill any government officials who would be a threat to the coup's organizers. Quite frequently the leaders of the coup d'état return power to the politicians after a fairly short period, once they believe that their aims of stabilizing and bringing order to the political system have been achieved. The tendency of the military to be involved in coups d'état stems from their virtual monopoly of coercive means and the way in which they are usually, at least in the context of any particular social system, seen as apolitical or even "above politics."

References: John Markoff and Silvio R. Duncan Baretta, "What We Don't Know about the Coups: Observations on Recent South American Politics," *Armed Forces and Society* 12 (Winter 1986); Edward Luttwak, *Coup d'État: A Practical Handbook* (Cambridge, Mass.: Harvard University Press, 1979); Pat McGowan and Thomas H. Johnson, "Forecasting African Coups D'État," *Politikon* 12 (December 1985); Thomas H. Johnson, Robert O. Slater, and Pat McGowan, "Explaining African Military Coups d'État, 1960–1982," *American Political Science Review* 78 (September 1984); Rosemary H. T. O'Kane, "Towards an Examination of the General Causes of Coups d'État," *European Journal of Political Research* 11 (March 1983).

THE COVENANT, THE SWORD, AND THE ARM OF THE LORD (CSA)

A U.S. right-wing, white supremacist, anti-Semitic organization. The group is connected to the larger ARYAN NATIONS Organization and is a sect dedicated to the construction of an ark in preparation for the coming Armegeddon. The CSA is a survivalist group, with sizeable stockpiles of food, supplies and weapons. After a 1985 shooting implicating CSA members, police in Arkansas uncovered a cache of automatic weapons, grenades, anti-tank artillery and other explosives at a CSA paramilitary training camp.

COVERT OPERATIONS

Military, police or intelligence activities that are planned and executed so as to conceal the identify of, or permit plausible denial by, the sponsor. They differ from clandestine operations in that emphasis is placed on concealment of the identity of the sponsor rather than on concealment of the operation.

References: Gregory F. Treverton, *Covert Action: The Limits of Intervention in the Postwar World* (New York: Basic Books, 1987); Jules Lobel, "Covert War and Congressional Authority: Hidden War and Forgotten Power," *University of Pennsylvania Law Review* 134 (June 1986); Stephen D. Wrage, "A Moral Framework for Covert Action," *Fletcher Forum* 4 (Summer 1980).

CROATIAN NATIONAL RESISTANCE

An organization dedicated to liberating Croatia from Yugoslav rule. In September 1976 five American members of the group hijacked a TWA jetliner. Their demand that Croatian nationalist propaganda be dropped from the plane over the cities of Paris, London, Montreal, New York and Chicago was met. The five were arrested in Paris and then extradited to the United States, where they were convicted of hijacking.

CUBA

Fidel CASTRO's Cuban revolution and the Communist regime he subsequently founded has been a role model and a source of support and training for Third-World revolutionary movements around the globe. At Havana in 1966 the First Conference for Afro-Asian-Latin American People's Solidarity, later known as the Trilateral Conference, outlined a grand revolutionary strategy to combat "American imperialism" through armed revolutionary groups. Since that time, the Cuban government has been a conspicuous supporter of left-wing guerrilla movements, particularly in Latin America and Africa. This support has included the supply of arms; weapons and tactical training; ideological indoctrination; and the use of military advisors and troops. Cuban revolutionary leader Che GUEVARA helped to inspire and direct the guerrilla war of ELN in rural Bolivia. In Chile the Cuban government sponsored the MIR, in Argentina the MONTENEROS and the ERP were supported by Havana. The TUPAMAROS of Uruguay were perhaps the greatest beneficiaries of the largesse of Cuban guerrilla warfare.

During the late 1960s and early 1970s, Havana became internationally infamous as a haven for terrorist hijackers, most notably Palestinian extremists. More recently, Cuba has been a sponsor of the Salvadoran FMLN and the Colombian M-19. Cuba has seemed willing to provide some degree of support to almost any organization espousing an anti-U.S. and anti-Israeli ideology and is considered by the U.S. Department of State to be one of the foremost state sponsors of terrorism.

References: Roger W. Fontaine, *Terrorism: The Cuban Connection* (New York: Crane Russack and Company, 1988); Pamela S. Falk, "Cuba in Africa," *Foreign Affairs* 65 (Summer 1987); Claire Sterling, *The Terror Network* (New York: Holt, Rinehart and Winston, 1981).

CUBAN NATIONAL LIBERATION FRONT

An anti-CASTRO, U.S.-based organization comprised primarily of Cuban exiles living in southern Florida. In the late 1960s and early 1970s the group staged a series of bombings and assaults against targets associated with or perceived to be sympathetic to the Castro government.

CURCIO, RENATO

Left-wing terrorist and one of the founders of the Italian RED BRIGADES. He became a leftist activist during his studies at the University of Trento during the 1960s. He, his wife, and several other extremists founded the Red Brigades in the early 1970s. Curcio is now serving a life sentence in an Italian prison.

Reference: Richard Drake, "The Red and the Black: Terrorism in Contemporary Italy," *International Political Science Review* 5 (July 1984).

CURIEL, HENRI (1915–78)

An Egyptian-born Communist who for many years ran a Parisian network of assistance for revolutionary organizations, under the name Aide et Amitie ("Help and Friendship"). It has been reported that he was a KGB agent in France, and French government operatives are thought to have been responsible for his shooting death on April 5, 1978.

References: Gilles Perrault, *A Man Apart: The Life of Henri Curiel* (London: Zed Books, 1987); Claire Sterling, "The Strange Case of Henri Curiel," *Washington Post Magazine* (March 15, 1981).

CZOLGOSZ, LEON (1872–1901)

The anarchist assassin of U.S. president William McKinley, whom he shot and mortally wounded at the Pan-American Exhibition in Buffalo, New York on September 6, 1901. Mckinley died on September 14. The Detroit-born Czolgosz was executed on November 29, 1901.

Reference: A. Wesley Johns, *The Man Who Shot McKinley* (South Brunswick, N.J.: A. S. Barnes, 1970).

D

DAL KHALSA

One of the oldest of the SIKH separatist groups, founded on April 13, 1978 and established with the avowed purpose of demanding an independent and sovereign Sikh state. The Sikh independence movement became involved in terrorism after turning violent under the influence of Sant Jarnail Singh BHINDRANWALE in 1981. The Dal Khalsa was officially banned by the Indian government after allegedly participating in Sikh–Hindu rioting in April 1982. The group's leader, Gurbachan Singh Manochahal, is one of the most wanted of Sikh extremists in the Punjab, and the Indian government has offered a reward for his capture, dead or alive. The membership of the Dal Khalsa is estimated at 200.

Reference: Pranay Gupte, *Vengeance: India and the Assassination of Indira Gandhi* (New York: W. W. Norton, 1985).

DASHMESH REGIMENT

A particularly violent SIKH terrorist organization dedicated to the establishment of an autonomous state in the Khalistan region of India. The Dashmesh ("Tenth") Regiment was probably organized under the aegis of Sant Jarnail Singh BHINDRANWALE in about 1982. The group was named after the Sikh's revered 10th and last guru, Gobind Singh, who in the 18th century greatly influenced the Sikh religion and forged the Sikhs into a warrior class.

The Dashmesh Regiment's founder is reputed to have been Major General Shaheg Singh, a Sikh officer with experience training irregulars in Bangladesh, who subsequently was cashiered from the Indian Army for corruption. (Shortly before his death in the attack on the GOLDEN TEMPLE OF AMRITSAR, however, the general vehemently disclaimed any connection with the Dashmesh Regiment or any knowledge about such an organization.) Following the assault on the Golden Temple, Dashmesh gained increased covert and popular support and has continued to claim responsibility for terrorist attacks throughout India.

The organization has assassinated many prominent Indian political, religious, and media figures and made attempts on the life of former prime minister Rajiv Gandhi. It has claimed credit for a June 1985 bomb, intended for an Air India jet, which exploded prematurely at Japan's Narita International Airport; two baggage handlers were killed in the blast. The group also claimed responsibility for the June 1985 destruction of an Air India jet off the coast of Ireland.

The membership of the Dashmesh Regiment is estimated to be about 200.

D'AUBISSON, ROBERTO

See ARENA.

DAWA, AL-

Arabic, al-Dawa al Islamiya; "The Call." Founded in Najaf, Iraq in the late 1950s by Muhammed Baqir al-Sadr as a SHI'ITE opposition political organization, al-Dawa is the oldest of the radical Shi'ite groups. At its inception it drew support from revolutionary factions and was repressed by Iraqi dictator Saddam Hussein. As a result, many followers of al-Sadr fled Iraq, and today the group has factions throughout the Middle East and Northern Africa. Baqir al-Sadr and his sister were arrested and executed in 1980 by the ruling Iraqi Ba'thist party, which felt threatened by the ever-increasing activism of Shi'ite extremists, especially in the wake of the Iranian revolution.

The group appears to have been plagued by internal dissension since the death of its leader, although members of the group have launched many terrorist attacks within Iraq during the 1980s. Members of al-Dawa played major roles in the series of bomb attacks in Kuwait on December 12, 1983. By the end of 1984 the radical al-Dawa organization in Lebanon was effectively subsumed in the momentum of the HEZBOLLAH movement. However, with the conclusion of the 1991 Gulf War, al-Dawa and other Shi'ite movements within Iraq began to assert themselves again. Their goal is the overthrow of the Ba'thist regime in Baghdad. At this writing, these revolts have been largely suppressed.

Reference: Christine M. Helms, *Iraq: Eastern Flank of the Arab World* (Washington, D.C.: Brookings Institution, 1984).

DAWSON'S FIELD

A landing strip north of Amman, Jordan that had been built by the British in World War II became the focal point of a nearly month-long series of terrorist incidents involving five commercial airliners and hundreds of hostages. Terrorists of the POPULAR FRONT FOR THE LIBERATION OF PALESTINE (PFLP) were responsible for coordinating the attacks, which began on September 6, 1970 with the simultaneous midair hijackings of a Swissair DC-8 and a TWA Boeing 707. Both planes were diverted to Dawson's Field. The PFLP also attempted to seize a third plane, an El Al aircraft, but plainclothes Israeli security guards thwarted the attempt, killing one hijacker, Patrick Arguello, a Nicaraguan in PFLP employ, and capturing the other, Leila Khaled. A Pan Am plane, the fourth grabbed that day, was seized in flight and diverted to Cairo, where the terrorists then destroyed it. On September 9th the fifth and final airliner was hijacked, this time a BOAC VC-10, and flown to Dawson's Field. Negotiations with the PFLP terrorists at Dawson's Field dragged on for weeks, until, on September 29th, authorities in Britain, Switzerland and West Germany agreed to release eight Palestinian prisoners, including the recently captured Khaled. The following day, after evacuating their hostages, the PFLP blew up the three planes at Dawson's Field as a startled international press corps looked on. That same day the Jordanian Army moved in and freed the nearly 400 hostages.

The Dawson's Field incident had far-ranging consequences. King Hussein of

Jordan viewed it as the final straw in his long-simmering dissatisfaction with the Palestinian guerrillas based in Jordan, and he ordered his armed forces to expel the guerrillas, most of whom fled to Lebanon.

See BLACK SEPTEMBER.

DEA

Greek, "Dimoria Eidikon Apostolon." An Athens police special mission SWAT team which acts as the primary Greek Hostage Rescue Unit. It was established in the mid 1970s and has about 50 members.

DEATH SQUADS

Terrorist gangs that have engaged in widespread torture and murder in Latin America of people targeted as leftists and sympathizers. The term probably first was used in Brazil in the 1960s, where "Escuadros da Morte," consisting of off-duty police, took vigilante action against criminals. After the Brazilian coup of 1964, however, the squads were used to silence dissidents. In Argentina, vigilante paramilitary groups such as the Liberators of America Commandos and the AAA preyed upon leftist and liberal elements of the population, their families, and friends. Argentinian military officers were often integral members of the squads. El Salvador's death squads are still operational. Often paramilitary in nature, the squads' clandestine attacks have been seen as both a cause and a product of the civil war in that troubled nation. Their attacks have not been limited to leftist guerrillas; it has been estimated that 40,000 Salvadoran noncombatants have been slain by government security forces and underground death squads.

References: Michael Stohl and George Lopez, eds., *The State as Terrorist* (Westport, Conn.: Greenwood Press, 1984); Neil C. Livingstone, "Death Squads," *World Affairs* 146 (Winter 1983–84); T. David Mason and Dale A. Krane, "The Political Economy of Death Squads: Towards a Theory of the Impact of State-Sanctioned Terror," *International Studies Quarterly* 33 (June 1989).

DEBRAY, REGIS

French left-wing revolutionary theorist and intellectual. Debray was a disciple of Che Guevara and helped to popularize both the legend of Guevara and Guevara's brand of rural GUERRILLA warfare. He was arrested in Bolivia while a member of Guevara's final expedition but was released after serving three years of a 30-year sentence. In recent years Debray has softened his violent rhetoric and has served as a Third-World advisor to French president Francois Mitterrand.

References: Regis Debray, *Strategy for Revolution: Essays on Latin America* (New York: Monthly Review, 1970); Regis Debray, *Revolution in the Revolution* (New York: Grove Press, 1967).

DEIR YASSIN

An Arab village outside the city of Jerusalem, where on April 9, 1948 more than 200 villagers were massacred by Jewish terrorists. Men, women and children died in the attack carried out by IRGUN and LEHI, militant Zionist organizations, which claimed that Deir Yassin was a hotbed of anti-Jewish activity. The Deir Yassin massacre was used by both Zionist organizations as a terror tactic to expel Palestinians from their homeland. This episode was followed by the declaration of the State of Israel on May 14, 1948. It is considered to be a turning point that culminated in the exodus of Palestinians from present-day Israel.

References: J. Bowyer Bell, *Terror Out of Zion: Irgun Zvai Leumi, LEHI, and the Palestine Underground, 1929–1949* (New York: St. Martin's Press, 1977); Rosemary Sayigh, *Palestinians: From Peasants to Revolutionaries* (London: Zed Press, 1979).

DELLE CHIAIE, STEFANO

Italian neo-FASCIST and right-wing terrorist leader. Known as the "Black Bomber," he formed the AVANGUARDIA NAZIONALE in 1959. He was implicated in the bombing of a bank in Milan in which 16 people were killed on December 12, 1969. In 1970 he was part of a flawed COUP D'ÉTAT in Rome. Della Chiaie has been extremely active in international circles and has been involved in anti-left terrorism around the world. He had close ties to the Chilean DINA secret police in the Pinochet regime and to the military government of Argentina, as well as to European right-wing terrorist and political groups.

Reference: Leonard Weinberg and William Eubank, *The Rise and Fall of Italian Terrorism* (Boulder, Colo.: Westview Press, 1987).

DELTA FORCE

The U.S. Army's elite anti-terrorist strike team, officially known as the 1st Special Forces Operational Detachment–Delta. It is based at Fort Bragg, N.C.

Delta Force was established in November 1977, in part due to the success of the West German GSG-9 anti-terrorist force in rescuing hostages at Mogadishu earlier that year. Delta Force was conceived by Colonel Charlie Beckwith, a U.S. Army Special Forces (Green Beret) officer who became the first Delta Force commander. The unit is closely patterned after Britain's Special Air Service (SAS). Although the detachment is kept in a state of constant readiness, it has not often been utilized.

Delta Force is best known for its unsuccessful rescue operation in April 1980, during the IRANIAN HOSTAGE CRISIS. Mechanical problems with helicopters and poor weather conditions caused Beckwith to abort the mission, code-named "Eagle Claw," in the Iranian desert. Eight men died and several more were injured when a helicopter crashed into a fixed-wing aircraft during the operation. The mission has been severely criticized for both its planning and implementation. In October 1985 the Delta Force was involved in the interception of the Egyptian airliner transporting ABU ABBAS and the four PLF hijackers of the ACHILLE LAURO. That mission ended in a stand-off with Italian authorities, who refused to allow the Delta Force team to seize the terrorists inside an Egyptian airliner that U.S. warplanes had forced to land in Sicily.

References: David C. Martin and John Walcott, *Best Laid Plans: The Inside Story of America's War Against Terrorism* (New York: Harper & Row, 1988); Charlie A. Beckwith and Donald Knox, *Delta Force* (New York: Harcourt Brace Jovanovich, 1983); Harry G. Summers, Jr., "Delta Force: America's Counterterrorist Unit and the Mission to Rescue the Hostages in Iran," *Military Review* (November 1983).

DEMOCRATIC ALLIANCE

One of the three factions of the PALESTINE LIBERATION ORGANIZATION that emerged following the break between Syria and Yasir ARAFAT in 1983–84. This group, sympathetic to the anti-Arafat rebels of al-FATAH, primarily consisted of the Marxist-Leninist Palestinian organizations, including the POPULAR FRONT FOR THE LIBERATION OF PALESTINE and the DEMOCRATIC FRONT FOR THE LIBERATION OF PALESTINE.

DEMOCRATIC FRONT FOR THE LIBERATION OF PALESTINE (DFLP)

Established in 1968, the DFLP is a Marxist-Leninist Palestinian nationalist group. It is pro-Soviet and maintains that the Palestinian national goal cannot be achieved without a working-class revolution. The DFLP has often opposed what it considers to be the "moderate" policies of the PLO under Yasir ARAFAT. The group's terrorist actions have always taken place within Israel or the occupied territories. Typical acts are bombings and grenade attacks, as well as spectacular operations to seize hostages and attempts to negotiate the return of Palestinian prisoners in Israeli jails. The most infamous DFLP incident occurred in May 1974, when DFLP terrorists disguised as Israeli Defense Force members killed 27 Israelis and wounded 134 in the MA'ALOT MASSACRE. In May 1988 Israeli security forces uncovered and arrested several DFLP terrorist squads after an attack on the vehicle of Israeli government minister Ariel Sharon.

Syria provided most of the DFLP's external support before March 1987, when the group refused to join the Syrian-backed NATIONAL SALVATION FRONT. The group reportedly has received training in the Soviet Union and accepts aid from Cuba. Outside sponsorship notwithstanding, the group is considered to be intensely independent. The DFLP is led by Naif HAWATMEH, and membership is thought to number about 500.

DEMOCRATIC REVOLUTIONARY FRONT FOR THE LIBERATION OF ARABISTAN

An Iranian Arab organization which was responsible for the siege of the Iranian embassy in London in April and May 1980. This anti-KHOMEINI group sought the establishment of an Arab state and government in the southwestern part of Iran, which is heavily populated by Arabs and is rich in oil. The area was given to Iran by the British, who ruled Iraq after World War I under the mandate of the League of Nations.

DINA (DIRECCION DE INTELLIGENCIA NACIONAL)

The secret police organization of the Pinochet regime in Chile, established in June 1974. DINA was a major instrument of state terror, using mass detention, torture and murder to squelch existing or potential criticism of the military government. DINA operated clandestine detention centers where, secretly and illegally, imprisoned Chileans were subjected to torture. Its operatives were active in right-wing DEATH SQUADS. DINA agents also operated abroad and were implicated in the September 1976 assassination in Washington, D.C., of Orlando LETELIER, former foreign minister of Chile under Salvador Allende. DINA was disbanded in 1978, and the Central Nacional de Informaciones (CNI) was established as its replacement.

Reference: Amnesty International, *Chilean Briefing* (London: Amnesty International, 1988).

DIRECT ACTION

See ACTION DIRECTE.

DIRTY WAR

Cynically known as the "Process of National Reorganization," the dirty war was the Argentine military junta's brutal program for stamping out political opposition, leftist guerrillas, labor organizers and the intelligentsia. The dirty war was begun soon after the military coup of March 24, 1976, and lasted until 1983. It was conducted by the military forces and by right-wing death squads such as AAA, which operated with the approval and sometimes the participation of the military.

Tens of thousands of Argentines were arrested and tortured in hundreds of secret government jails. Many were killed, and their bodies were disposed of in unmarked graves or dumped at sea. The basis of the dirty war lay in its clandestine approach; the government seized its victims with no formal or legal basis or controls. No documentation was made, so as to preclude any "paper trail" of the atrocities. The victims of the dirty war, which number perhaps 20,000–30,000, simply "disappeared." The ruling junta declared any inquiries into the conduct of the security forces and into the whereabouts of the "disappeared" to be illegal, and the declaration was brutally enforced. The international community did, slowly, discover what was occurring in Argentina and brought some amount of pressure to bear on the military government. The government did not topple, however, until its defeat in the Falklands War with Britain and until its economic policies brought the Argentine economy to the brink of ruin.

See CODEP.

References: Donna Schlagheck, "State Terrorism," in *International Terrorism* (Lexington, Mass.: Lexington Books, 1988); John Simpson and Jana Bennett, *The Disappeared* (London: Robson Books, 1985); "The Argentine Military Junta's Final Report on the War Against Subversion and Terrorism, April 1983," *Terrorism* 7 (1984); Jacobo Timerman, *Prisoner Without a Name, Cell Without a Number* (New York: Knopf, 1981).

DISAPPEARED

Broad term referring to those, especially in Latin America, who have fallen victim to covert government-sponsored or condoned campaigns to eliminate opposition liberals, leftists, labor unionists and the intelligencia. In many cases the disappeared are the victims of DEATH SQUADS. In Spanish the disappeared are called *Desparecidos* or the "disappeared ones." While accurate statistics are impossible to come by, the problem has been endemic in most of Latin America—including Mexico. But the worse examples, with literally thousands of victims, were the military regimes in Chile and Argentina during the 1970s and early 1980s.

See ARGENTINA; DIRTY WAR; URUGUAY; CHILE.

References: Maureen R. Berman and R. S. Clark, "State Terrorism: Disappearances," *Rutgers Law Journal* 13 (Spring 1982); Steve Robinson, "Argentina's Disappeared," *Life* (September 1981).

DISIP

The secret police of Venezuela. DISIP has anti-terrorist and anti-guerrilla responsibilities. In November 1988 the organization was found to have been responsible for the murder of 14 fishermen mistaken for guerrillas, and the subsequent cover-up of the incident unleashed considerable public outrage.

DOZIER, JAMES

U.S. Army Brigadier General and NATO Deputy Commander, abducted by the Italian RED BRIGADES in Verona on December 17, 1981. He was freed by the Italian government's anti-terrorist units, NOCS, in Padua on January 28, 1982, as 10 members of the elite Italian rescue team stormed the apartment in which he was being held.

References: Alison Jamieson, "Political Kidnapping in Italy," *Conflict* 8 (1988); Vittorfranco Pisano, "Terrorism in Italy: The 'Dozier Affair'," *Police Chief* 49 (April 1982).

E

EELAM PEOPLE'S REVOLUTIONARY LIBERATION FRONT (EPRLF)

A Marxist-Leninist TAMIL separatist organization, originally dedicated to the establishment of a communist "Eelam," the name given by Tamil separatists to their envisioned sovereign nation-state in the northern and eastern sections of the island nation of SRI LANKA. The EPRLF suffered heavy losses in battles with their more powerful rival, the Liberation Tigers of Tamil Eelam, in the mid-1980s. Recently, however, the EPRLF has received the support of Indian elements, who see the group as a viable alternative to more hostile Tamil organizations, offering greater potential for political approaches to Sri Lankan ethnic strife. The EPRLF has emerged as a political force in the Tamil city of Jaffna, in the new Northeast Province.

References: R. Kearney, "Tension and Conflict in Sri Lanka," *Current History* (March 1986); S. V. Kodikara, "The Separatist Eelam Movement in Sri Lanka: An Overview," *India Quarterly* 37 (April–June 1981).

EELAM REVOLUTIONARY ORGANIZATION

A minor left-wing TAMIL separatist organization.

EJERCITO BORICAN POPULAR (EBP)

See MACHETEROS.

EKSUND

A trawler seized by French customs officials off the coast of Brittany on October 30, 1987. The vessel had inadvertently strayed into French territorial waters as it sailed from LIBYA to Ireland. When it was challenged, the ship was discovered to be carrying more than 150 tons of munitions and explosives. The five crew members, three of whom were members of the IRISH REPUBLICAN ARMY, had taken on their deadly cargo in the Libyan port of Tripoli. Included among the seized weapons were 1,000 Kalashnikov rifles, 20 SAM-7 anti-aircraft missiles, and two and one-half tons of Semtex explosive. The four crewmen were placed on trial in France in January 1991; the captain of the vessel, Adrian Hopkins, jumped bail in France and is now in custody in Ireland. All five were originally charged with arms trafficking and other violations of French law. Hopkins has admitted making four successful arms shipments to the IRA between 1985 and 1987. He has also implicated the Libyan government directly in the supply of arms. According to Hopkins, Libyan navy personnel loaded the munitions on the *Eksund*.

EL AL

The national airline of Israel. Because it is such a high-profile target, the airline has developed the most comprehensive security procedures of any international air carrier.

ELA (EPANASTIKOS LAIKOS AGONAS)

Greek, "Revolutionary Popular Struggle." A Greek extreme leftist group that developed out of the opposition to the military junta that ruled Greece from 1967 to 1974. It has declared its opposition to "imperialist domination, exploitation, and oppression." The ELA is strongly opposed to U.S. influence and seeks the removal of U.S. military forces from Greece. To support its goals, the group has carried out a series of relatively unsophisticated bombings against Greek government and economic targets, as well as against U.S. interests. To date, ELA-claimed incidents have caused only property damage and no injuries.

Little is known about the ELA's structure, membership and relationships (if any) to other Greek terrorist groups. There has been speculation that the ELA in some way provides support or coordination to other terrorist organizations in Greece. Analysis of the ELA is further complicated by the periodic appearance of apparently new groups that claim responsibility for acts of terrorism in Greece. It is possible that these names are nothing more than covers used by the ELA or another group to confuse authorities and to project a growing revolutionary movement. Although details concerning the relationships between Greek terrorist groups are sketchy, Greek police believe that they have established a linkage between the ELA and another Greek organization, the REVOLUTIONARY ORGANIZATION 17 NOVEMBER. Although the ELA has expressed solidarity with other terrorist groups and revolutionary movements, including the West German RED ARMY FACTION (RAF) and the French ACTION DIRECTE (AD), there is no evidence that the group maintains ties to any foreign terrorist groups.

ELN (EJERCITO DE LIBERACION NACIONAL)

Spanish, "National Liberation Army." A Colombian left-wing revolutionary organization, organized in 1965 as a guerrilla movement to overthrow the existing regime. The ELN is heavily influenced by LIBERATION THEOLOGY and by the CASTRO government in CUBA. The ELN is a political-military operation drawing members from across the spectrum of Colombian society, from students and intellectuals to peasants and middle-class workers. It has several factions and fronts, including the "Camilo Terres Restropo," the "Jose Antonio Galan," and the "Domingo Lain Sanz." The "Simon Bolivar" faction opposes the more hard-line elements of the ELN. Since early 1988, the ELN has been the most active of Colombian guerrilla groups.

The ELN has a long history of assassinations, kidnappings of wealthy ranchers and industrialists, armed robberies, village raids and bombings. On October 6, 1975 it assassinated its nemesis, the Inspector General of the Army, Ramon Arthur Rincon Quinones, who had directed many anti-guerrilla campaigns. The ELN bombed the Spanish Embassy in Bogota on January 21, 1976. In November 1983 it kidnapped Dr. Jaime Betancur Cuartas, brother of the president of Colombia. Most recently the ELN has concentrated its efforts on attacking petroleum pipelines and facilities, thereby damaging Colombia's economic infrastructure and injuring the investment climate.

Despite truces agreed to by allied organizations, including the FARC, the ELN has remained an active guerrilla force. The ELN is the one group that refused to agree to a government truce in 1984. The ELN is a part of the National Guerrilla Coordinator (CNG) and the recently formed Simon Bolivar Guerrilla Coordinator (SBGC). The group operates primarily in the northern and northeastern part of Colombia. The ELN is thought to receive support from CUBA, and its membership is thought to number less than 1,000.

Reference: Gary Hoskin, "Colombia's Political Crisis," *Current History* (January 1988).

EL SALVADOR

This tiny Central American nation has been rocked by civil war and terrorist violence since 1979. Terror is a common tool of both the left and the right. Marxist rebels, banded together in the FARABUNDO MARTI NATIONAL LIBERATION FRONT (FMLN) coalition, battle the U.S.-backed Salvadoran military and seek to overthrow the existing government and establish a communist state. Their strategy in essence is to challenge the oligarchic nature of Salvadoran society in order to create a level of social and political chaos conducive to popular revolution. The present institutional instability of the country is testament to the partial success of the guerrilla efforts. Rural El Salvador has been politically paralyzed, as more than 40% of the nation's municipalities are presently without an elected mayor, a situation created by FMLN death threats and assassinations. Urban guerrilla warfare has created a climate of intense fear and instability in the capital

of San Salvador and in many of the nation's other large communities. In November 1989 the FMLN launched a massive offensive against the capital, seizing whole districts of the city.

Leftist violence has helped to spawn right-wing terrorist activity. The country's infamous DEATH SQUADS often operate in tandem with El Salvador's security forces, targeting left-wing guerrillas, perceived sympathizers, human rights workers, religious leaders, liberals, and indeed any individual who dares to criticize the right. Members of the ARENA party, which was victorious in the 1989 presidential election, have been clearly identified with death squad terrorism. Roberto D'AUBISSON, leader of ARENA, has been implicated in the activities of the ORDEN right-wing paramilitary organization and in the 1980 assassination of Archbishop Oscar ROMERO. Death squad violence increased to alarming levels in the early 1980s and then subsided temporarily during the early years of Christian Democratic Jose Napolean Duarte's presidency; it rose again in late 1988 and early 1989. By April 1989 victims of the death squads had reached an average of 20 dead per month. In November of that year the brutal execution-style murders of six Salvadoran Catholic priests threatened to undermine the U.S. government's support for the elected government.

See CLARA ELIZABETH RAMIREZ FRONT.

References: Thomas P. Anderson, *Matanza: El Salvador's Communist Revolt of 1932* (Lincoln: University of Nebraska Press, 1971); Richard L. Millett, "The Politics of Violence: Guatemala and El Salvador," *Current History* (February 1981); "Salvadoran Death Threats: A Dialogue," *Harpers* 278 (April 1989); James LeMoyne, "The Guns of Salvador," *The New York Times Magazine* (February 5, 1989); Lindsey Gruson, "Salvador

Rebels' Drive on Mayors is Bringing Chaos to Rural Area," *New York Times* (January 6, 1989); Frances FitzGerald, "In the Artificial Gardens of War," *Esquire* 110, (August 1988); Stewart W. Fisher, "Human Rights in El Salvador and U.S. Foreign Policy," *Human Rights Quarterly* (Spring 1982).

EM

See ESA.

ENFORCEMENT TERRORISM

The term applied to the guerrilla technique of inspiring fear in the populous, so as to terrify the masses into supporting the cause of the rebel organization. At a minimum, enforcement terrorism seeks to prevent people from collaborating with government authorities. This term has been used to characterize the seeming irony of the SENDERO LUMINOSO's massive violence against the Peruvian campesinos, who are obstensibly the people that the Senderos are dedicated to "liberating." The term similarly may be applied to inter-Palestinian terrorism, in which individuals or groups use terrorist acts to eliminate or intimidate rivals. The U.S. Department of State estimates that 63 percent of all attacks by the Abu Nidal Organization have been directed against other Palestinian and Arab targets.

Reference: Paul L. Bremer, "Terrorism: Myths and Reality," U.S. State Department Current Policy Paper no. 1047 (Washington, D.C.: U.S. Department of State, 1988).

ENSSLIN, GUDRUN

West German left-wing revolutionary and member of the RED ARMY FACTION or (Baader-Meinhof Gang). Ensslin was active in student demonstrations in the late 1960s. She and Andreas BAADER committed their first act of terrorism on April 2, 1968 as they set fire to two Frankfurt department stores. Ensslin and Ulrike MEINHOF conducted an armed "liberation" of Baader from prison in 1970. Following the escape plot, she and her colleagues trained in a camp run by the POPULAR FRONT FOR THE LIBERATION OF PALESTINE (PFLP) in Jordan. They returned to West Germany to launch a campaign of bombings, abductions, and shootings. Ensslin and many of her fellow RAF members were arrested in 1972. Several terrorist attempts to force the releases of the jailed RAF leaders failed, including the kidnapping of German businessman Hans-Martin SCHLEYER on September 5, 1977. After the most spectacular of these attempts—the skyjacking of a Lufthansa flight by PFLP terrorists—was foiled by a West German anti-terrorist team, Ensslin, Baader, and another RAF member committed suicide in their prison cells on October 18, 1977.

ENTEBBE RAID

The rescue on July 1, 1976, by the Israeli military of 103 passengers from the hijacked Air France Flight 139. The hostages were being held at the Entebbe airport in Uganda by terrorists of the POPULAR FRONT FOR THE LIBERATION OF PALESTINE (PFLP). Because most of the hostages were Jewish, and because the hijackers seemed to have the cooperation of Ugandan dictator Idi Amin, the Israeli government decided to attempt a rescue mission despite the enormous distance between Israel and Uganda and the difficulty of transporting forces. The difficulties notwithstanding, the rescue was an astounding success. Israeli soldiers stormed the airport, killed seven hijackers and 20 Ugandan soldiers, and saved all but four of the hostages while losing only one Israeli soldier (the expedition commander, Jonathan Netanyahu).

References: Zeev Maoz, "The Decision to Raid Entebbe: Decision Analysis Applied to Crisis Behavior," *Journal of Conflict Resolution* 25 (December 1981); Francis A. Boyle, "International Law in Time of Crisis: From the Entebbe Raid to the Hostages Convention," *Northwestern University Law Review* 75 (December 1980); Jeffrey A. Sheehan, "The Entebbe Raid: The Principle of Self-Help in International Law as Justification for State Use of Armed Force," *The Fletcher Forum* 1 (Spring 1977).

EPL (EJERCITO POPULAR DE LIBERACION)

Spanish, "Popular Liberation Army." A Colombian left-wing revolutionary organization. Founded in 1967, EPL is a rural guerrilla group with a Maoist orientation and is the armed branch of the small pro-Beijing party PCC-ML, Partido Communista de Colombia-Marxista-Leninista (the Communist Party of Columbia–Marxist-Leninist). During the late 1970s the group was responsible for a number of sabotage attacks, kidnappings, bank robberies and bombings. Beginning in early 1987, the EPL began an active campaign in the Uraba region, making it one of the most consistently active guerrilla zones in the violence-plagued country. The EPL, the ELN, M-19, and two smaller groups compose the National Guerrilla Coordinator (CNG). The CNG was largely overcome by the advent of the Simon Bolivar Guerrilla Coordinator (SBGC), which the EPL also joined. The Maoist ideological stance of the EPL continued to appeal to a small circle of university intellectuals who provide aid to the terrorist movement. The group presently numbers about 600–800 members and remains active despite damaging arrests.

ERITREAN LIBERATION FRONT (ELF)

Organization that seeks autonomy for Muslim Eritrea from Ethiopia. It was founded in Cairo in 1958 by three Eritrean expatriates, Ibrahim Sultan, Osman Saleh Sabbeh and Welde-Ab Welde-Miriam. In 1971 the group split and the more militant Eritrean People's Liberation Front became the dominant faction. ELF has been responsible for the hijacking of a number of Ethiopian Airlines flights.

ERP (EJERCITO REVOLUCIONARIO DE PUEBLO)

1. "People's Revolutionary Army." An Argentine left-wing organization founded in 1970. Influenced by the TUPAMAROS of Uruguay, ERP adopted a Trotskyite philosophy and recruited from the lower economic classes of Argentine society. Like the Tupamaros, the group used "Robin Hood" tactics to win popular support. It carried out a campaign of kidnappings, assassinations, and assaults on military targets. It was especially adept at obtaining large ransoms through its abductions, including the $14.2 million paid by Exxon in 1973 to obtain the release of employee Victor Samuelson. ERP, like the Argentine MONTENEROS, was largely undone by the military government's DIRTY WAR in the mid- and late 1970s.

2. "People's Revolutionary Army." One of the left-wing Salvadoran guerrilla groups encompassed under the umbrella organization FMLN.

ESA (EJERCITO SECRETO ANTICOMUNISTA)

1. "Secret Anti-Communist Army." A Guatemalan right-wing death squad that played a major role in that country's extremist violence of the 1960s, 1970s and 1980s. ESA was a paramilitary organization with strong ties to the government, military and police. It carried on a government-condoned, extralegal, anti-leftist campaign with impunity. ESA issued death lists, carried out kidnappings and assassinations and conducted its own "trials" of suspected leftists and leftist sympathizers. The group was reportedly led by Lucas Garcia, the Guatemalan minister of the interior.

2. "Secret Anti-Communist Army." A Salvadoran right-wing death squad, thought to have been led by Colonel Reynaldo Lopez Nuila, the deputy minister of defence of El Salvador.

Reference: George Black, *Garrison Guatemala* (London: Zed Press, 1984).

ESCOBAR GAVIRIA, PABLO

One of the principal leaders of Colombia's cocaine trafficking cartel. Escobar and Jose Gonzalo RODRIGUEZ GACHA were said to control 80% of the cocaine entering the United States. Their vast drug empire, known as the MEDELLIN CARTEL for the central Colombian city in which it was traditionally based, generated billions of dollars of illegal profits. In late 1989 Colombian president Virgilio Barco Vargas launched an all-out war against the cartel and its leaders, and since that time Escobar has been in hiding. In an attempt to break the government's resolve, Escobar and Rodriguez Gacha stepped up their own campaign of NARCO-TERRORISM within Colombia, conducting bombings, assassinations and kidnappings in the name of the EXTRADITABLES. By the end of 1990 Rodriguez Gacha was dead, killed by police, and the Extraditables organization was reported to be seeking to make a bargain with the Colombian government.

References: Peter Andreas and Coletta Youngers, " 'Busting' The Andean Cocaine Industry: America's Counterproductive War on Drugs," *World Policy Journal* 6 (Summer 1989); Rensselaer Lee III, "Dimensions of the South American Cocaine Industry," *Journal of InterAmerican Studies and World Affairs* 30 (Summer/Fall 1988).

ESI (ESCADRON SPECIAL D'INTERVENTION)

The anti-terrorist unit of Belgium, often referred to by its codename, "Diana." The ESI is about 200 members strong and has trained with the French GIGN and the West German GSG-9.

ETA (EUZKADI TA ASKATASUNA)

"Basque Fatherland and Liberty." A radical and violent BASQUE separatist movement founded on August 31, 1959. The group was formed by a group of young members of the Basque Nationalist Party (PNV). Originally an organization dedicated to democratic ideals and the preservation of Basque heritage and language, by 1962 ETA had evolved into a group prepared to use violent measures in its quest to secure Basque independence. The group first incurred the wrath of the Spanish government in 1968, when it murdered Meliton Manzanas, chief of police in the city of San Sebastian. Since that time, the group has maintained a consistent agenda of shootings, bombings, and arson and has remained one of the most active and violent terrorist organizations in the world. More than 600 people have died in ETA violence. Perhaps ETA's most infamous terrorist attack was the assassination on December 20, 1973 of Luis CARRERO BLANCO, the prime minister of Spain.

In 1974 the group split into two factions, ETA/M (Militant) and ETA/PM (Political-Military). Following the death of the Spanish dictator General Francisco Franco, and the reforms of King Juan Carlos, ETA/PM chose to pursue politically their separatist goals, and they renounced violence. Only the ETA/M remains active today. ETA has a history of kidnappings for ransom, from which it has obtained huge amounts of money. In January 1981 members abducted one of the wealthiest men in Spain, eventually receiving a $3.29 million ransom. In January 1982 members kidnapped an industrialist and netted $1.3 million in ransom. In 1982 ETA caused millions of dollars in damages when it bombed the central telephone exchange in Madrid, disrupting service for much of the country. In October 1986 the group assassinated a provincial governor in an attack with plastic explosives. In the spring of 1988 the group seized industrialist Emiliano Revilla, and he is still believed to be captive somewhere near Madrid.

The U.S. Department of State believes that the organization has received training in Libya, Lebanon, and Nicaragua and has close ties with the Provisional Wing of the Irish Republican Army. The Spanish government has stated that ETA members have trained in Cuba and Czechoslovakia. Although many members of the top ETA leadership have been arrested by Spanish and French police in recent years, ETA seems able to rebound from even the most successful COUNTERTERRORIST operations. Because of the large size of the group's support base and the high level of nationalist sentiment among Basques, many experts have predicted that ETA violence will continue for the foreseeable future. Nonetheless, in 1988 and 1989 the Spanish government of Felipe Gonzalez was conducting secret negotiations in an effort to dissuade ETA from continuing its violent approach to the Basque question. A three-month truce arranged in Algiers took effect in early 1989, but in April 1989 ETA declared the agreement officially ended, attributing the breakdown to the Spanish government's breach of promises.

References: Peter Janke, "Spanish Separatism: ETA's Threat to Basque Democracy," in *The New Terrorism*, William Gutteridge, ed. (London: Mansell, 1986); Robert P. Clark, "Patterns in the Lives of ETA Members," *Terrorism* 6 (1983). Robert P. Clark, *The Basque Insurgents* (Madison: University of Wisconsin Press, 1984).

EUROTERRORISM

The efforts of left-wing ideological terrorists directed mainly against NATO and establishment targets. The Euroterrorists include ACTION DIRECTE in France, the RED ARMY FACTION in West Germany, the RED BRIGADES in Italy, the COMMUNIST COMBATANT CELLS in Belgium, the POPULAR FORCES OF APRIL 25TH in Portugal, and GRAPO in Spain.

References: Naomi Gal-Or, *International Cooperation to Suppress Terrorism* (London: Croom Helm, 1985); Hans J. Horchem, "European Terrorism: A German Perspective," *Terrorism* 6, no. 1 (1983).

EUZKADI

The Basque name meaning "homeland" given to the independent Basque nation envisioned by separatists.

EUZKADI TA ASKATASUNA

See ETA.

EXTRADITABLES

The Medellin drug cartel's shadow organization for conducting NARCO-TERRORISM. The group was spawned as a response to the Colombian government's crackdown on the cocaine smuggling operations of Pablo ESCOBAR GAVIRIA and Jose Gonzalo RODRIGUEZ GACHA. The Extraditables had, through the end of 1989, killed 261 persons and wounded more than 1,200 others in 200 separate bombings. The most heinous of their crimes were the November 1989 bombing of an Avianca jetliner, which killed 107, and the truck bombing of the Bogota police headquarters, which killed more than 60 persons. In January 1990 the Extraditables approached the government in search of a deal, declaring that the government had won the drug war. The Bogota government rejected the offer.

Reference: Rensselaer Lee III, "Dimensions of the South American Cocaine Industry," *Journal of InterAmerican Studies and World Affairs* 30 (Summer/Fall 1988).

EXTRADITION

The surrender by one state to another of an individual accused or convicted of an offense in the latter state. Even among long-standing Western allies, requests for the extradition of suspected or even convicted terrorists have proven to be problematic and have led to strained diplomatic relations between nations. The ABU DAOUD case, the ACHILLE LAURO episode, the Greek government's refusal to extradite Mohammed RASHID, and the U.S. hesitancy to cooperate with some British requests to extradite IRISH REPUBLICAN ARMY terrorists are well-known examples.

References: Barbara Ann Anoff and Christopher H. Pyle, " 'To Surrender Political Offenders': The Political Offense Exception to Extradition in United States Law," *New York University Journal of International Law and Politics* 16 (Winter 1984); James G. Clark, "Political Offenses in Extradition: Time for Judicial Abstention," *Hastings International and Comparative Law Review* 5 (Fall 1981).

F

FACTIONS ARMEES REVOLUTIONNAIRES LIBANAISES

See FARL.

FADLALLAH, SHEIKH MUHAMMED HASSAN

Lebanese Shi'ite religious leader, and spiritual father to HEZBOLLAH and other Lebanese Shi'ite extremists. Fadlallah, often described as the founder and leader of Hezbollah, has in reality played a far less direct role in that loosely structured organization. He was himself the target of a terrorist car-bomb attack in Beirut in 1985, believed to have been the work of the Lebanese intelligence agency. Fadlallah's followers have accused the CIA of involvement in the attempted assassination, as the CIA has been active in Lebanese intelligence training.

Reference: A.R. Norton, ''Shi'ism and Social Protest in Lebanon,'' in Juan R. I. Cole and Nikki R. Keddie, eds. *Shi'ism and Social Protest* (New Haven: Yale University Press, 1986).

FAL (FUERZAS ARMADAS DE LIBERACION)

''Armed Forces of Liberation,'' a Salvadoran left-wing guerrilla group affiliated with the Communist Party of El Salvador. The FAL, founded in 1930, is one of the constituent groups in the umbrella organization FMLN.

FALN (FUERZAS ARMADAS DE LIBERACION NACIONAL)

Spanish, ''Armed Forces, of National Liberation.'' **1.** Puerto Rican separatist organization, founded in 1974 from the remnants of two earlier separatist organizations. The FALN's first terrorist acts were the bombings of five New York City banks on October 26, 1974. On January 24, 1975 the group bombed Fraunces Tavern in the Wall Street area, killing four people and wounding more than 60 others. Many of the FALN's operations have been staged against perceived symbols of American capitalism and imperialism, both in the United States and on the island of Puerto Rico. The group is believed to be responsible for more than 100 bombings in New York, Chicago, and Washington, with targets including department stores, hotels, corporate offices, and airports. FALN terrorist activity has greatly subsided since the April 1980 arrests of 11 members in Evanston, Illinois during an attempted armed robbery. On

December 31, 1983 the group detonated a series of explosions in New York City, damaging such targets as the FBI offices, a police headquarters, and a federal courthouse.

2. Venezuelan Marxist guerrilla group active in the 1960s and early 1970s. In the early 1960s the FALN began a series of violent actions, ranging from the shooting of police officers to attacks on Venezuelan oil field facilities. By the late 1960s the group had so disrupted Venezuelan society that the government declared a state of siege. Government security forces zeroed in on the FALN and by the mid-1970s had rendered the group inactive. Douglas Bravo, the FALN leader, opted to accept amnesty in 1979 and enter the legitimate political arena.

Reference: Ronald Fernandez, *Los Macheteros* (Englewood Cliffs, N.J.: Prentice Hall, 1987).

FANE (FEDERATION D'ACTION NATIONALE EUROPEENE)

A French extreme right-wing, neo-fascist organization founded in 1966 and banned by the French government in 1980. FANE actively disseminated anti-minority propaganda and was responsible for a number of attacks against Jewish targets in Paris. Members of FANE were thought to be involved in a wave of anti-Semitic attacks that swept France in 1980, in which more than 30 Jewish synagogues, offices, apartments and persons were attacked. After French authorities outlawed FANE in September 1980, the group was succeeded by FNE.

Reference: Edward Moxon-Browne, "Terrorism in France," *Conflict Studies* 144 (1983).

FAR

See GUATEMALAN NATIONAL REVOLUTIONARY UNITY.

FARABUNDO MARTI LIBERATION FRONT

See FMLN.

FARC (FUERZAS ARMADAS REVOLUTIONARIAS DE COLOMBIA)

Spanish, "Revolutionary Armed Forces of Colombia." The largest of the leftist guerrilla movements in Colombia. The FARC was established in 1966 as the military wing of the Colombian Communist Party. Its primary goal is to overthrow the government and the ruling class. It is pro-Soviet, pro-Cuban and vehemently anti-American. The group is run as a military organization, and its guerrillas number perhaps 5,000. The FARC is considered to be the best-trained, best-equipped, and most effective insurgent organization in South America. It conducts armed attacks against domestic Colombian targets and bombings of U.S. businesses. In May 1984 the FARC agreed to a cease-fire accord with the Government of Colombia, but it has not given up its armed struggle. During the cease-fire, FARC forces have carried out terrorist actions such as extortion, kidnappings and killings, as well as attacks against military units. The FARC's peace gestures appear to be a method for preparing for its political path, inhibiting pressure from Colombian security forces, and allowing the FARC time to regroup.

The FARC's leadership is largely composed of disaffected middle and upper class intellectuals, although it also recruits from, and attempts to appeal to, the peasant population. The FARC also has received support from other elements of Colombian society, including workers, students, and priests supportive of LIBERATION THEOLOGY. FARC popularity has been undermined by the occasional practice of kidnapping peasants, branding them as collaborators, and killing them if they do not cooperate. The FARC has attempted to strengthen its influence over other insurgent factions by leading the recent efforts to establish the national Simon Bolivar Guerrilla Coordinator (SBGC), which includes all major Colombian insurgent groups. In 1985 the group spawned a political movement, the Patriotic Union (UP) and a radical dissent faction. The RICARDO FRANCO FRONT (RFF) broke away the FARC in March 1984 over differences in tactics and became an active terrorist organization in its own right.

The FARC has a closer relationship with Colombian narcotics traffickers than do other Colombian insurgent groups. In return for FARC protection of narcotics interests, the guerrillas have received money to purchase weapons and supplies. There are continuing reports of actual FARC involvement in the cocaine industry. Drug money supplements revenues from extortion, robberies, and kidnappings. FARC has a history of abductions for ransom, including the February 14, 1977 kidnapping of a U.S. Peace Corps worker. (The captive was released on February 11, 1980 after a $250,000 ransom was delivered to the FARC.) In January 1986, FARC attempted to extort $100 million from Shell Oil Company, but the company opted to suspend its operations in guerrilla-controlled regions rather than meet the demand.

References: Gary Hoskin, "Colombia's Political Crisis," *Current History* (January 1988); James Adams, "The Narc-Farc Connection," in *The Financing of Terror* (London: New English Library, 1986).

FARL (FACTIONS ARMEES REVOLUTIONNAIRES LIBANAISES)

French, "Lebanese Armed Revolutionary Faction," sometimes called LARF. A Lebanese left-wing, anti-Zionist terror group, dedicated to the establishment of a Marxist-Leninist state in Lebanon, with its roots in the POPULAR FRONT FOR THE LIBERATION OF PALESTINE (PFLP). Few, if any, members of the group are of Palestinian origin. The group consists mostly of Lebanese Christians from the villages of Qubayyat and Andraqat in northern Lebanon. The FARL, along with the MAY 15 GROUP and the PFLP-SC, arose from the remnants of the PFLP Special Operations Group after its leader, Wadi Haddad, died in 1978. Georges Ibrahim Abdallah is believed to have founded the FARL in 1978 or 1979, and its first operations may have been against Christian Phalange targets in Lebanon in 1979. Abdallah moved the group's operations in Europe sometime around mid-1980.

The FARL established its terrorist reputation with a series of killings of U.S. and Israeli diplomats in France. The group conducted most of its operations in Western Europe, where it created an extensive network of safehouses, bank accounts, and arms caches. In January 1982 members of the group murdered U.S. Army Lieutenant Colonel Charles Ray, Assistant Army Attaché, in Paris. In 1982 the group bombed several targets in Paris. American diplomat Leamon Hunt, head of the Multinational Peacekeeping force in the Sinai, was assassinated by FARL gunmen in Rome in February 1984.

Abdallah was arrested by French police in 1984. The arrest of the organization's leader, along with a number of other significant arrests in Italy and France, dealt a serious but not fatal blow to the group's operations. FARL bombers launched several attacks in Paris in 1986 in efforts to obtain their leader's freedom; 15 people died and more than 150 were wounded.

FARN (FUERZAS ARMADAS DE LA RESISTENCIA NACIONAL)

Spanish, "Armed Forces of National Resistance." A left-wing Salvadoran guerrilla group, and one of the constituent groups in the umbrella organization FMLN.

FARP

See PUERTO RICAN TERRORISM.

FAS

See FRENTE AMERICO SILVIO.

FASCISM

A right-wing political philosophy of intense nationalism and authoritarianism, which places the national interest above individual rights. Fascism promotes militarism and racism and is opposed to both democracy and socialism. It places great emphasis on order and is intolerant of dissent. The main difference between totalitarian fascism and totalitarian communism is that fascism professes sympathy toward many aspects of private capitalism and would resolve the conflict between capital and labor by using the government to enforce their relations to one another in the interest of full employment and high productivity. The term was first applied to the political movement of Benito Mussolini in Italy in the 1920s. It has also been applied to the NAZI party in Germany and the Franco regime in Spain. It

has been used to describe a wide range of extreme right-wing contemporary movements which adhere to some or all of its primary facets.

References: Dennis King, *Lyndon La-Rouche and the New American Fascism* (New York: Doubleday, 1989); Bruce Hoffman, *Right-wing Terrorism in Europe* (Santa Monica, Calif.: Rand, 1982).

FATAH, AL-

Reverse acronym for the Arabic, Harakat al-Tahrir al Filistini ("Palestine Liberation Movement"). The largest organization in the PLO. Founded in 1957 in Kuwait as an anti-Israeli guerrilla force independent of the control of any Arab state, al-Fatah has been led since 1964 by Yasir ARAFAT. Al-Fatah emerged as the preeminent PLO group in 1969, and Arafat became the Chairman of the PLO Executive Committee at that time; it retains majorities in both the Executive Committee and the Palestinian National Assembly. The group has received funding from Arab states such as Saudi Arabia and Iraq, and the Soviet Union is a primary supplier of arms and training. It describes itself as a "revolutionary patriotic movement that aims to liberate the whole of Palestine and to establish a democratic Palestinian state," and holds that "armed revolution and armed struggle are the only ways to liberate Palestine." The U.S. Department of State estimates the personnel strength of al-Fatah to be 6,000–8,000.

During the 1960s the organization became known for its small but violent forays into Israeli territory from bases in Jordan. In September 1970 King Hussein of Jordan responded to confrontations between his troops and Fatah forces by expelling al-Fatah from Jordanian soil; the vanquished forces retreated to Syria and Lebanon. BLACK

SEPTEMBER, the violent Fatah splinter group which carried out the MUNICH MASSACRE at the 1972 Olympic Games, was born of, and named for, the fateful month of this expulsion. It has sought to function as a separate terrorist wing of the organization in order to keep Arafat and his political organization above the bloody fray. Al-Fatah carried out terrorist activities in Western Europe and the Middle East in the 1970s and offered training facilities and instruction to a wide array of international terrorist groups and individuals. Al-Fatah's resort to terrorism is often regarded as the group's response to its failures as a guerrilla force. It has never proven to be a true military threat to the state of Israel. Al-Fatah was forced to flee its bases in southern Lebanon in 1982 when the Israeli army launched its offensive across the Lebanese border, dispersing al-Fatah and other PLO groups to Tunisia, South Yemen, Algeria and a number of other countries throughout the Middle East. The group has been reinfiltrating Lebanon for several years. Its headquarters are currently in Tunis. Though considered to be one of the "moderate" factions of the PLO, al-Fatah is nonetheless capable of extreme violence, as it demonstrated during its March 7, 1988 storming of an Israeli bus, in which six people, including two women, were killed by automatic weapons.

See REJECTIONIST FRONT.

Reference: William Quandt et al., The Politics of Palestinian Nationalism (Berkeley: University of California Press, 1973); Adam M. Garfinkle, "Sources of the Al-Fatah Mutiny," Orbis 27 (Summer 1983); Gerard Chaliand, The Palestinian Resistance (Harmondsworth: Penguin Books, 1972); Richard A. Norton and Martin H. Greenberg, eds., The International Relations of the Palestine Liberation Organization (Carbondale: Southern Illinois University Press, 1989).

FATAH REVOLUTIONARY COUNCIL (FRC)

The terrorist organization of ABU NIDAL founded in 1974. Abu Nidal and his operatives operate under a variety of organizational guises, which the U.S. Department of State groups together under the umbrella term "Abu Nidal Organization," or ANO. The Abu Nidal group does not use the FRC name when claiming responsibility for a terrorist attack, but instead uses one of its many aliases.

FEDAYEEN

Plural of the Arabic word fedayee meaning commando or fighter. It is derived from the Arabic word fidai, which means to martyr oneself for one's country. Anti-Israeli guerrilla organizations frequently use the term fedayeen to refer to their cadres of fighters.

FEDERAL BUREAU OF INVESTIGATION (FBI)

The principal investigative arm of the U.S. Department of Justice, established in 1908 as the Bureau of Investigation. It is charged with gathering and reporting facts, locating witnesses and compiling evidence in matters in which the federal government is, or may be, a party in interest. Cooperative services of the FBI for other duly authorized law enforcement agencies include fingerprint identification, laboratory services, police training and the National Crime Information Center.

The FBI directs a Terrorist Research and Analytical Center (TRAC), founded in 1981. TRAC gathers intelligence on domestic terrorism, conducts criminal investigations and makes arrests. The FBI's Hostage Response Team (HURT), a 50-member elite unit, is the primary national anti-terrorist hostage rescue unit. In recent years HURT has ceased to be a full-time organization, drawing criticism from experts who argue that the United States has neither the resources nor the need to maintain a full time domestic hostage rescue unit.

See CHURCH COMMITTEE.

FELTRINELLI, GIANGIACOMO (1926–1972)

Italian millionaire and proponent of European revolution and terrorism. He was very much influenced by the Uruguayan TUPA-MAROS movement and styled himself a revolutionary guerrilla leader. A wealthy publisher, Feltrinelli was widely known for his extremist views, but in most circles his ramblings on Euro-revolution and urban guerrilla warfare were considered to be the rantings of a wealthy eccentric. A shocked Italian public discovered the seriousness of his commitment when, on March 15, 1972, he was killed, the accidental victim of the TNT explosives strapped to his body. He was a founder and member of the Italian terrorist organization Gruppi di Azione Partigiana ("Partisan Action Group").

FIGHTING SECTION

In pre-revolutionary Russia, the terrorist wing of the Russian SOCIAL REVOLUTIONARY PARTY. Led for much of its existence by Yevno Azev (1869–1918), it carried out a series of bombings and attacks against the Russian elite and the Tsarist government.

FIRST OF OCTOBER ANTI-FASCIST RESISTANCE GROUP

See GRAPO.

FLN (FRONT DE LIBERATION NATIONALE)

French, "National Liberation Front." The Algerian nationalist party dedicated to the establishment of Algerian autonomy and independence from France. Formed on November 1, 1954 by a radical transformation of the CRUA (Revolutionary Council for Unity and Action), the FLN waged a violent offensive against French colonial rule. In 1956 and 1957 widespread FLN terrorism, most often in the form of bombings, caused many deaths and injuries. French authorities in turn responded with force and repressive measures against the native population. The FLN's military wing, the ALN ("Armee de Liberation Nationale"), staged a guerrilla war against the French. European settlers, through the OAS, responded with mass terrorism of their own, and several bloody years preceded the eventual establishment of the Algerian state in 1962.

References: Martha C. Hutchinson, *Revolutionary Terrorism* (Stanford, Calif.: Hoover Institution Press, 1978); Martha C. Hutchinson, "The Concept of Revolutionary Terrorism," *The Journal of Conflict Resolution* 16 (September 1972).

FLNC (FRONT DE LIBERATION NATIONALE CORSE)

French, "Corsican National Liberation Front." A separatist, anti-French organization founded in 1976, which has carried out a series of bombings and assassinations in the name of Corsican independence. Although violence in the name of Corsican sovereignty has been widespread among many small groups and individuals, the FLNC, the largest of Corsican terrorist groups, is responsible for the majority of Corsican terrorism. Its frequent targets include French military installations, French banks and tourist areas. In May 1988 the group announced a four-month halt to active hostilities in order to facilitate French acquiescence to Corsican separatist proposals and demands that the Corsican assembly be dissolved and convicted Corsican terrorists be released.

See FRANCIA.

References: Peter Savigear, "Corsica: Regional Autonomy or Violence," *Conflict Studies* 149 (1983); Robert Ramsay, *The Corsican Time Bomb* (Manchester, U.K.: Manchester University Press, 1983); Edward Moxon-Browne, "Terrorist in France," *Conflict Studies* 144 (1983).

FLQ (FRONT DE LIBERATION DU QUEBEC)

A violent separatist movement founded in the early 1960s. FLQ began a campaign of bombings against Canadian public and government buildings in 1963. By 1970 these bombings had resulted in six deaths, all apparently inadvertent. On October 5, 1970 the group kidnapped senior British Trade Commissioner James R. Cross in Montreal and demanded the release of 23 FLQ prisoners, $500,000 in gold, and transport to safe asylum. Pierre Trudeau, Prime Minister of Canada, stood steadfastly against any release of imprisoned terrorists. On October 10, Pierre Laporte, Quebec's Minister of Labor and Immigration, was abducted by the frustrated FLQ; on October 17, he was found strangled to death. A massive police mobilization located the terrorist's haven on December 2, and Cross's release was obtained in exchange for the terrorists' safe passage to Cuba.

FMLN (FRENTE FARABUNDO MARTI DE LIBERACION NACIONAL)

Spanish, "Farabundo Marti National Liberation Front." The umbrella organization for five Salvadoran left-wing guerrilla groups: the People's Revolutionary Army (ERP), the Farabundo Marti Popular Liberation Forces (FPL), the Armed Forces of National Resistance (FARN), the Revolutionary Party of Central American Workers (PRTC), and the Communist Party of El Salvador's Armed Forces of Liberation (FAL). This alliance was formed in 1980 as a means to create a more effective insurgency and as a prerequisite for Cuban aid and materiel. Its total membership is estimated to be approximately 7,500.

The FMLN external headquarters is located near Managua, Nicaragua, but it maintains "political-diplomatic" offices in Panama, Mexico and Europe. The group receives external support from Communist countries that channel arms and supplies primarily through Nicaragua. FMLN members are routinely trained at camps in Cuba, and the primary safe havens for the FMLN hard-core members are Nicaragua and the ill-defined border region between EL SALVADOR and HONDURAS. The scope of FMLN activities is broad. It regularly conducts guerrilla warfare in rural regions and conducts political operations through the Revolutionary Democratic Front (FDR). FMLN guerrillas have actively sought through terrorism to prevent the establishment of an operational, legitimate political process in El Salvador. The organization has sought to deter voter participation in local and national elections through the threat and use of violence and has forced the resignation of several mayors.

Operational funding for the FMLN comes from a variety of sources. Most external funding probably comes through Cuba, and the Soviet Union and Vietnam are also believed to contribute. Some money is thought to come from radical Middle Eastern states. As with many Latin American groups, the FMLN conducts kidnapping and ransom operations and collects "taxes" from businesses and private citizens in contested areas. Overseas front or "solidarity" organizations are also an important source of funding.

References: R. Armstrong and J. Shenk, *El Salvador: The Face of Revolution* (Boston: South End Press, 1982); T. S. Montgomery, *Revolution in El Salvador: Origins and Evolution* (Boulder, Colo.: Westview Press, 1982).

FNE (FASCEAUX NATIONALES EUROPEENS)

A French neo-FASCIST organization, founded in the early 1980s. It is considered to be a replacement of FANE, European National Fascists, which was banned by the French government. Like FANE, the FNE is violently rascist and has been responsible for threats and physical attacks against minorities, especially members of the French Jewish community.

Reference: Edward Moxon-Browne, "Terrorism in France," *Conflict Studies* 144 (1983).

FNSA (FRENTE NACIONAL SOCIALISTA ARGENTINO)

Spanish, "Argentine National Socialist Front." A fascist organization very active in the turbulent Argentina of the mid-1970s. The group was violently anti-Semitic and was responsible for a wave of bombings of synagogues in Buenos Aires.

FOCO

The rural guerrilla concept of a revolutionary guerrilla group living as a community, living and raiding as a united entity. The foco, a concept developed by "Che" GUEVARA in Latin America, is believed to be the necessary basis of a successful guerrilla movement.

Reference: Jose Moreno, "Che Guevara on Guerrilla Warfare: Doctrine, Practice and Evaluation," *Comparative Studies in Society and History,* 12 (April 1972).

FORCES POPULARES 25 DE ABRIL

See FP-25.

FORCE 17

A violent Palestinian group formed in the early 1970s as a personal security force for Yasir ARAFAT. In 1985 it began to launch attacks against Israeli targets. In September of that year the organization killed three Israelis in Cyprus believed to be agents of MOSSAD, the Israeli intelligence agency, spying on PLO officials and installations on the island. The Israeli Labor government responded to the attack by launching an air raid on the PLO headquarters in Tunisia, in which several civilians were killed.

FPL (FUERZAS POPULARES DE LIBERACION)

Spanish, "(Farabundo Marti) Popular Revolutionary Forces." One of the constituent left-wing guerrilla groups in the Salvadoran FMLN coalition.

FPMR

See MANUEL RODRIGUEZ PATRIOTIC FRONT.

FP-25 (FORCAS POPULARES 25 DE ABRIL)

A Portuguese left-wing terrorist organization, named for the date in 1974 when the right-wing dictatorship that had led Portugal since 1926 was overthrown. The group seeks the violent overthrow of the Portuguese government and the establishment of a Marxist state. Its stated goals are to "use armed force against imperialism" and to lead a "workers' assault on bourgeois power." It is strongly anti-NATO and anti-American. The group has committed a series of assassinations, bombings and rocket attacks against Portuguese government and economic targets, as well as against American and NATO installations in Portugal.

Few details concerning the organizational structure of the FP-25 are known. In an interview given to a Portuguese Communist Party journalist in 1984, two men who claimed to be FP-25 members said that the group's structure was cellular and that it placed a high degree of emphasis on security. Reportedly only armed militants are allowed to assume leadership positions. Support elements are kept at a distance to minimize the potential for police infiltration.

There is no evidence of extensive foreign support for the FP-25. Press reports have claimed that Portuguese authorities are aware of some financial support from Libya. There also is no evidence of direct ties to other European terrorist groups, despite the fact that the FP-25 had conducted acts of terrorism directed at American, British, French, and West German targets to express solidarity with various groups.

The FP-25's capabilities have been damaged by a series of Portuguese counterterrorist successes, including the arrest of 56 of the group's members in 1984. It is pos-sible that the group is currently reorganizing after a period of disarray.

FRANCIA (FRONT D'ACTION NOUVELLE CONTRE L'INDEPENDENCE ET L'AUTONOMIE)

French, "New Action Front Against Independence and Autonomy." A militant organization that stands in violent opposition to the Corsican separatist movement. Comprised primarily of French settlers on Corsica, FRANCIA seeks to counter the activities of the FLNC and other Corsican separatist groups.

FRANZ FERDINAND (1863–1914)

Archduke of Austria and heir-apparent to the throne of Austria-Hungary, assassinated along with his wife Sophie in Sarejevo on June 28, 1914. His assassin, Gavrilo PRINCIP, was a member of a Serbian nationalist conspiracy, "Young Serbia," which had ties to the Serbian Black Hand organization. The murder of Franz Ferdinand was the pretext for Austria's showdown with Serbia, a seminal incident in the chain of events leading to World War I.

Reference: R. W. Seton-Watson, "The Murder at Sarajevo," *Foreign Affairs* (April 1925).

FRENTE AMERICO SILVIO

The armed wing of the Venezuelan guerrilla organization BANDERA ROJA.

FRENTE CLARA ELIZABETH RAMIREZ

See CLARA ELIZABETH RAMIREZ FRONT.

FRENTE RICARDO FRANCO

See RICARDO FRANCO FRONT.

FRONT DE LIBERATION DU QUEBEC

See FLQ.

FRP-LZ (FUERZAS REVOLUTIONNARIOS POPULARES LORENZO ZELAYA)

Spanish, "Popular Revolutionary Forces-Lorenzo Zelaya." A Honduran leftist guerrilla group formed in 1978. FRP-LZ is engaged in a war on U.S. "imperialism" and on U.S. allies in Honduras. The group has carried out terrorist activities against several foreign embassies. It first surfaced in 1980, and in the early years of the decade it claimed responsibility for numerous bombings in Tegucigalpa, including attacks on U.S. military and commercial facilities. In April 1982 the group bombed the embassies of Argentina and Chile. Reprisals by right-wing DEATH SQUAD and the arrests of several of the FRP-LZ leader in 1983 and 1987 have led to a substantial reduction in the group's activity. FRP-LZ has stated publicly that its members have received training in Nicaragua and Cuba. The estimated membership of the group is 150–300. Also known as FRP.

FUERZA UNIDA REVOLUCIONARIA PRO INDEPENDENCIA ARMADAN

See FALN.

FUERZAS ARMADAS DE LIBERACION NACIONAL

See FALN.

G

GAL (GRUPOS ANTITERRORISTAS DE LIBERACION)

Spanish, "Anti-terrorist Group of Liberation." A right-wing Spanish organization that carries out attacks against members of the Basque ETA movement. Founded in 1983, GAL considers itself an anti-terrorist group. ETA asserts that GAL is at least partially comprised of Spanish police operatives. Many of GAL's "hits" against ETA have occurred in southern France, where there is a large Basque population. In late 1988 questions were raised about the alleged involvement of the government of Spanish prime minister Felipe Gonzalez Marquez in the GAL murders.

Reference: David A. Korn, "State Terrorism: A Spanish Watergate?" *Freedom at Issue* (November–December 1988).

GANDHI, INDIRA (1917–84)

Prime Minister of India, assassinated by her SIKH bodyguards Beant Singh and Satwant Singh on October 31, 1984. Mrs. Gandhi's shooting occurred in a period of extreme tension between the Sikh community and the Indian government resulting from the military's assault on the Sikh GOLDEN TEMPLE OF AMRITSAR. Mrs. Gandhi's death, in turn, caused an outbreak of violence in the northern provinces.

GAZA STRIP

The Arab territory that was occupied, along with the WEST BANK, by Israel during the Six-Day War in 1967. The Gaza Strip is a narrow area bordered by Egypt on the southwest, the Mediterranean Sea on the west, and Israel on the north and east. Its 140 square miles of territory supports a population, mostly Arab, of over half a million. In November 1988 the Gaza Strip was declared part of the independent Palestinian state by the PALESTINIAN NATIONAL COUNCIL. Since December 1987 Gaza and the West Bank have been the scene of the INTIFADA. A large number of PLO leaders come from this area, including the late Khalil al-WAZIR.

Reference: Jamal R. Nassar and Roger Heacock, *Intifada: Palestine at the Crossroads* (New York: Praeger, 1990).

GENOCIDE

Acting with intent to destroy a national, ethnic, racial or religious group; an attempt at wholesale extermination of any category of people by a political authority controlling them. This term was coined by Raphael Lemkin, a Polish-born legal scholar who lost 49 members of his family in the HOLOCAUST. He devoted the remainder of his life to lobbying for international laws against genocide. The word is constructed from the Greek word for "race" and the Latin for word "murder." The United Nations resolution against genocide, passed in 1948, is a result of the tireless lobbying of Lemkin.

References: A. M. Rosenthal, "A Man Called Lemkin," *New York Times* (October 18, 1988); Jack Nusan Porter, ed., *Genocide and Human Rights* (Washington, D.C.: University Press of America, 1982); Israel W. Charney, *How Can We Commit the Unthinkable? Genocide: The Human Cancer* (Boulder, Colo.: Westview Press, 1982).

GEO (GRUPO ESPECIAL DE OPERACIONES)

Spanish, "Special Operations Group." The national anti-terrorist and hostage rescue team of Spain. GEO has a number of successes to its credit, including the dramatic ending of a siege at a bank in Barcelona, where more than 200 hostages were being held by 24 right-wing terrorists in April 1981. In the course of the GEO's rescue, only one hostage was killed.

GEORGE JACKSON BRIGADE

A militant left-wing U.S. organization active in the northwestern United States during the late 1970s. It was named for a black militant who was killed at San Quentin on August 21, 1971. The George Jackson Brigade carried out a series of small-scale thefts and bombings in the western United States. For a sampling of Jackson's philosophy, see his *Blood in My Eye* (New York: Random House, 1972).

GHAWSHAH, SAMIR

See GOSHEH, SAMIR.

GIGN (GROUPEMENT D'INTERVENTION DE LA GENDARERIE NATIONALE)

France's elite anti-terrorist hostage rescue unit (HRU). Formed in 1973, it is now considered to be one of the world's best HRUs. Indeed, it is often used to train HRUs for Third World countries. Its organization is similar to that of the United Kingdom's Special Air Service in that it is small (about 50 members) and trains with the most sophisticated gear.

GIS (GROUPE INTERVENTIONAL SPECIALE)

The primary Italian anti-terrorist hostage rescue unit. While the members of GIS are highly capable, they suffer from poor intelligence backup and a weak national political will to fight terrorism.

GLOCK-17

A plastic pistol with some metal parts. It is of great concern to counterterrorism operations because it might escape detection by X-ray imaging equipment used at airports, especially if it is broken down into its parts. The existence of this pistol, first manufactured in Europe in the 1980s directly led to the passage of the Terrorist Firearms Detection Act of 1988, which amends the Gun Control Act to prohibit the import, manufacture, sale or possession of any firearm: (1) containing less than 3.7 ounces of electromagnetically detectable metal; or (2) of which any major component, when subjected to inspection by x-ray machines commonly used at airports, does not generate an image that accurately depicts the shape of the component.

GOLDEN TEMPLE OF AMRITSAR

The holiest of SIKH shrines, located in Amritsar, in the northern Indian state of Punjab. On June 5–6 1984, the Indian military attacked the Golden Temple in an assault on Sikh extremists led by Jarnail Singh Bhindranwale. More than 500 Sikhs died in the bloody onslaught, and the shrine itself sustained structural damage from artillery fire. Indian army casualties also numbered in the hundreds, and many civilian deaths have also been reported. The assault on the temple signaled the beginning of a new wave of Sikh violence, which culminated in the assassination of Prime Minister Indira GANDHI in October 1984.

GORRIARAN MERLO, ENRIQUE

Argentinian leftist and a leader of the People's Revolutionary Army in the 1970s. On January 23, 1989 Gorriaran Merlo led a guerrilla assault on the Buenos Aires army base at La Tablada, in which 21 people were killed. He is also thought to have been involved in the 1980 assassination of deposed Nicaraguan strongman Anastasio Somoza Debayle in Paraguay.

GOSHEH, SAMIR

Leader of the Palestinian POPULAR STRUGGLE FRONT, a splinter group of the PFLP, formed after Gosheh's split with George HABASH in the late 1960s. He is considered to be among the "Syrian camp" of Palestinian leaders but is thought to be a more independent leader than other Syrian-aligned figures such as Ahmed JABRIL.

GRAND MOSQUE

Also known as the Great Mosque. The Mosque is the holiest of all Islamic shrines.

Located in Mecca, Saudi Arabia, it houses the Kaaba, the Muslim holy of holies, toward which all Muslims face in prayer. On November 20, 1979, while the Mosque was filled with religious pilgrims, it was seized by a large band of armed Sunni fundamentalists. The attack sent a shock through the Islamic world. After a five-day siege, several thousand Saudi troops and police assaulted the massive structure, retaking it after a bloody room-to-room battle with the well-armed terrorists. In the end, 127 people were killed and 451 injured.

Reference: Robin Wright, *Sacred Rage* (New York: Simon & Schuster, 1985).

GRAPO (GRUPO DE RESISTENCIA ANTIFASCISTA, PRIMERO DE OCTUBRE)

Spanish, "October 1st Anti-fascist Resistance Group." A Maoist urban terrorist group in Spain which is dedicated to the removal of U.S. and NATO military installations from Spanish soil, and to the establishment of a revolutionary regime. Formed in 1975, GRAPO has committed assassinations, bombings and kidnappings against Spanish personnel and facilities. The group has preferred ambushes using automatic weapons. Like ETA, the Basque terrorist group operating in Spain, GRAPO has financed its operations through kidnap ransoms, bank robberies and the extortion of "revolutionary taxes," from individuals and businesses. Direct ties between GRAPO and foreign terrorist groups or state sponsors have not been established. GRAPO, however, has made public statements in support of a number of other terrorist groups, including the German RED ARMY FACTION and the Italian RED BRIGADES.

The group is organized in a cellular structure for maximum internal security. These cells are probably quite small, in view of the group's estimated membership of less than 25. These members fall into one of two categories. "Legal Commandos," whose identities are unknown to Spanish authorities, lead outwardly normal lives, periodically carrying out terrorist activities. "Liberated Commandos" are full-time terrorists and are forced to live underground, as their identities are known to the police.

GRAPO surfaced in 1977, when it abducted two senior members of the Spanish military command. Later that year it bombed a U.S. Cultural Center on the day Vice President Walter Mondale arrived for an official visit. In 1979 the group killed eight people and wounded 40 in a bomb attack on a Madrid café frequented by rightists. In the early 1980s GRAPO carried out several bombings against U.S. and NATO bases. A government sting operation in January 1985 netted many of the group's members, rendering GRAPO inactive for several years. In 1987 the group resurfaced in a machine-gun attack at a national police station. In 1988 members were reportedly responsible for the murder of a prominent banking executive in May and the shooting of a Madrid police officer in October.

GREAT MOSQUE

See GRAND MOSQUE.

GREAT TERROR

Joseph Stalin's period of upheaval of Soviet society and politics from 1935–1938. Widespread terror was employed as a means of tightening Stalin's autocratic control of the Soviet Union. The Communist Party was "purged" of those individuals perceived to be competitors of Stalin. The Great Terror spanned social and political divisions, encompassing common Soviet citizens as well

as most of the Central Committee. Millions were sent to the GULAGS or to prisons, and hundreds of thousands were executed. The Soviet military was especially hard hit, losing the great majority of its officer corps.

The Great Terror was implemented by Stalin's secret police, the NKVD. "Show trials" were utilized to discredit public figures. The terroristic nature of the purges left Stalin with a bowed and broken Soviet Union, Soviet Army, and Communist Party, all entirely under his personal control.

References: Robert W. Thurston, "Fear and Belief in the USSR's 'Great Terror'," *Slavic Review* 45 (Summer 1986); Robert Conquest, *The Great Terror* (New York, 1968).

GREEN LINE

1. The line in Nicosia, Cyprus, dividing the Greek Cypriot and Turkish Cypriot sectors. The line was established in 1963 following an outbreak of fighting between the two communities.

2. The line separating warring Christian and Muslim factions in Beirut, Lebanon.

GREENSBORO FIVE

Five members of the U.S. Communist Worker's Party (CWP) slain by the KU KLUX KLAN and other far-right radicals at a CWP demonstration in Greensboro, North Carolina on November 3, 1979. The demonstration, specifically billed as a "Death to the Klan" march, occurred in the southern city, Greensboro, that was the location of the first lunch-counter "sit-ins" of the civil rights movement in 1960. The police arrested 12 men associated with the Klan and charged them with various counts of murder and conspiracy to commit murder. In 1980 six of the Klan members involved in the shooting were tried and acquitted by an all-white jury.

References: Nan Chase, "Klan Marches at Scene of 1979 Killings," *Washington Post* (June 8, 1987); William E. Schmidt, "Jim Crow is Gone, But White Resistance Remains," *New York Times* (April 6, 1985).

GREY WOLVES

The ultra-right-wing Turkish youth movement of the National Action Party, which is dedicated to the extinguishing of all leftist institutions and influences in Turkey. The Grey Wolves evolved from a student strong-arm society of the early 1970s to become a terrorist organization carrying out assassinations by the end of the decade. The murderer of Turkish newspaper editor Abdi Ipekci was Grey Wolf member Mehmet Ali AGCA, who later tried to assassinate Pope John Paul II.

Reference: Dietrich Orlow, "Political Violence in Pre-Coup Turkey," *Terrorism 6*, no. 1 (1982).

GSG-9 (GRENZCHUTZGRUPPE 9)

The West German elite anti-terrorist force. GSG-9 was established following the tragedy of the MUNICH MASSACRE at the 1972 Olympics. On October 17, 1977, GSG-9 staged a hugely successful anti-terrorist operation at Mogadishu, Somalia, as it freed 91 hostages held aboard a hijacked Lufthansa airliner. GSG-9 is considered to be one of the best hostage rescue units in the world, in part because it is backed up by one of the best intelligence systems.

GUARDIANS OF THE ISLAMIC REVOLUTION

A pro-Iranian Shi'ite extremist terrorist organization. The group first came to light in 1980 when it claimed responsibility for bombings at a Rome industrial facility. In May 1987 the group asserted responsibility for the shootings of two anti-KHOMEINI dissidents and the wounding of a former official in the Shah's government. The Guardians are believed to have been responsible for the murder in May 1988 of a West German banker who was identified with the Iraqi military effort. Also in 1988 the group killed a former minister in the Shah's government and a Palestinian cartoonist in London. The group is known to claim responsibility for acts which it almost certainly has not committed, such as the bombing on December 21, 1988, of PAN AM 103.

GUATEMALA

During the period of military rule in this Central American country from 1954 until 1986, there were an estimated 26,000 victims of government terror, much of it carried out by DEATH SQUADS with ties to the military. The government of President Julio Cesar Mendez Montenegro took office in 1966 and upon assuming power launched a major counterinsurgency campaign that largely broke up the rural guerrilla movements running rampant in Guatemala during the early and mid-1960s. The guerrillas, with a leftist orientation, demanding land reform and political freedom, then concentrated their activities in urban areas, especially Guatemala City. The succeeding government of General Carlos Arana (1970–74) declared a state of siege and carried out a fierce counterterrorist strategy. Political violence decreased under the administration of General Laugerud Garcia (1974–78), and civil rights enjoyed a temporary resurgence.

The government of General Fernando Romero Lucas Garcia (1978–82) witnessed a return to both left-wing guerrilla violence and state-sponsored violent reaction. During this period, right-wing extremist groups such as the Secret Anti-Communist Army (ESA) and the WHITE HAND tortured and murdered students, professionals and peasants whom they considered to be involved in or sympathetic to leftist activities. These death squads are thought to have had substantial connections to the police and military forces of Guatemala. The government of Rios Montt, who succeeded to power in 1982, instituted a system of secret courts and brutal anti-subversive tactics. He was deposed in 1983. Government forces were primarily responsible for the deaths of many thousands of Indians, while the right-wing death squads directed their violence against "opponents" of the government. The Christian Democratic Party was especially hard hit by the right-wing, government-condoned terror.

Since the re-establishment of civilian rule in 1986, state-condoned terror has decreased, although there are still reports of military abuse of the destitute rural Indian population. Recent reports indicate that the military is no longer involved in death squad activities.

References: Stephen Kinzer, "Guatemala: What Has Democracy Wrought?", *The New York Times Magazine* (March 26, 1989); Victor Montejo, *Testimony: Death of a Guatemalan Village*, translated by Victor Parera (New York: Talman Co., 1987); Peter Ford, "After Years of Civilian Rule, Guatemalan Death Squads Still Active," *Christian Science Monitor* (March 23, 1987); Cheryl A. Rubenberg, "Israel in Central America: Arms, Aid and Counterinsurgency," *MERIP*, 16 (May–June 1986); Colman McCarthy, "Facing the Hor-

ror in Guatemala," *Washington Post* (October 20, 1985).

GUATEMALAN NATIONAL REVOLUTIONARY UNITY (URNG)

A loose coalition of three of the major Guatemalan insurgent groups using terrorist tactics: the Revolutionary Organization of the People in Arms (ORPA), the Guerrilla Army of the Poor (EGP), and the Rebel Armed Forces (FAR). The three groups signed a unity agreement that was a precondition for increased Cuban support in 1980, and the URNG was formalized in Havana in 1982. As a result, the government of Guatemala launched a large counteroffensive in an attempt to eliminate the guerrillas' popular support. By the end of that year, the guerrillas were on the defensive and decreased activity for the next two years. In February 1985 the coalition announced a "new stage of military struggle" but showed no evidence of being able to expand their operations. Cooperation and coordination among the groups is incomplete and irregular. Nonetheless, the URNG stresses joint political-military operations and coordination among its member groups on matters pertaining to territorial responsibilities, tactics, strategy and external support. Cooperation among groups seems to work best in rural areas, mainly between the ORPA and the FAR.

Cuba in the past has made significant arms supplies to the coalition, but in recent years Cuban support is thought to have been limited to minor financial aid for black-market arms purchases. All three of the member groups are strongly anti-U.S., though most of their activities have been directed against the Guatemalan Army.

The FAR, the oldest and most established of the organizations, seems to recover rapidly from serious losses, although it has not been as severely threatened as have the ORPA and the EGP. When guerrilla activity is too difficult to undertake, the FAR seems the most willing to resort to terrorist operations to remind the country that it still exists. UNRG has an estimated 1,500 members, as well as active delegations in Mexico City, Havana and Managua. The coalition operates mainly in rural regions of the country, with the ORPA in the southwest, the EGP mainly in the northwest highlands and the FAR in the extreme north ("the Peten").

GUERRILLA FORCES OF LIBERATION (GFL)

A Puerto Rican separatist organization that was unknown until it claimed responsibility for a series of bomb placements in Puerto Rico on May 25, 1987. Eight crude pipe bombs were placed at seven locations on that day and four were detonated, causing minimal damage and no injuries.

GUERRILLA WARFARE

Military operations conducted by irregular troops against conventional government forces. The term was first used to refer to the Spanish partisans who fought against Napoleon's troops in the early 1800s, but any armed uprising by the people of a nation against their perceived oppressors is today considered to be guerrilla warfare.

Because guerrilla troops do not follow normal battle tactics or use standard weapons systems in open combat, they are much more difficult for regular battle troops to control. By never forming into large units and allowing themselves to be trapped into fighting pitched battles, guerrillas are able to avoid the damage that the massed fire-power and superior numbers of a regular army could inflict. Very large armies can have their effective personnel substantially reduced when forced to garrison hundreds of villages and towns and to send guard detachments with every supply convoy. It is widely believed that a drawn-out guerrilla war will prove the undoing and eventual defeat of an orthodox army, but history provides little evidence for this. The Napoleonic armies were only defeated by Wellington's British army, and the French Resistance was of use only in support of the 1944 Allied invasion. The U.S. Army was almost invariably successful in actual operations against the Vietcong, which was almost completely destroyed in the 1968 Tet Offensive; thereafter it was the regular army of North Vietnam which the Americans were fighting, an army that had already shown its worth in the entirely orthodox campaign against the French in 1954.

The reason for the apparent success of guerrilla warfare is that it is usually practiced in countries where a foreign "army of occupation" has no support among the indigenous population. Although there is generally no significant military success, the costs of continuing to garrison a foreign country and maintain a presence by force is often too much for the political will of the occupying power, which may decide to withdraw, or to accommodate the guerrilla leaders, although militarily undefeated.

It was China's Mao Zedong who summed up the essence of guerrilla strategy: "The enemy advances, we retreat; the enemy camps, we harass; the enemy tires, we attack; the enemy retreats, we pursue." And it was former U.S. Secretary of State Henry Kissinger who summed up its result: "The conventional army loses if it does not win. The guerrilla wins if he does not lose." (*Foreign Affairs* 13 [January 1969]).

References: Gerard Chaliand, *Guerrilla Strategies: A Historical Anthology from the Long March to Afghanistan* (Berkeley: University of California Press, 1982); John J. Tierney, Jr., "America's Forgotten Wars: Guerrilla Campaigns in U.S. History," *Conflict: An International Journal for Conflict and Policy Studies* 2 (1980); Richard Schultz, "The Limits of Terrorism in Insurgency Warfare: The Case of the Viet Cong," *Polity* 11 (Fall 1978); Burton M. Leiser, "Terrorism, Guerrilla Warfare, and International Morality," *Stanford Journal of International Studies* 12 (Spring 1977); Walter Laqueur, "The Origins of Guerrilla Doctrine," *Journal of Contemporary History* 10 (July 1975); Thomas O. Schelsinger, "The Army and the Guerrilla," *Polity* 4 (Spring 1972).

GUERRILLA WARFARE, RURAL

Revolutionary guerrilla tactics and strategy designed to foment popular rebellion in the rural areas of underdeveloped nations in the interest of overthrowing the political status quo and establishing a revolutionary government. Rural guerrilla theory looks to the countryside as the vanguard of the revolution and has as its model the Cuban revolution of Fidel CASTRO and Che GUEVARA. Guevara and Regis DEBRAY stand as the two foremost theorists of revolution through rural uprising. The FOCO, the concept of a revolutionary guerrilla group living as a community, of living and raiding as a united entity, forms the basis of rural guerrilla theory and is the essence of a successful guerrilla movement. Rural guerrilla insurgency theory finds value in urban insurgencies, but only as complements to the primary revolutionary thrust of rural guerrilla warfare.

Reference: Regis Debray, *Revolution in the Revolution* (New York: Grove Press, 1967).

GUERRILLA WARFARE, URBAN

Revolutionary guerrilla tactics and strategy practiced in urban and metropolitan settings, utilizing armed attacks, assassinations, kidnappings and robberies as means of upsetting the political status quo and establishing a revolutionary state. The evolution of modern urban guerrilla practice and theory is in large part a function of the decline and defeat of many of the rural-based Latin American insurgencies of the 1960s. By the late 1960s, rural guerrilla movements in Colombia, Bolivia and Guatemala, among others, were displaying symptoms of collapse and strategic failure. Leftist revolutionaries in Brazil, Uruguay and Argentina found that urban strategies offered many improvements over the rural insurgencies advocated by Che GUEVARA, Regis DEBRAY and other more traditional theorists. Urban warfare seemed to offer more accessible targets, improved sources of supplies and funds and an expanded recruiting pool. Urban areas contain most of the students and intelligentsia of a nation, which comprise the greatest percentage of Marxist devotees.

The father of modern urban guerrilla thought is Abraham GUILLEN, who wrote *Philosophy of the Urban Guerrilla*. He was a primary influence on Carlos MARIGHELLA, author of *The Mini-manual of the Urban Guerrilla*, a "how-to" book that became very popular with Latin American revolutionaries in the late 1960s and the 1970s. The Uruguayan TUPAMAROS were the first guerrilla group to recognize the potential of the urban area as a focus of revolutionary activity, rather than simply a complement to the rural struggle. They found the urban strategy to be an ideal method of provoking the government into repressive counterinsurgency measures. It was the Tupamaros' goal—and it remains a goal of the urban guerrilla today—to provoke the authorities into taking actions that could incite the general population into mass rebellion. The Tupamaros' goal was only partially met, for although they succeeded in provocation, their urban guerrilla strategy so weakened the Uruguayan civilian government that the military assumed control of the country and destroyed the Tupamaros through an intense campaign of repression.

See NEW PEOPLE'S ARMY; ERP.

References: Richard Gillespie, "The Urban Guerrilla in Latin America," in *Terrorism, Ideology, and Revolution,* Noel O'Sullivan, ed. (Worcester, U.K.: Harvester Press, 1986); James A. Miller, "Urban Terrorism in Uruguay: The Tupamaros," in Brad E. O'Neill, *et al.,* eds., *Insurgency in the Modern World* (Boulder, Colo.: Westview Press, 1980); Anthony M. Burton, *Urban Terrorism: Theory, Practice and Response* (New York: Free Press, 1975); J. Kohl and J. Litt, eds., *Urban Guerrilla Warfare in Latin America* (Cambridge, Mass.: MIT Press, 1974).

GUEVARA, ERNESTO ("CHE") (1928–67)

Legendary guerrilla leader, born in Argentina, who fought with Fidel CASTRO in the Cuban revolution. He is one of the most influential of revolutionary theorists, and his treatise *The Guerrilla War* has become a standard among modern revolutionaries, especially in Latin America. Guevara became one of the leaders of Castro's Cuba after the successful overthrow of Batista, but in 1965 he left Cuba to foment and lead revolutionary guerrilla movements elsewhere. In October 1967 he was captured by Bolivian government forces and executed.

See also FOCO.

References: Donald C. Hodges, *The Legacy of Che Guevara* (London: Thames and Hudson, 1977); Jose Moreno, "Che Guevara on Guerrilla Warfare: Doctrine, Practice and Evaluation," *Comparative Studies in Society and History* 12 (April 1970); Robert F. Lamberg, "Che in Bolivia: The "Revolution' That Failed," *Problems of Communism* 19 (July–August 1970); Martin Ebon, *Che: The Making of a Legend* (New York: Signet, 1969).

GUILLEN, ABRAHAM

Latin American revolutionary, leftist theorist and author. Born in Guadalajara, Mexico to a peasant family, he became, during the 1960s, one of the earliest and most influential proponents of Marxist urban guerrilla warfare. His influence was particularly great among the TUPAMAROS of Uruguay and the ERP of Argentina.

Reference: Abraham Guillen, *Philosophy of the Urban Guerrilla,* edited by Donald C. Hodges (New York: William Morrow, 1973).

GULAG

Term for the system of government prison camps and forced labor camps of the Soviet Union. The Soviet dissident Alexandr Solzhenitsyn traces the gulag system to Lenin, but it was under Stalin that the brutal system reached its terrifying zenith. Solzhenitsyn himself was sent to a gulag for referring to Stalin as "the man with the mustache" in personal correspondence. Gulag is the Russian acronym for Chief Administration of Corrective Labor Camps. The term gulag came into English with the publication of Solzhenitsyn's *Gulag Archipelago* in 1974. This was the first major account of the horrors of prison labor camps in the Soviet Union. The gulag killed millions of innocent people. Major groupings of victims include peasants during Stalin's collectivization drive; millions more sentenced during the purges of the 1930s; and returning Soviet prisoners of war from World War II deemed "traitors to the fatherland" for not having died for their country. The gulag was part of the Soviet plan for economic development; convict labor built up Siberia, Central Asia and the Far North. Prisoners were often taken and sentenced just to fulfill labor quotas. According to Solzhenitsyn, an estimated 13 to 25 million died because of the harsh conditions in these labor camps.

See also GREAT TERROR.

Reference: Steven Rosefielde, "An Assessment of the Sources and Uses of Gulag Forced Labour, 1929–1956," *Soviet Studies* 33 (January 1981).

GUSH EMUNIM

Hebrew, "The Bloc of the Faithful." An Israeli right-wing, strictly orthodox organization, founded in 1974 and dedicated to the permanent and formal annexation of the Israeli-occupied Arab territories. This organization was responsible for much of the Israeli terrorism carried out on the West Bank in the early 1980s, including bombings that injured the Arab mayors of Nablus and Ramallah. The group continues to call for the expansion of Jewish settlements in the occupied territories and the expulsion of the Arab population from their homes.

References: Kevin Avruch, "Gush Emunim: The 'Iceberg Model' of Extremism Reconsidered," *Middle East Review* 21 (Fall 1988); David Newman, ed., *The Impact of Gush Emunim: Politics and Settlement of the West Bank* (New York: St. Martin's Press, 1985); Robert I. Friedman, "Where Gush and Kash Get Their Cash," *Middle East International* 273 (April 18, 1986).

GUZMAN, ABIMAEL

Former college professor, and founder and leader of SENDERO LUMINOSO, the violent Peruvian guerrilla organization. In July 1988 he offered the Lima newspaper *El Diaro* his first interview in a decade, in which he reiterated his commitment to Maoist revolutionary dogma. He also stated categorically that Sendero Luminoso would not enter the political process and would do all that it could to disrupt the electoral system.

Reference: David Scott Palmer, "Rebellion in Rural Peru: The Origins and Evolution of Sendero Luminoso," *Comparative Politics* 18 (January 1986).

H

HABASH, GEORGE

Leader of the POPULAR FRONT FOR THE LIB-
ERATION OF PALESTINE (PFLP), one of the
most radical groups in the PLO. He was born
in Lydda, now the city of Lod, Israel, to a
Greek Orthodox Christian family. A medical doctor, he earned his degree at the
American University in Beirut. Habash is a
staunch Arab nationalist and Marxist-Leninist. He is called "al-Hakim" by his followers, which means "physician and wise man."

Habash founded the PFLP in 1968. It is
now the second largest group in the PLO.
The PFLP, under Habash's direction, conducted some of the most infamous of Palestinian terrorist acts, including the DAW-
SON'S FIELD incident, which led to the BLACK
SEPTEMBER ouster of the Palestinian guerrilla
groups from Jordan. His organization has
provided training and support for international terrorists from around the globe. He
has often proven to be the nemesis of Yasir
ARAFAT, whom he finds too prone to compromise; the hard-line Habash is Arafat's
most serious leadership rival. Habash was
the leader of the REJECTIONIST FRONT within
the PLO and is motivated by a leftist ideology in a way that Arafat is not. Habash
supported the PALESTINIAN NATIONAL
COUNCIL's declaration in 1988 of Palestinian
statehood, but he has stated that he does
not consider Arafat's renunciation of terrorism to be official PLO policy. He remains
firmly opposed to the recognition of Israel.
His strongest state supporters are SYRIA and
LIBYA, and more recently, IRAQ. In 1980
Habash suffered a massive stroke, and his
health has remained a persistent question
in recent years.

References: Abu Khalil As'ad, "Internal
Contradiction in the PFLP: Decision Making
and Policy Determination," *The Middle East
Journal* 4 (Summer 1987); Walid W. Kazziha,
*Revolutionary Transformation in the Arab World:
Habash and his Comrades from Nationalism to
Marxism* (New York: St. Martin's Press, 1975);
Oriana Fallaci, "A Leader of Fedayeen: 'Why
We Want a War Like the Vietnam War':
Interview with George Habash," *Life* (June
12, 1970).

HAGUE CONVENTION, THE

Official name: Convention for the Suppression of Unlawful Seizure of Aircraft, of the
United Nations International Civil Aviation
Organization. The convention was signed
at The Hague on December 16, 1970. It is
the main international agreement that deals
specifically with seizure of aircraft in flight.
It defines the offense and obliges each signatory state to make it punishable by "severe penalties." Thus each state must make
aircraft hijacking a part of its domestic crim-

inal law. While 130 countries have signed this convention, none of them is obliged to extradite a hijacker except under the terms of a separate extradition treaty. This means that extradition of hijackers may still be refused on the basis of provisions in a treaty that exclude extradition for political offenses or deny the extradition of a state's own citizens.

See BONN DECLARATION; MONTREAL CONVENTION.

Reference: Geoffrey M. Levitt, *Democracies Against Terror* (New York: Praeger, 1988).

HAMAH

A city in SYRIA, long a hotbed of activity against Syria's president, Hafez al-ASSAD. On February 2, 1982 Assad ordered the Syrian army to crush the opposition group MUSLIM BROTHERHOOD by attacking its base at HAMAH. Over a two-week span much of the city was leveled and an estimated 25,000 civilians were killed. Several thousand members of the Muslim Brotherhood were estimated to have been killed. What is certain is that the Brotherhood lost Hamah as a base of support. The Hamah incident also caused Syria to break diplomatic relations with Iraq later in 1982; Syria accused Iraq of supporting the Brotherhood's efforts to destabilize the Syrian regime.

Reference: Fred H. Lawson, "Social Bases for the Hamah Revolt," *MERIP Reports* 12 (November–December 1982).

HAMMAMI, SAID

PLO representative to London who was assassinated on January 5, 1978 by a member of the BLACK JUNE group of the ABU NIDAL Organization. The motive for the assassination was the perception within the Abu Nidal Organization that Yasir ARAFAT was

compromising his negotiating position for the PLO by dealing indirectly with the United States through Hammami.

HAMZA

The popular name of Hamza al-Hamieh, a radical SHI'ITE terrorist and military commander of the AMAL militia in Lebanon. Hamza is a militant and charismatic follower of Imam Musa al-SADR; after the Imam's failure to return from a trip to Libya in September 1978, Hamza led a campaign to obtain the release of his spiritual leader, whom most experts believe was killed by the Libyan leader Muammar al-QADAFFI. Hamza and his "Sons of Musa al-Sadr" staged six hijackings to attract popular attention to the plight of al-Sadr. The most recent and spectacular of these was the seizure on February 24, 1982 of a Kuwaiti Airways jet at Beirut International Airport. He also led attacks against the U.S. peacekeeping forces in LEBANON in 1984. Hamza is perhaps the most influential of the younger generation of radical Shi'ites in Lebanon.

HARIRI, HUSSEIN ALI MOHAMMED

Lebanese SHI'ITE terrorist, convicted of murdering a passenger during the hijacking of an Air Afrique jetliner on July 24, 1987. Hariri, affiliated with and trained by HEZBOLLAH, had explosives strapped to his body when he hijacked the plane in an effort to force the release of imprisoned fellow terrorists. He was sentenced to life imprisonment by a Swiss court in February 1989.

HASI, AHMAD

Convicted, along with a fellow Arab conspirator, in the March 29, 1986 bombing of the West Berlin German-Arab Friendship Union, in which 11 were injured. He named the Syrian embassy as the source of his explosive device. Hasi is the brother of another convicted terrorist, Nazir HINDAWI.

See also LA BELLE DISCO.

HASSAN, KHALED AL-

A senior member of al-FATAH and advisor to Yasir ARAFAT. Born in Haifa, Israel, Hassan is considered to be an intellectual leader of al-Fatah and part of the moderate PLO braintrust.

HAWARI, COLONEL

The pseudonym of Abdullah Hamid Labib, leader of the MAY 15 GROUP. A former bodyguard to Yasir ARAFAT, Hawari was the leader of the PLO's Special Operations Group. He is best known for his 1982 bombing of a Pan Am flight from Tokyo to Honolulu, in which one person was killed.

HAWATMEH, NAIF

One of the cofounders of the POPULAR FRONT FOR THE LIBERATION OF PALESTINE (PFLP), he soon broke away and formed his own group, the DEMOCRATIC FRONT FOR THE LIBERATION OF PALESTINE (DFLP). Born in Salt, Jordan, to a Greek Orthodox family, he studied psychology at the Arab University in Beirut. He was the first major Palestinian leader to publicly call for a Palestinian state in the Israeli-occupied Arab territories (1974) of the West Bank and Gaza.

Reference: William Quandt *et al., The Politics of Palestinian Nationalism* (Berkeley: University of California Press, 1973).

HEARST, PATRICIA

The young heiress to the Hearst media empire kidnapped by the SYMBIONESE LIBERATION ARMY (SLA) in Berkeley, California on February 4, 1974. Months of subsequent brainwashing eventually converted her into an active member of the left-wing group, and she took the revolutionary name "Tania." She was arrested by the FBI in August 1975 for her role in the armed robbery of a San Francisco bank, convicted in Federal District Court in 1976, and later sentenced to seven years imprisonment. Her sentence was commuted by President Jimmy Carter in September 1979. She later married her former police bodyguard, Bernard Shaw. Her abduction, conversion and tribulations were one of the major terrorist media stories of the decade. On August 4, 1988 Mrs. Shaw's lawyer filed a petition for a full presidential pardon; the request was denied by outgoing president Ronald Reagan.

References: Marilyn Baker, *Exclusive! The Inside Story of Patricia Hearst and the SLA* (New York: Macmillan, 1974); Shana Alexander, *Anyone's Daughter* (New York: Viking, 1979).

HELSINKI AGREEMENT

Refers to the Final Act of the Conference on Security and Cooperation in Europe signed on August 1, 1975 by the United States, Canada, and 33 European countries (including the Soviet Union) in Helsinki, Finland. The Final Act is not a treaty and is not legally binding, yet it carries considerable moral weight because it was signed by the heads of government. The agreement included an endorsement of human rights which has become controversial because of its "observance in the breach" by Soviet Bloc countries, prior to the recent revolutions that ended Soviet domination in Eastern Europe.

References: Harold Molineu, "Negotiating Human Rights: The Helsinki Agreement," *World Affairs* 141 (Summer 1978); Arthur J. Goldberg and James S. Fay, "Human Rights in the Wake of the Helsinki Accords," *Hastings International and Comparative Law Review* 3 (Fall 1979); Margaret E. Galey, "Congress, Foreign Policy, and Human Rights Ten Years After Helsinki," *Human Rights Quarterly* 7 (August 1985).

HEZBOLLAH

Arabic, "The Party of God" or "The Party of Allah." A radical SHI'ITE organization founded in 1978 and devoted to the establishment of a fundamentalist Islamic state in Lebanon and the destruction of all non-Islamic institutions in that nation. Hezbollah is largely influenced by the Islamic revolution in Iran. Amir Taheri, in *Holy Terror* (1987), wrote that Hezbollah was motivated by two main concepts: a leadership seen to represent Allah's will on earth (in the person of the Ayatollah Khomeini until his death in 1989) and a very personal concept of MARTYRDOM. Iran's REVOLUTIONARY GUARDS have provided Hezbollah with political indoctrination, financing and material support.

Hezbollah is an amorphous organization by Western standards, loose-knit and quite informal. It is believed to have been formed in 1982. The group is vehemently anti-American and anti-Israeli, and much of Hezbollah's terrorist activity has been directed against U.S. and Israeli targets. By 1984 Hezbollah had effectively absorbed all of the other Lebanese extremist Shi'ite factions. One member is quoted in Robin Wright's *Sacred Rage* (1985) as saying that "every believer who fights Israel in the south and who defends the honor of the Muslims in Beirut or the Bekaa Valley and has links with the Islamic revolution belongs to [Hezbollah]. . . ." It is widely supposed that the terrorists who have carried out the deadly

missions of the shadowy ISLAMIC JIHAD have been tied to Hezbollah. In 1985 and 1986 Hezbollah joined forces with Palestinian guerrillas and battled the more moderate Shi'ite AMAL militia in Beirut. Israeli security forces in October 1988 were the victims of a Hezbollah suicide attack in which eight Israeli soldiers died. Hostage taking is a major component of Hezbollah terrorism, and the U.S. Department of State believes that the group is responsible for most if not all of the Western hostages being held in Lebanon at this time. The membership of Hezbollah is thought to number in the thousands.

References: Robin Wright, *Sacred Rage* (New York: Simon & Schuster, 1985); Helena Cobban, "The Growth of Shi'ite Power in Lebanon and Its Implications for the Future," in Juan Cole and Nikki Keddie, ed., *Shi'ism and Social Protest* (New Haven: Yale University Press, 1986).

HIGGINS, LT. COL. WILLIAM R.

A U.S. Marine and a member of the multinational peacekeeping force in Lebanon. Higgins was taken hostage in February 1988 as he drove along a highway outside the city of Sidon. He was murdered on or about July 31, 1989 by his terrorist captors in retaliation for the Israeli kidnapping on July 27, 1989 of HEZBOLLAH leader Sheikh Abdel Karim Obeid. The killers provided graphic proof that they had carried out their death threat in the form of a videotape which showed the lifeless body of Higgins slowly twisting at the end of a rope.

HIGHER LAW

The notion that no matter what the laws of a state may be, there remains a "higher" law to which individuals have an even greater obligation. A "higher" law is often appealed to by those who wish to attack an existing law or practice that courts or legislators are unlikely or unwilling to change. Martyrs throughout the ages have asserted that they adhere to a higher law in defiance of the state, thereby earning their martyrdom. The classic presentation of this concept is in the play *Antigone*, by the Greek playwright Sophocles (496–406 B.C.). The heroine, Antigone, defies the king, asserts a higher law as her justification, and "forces" the king to have her killed for her defiance. Because the courts of any state will only enforce the law of the land, appealing to a higher law puts one at risk of punishment. Examples of Americans who have appealed to a "higher" law and gone to jail as a result are Henry David Thoreau, for resisting a tax; Martin Luther King Jr., for flaunting segregationist laws; and conscientious objectors who served time in jails rather than serve in the U.S. military during the Vietnam War.

HINDAWI, NIZAR

A Jordanian convicted in Great Britain for plotting to use his pregnant British girlfriend as the unwitting carrier of a suitcase bomb, intended to destroy an EL AL airliner with 375 people aboard on April 17, 1985. The plot was foiled at an airport security checkpoint. Hindawi's Syrian connections were soon exposed, including his recruitment by Syrian Air Force personnel, Syrian funding, a passport provided by Syria, and his use of the Syrian Embassy in London as a safe house after the incident. Hindawi's brother, Ahmad HASI, is also a convicted terrorist with ties to Syria.

HOFFMAN MILITARY SPORTS GROUP (WEHRSPORTGRUPPE HOFFMAN)

A violent West German right-wing paramilitary organization, founded by Karl Heinz Hoffman during the 1970s. This group is a NEO-NAZI group with a penchant for military training. The group has been suppressed by West German authorities since 1980, the year in which its founder was linked to the killing of a Jewish publisher. Members of the organization are believed to have trained in FATAH bases in Lebanon and to have participated in Palestinian operations in Beirut.

At the 1980 Munich Oktoberfest, a bomb belonging to the Sports Group exploded prematurely, killing 12 people (including the terrorist responsible for it) and injuring more than 200 others.

Reference: Peter H. Merkyl, "Rollerball or Neo-Nazi Violence," in *Political Violence and Terror* (Berkeley: University of California Press, 1986).

HOLOCAUST

NAZI Germany's systematic persecution and murder of European Jews from 1933 to 1945, and the foremost act of terror of the 20th century. State-condoned and directed persecution of Jews began soon after the rise to power of Adolf Hitler in 1933, although many authorities date the beginning of the Holocaust from the 1938 KRISTALLNACHT. Many German Jews fled the country; millions of those who remained behind were interned in CONCENTRATION CAMPS. Hitler's "final solution" to the Nazis' so-called "Jewish problem" was the wholesale extermination of European Jews. By the end of World War II, an estimated 6,000,000 Jews had died in the Holocaust.

HOME GUARD

The Norwegian military's anti-terrorist force, created in 1988. The Home Guard is reportedly modeled on the Soviet Union's SPETSNAZ special forces.

HOSTAGE

1. A person held against his will by captors who seek to secure certain terms in exchange for his release.

2. General term for the Western hostages currently being held in Lebanon. As of late 1990 there are believed to be six Americans and perhaps as many more Europeans of various nationalities held by an assortment of terrorist groups in Lebanon. An American, Terry Anderson, an Associated Press correspondent, has been held the longest, having been originally kidnapped in March 1985. Other Americans, with their date of abduction, include: Thomas M. Sutherland (June 1985), Joseph J. Cicippio (September 1986), Edward A. Tracy (October 1986), Jesse Turner (January 1987) and Alann Steen (January 1987). Robert Polhill (January 1987) and Frank H. Reed (September 1986) were released in 1989 and 1990, respectively, the first for health reasons and the second due to intervention of the Syrian government.

HRU (HOSTAGE RESCUE UNIT)

General term for a specially trained and equipped anti-terrorist strike force, with particular expertise in the safe rescue of hostages. Well-known HRUs include the U.S. Delta Force, the French GIGN, and the West German GSG-9.

Reference: Leroy Thompson, *The Rescuers: The World's Top Anti-Terrorist Units* (Devon, U.K.: David and Charles, 1986).

HUKS

Diminutive of "Hukbalahap," a guerrilla organization in the Philippines during the 1940s and early 1950s. The Huks were originally formed to oppose the occupation of the Japanese Army. After the end of World War II, the group fought the Philippine Army, which was widely considered to be the corrupt military establishment of a contemptible regime. The Huk insurgency is credited with helping to usher in the governmental and social reforms of the early 1950s. The Huks were dissolved in the mid-1950s.

HUMAN RIGHTS

1. Minimal rights to which all people are entitled as humans. In 1948 the United Nations adopted a Universal Declaration of Human Rights to establish a "common standard of achievement for all peoples and all nations." But since this declaration was never legally binding (among other reasons), it has not been widely implemented.

2. Whatever rights and privileges are given or guaranteed to a people by its government.

3. A U.S. foreign policy initiative of the Carter administration (1976–80) which called for all people (a) to be free from government-sponsored physical violence; (b) to have such vital needs as food, shelter, health care, and education; and (c) to enjoy civil and political liberties.

See HELSINKI AGREEMENT.

References: David P. Forsythe, "The United Nations and Human Rights, 1945–1985," *Political Science Quarterly* 100 (Summer 1985); Tamar Jacoby, "The Reagan Turnaround on Human Rights," *Foreign Affairs* 64 (Summer 1986); Jordan J. Paust, "The Link Between Human Rights and Terrorism. . . ,'' *Hastings International and Comparative Law Review* 11 (Fall 1987).

HUMAN RIGHTS WATCH

A U.S. organization that monitors and reports on the status of human rights around the globe. Founded in 1978, Human Rights Watch operates through a network of approximately 3,000 citizens who monitor events in their homeland. The degree of personal danger which many monitors assume is demonstrated by the fact that 29 monitors were killed in 1988, including a South African high school student and a Czech social worker. Many more were beaten and/or imprisoned.

HUSSEIN SUICIDE SQUAD

A radical Shi'ite organization named after the third Shi'ite Imam. The group is now considered to have been subsumed under the HEZBOLLAH umbrella of militant groups.

I

IMRO (INNER MACEDONIAN REVOLUTIONARY ORGANIZATION)

A Macedonian separatist group active in the first half of the 20th century. Fiercely nationalistic, IMRO battled the Ottoman Empire and later Greece, Bulgaria and Serbia in efforts to establish Macedonian sovereignty.

INCURSION

1. A political euphemism for a military invasion of another state's territory, such as the Israeli incursion into Lebanon in 1978.

2. A sudden, hostile but short-lived raid, such as the frequent incursions by Palestinian terrorists into Israel.

INFILTRATION

1. The secret movement of forces into or through an area or territory occupied by enemy troops or organizations. The movement is made either by individuals or by small groups at irregular or extended intervals. When used in connection with enemy territory, the word "infiltration" implies that movement has gone undetected.

2. In intelligence or espionage, placing an agent or other person in a target area in hostile territory. This usually involves crossing a frontier or other guarded line. Methods of infiltration are: black (clandestine), grey (through a legal crossing point but under false documentation) and white (legal).

INFRASTRUCTURE

1. The administrative structure of a political party or a government, as well as the people and processes that make it work.

2. The institutional framework of a society that supports the educational, religious and social ideology which in turn support the political order.

3. The permanent installations and facilities for the support, maintenance and control of naval, land or air forces. A military organization such as NATO, with large forward-based strength and even larger reinforcement needs during mobilization, is necessarily deeply concerned with infrastructure provisions.

INSURGENCY

1. An armed attempt to foster a revolution through attacks against governmental or societal targets. Insurgencies usually take the

form of guerrilla warfare and are often identified with Latin American guerrilla movements. Insurgencies often rely on terrorist acts to (a) publicize their cause, both domestically and internationally; (b) attract popular support and participation; (c) seek retribution; (d) spark governmental repression so as to incite popular insurrection and anti-government sentiment; and (e) make strategic gains against a far stronger adversary with the use of limited resources.

2. An organization or movement aimed at the overthrow of a constituted government through use of subversion and armed conflict.

Dealing with insurgents who use terrorism is always difficult. Sir Robert G.K. Thompson, in *Defeating Communist Insurgency* (1966), recommends giving them a dose of their own medicine. "Getting government forces into the same element as the insurgent is rather like trying to deal with a tomcat in an alley. It is no good inserting a large, fierce dog. The dog may not find the tomcat; if he does, the tomcat will escape to a tree; the dog will then chase the female cats in the alley. The answer is to put in a fiercer tomcat. The two cannot fail to meet because they are both in exactly the same element and have exactly the same purpose in life. The weaker will be eliminated."

References: Mohammed E. Ahrari, "Theological Insurgency: Iran in the Region," *Washington Quarterly* 8 (Spring 1985); John M. Gates, "Indians and Insurrectos: The U.S. Army's Experience with Insurgency," *Parameters: Journal of the US Army War College* 13 (March 1983); Thomas J. Kuster Jr., "Dealing with the Insurgency Spectre," *Military Review* 67 (February 1987); Richard Schultz, "The Limits of Terrorism in Insurgency Warfare: The Case of the Viet Cong," *Polity* 11 (Fall 1978).

INTIFADA

Arabic, "Uprising" or "shaking off." The term applied to the unrest which began in early December 1987 in the Israeli-occupied GAZA STRIP and the West Bank. The intifada was initially a reaction to a December 8 automobile accident, in which several Gaza Arabs were killed when their vehicle collided with an Israeli vehicle. Rumors soon spread throughout the Gaza Strip that the collision had not been an accident, and the rumors incited riots. Civil disobedience mounted after a 17-year-old Palestinian was killed on December 9, and the Israeli occupying forces attempted to quell the protests. The demonstrations were staged primarily by young Palestinians from the refugee camps, most of whom had grown up under Israeli occupation and seemed unafraid to meet the Israeli military in the streets.

The intifada is manifested primarily in the taunting of the Israeli forces of occupation, the throwing of stones and Molotov cocktails, during street demonstrations, and the proliferation of political graffitti. Commercial strikes occur with regularity, and there are routine demonstrations against the continued Israeli presence. The Israeli response has been the object of criticism from many quarters. Israeli troops have answered stones with bullets; many residents have been jailed or deported by the Israeli government. In late 1988 the Israeli government began to destroy the homes of Palestinian activists. In its February 1989 annual report on human rights, the U.S. Department of State charged Israel with substantial human rights violations as a result of its response to the intifada, asserting that troops had caused "many avoidable deaths and injuries." Many participants in the intifada, as well as many analysts, cite the uprising as a major impetus to the PALESTINIAN NATIONAL COUNCIL'S declaration of Palestinian statehood in November 1988. By the end of 1990, more than 720 Palestinians and 47 Israelis had been killed in the intifada.

References: Jamal R. Nassar and Roger Heacock, eds., *Intifada: Palestine at the Crossroads* (New York: Praeger, 1990); Ze'ev Schiff and Ehud Ya'ari, *Intifada* (New York: Simon & Schuster, 1990); Emile Sahliyeh, *In Search of Leadership: West Bank Politics Since 1967* (Washington, D.C.: Brookings Institution, 1988); Alan Dowty, ''The Use of Emergency Powers in Israel,'' *Middle East Review* 21 (Fall 1988); Adam Roberts, ''Decline of Illusions: The Status of the Israeli-occupied Territories over 21 Years,'' *International Affairs* 64 (Summer 1988).

INVISIBLE BOMB

The term applied to explosives that are impervious to X-rays and other scanning security devices, as well as to vapor-sniffing devices. Invisible bombs have been implicated in the explosion aboard TWA Flight 840 on April 2, 1986, which left four dead, and in the bombing of Korean Air Flight 858 on November 29, 1987, which killed 115.

See C-4.

IRAN

Iran is currently one of the world's most active states supporting international terrorism and subversion against other countries. The SHI'ITE Muslim fundamentalist government of Ayatollah Ruhollah KHOMEINI, after it came to power in 1979, demonstrated an exceptional readiness to use terrorism and subversion as a policy tool to spread its Islamic revolution to other nations and to rid the Middle East of Western influence. The government, and groups over which it has strong influence, have attacked civilians, government officials, international peacekeeping forces, Iranian dissidents at home and abroad, and the economic assets of other states. While Iranian government personnel have been used directly in terrorist operations, particularly those against Iranian dissidents, the government prefers to support (directly or indirectly) extremist groups such as the Lebanese HEZBOLLAH.

Iran used terrorism during the Iran–Iraq Gulf War (1980–1988) as part of a broader strategy to deter Kuwait, Saudi Arabia, and other Arab states from supporting the Iraqi cause. Iran recruits disgruntled Shi'ite Muslims from the Gulf States and elsewhere, trains them in paramilitary and terrorist activities, and returns them home. Most of the Iranian-backed terrorist acts that have been perpetrated in the Gulf area have been conducted by Iranian-inspired and sponsored Shi'ite radicals. Several have been convicted of a number of sabotage acts at Kuwaiti oil facilities since June 1986. Groups in the Gulf area promoted by Iran include the ISLAMIC FRONT FOR THE LIBERATION OF BAHRAIN, DAWA and the ISLAMIC JIHAD IN HEJAZ.

Iranian terrorist-related activities have reached well beyond the Gulf. Egyptian officials announced in July 1987 that they had apprehended members of what they described as a new Iranian-backed terrorist ring with explosives in their possession. In March 1987, Tunisia broke relations with Iran, charging that Iran was supporting fundamentalist groups trying to undermine the Tunisian government. The Iranian-inspired and supported Hezbollah in Lebanon is an amorphous group, with no true organizational structure in the Western sense, and it has become an organization which more or less encompasses smaller, shadowy Iranian-influenced Shi'ite extremist groups such as ISLAMIC JIHAD and the Revolutionary Justice Organization. In Iraq, DAWA is considered to be an Iranian surrogate. Iran has nurtured these groups with financial assistance, arms and training. In Lebanon, Iranian REVOLUTIONARY GUARDS coordinate closely with Hezbollah leaders and maintain mutual headquarters. Iran has made clear its ability to manipulate Hezbollah's foreign hostages.

Iran has also shown a disregard for internationally accepted conventions and norms, including those applying to diplomats. On November 4, 1979, the U.S. Embassy in Teheran was seized and its staff was held hostage in what came to be known as the IRANIAN HOSTAGE CRISIS. British and French diplomats have also been the victims of Iranian violations of diplomatic standards.

See IRAN-CONTRA SCANDAL; ORGANIZATION OF THE OPPRESSED ON EARTH; RUSHDIE.

References: James Bill, *The Eagle and the Lion* (Cambridge, Mass.: Yale University Press, 1989); Richard Cottam, *Iran and the United States: A Cold War Case Study* (Pittsburgh: University of Pittsburgh Press, 1988); Shireen T. Hunter, ed., *The Politics of Islamic Revivalism* (Bloomington: University of Indiana Press, 1988); Amir Taheri, *Holy Terror: The Inside Story of Islamic Terrorism* (London: Hutchinson, 1987); Shireen T. Hunter, "Islamic Fundamentalism: What It Really Is and Why It Frightens the West," *SAIS Review* 6 (Winter–Spring 1986); Dilip Hiro, *Iran Under the Ayatollahs* (Boston: Routledge and Kegan Paul, 1985); Gary Sick, *All Fall Down* (New York: Random House, 1985).

IRAN-CONTRA AFFAIR

The controversy that first arose in the fall of 1986 when it was revealed in the United States that members of the Reagan administration had secretly sold arms to the government of IRAN in the hope that Iran would then use its "good offices" to gain the release of American hostages in LEBANON. The sale had taken place at exorbitant prices, and the "profits" had been used to fund the CONTRA movement in Nicaragua. A scandal ensued because it was illegal to sell arms to Iran, illegal to fund the Contras beyond limits set by Congress, and against the expressed policy of the United States to negotiate for (let alone trade arms for) the release of hostages. Because the Iran-Contra operation was undertaken primarily by the National Security Council without the formal approval of the departments of Defense and State, the affair called into question the cohesiveness of the Reagan administration's foreign policy.

References: Michael A. Ledeen, *Perilous Statecraft: An Insider's Account of the Iran-Contra Affair* (New York: Charles Scribner's Sons, 1988); Samuel Segev, *The Iranian Triangle: The Untold Story of Israel's Role in the Iran-Contra Affair*, translated by Haim Watzman (New York: The Free Press, 1988).

IRANIAN HOSTAGE CRISIS

The wholesale violation of diplomatic privileges and immunities which occurred when Iranian "students" backed by their government captured the American Embassy complex in Teheran on November 4, 1979. They held 53 Americans hostage for 444 days, until January 20, 1981. The crisis so dominated the last year of the presidency of Jimmy CARTER that it badly damaged Carter's reelection prospects, especially after a rescue effort failed on April 24, 1980. In Iran, the urban lower class and lower-middle class supported the hostage taking, for they perceived it as an act that finally shed the yoke of domination from the West. Ayatollah KHOMEINI wished to illustrate to the West and particularly the United States that foreign powers could no longer dictate events in Iran. The Khomeini government felt that the previous regime of the Shah acted too much in the interests of the United States. The Iranians agreed to free the hostages only after the Carter administration agreed to some of the Iranian demands "in principle." As one last insult to the Carter administration, Iran did not free the hostages until the day Ronald Reagan formally succeeded Carter as president.

References: Kazimierz Grzybowski, "The Regime of Diplomacy and the Teheran Hostages," *International and Comparative Law Quarterly* 30 (January 1981); Anthony Root, "Settlement of the Iranian Hostage Crisis: An Exercise of Constitutional and Statutory Executive Prerogative in Foreign Affairs," *New York University Journal of International Law and Politics* 13 (Spring 1981); Oscar Schachter, "Self-Help in International Law: U.S. Action in the Iranian Hostage Crisis," *Journal of International Affairs* 37 (Winter 1984); Warren Christopher *et al.*, *American Hostages in Iran: The Conduct of a Crisis* (New Haven: Yale University Press, 1985).

IRANIAN REVOLUTIONARY GUARDS

See REVOLUTIONARY GUARDS.

IRAQ

The independent state of Iraq came into existence in 1932 with the ceding of the British mandate established by the LEAGUE OF NATIONS at the end of World War I. The country was governed by a Hashimite king from independence until 1958, when a bloody palace coup ended the monarchy. The decade between 1958 and 1968 saw a succession of coups as various factions struggled for power. It was in 1968 that

Ahmad Hassan al-Bakr and the Iraqi Ba'th Party first seized control of the government. Although al-Bakr was forced out in 1978 in favor of Saddam Hussein, the Ba'th Party itself has controlled the country since 1968.

President Hussein's regime has been one of the foremost state sponsors of terrorism and has also practiced state terrorism within Iraq. Hussein espouses a pan-Arab ideology and sees himself as an Arab leader on a par with the late Gamal Abdel Nasser. He has also provided substantial support for the Palestinian cause, including providing safe haven for terrorists belonging to both ABU ABBAS' and ABU NIDAL's groups. Yasir Arafat took up residence in Baghdad at the end of 1990 and had thrown the PLO's lot in with that of Iraq in the Kuwait crisis, which was dividing the Arab world at that time. In the latter stages of that crisis Hussein attempted to link his own withdrawal from Kuwait with demands for an Israeli withdrawal from the occupied territories. However, while his invoking of the Palestinian issue endeared him to some, he is feared by others, including many of his own people. In some of the most infamous acts of state terrorism witnessed in recent history he has used poison gas against thousands of innocent people belonging to Iraq's Kurdish minority. In addition, his desires for territorial expansion have made him a threat to his neighbors. In 1980 he attacked Iran and waged a bloody eight-year war with that country which ended in stalemate. And on August 2, 1990 he invaded and annexed Kuwait, precipitating the 1991 Gulf War, which restored the independence of Kuwait. Before Kuwait was liberated, Iraqi forces sacked the entire country and kidnapped, tortured and murdered thousands of Kuwaiti civilians. In the aftermath of Iraq's humiliating defeat in that conflict, Hussein once again turned the remnants of his army against his own people as he brutally put down simultaneous revolts among the SHI'ITES, who predominate in southern Iraq, and the Kurds, who are centered in the northernmost areas of the country.

Immediately before the outbreak of the 1991 Gulf War there were reported to be more than 1,500 terrorists assembled in Baghdad. Hussein promised throughout the crisis and the ensuing war to unleash a global terror campaign against those arrayed against him. Although there was a substantial increase in terrorist incidents worldwide during the period between the onset of the air war on January 17, 1991 and the cease-fire of February 27, 1991, the great majority were minor, symbolic incidents. By one estimate 120 incidents during this period resulted in a half dozen fatalities.

References: Hanna Batatu, *The Old Social Classes and the Revolutionary Movements of Iraq* (Princeton, N.J.: Princeton University Press, 1978); Edith and E. F. Penrose, *Iraq: International Relations and National Development* (London: Ernest Benn Limited, 1978); Amazia Baram, "The Ruling Political Elite in Ba'thi Iraq, 1968–1986: The Changing Features of a Collective Profile," *International Journal of Middle East Studies* 21, no. 4 (November 1989); Phebe Marr, *The Modern History of Iraq* (Boulder, Colo.: Westview Press, 1985); Christine Moss Helms, *Iraq: Eastern Flank of the Arab World* (Washington, D.C.: Brookings Institution, 1984).

IRAULTZA

An obscure left-wing Basque separatist group thought to have been formed in 1982. Marxist and strongly anti-American, Iraultza seeks to establish an independent, Marxist Basque nation in northern Spain, and to end investments by foreign interests (particularly the United States) in the Basque region. The group also stands in violent opposition to U.S. foreign policy in the Third World, particularly in Latin America, where Iraultza has expressed solidarity with radical leftists.

Although it consists of fewer than 20 members, Iraultza has committed numerous bombings against U.S. and French economic interests in the Basque region and indeed may have committed more bombings against U.S. business interests than any other European terrorist group. Corporate victims of bombings include Ford, NCR, 3M, Citibank and Xerox. Anonymous callers claiming responsibility for Iraultza attacks have voiced opposition to U.S. aid to the CONTRAS, to U.S. actions in Grenada and Lebanon and to Spain's participation in NATO. The group has not directly attacked U.S. Government personnel or facilities. Attacks against French interests have been prompted by the arrest and expulsion of Basque terrorists from France.

Iraultza members typically leave small, unsophisticated bombs on the sidewalk or in the street outside an intended target, late at night. Although an anonymous caller then warns the police, there usually is not enough time for the police to react before the bomb explodes. Intended only to cause property damage, Iraultza's "midnight" bombs have injured several people, and a construction worker was killed when an Iraultza bomb malfunctioned.

Reference: Robert P. Clark, "Patterns in the Lives of ETA Members," *Terrorism* 6 (1983).

IRGUN (IRGUN ZVAI LEUMI)

An Israeli terrorist group, whose name in English means national military organization; founded in 1938, that directed a broad campaign of terror against Palestinian and

British targets. On July 22, 1946 Irgun bombed the King David Hotel in Jerusalem, which housed the British headquarters in Palestine. More than 90 people, many of them not British officials, died in the attack. The group's most infamous act was the massacre of Arab villagers at DEIR YASSIN on April 9, 1948. Irgun was led by Menachem BEGIN, who later became prime minister of Israel. The Irgun became part of the Israel's Defense Forces in 1948.

References: J. Bowyer Bell, *Terror Out of Zion: Irgun Zvai Leumi, LEHI, and the Palestine Underground, 1929–1949* (New York: St. Martin's Press, 1977); Thurston Clarke, *By Blood and Fire: The Attack on the King David Hotel* (New York: Putnam, 1981); Samuel Merlin, ''Menachem Begin: Orator, Commander, Statesman,'' *National Jewish Monthly* (July 1977).

IRISH NATIONAL LIBERATION ARMY (INLA)

The military arm of the Irish Socialist Party (IRSP) and a political splinter group of the IRISH REPUBLICAN ARMY, dedicated to the formation of a unified and socialist Ireland. The IRSP has repeatedly denied any connection with the INLA.

A small group of less than 20 members, headquartered in Dublin, the INLA has staged a campaign of anti-British and anti-Protestant violence since its founding in 1975 by Seamus Costello. In the first few years following its creation, the INLA fueded with both wings (Official and Provisional) of the IRA. Many militants were killed, including Costello, who was gunned down in 1977. Despite ideological and tactical differences, the INLA has collaborated with the Provisional Wing of the IRA (PIRA). At one time, this cooperation reportedly involved regular weekly meetings. Occasional friction be-

tween the groups continues to occur, though their differences no longer erupt into the bloody killing seen in the mid-1970s.

Although the INLA has engaged in bombings and shootings since its inception, it achieved widespread notoriety only after the March 1979 assassination of leading British Conservative Party member Airey Neave in Great Britain. This INLA attack shocked British authorities, and it represented an expansion of INLA activities outside of Ireland. In typical operations in the urban areas of Belfast and Londonderry, INLA attacks target British soldiers, members of Northern Ireland's security forces, Ulster government officials, and members of loyalist political parties and paramilitary groups. Bank, armored cars, and train robberies in both Ulster and the Republic of Ireland appear to be the primary sources of INLA funding. The group apparently does not have the access to the international funding enjoyed by the PIRA and may have started to resort to extortion to meet operational expenses.

There is evidence of INLA contacts with the West German REVOLUTIONARY CELLS (RZ) and the French ACTION DIRECTE (AD). British sources claim that the explosives used in INLA's aborted 1985 plot to bomb the Chelsea Barracks in London were stolen by AD members in France in 1984. In accordance with its Marxist ideology, the INLA also has expressed solidarity with numerous national liberation and terrorist movements throughout the world. Numerous arrests of INLA members and testimony by Irish militant informers (known as SUPERGRASS informers) have reduced INLA operational capabilities significantly and have caused the group to limit its activities. Problems in permitting the use of supergrass testimony in court, however, led to the release in 1987 of many captured INLA militants. Upon their release, a bloody feud erupted over whether to disband the organization, and many militants were killed. Despite this preoccupation with internal leadership conflicts, the INLA remains a lethal and unpredictable organization.

The group's most notorious episode occurred on December 7, 1982, when it bombed a public house in Ballykelly, Northern Ireland, killing 11 soldiers and six civilians and wounding 66. It is believed that some of the terrorist incidents in Northern Ireland attributed to the better-known Irish Republican Army in reality have been carried out by the INLA.

IRISH REPUBLICAN ARMY

The militant organization dedicated to forcing the withdrawal of Britain from Northern Ireland and the reunification of the Irish nation.

The IRA has its roots in the National Volunteer Force, an anti-British, republican (meaning "from the people") organization. The IRA was born out of the Easter Uprising of 1916, in which Irish republicans in Dublin unsuccessfully rebelled against British authorities. IRA guerrilla tactics were a major contributing factor in the creation in 1921 of the Irish Free State. A split then developed in the republican movement between those opposed to a divided Ireland (under the leadership of Eamon de Valera), and those who favored acceptance of a separate Irish Free State (the current state of Ireland) as the most feasible political solution. The IRA battled the Free State Army during the Irish Civil War in 1921–23 but was defeated by former IRA leader Michael Collins and his Free State forces.

In the 1930s, the IRA mounted a campaign of violence to drive Great Britain out of Northern Ireland, staging attacks and bombings in Great Britain as well as in the Irish Free State and in Northern Ireland. As a result of this wave of violence, in June 1939 the group was banned by the Irish Free State. After the declaration of the Republic of Ireland in 1949, the IRA focused its energies on Northern Ireland. During the late 1950s and early 1960s the IRA maintained a military presence at the Northern Ireland border and was responsible for the deaths of many British and Northern Irish security forces. This border strategy was effectively terminated in 1961 through the successful Northern Irish policy of internment of IRA suspects, which was tacitly supported by the southern Republic.

Following the failure of their strategy, the IRA turned to a nonviolent approach and supported campaigns of civil disobedience organized to further civil rights causes. However, this approach did not satisfy the more radical members of the IRA. Many such members, partly in response to a wave of Protestant violence against Irish Catholics, split from the IRA (which then became known as the Official IRA) and formed the PROVISIONAL WING OF THE IRISH REPUBLICAN ARMY (PIRA) in 1969.

The Official IRA pressed for a socialist, unified Irish state primarily through nonviolent means. The Provos, as PIRA members are called, stress nationalistic and Catholic goals to be obtained by force. As the conflict in Northern Ireland became more bitter and violent, the Official IRA became less visible and popular, and the PIRA became the predominant organization. The political wing of the IRA is SINN FEIN, which supports the PIRA in its campaign of violence. Since the "troubles" (as the current wave of violence is known) began in 1969 almost 2,800 people have died in Northern Ireland.

References: Michael McKinley, " 'Irish Mist:' Eight Clouded Views of the Provisional Irish Republican Army," *Australian Quarterly* 57 (Spring 1985); John Darby,

Northern Ireland: The Background to the Conflict (Syracuse, N.Y.: Syracuse University Press, 1983); Yonah Alexander and Alan O'Day, eds., *Terrorism in Ireland* (New York: St. Martin's Press, 1984); Padraig O'Malley, *Uncivil Wars: Ireland Today* (Boston: Houghton Mifflin, 1983); Paul Wilkinson, "The Provisional IRA: An Assessment in the Wake of the 1981 Hunger Strike," *Government and Opposition* 17 (Spring 1982).

IRREDENTISM

From the Italian "irredenta," meaning unredeemed. The long-standing and frustrated desire of the people of one state to annex some area of an adjoining state that contains peoples of the same cultural or ethnic group. Irredentism is an ideological element of many terrorist organizations.

IRON GUARD

An Eastern European fascist organization that was active between World War I and World War II. The Iron Guard assassinated Rumanian prime minister Ion Duca in 1933 and Prime Minister Armand Calinescu in 1939.

ISLAMIC AMAL

A clandestine splinter group of the AMAL militia, established in 1982 by Hussein Musawi as a reaction against the more moderate leadership of Nabih BERRI. By 1984 the group was considered to be a part of HEZBOLLAH.

ISLAMIC FRONT FOR THE LIBERATION OF BAHRAIN

A SHI'ITE Muslim fundamentalist group which seeks to establish a revolutionary Islamic state in the tiny Gulf nation of Bahrain. The group has strong ties to IRAN and has offices at Teheran's TALEGHANI CENTER. A major plot to attack several targets in Bahrain in December 1981, involving 150 men, was uncovered by authorities in the United Arab Emirates. Seventy-three members of the group were arrested.

ISLAMIC GUERRILLAS IN AMERICA

A U.S. pro-Iranian, pro-Khomeini group that has been active in the suppression of Iranian dissident critics of the revolutionary regime in Teheran. In July 1980 Ali Tabatabai, a member of the government of the deposed Shah of Iran, was killed by Islamic Guerrilla David Belfield in Washington, D.C. Belfield eluded U.S. authorities and fled to Iran.

ISLAMIC JIHAD

A radical and violent SHI'ITE group, which has claimed responsibility for many of the bloodiest terrorist acts in Lebanon. The group is shadowy, and some experts suspect that Islamic Jihad is simply an umbrella cover name used by various pro-Iranian Lebanese Shi'ite organizations, including HEZBOLLAH. Acts for which the group has claimed responsibility include the April 1983 bombing of the U.S. Embassy in Beirut, which killed 49 people; the October 1983 suicide bombings of the U.S. Marine barracks in Beirut, which killed 241, and of the French peacekeeping forces in Beirut, which left 58 French soldiers dead; the November 1983 attack against an Israeli army post in Tyre, Lebanon, which killed 63 people; and the September 20, 1984 bombing of the U.S. Embassy annex in East Beirut. The group also is believed to have kidnapped four American college instructors at Beirut University College on January 24, 1987. One of the four was released in October 1988. The group claimed responsibility for the downing of a ULA flight in September 1989 in which 70 people were killed.

References: Juan Cole and Nikki Keddie, eds., *Shi'ism and Social Protest* (New Haven: Yale University Press, 1986); R. Norton, *Amal and The Shi'a: Struggle for the Soul of Lebanon* (Austin: University of Texas Press, 1988).

ISLAMIC JIHAD IN HEJAZ

A Saudi SHI'ITE extremist organization, linked to IRAN, the Lebanese ISLAMIC JIHAD and HEZBOLLAH, which undertakes terrorist missions against the SUNNI Muslim government of Saudi Arabia. Hejaz, sometimes spelled "Hasa" in English-language texts, is an oil-rich eastern Saudi province with a Shi'ite population of 100,000. Shi'ites in that province have long complained of official discrimination by the ruling majority Sunnis, and the Islamic Jihad in Hejaz mounts terrorist attacks designed to destabilize the Sunni regime. It has claimed responsibility for the shootings of Saudi diplomats abroad in Ankara, Turkey in October 1988, in Karachi, Pakistan in December 1988, and in Bangkok, Thailand in January 1989. The Saudi government, in turn, has sought to contain the growing Shi'ite unrest and violence by instituting harsh reprisals against suspected Shi'ite extremists. In September 1988 the government executed four Shi'ites convicted of subversive activity in Hejaz.

ISLAMIC LIBERATION ORGANIZATION (ILO)

A Lebanese Islamic fundamentalist group responsible for the seizure of four Soviet diplomats in Beirut on September 30, 1985. The body of one of the Soviet Embassy officials, Arkady Katkov, was discovered two days later. The ILO demanded that the Soviet Union intervene in the Lebanese conflict and stop the Syrian attacks on Muslim forces. It has been reported that the Soviet Union did press Syria to accept a ceasefire. The remaining three Soviet officials were released on October 30, 1985.

ISLAMIC REVOLUTIONARY ORGANIZATION

A SHI'ITE Muslim organization believed to be linked to the revolutionary government in IRAN. The group has waged a campaign of violence and propaganda against the government of Saudi Arabia. This campaign has included violence in the heavily Shi'ite Saudi province of Hejaz and broadcasting of anti-Saudi radio programming.

ISLAMIC TENDENCY MOVEMENT

A fundamentalist Islamic organization at the forefront of the anti-Western, Islamic revivalist movement in Tunisia. The group has been responsible for violent protests against Tunisia's large European tourist industry.

ISRAEL

Israel is a predominately Jewish state surrounded by hostile Arab nations. It has been the focus, directly or indirectly, of much of the terrorism in the world. Since its independence in 1948, won by transforming the British mandate in Palestine into Israel, it has occupied substantial additional territory in the WEST BANK and East Jerusalem, the GAZA STRIP and the Golan Heights as a result of a succession of wars with its Arab neighbors. The Palestinians who live in these occupied areas are a stateless people held together by their common plight: Israel's denial of their national rights. The frustration of being denied the right of self-determination has manifested itself in the form of literally thousands of attacks on Jews within Israel and on symbols of the Israeli state abroad. Diplomats, embassies and the national Israeli air carrier El Al, have been frequent targets, as have Western nations, most notably the United States. The disenfranchised Palestinians blame the Western nations because they have not used their power to compel the Israelis to respond to the Palestinian demands. The state of siege that has characterized Israel's existence has led it to build one of the best trained and most efficient armies in the world.

Terror tactics, adopted as a means of publicizing the Palestinian plight, did little to foster support for the cause of the thousands who have grown up in refugee camps just outside the borders of Israel. However, in December 1987 a popular uprising, known as the INTIFADA, began in the Gaza Strip and quickly spread to the West Bank. This spontaneous mass civil unrest, which pits rock-throwing youths against heavily armed Israeli soldiers, has continued ever since and has had a far more positive impact on world opinion than the two decades of random and senseless terrorism that preceded it. For the first time there is the possibility serious discussions might take place that could ultimately lead to free elections and a degree of autonomy for Israel's Arabs.

References: David A. Shipler, *Arab and Jew: Wounded Spirits in the Promised Land* (London: Bloomsbury, 1987); Lenni Brenner, *The Iron Wall: Zionist Revisionism from Jabotinsky to Shamir* (London: Zed Press, 1984); Jacobo Timerman, *The Longest War: Israel in Lebanon* (New York: Alfred A. Knopf, 1982).

ISTANBUL SYNAGOGUE MASSACRE

On September 6, 1986 terrorists brandishing automatic weapons attacked Neve Shalom, Istanbul's oldest Jewish temple, interrupting a Sabbath worship service. The terrorists fired upon the congregation, leaving 21 dead. The terrorists then poured gasoline on the bodies of their victims, set them afire, then committed suicide. The terrorists are thought to have been operatives of the ABU NIDAL organization acting with the assistance of the Syrian, Iranian and Libyan governments.

Reference: Judith Miller, "The Istanbul Synagogue Massacre: An Investigation," *New York Times Magazine* (January 4, 1987).

ITERATE

"International Terrorism—Attributes of Terrorist Events," a database developed by Edward Mickolaus, an intelligence analyst for the CIA. ITERATE groups terrorist incidents according to factors such as educational level of terrorists, terrorist demands, and whether terrorists gave an advance warning of an incident.

J

JABRIL, AHMED

The leader of the militant, pro-Syrian Ba'athist POPULAR FRONT FOR THE LIBERATION OF PALESTINE-GENERAL COMMAND (PFLP-GC), which he established in 1968 after splitting from the PFLP in reaction against its left-wing ideological emphasis. Jabril is a former captain in the Syrian army and is a hard-line Palestinian nationalist opposed to the more moderate policies of Yasir ARAFAT's PLO. His group has been linked to several technologically sophisticated bombing attacks, and its members are the prime suspects in the downing of PAN AM FLIGHT 103 in December 1988. Jabril made additional headlines in 1989 when he voiced support for the death sentence passed on controversial author Salman RUSHDIE by the Ayatollah KHOMEINI.

JAMMU-KASHMIR LIBERATION FRONT

The leading Kashmiri separatist movement operating in the Indian province of Kashmir. Kashmir is Muslim-dominated and ethnically and culturally different than Hindu India. Jammu is the adjacent province of Pakistan. Pakistan also lays claim to Kashmir. Until recently the spiritual leader of the group was Maulvi Mohammed Farooq, known by the religious title of the Mirwaiz of Kashmir. Mohammed Farooq was assassinated on May 21, 1990 by Hindu fundamentalists.

JAPANESE RED ARMY (JRA)

In Japanese, "Nippon Sekigun." A small but extremely dangerous Japanese left-wing revolutionary organization, with an estimated membership of 25. The JRA was formed in 1971, a product of radical Japanese student unrest in the late 1960s, and is considered to be a splinter group of the Japanese Communist League Red Army Faction. Its founder, Fusako Shigenobu, served as a liaison between the Japanese Red Army and Palestinian terrorists and formed the group with a small cadre of personnel who joined her in Lebanon. Many JRA members have been educated at universities, and many are products of the prosperous Japanese middle class. The core strength of the organization probably never exceeded its present level, and a base of sympathizers in Japan numbers about 100. Palestinian homeland sympathizers provided some moral support and financial aid as well as an audience for JRA propaganda. The group's primary sources of funds, however, are believed to be Palestinian factions and LIBYA.

The stated ultimate goal of the JRA is the overthrow of the Japanese government and monarchy and the establishment of a people's republic in Japan. The group has a fierce devotion to its cause, rooted in traditional cultural militaristic ideals. In its initial terrorist act, the 1970 hijacking of a Japanese airliner, JRA operatives brandished an assortment of samurai swords and other ritual weapons. The JRA conducted terrorist acts on behalf of the POPULAR FRONT FOR THE LIBERATION OF PALESTINE (PFLP) from 1972 to 1977, most notably the LOD AIRPORT MASSACRE in Israel in 1972. In September 1974 the group seized the French Embassy and 12 hostages in The Hague, holding the French ambassador until the French government released a jailed JRA operative, Joshiaka Yamada, on the fifth day of the crisis. The JRA has acted independently for years, although its leaders probably consult with the PFLP prior to conducting any attacks for its own purposes. JRA members still at large are believed to operate out of Lebanon with the PFLP. Since 1977 the JRA has not claimed credit for violent actions; however, individuals associated with the group have been linked to acts of terrorism as recently as 1988. The group is suspected of perpetrating terrorist acts under the guise of the ANTI-IMPERIALIST INTERNATIONAL BRIGADE (AIIB). In 1986 and 1987 terrorists claiming to represent the AIIB carried out a series of rocket and mortar assaults against U.S. embassies in Jakarta, Rome and Madrid.

Reference: Yoshihiro Kuriyama, "Terrorism at Tel Aviv Airport and a 'New Left' Group in Japan," *Asian Survey* 13 (March 1973).

JEWISH DEFENSE LEAGUE (JDL)

A militant U.S. Jewish pressure group founded in Brooklyn in 1968 by Rabbi Meir KAHANE (1932–1990). In its earliest days the group functioned as a local anticrime organization, but by 1969 it had developed an ambitious political agenda aimed at protecting Jewish interests throughout the world. Though it has a history of terrorist activities, the group is legally incorporated in New York State as a religious non-profit religious organization and enjoys tax-exempt status as a religious group.

More than 30 JDL members have been convicted in U.S. courts of terrorist acts or terrorist conspiracy, and the FBI estimates that 37 such acts were carried out by the group between 1977 and 1984. The targets of these acts are individuals, organizations, and institutions considered to be hostile to Israeli or Jewish interests. Traditionally, targets connected with the Soviet Union, as the nemesis of Soviet Jewry, have borne the brunt of JDL attacks. Victims of JDL attacks include Soviet dance companies and Aeroflot airline offices. In recent years Arab and Palestinian targets have risen to prominence as JDL targets. On October 11, 1985 the group may have bombed the Los Angeles office of the American-Arab Anti-Discrimination League, killing director Alex Odeh, who had appeared on television the previous day to offer a Palestinian perspective on the ACHILLE LAURO incident. In December 1985 the JDL may have bombed the Anti-Discrimination League's headquarters in Washington, D.C. In 1987 several members of the group were arrested and convicted of a variety of criminal charges, and since that time no violent acts by members of Jewish radical organizations have been recorded in the United States.

Reference: Bruce Hoffman, "The Jewish Defense League," *TVI Journal* 5 (Summer 1984).

JIHAD

Arabic Islamic term usually translated as "holy war," and characterized by the conviction among Shi'ite Muslims to spread the Islamic revolution. The concept of jihad grants divine approval to the Islamic battle against infidels; hence, terrorist acts are seen by Shi'ite revolutionaries as justifiable efforts to overthrow the corrupt institutions and states that are the enemies of Islam.

JINDA

The alias of Harjinder Singh, a Sikh terrorist personally responsible for more than two dozen murders, including the 1986 assassination of Arn Vaidya, the Indian Army General who led the military assault against the Sikh GOLDEN TEMPLE OF AMRITSAR. Jinda, a leader of the Khalistan Commando Force, was captured by Delhi police in August 1986.

JUNE 2ND MOVEMENT

A West German left-wing terrorist organization of the 1970s. Heavily influenced by the writing of Mao Zedong, the group trained in camps of the POPULAR FRONT FOR THE LIBERATION OF PALESTINE in the Middle East and was linked to the infamous CARLOS. Numerous arrests rendered the June 2nd Movement's small membership inactive by the late 1970s.

JUSTICE COMMANDOS OF THE ARMENIAN GENOCIDE (JCAG)

An extremely violent organization which pursues its stated goal of Armenian autonomy by attacking Turkish diplomats around the globe. The JCAG is, in its political leanings, far to the right of the Marxist ARMENIAN SECRET ARMY FOR THE LIBERATION OF ARMENIA (ASALA). It seeks to re-establish the Independent Republic of Armenia, which existed briefly in eastern Turkey after World War I, and, unlike the ASALA, the JCAG does not seek reunification with the Armenian Soviet Socialist Republic in the Soviet Union.

Drawing on elements from the large Armenian communities abroad for support, the JCAG has committed a series of assassinations and bombings against official Turkish personnel and facilities worldwide. JCAG operations usually favor either ambushes of Turkish officials in or near their automobiles, or bombings of facilities. In the belief that Western public opinion is too valuable to its cause to risk alienation through indiscriminate violence, the JCAG has limited its attacks to Turkish targets. Despite these intentions, however, other nationalities have been victims of JCAG terrorism.

JCAG victims include the Turkish Consul General in Los Angeles (January 28, 1982) and the Turkish Consul General in Sydney, Australia (December 17, 1980). The Justice Commandos also claimed responsibility for the bombing of the Turkish mission to the United Nations in New York City on October 12, 1980. The group is thought to be based in Lebanon. Little is known about its leadership or ties to other groups. Although the JCAG has expressed solidarity with other movements such as the Basque ETA and the Turkish Kurds, it is not known whether the JCAG maintains operational ties with other groups.

In about 1983 a group called the Armenian Revolutionary Army (ARA) began claiming responsibility for anti-Turkish attacks, and the name JCAG fell from usage. The similarity of ARA attacks to past JCAG attacks may indicate that ARA is a cover name for JCAG.

JVP

"People's Liberation Front." An extremely violent, ultra-left Sri Lankan Sinhalese political party and terrorist organization. The JVP has been responsible for much of the anti-Tamil violence that has occurred in the small island nation of Sri Lanka since 1983. The majority of its members are young men. The group has capitalized on the intervention of the Indian Peace-Keeping Force. As a movement of the Sinhalese majority, the JVP has not incurred the same level of government wrath that violent young Tamils have borne.

K

KADAR, SAMIR

An operative of the ABU NIDAL Organization and one of the world's most wanted terrorists. Mystery surrounds his connection to an explosion in Athens on July 11, 1988. Press reports initially speculated that Kadar had died in the blast, which occurred on the day of the terrorist attack on the Greek tourist ship CITY OF POROS in the Saronic Gulf. However, Greek police forensic analysis raised doubts about Kadar's reported demise, and Italian authorities announced their belief that Kadar remained alive and well. Evidence gleaned from the Athens explosion led police to a Stockholm terrorist hideaway, in which a large cache of weapons and explosives (including the plastic explosive Semtex) was found. It is believed that Kadar organized the attack on the *City of Poros*. He is also believed to have been connected with an attack on a synagogue in Rome in 1982 and the Rome airport attack on December 27, 1985 in which 15 civilians were killed. Authorities have traced his frequent travels to Syria and Libya through forged passports confiscated in the Stockholm raid.

KADDOUMI, FAROUK

Senior member of al-FATAH and chief of that group's political apparatus. Born in the West Bank town of Nablus, Kaddoumi is the most left-wing of the Fatah leadership and is the Soviet Union's primary advocate in the organization. He has adopted the nom de guerre "Abu Lutf."

KAFFIYEH

A cloth head covering worn by Arabs as protection against the elements. The kaffiyeh has been frequently worn by and identified with Palestinian terrorists, who have worn the headdress over their faces to conceal their identities. The kaffiyeh worn in this fashion has become a symbol of the INTIFADA. Yasir ARAFAT's ubiquitous kaffiyeh is worn in the more traditional fashion.

KAFIR

Arabic, "the unbeliever." To the Islamic fundamentalist, the kafir is defined by his rejection of the faith of Mohammed and is thus an enemy of the faith and a just target of the rightful wrath of Islam.

KAHANE, MEIR (1932–1990)

The American Rabbi who founded the JEWISH DEFENSE LEAGUE in 1968. He emigrated to Israel in 1971 and resigned as head of the JDL in 1985. He became a right-wing Israeli politician and was elected to the Knesset. His party was excluded from the general elections in October 1988, however, because its ideology called for the expulsion of all Arabs from Israel and the occupied territories. His group has been involved in several attacks on Palestinian civilians, attempting to intimidate them in order to quicken the process of expulsion from the occupied territories. Kahane was shot to death on Nov. 5, 1990 by an Egyptian Arab in New York after Kahane finished a speech to a group of American-Jewish supporters.

Reference: Yair Kotler, *Heil Kahane* (New York: Adama, 1986).

KANAK SOCIALIST NATIONAL LIBERATION FRONT (KSNLF)

A left-wing Kanak nationalist organization that seeks independence from France for New Caledonia. The French annexed the South Pacific island of New Caledonia and the surrounding smaller islands that compose the overseas territory in 1853. Tensions between French settlers and the native Kanaks have increased in recent years and have erupted into violence resulting in casualties on both sides. The KSNLF has received encouragement and support from the Libyan government of Muammar Qaddafi.

KANSAI REVOLUTIONARY ARMY

The covert action wing of CHUKAKU-HA, a militant left-wing Japanese organization.

KASHIMIRI LIBERATION FRONT

One of the larger of the many separatist movements in the northern India province of Kashmir. Kashmiris are Muslims and are ethnically and culturally distinct from India's Hindus. Terrorism by the group is targeted primarily against Hindus. Many groups receive support from Muslim Pakistan, which has laid claim to the region.

KGB (KOMITET GOSUDARSTUENNOE BEZOPASNOSTI)

Committee for State Security, the internal security police and international espionage organization of the Soviet Union. It is the equivalent of a combined CIA and FBI with elements of local police. But unlike U.S. internal security forces, the KGB has a history of terror against its own people as well as support for terrorism abroad.

References: Amy W. Knight, "The KGBs Special Departments in the Soviet Armed Forces," *Orbis* 28 (Summer 1984); Amy W. Knight, "The Powers of the Soviet KGB," *Survey* 25 (Summer 1980).

KHALED, LEILA

Member of the Popular Front for the Liberation of Palestine, and one of the most renowned female terrorists. She was a key player in the September 1970 hijacking incidents that became known as the DAWSON'S FIELD affair. Captured while attempting to hijack an EL AL airliner at London airport, she was soon released by British authorities in exchange for the release of hostages aboard a BOAC aircraft at Dawson's Field. She is a Palestinian and has been elevated to the status of heroine in the Arab and Palestinian communities. She is perceived by many women in the region to be at the helm of the feminist movement.

KHALEF, SALEH

Born in Jaffa in 1933, he was among the Palestinians who fled the area after the establishment of the state of Israel in 1948. Khalef first met Yasir ARAFAT in Cairo in 1951. In 1957 he helped Arafat found al-FATAH in which he was second-in-command until his death in 1991. Khalef, who adopted the nom de guerre of Abu Iyad, has been linked to Black September and the 1972 Munich Massacre. Although originally considered to be more radical than Arafat he was instrumental in pushing through the Palestinian National Council the 1988 resolution that effectively recognized Israel's right to exist alongside an independent Palestinian state. During the 1990–91 Kuwait crisis Khalef warned Arafat against becoming too reliant on Iraq's Saddam Hussein. On January 14, 1991, Khalef, along with Mohammad Fakhuri al-Umari, and PLO security chief Hail Abd al-Hamid were killed in Tunis by Hamza Abu Zeid. Hamza was a member of the Abu Nidal Organization, a fact which has led many to speculate that Nidal's sponsor, Saddam Hussein, was behind the killings.

References: Paul A. Jureidini and William E. Hazen, *The Palestinian Movement in Politics* (Lexington, Mass.: Lexington Books, 1976); Gerard Chaliand, *The Palestinian Resistance* (Harmondsworth: Penguin Books, 1972); Richard A. Norton and Martin H. Greenberg, eds., *The International Relations of the Palestine Liberation Organization* (Carbondale, Ill.: Southern Illinois University Press, 1989); Abu Iyad, *My Home, My Land* (New York: Times Books, 1981).

KHMER ROUGE

Cambodian radical communist organization that rose to power in the 1970s. Beginning in 1975 POL POT, the Khmer Rouge commander, instituted a reign of terror that resulted in an estimated 1,000,000 deaths by torture, starvation, disease, overwork and outright murder. The organization presently operates out of heavily populated refugee camps on the Thai–Cambodian border and is amassing manpower and firepower for a future attempt to retake control of Cambodia, which was occupied from 1978 to 1989 by the Vietnamese army. The Khmer Rouge has received vast amounts of arms, supplies and funding from the People's Republic of China. Extortion has proven to be a primary source of funds for the group; for instance, the organization has earned tens of thousands of dollars a week by selling mining passes to prospective ruby miners in the areas it controls in Cambodia.

References: Steven Erlanger, "The Endless War: The Return of the Khmer Rouge," *New York Times Magazine* (March 5, 1989); Ross H. Munro, "The New Khmer Rouge," *Commentary* 80 (December 1985); William Shawcross, *Sideshow: Kissinger, Nixon and the Destruction of Cambodia* (New York: Simon and Schuster, 1979).

KHOMEINI, AYATOLLAH RUHOLLAH (1901–89)

SHI'ITE Muslim spiritual leader of the Iranian revolution, and political leader of the Islamic Republic of IRAN, a nation at the forefront of STATE-SPONSORED TERRORISM. Largely unknown in the West before his unseating of the Shah of Iran in 1979, Khomeini had been an active leader of dissent in Iran since the 1940s. He despised all things Western and referred to the United States as the "Great Satan." Through his charismatic leadership he inflamed the Iranian people. Almost as soon as he gained control of Iran he began to export Islamic fundamentalism to Arab states throughout the Persian Gulf.

References: Amir Taheri, *Holy Terror* (London: Hutchinson, 1987); Shaul Bakhash, *The Reign of the Ayatollahs: Iran and the Islamic Revolution* (New York: Basic Books, 1984); Ramy Nima, *The Wrath of Allah: Islamic Revolution and Reaction in Iran* (London: Pluto Press, 1983); Imam Khomeini, *Islam and Revolution: Writings and Declarations of Imam Khomeini*, translated and annotated by Hamid Algar (Berkeley, Calif.: Mizan Press, 1981).

KIKUMURA, YU

An operative of the JAPANESE RED ARMY who was arrested in April 1988 in New Jersey, after three bombs were discovered in his car by a state trooper at a New Jersey Turnpike rest stop. He was convicted of federal weapons and explosives violations in December 1988. It is believed that Kikumura planned to detonate the bombs on April 14, 1988, the second anniversary of the U.S. air raid against Libya.

KIM HYUN HEE

One of the two agents of the government of North Korea responsible for the bombing on November 29, 1987 of Korean Air Flight 858, in which 115 people died. Kim and her accomplice took poison upon their apprehension in Bahrain; her 70-year-old partner died, but she, a young woman, survived to confess her involvement. Kim recanted and expressed tearful remorse at a South Korean press conference in January 1988. She claimed to be part of a conspiracy to dampen enthusiasm for the 1988 Seoul Olympics.

KING DAVID HOTEL

On July 22, 1946 the King David Hotel, which housed the British military headquarters in Jerusalem, was bombed by the Jewish terrorist organization IRGUN, led by Menachem BEGIN. More than 90 people died in the attack which, though directed against the British military, killed many civilians.

Reference: Thurston Clarke, *By Blood and Fire: The Attack on the King David Hotel* (New York: G. P. Putnam, 1981).

KLINGHOFFER, LEON

See ACHILLE LAURO.

KNEECAPPING

A brutal form of intimidation or revenge, wherein a person's kneecaps are broken, crippling the victim. Kneecapping has been common in Northern Ireland.

KRISTALLNACHT

German, ''The Night of Broken Glass.'' This is considered by many to be the night when the HOLOCAUST began. On the night of November 9, 1938 mobs in Germany and Austria, inspired and led by Nazi authorities and troops, attacked Jews and Jewish homes and places of business. Stores were looted, windows were broken; more than 20,000 Jews were arrested; and many were murdered as authorities stood by. Synagogues were sacked and burnt to the ground as fire departments watched.

KU KLUX KLAN (KKK)

A racist, white-supremacist group established in the U.S. South following the Civil War. The KKK has a long history of intimidation, beatings and murders of blacks, as well as other racial and religious minorities. Lynchings are a hallmark of the KKK, as are the burning of crosses, designed to instill fear into the hearts of black onlookers. Klansmen traditionally cloak themselves in the anonymity of robes and hoods fashioned out of white sheets.

There are three major Klan organizations in the United States today: the United Klans of America (membership 1,500); the Invisible Empire (1,500); and the Knights of the Ku Klux Klan (1,000). In recent years, successful lawsuits brought against the Klan by KKK victims have dealt the organizations severe setbacks.

See GREENSBORO FIVE.

References: Irwin Suall and David Lowe, "The Hate Movement Today," *Terrorism* 10 (1987); Allen W. Trelease, *White Terror: The Ku Klux Klan Conspiracy and Southern Reconstruction* (Westport, Conn.: Greenwood Press, 1979); David M. Chalmers, *Hooded Americanism* (Chicago: Quadrangle, 1965).

KURDISH WORKERS' PARTY (PKK)

"Partiya Karkeren Kurdistan." A small Marxist-Leninist Turkish terrorist group established in the mid-1970s. The PKK seeks to set up a Marxist state in the Kurdish region of southeastern Turkey. Its primary targets are Turkish government forces and civilians in the southeastern region, but the group is becoming increasingly more active against Turkish targets in Western Europe. In 1986 the PKK attacked a NATO target in Mardin, Turkey. In 1984, the group murdered two exiles in Sweden who had fallen out of favor with the PKK. The group is thought by some experts to be responsible for the 1986 assassination of Olaf Palme, the Swedish prime minister; but such speculation is at the present time unsubstantiated. The group has strongholds in Iraq and in Syria and is thought to receive Syrian support.

Reference: Gerard Chaliand, ed., *People Without A Country: The Kurds and Kurdistan* (London: Zed Press, 1978).

KUWAITI 17

Refers to the 17 pro-Iranian SHI'ITE Islamic fundamentalists convicted of terrorist bombings of Western installations, including the U.S. Embassy in Kuwait in December 1983. The 17 were convicted in March 1984 and were imprisoned in Kuwaiti jails. At least five people died in the bombings, and more than 80 were injured. Fellow Shi'ite terrorists have committed many acts in the unrealized hope of obtaining the release of the Kuwaiti 17. These have included the abduction of Western hostages, and the hijacking of Kuwait Airways Flight 422 in April 1988. The Kuwaiti government has been steadfast in its refusal to bow to demands for the release of these and other jailed terrorists, but the government has not proceeded with the death sentences handed down to three of the Kuwaiti 17 in March 1984. In February 1989 two of the 17 were released after serving complete five-year terms. The remaining 15 were thought to have been sent to Iran by Iraq after its conquest of Kuwait in August 1990.

LA BELLE DISCO

West Berlin nightspot, frequented by off-duty American servicemen, which was bombed early on the morning of April 5, 1986. One U.S. soldier and a Turkish woman died in the attack, and more than 200 were injured. The Reagan administration stated that it had evidence that Libya was involved in the attack, and on April 15, 1986 the United States launched a retaliatory air strike against the Libyan cities of Tripoli and Benghazi. Libya has denied complicity in the bombing, and some analysts have asserted that Syrian elements may actually have been behind the action. West German police charged a West German woman and a Palestinian man in the bombing but dropped the charges in December 1988 due to a lack of evidence. The Palestinian, Ahmad HASI, had earlier been convicted of a May 1986 bombing also in West Berlin.

LEAGUE OF NATIONS

The international organization that preceded the United Nations. It was first called for by President Woodrow Wilson in an address to Congress (this was the last of the "Fourteen Points"), January 8, 1918: "A general association of nations must be formed under specific covenants for the purpose of affording mutual guarantees of political independence and territorial integrity to great and small states alike." However the U.S. never joined it.

LEBANESE ARMED REVOLUTIONARY FACTION

See FARL.

LEBANON

A troubled Middle Eastern nation on the eastern shore of the Mediterranean Sea. Lebanon is most importantly a religiously diverse state. Although the country has flourished economically since ancient times, the Lebanese state, created out of France's post-World War I mandate territory, has existed independently for less than 50 years. Lebanon has a large Christian minority. The Muslim peoples of the area are predominantly of the SUNNI sect. There is also a small but politically significant Druse population.

This multi-sectarian state exploded into civil war on April 13, 1975 after a succession of religiously motivated assassinations by both Muslims and Christians. The civil war has continued for more than fourteen years. During that time the country has been forcibly invaded by both SYRIA and ISRAEL, the United Nations has dispatched multinational peacekeeping forces, and the United

States temporarily sent in Marines. In 1982 and again in 1989 Lebanese presidents were assassinated by their religious rivals. The anarchy within the country has made it a fertile area for terrorism, and its proximity to Israel has made it an attractive base of operation for terrorist INFILTRATION of its southern neighbor. Numerous terrorist organizations have operated out of Lebanon, including: HEZBOLLAH, the PALESTINE LIBERATION ORGANIZATION and various ARMENIAN TERRORISM groups.

References: Michael Hudson, *The Precarious Republic: Political Modernization in Lebanon* (New York: Random House, 1968); Kamal Joumblatt, *I Speak for Lebanon* (London: Zed Press, 1982); Kamal Salibi, *A House of Many Mansions: The History of Lebanon Reconsidered* (Berkeley & Los Angeles: University of California Press, 1988).

LEHI

See STERN GANG.

LENIN, VLADIMIR ILYICH (1870–1924)

Russian revolutionary and leader of the Bolsheviks, considered to be the primary founder of the Soviet Union. Lenin's attitude toward terrorist acts committed in the name of revolution and political progress was undoubtedly shaped by the deeds of his brother Alexander, who was executed in 1887 for plotting to kill the tsar. Lenin supported "necessary measures" against both the imperial state and rival political groups; these acts of terror were often carried out under the direction of Joseph STALIN.

LETELIER, ORLANDO (1932–76)

Former Foreign Minister in the Chilean government (1970–73) of Salvador Allende. Letelier was assassinated on Embassy Row in Washington, D.C. on September 21, 1976. An American associate, Ronni Moffit, also died in the attack. In 1980 a Federal District Court concluded that the assassins were agents of the right-wing regime of General Pinochet. The United States has requested Chile to extradite a number of senior Chilean military officers implicated in the crime. In October 1988 the Reagan administration demanded that the Chilean government pay the U.S. $12 million in compensation for the victims' families and for costs incurred in the criminal investigation. So far the government of Chile has refused to honor the U.S. claims.

References: Taylor Branch and Eugene M. Propper, *Labyrinth* (New York: Viking, 1982); Donald Freed and F. Landis, *Death in Washington: The Murder of Orlando Letelier* (London: Zed Press, 1980); John Dinges and Saul Landau, *Assassination on Embassy Row* (New York: Pantheon Books, 1980).

LIBERATION THEOLOGY

A brand of Christian theology which proposes that corrupt political and social systems should be overthrown, by violent means if necessary, so as to permit the formation of a political and social order closer to the ideals expressed and implicit in the teachings of Jesus Christ. Liberation theology is most clearly identified with the Roman Catholic Church in Latin America, where activist priests and lay Catholics have found in their liberation theology justification for armed revolution against repressive conditions. The Vatican of Pope John Paul II has been very critical of armed insurrection under the banner of Catholic theology.

References: Richard L. Rubenstein, "The Political Significance of Latin American Liberation Theology," *World Affairs* 148 (Winter

1985–86); Roberta Steinfeld Jacobson, "Liberation Theology as a Revolutionary Ideology in Latin America," *Fletcher Forum* 10 (Summer 1986); Manzar Foroohar, "Liberation Theology: The Response of Latin American Catholics to Socioeconomic Problems," *Latin American Perspectives* 13 (Summer 1986).

LIBERATION TIGERS OF TAMIL EELAM (LTTE)

A Sri Lankan Tamil separatist guerrilla organization, founded in 1972. The group developed partly in reaction to the repression of Sinhalese security forces. The Tigers are the strongest of the Tamil militant organizations and are the only major group that has fought the Indian Peace Keeping Force in Sri Lanka. The group is based in Jaffna and is thought to have membership of 2,000. The Tigers are led by Vellupillai Probhakaran.

Tamil separatists seek an autonomous state in the northern and eastern portions of the island nation of Sri Lanka. The Tamils are primarily Hindu and are a minority, accounting for about 22% of the Sri Lankan population, while the Sinhalese, primarily Buddhist, account for approximately 71%. In 1981 the Tigers were responsible for numerous assassinations of moderate political candidates and policemen. In late July 1983, 13 soldiers were killed in a Tiger ambush, and after their funeral in the city of Colombo, hysteria broke out among the mourners and savage anti-Tamil violence followed. Many innocent Tamils were slaughtered and many homes and businesses destroyed.

In March 1987 the government of Sri Lanka requested help in battling the separatists, and the Indian government subsequently sent more than 40,000 troops to battle the guerrillas. The LTTE has refused to compromise and disarm, frequently battling with other Tamils. The LTTE is dedicated to total sovereignty, and the level of Tiger commitment to this cause is evidenced by the vial of cianide which many Tigers wear around their necks, to facilitate suicide in the event of capture. Meanwhile, the Indian Peace Keeping Force has begun withdrawing from the island at the request of the Sri Lankan government.

See JVP.

References: Robert C. Oberst, "Sri Lanka's Tamil Tigers." *Conflict* 8 (1988); James Manor, ed., *Sri Lanka: In Change and in Crises* (New York: St. Martin's Press, 1984).

LIBYA

The North African state between Egypt and Tunisia, its small population, about 4 million, lives in an area much larger than Egypt, which has more than ten times Libya's population. In 1969 Colonel Muammar QADDAFI took power in a military coup and closed American and British military bases on Libyan territory and partially nationalized all foreign oil and commercial interests in Libya. He played a key role in introducing oil as a political weapon to make the West alter support for Israel. In pursuit of his goal of Arab unity, Qaddafi has tried unsuccessfully at various times to merge with Egypt, Sudan, Tunisia, Algeria and Syria.

After the 1969 coup, U.S.-Libyan relations became increasingly strained because of Libya's foreign policies supporting international terrorism and subversion against moderate Arab and African governments. In 1972, the United States recalled its ambassador and did not replace him. U.S. Embassy staff members were withdrawn from Tripoli after a mob attacked and set fire to the embassy in December 1979. In May 1981, the U.S. government closed the Libyan People's Bureau (embassy) in Washington and expelled the Libyan staff in response to a general pattern of conduct by the People's Bureau contrary to internationally accepted standards of diplomatic behavior. In August 1981, over international waters of the Mediterranean illegally claimed by Libya, two Libyan jets fired upon U.S. Aircraft participating in a routine U.S. naval exercise. The U.S. planes returned fire and shot down the attacking Libyan aircraft. In December 1981, the State Department invalidated U.S. passports for travel to Libya and asked all U.S. citizens in Libya to leave.

In view of Libya's continuing support for terrorism, the United States adopted economic sanctions against Libya in 1986, including a total ban on trade. In addition, Libyan government assets in the United States were frozen. When evidence of Libyan complicity was discovered in a Berlin discotheque terrorist bombing that killed one American serviceman, the United States responded by launching an aerial bombing attack against targets near Tripoli and Benghazi in April 1986.

In 1988, it was discovered that Libya was in the process of constructing a chemical weapons plant, which was the largest such facility in the Third World. Libya's support for terrorism and its past regional aggressions made this development a matter of major concern to the United States. In cooperation with like-minded countries, the United States has since sought to bring to a halt the foreign technical assistance deemed essential to the completion of this facility.

According to the U.S. Department of State, Libya under the leadership of Muammar Qaddafi has provided weapons, training, funding and other forms of support to approximately 30 insurgent and terrorist groups around the world. These organizations include ASALA, the JAPANESE RED ARMY, M-19, MRTA, and several of the most lethal Pales-

tinian groups, including the ABU NIDAL Organization and the POPULAR STRUGGLE FRONT.

In June 1989 several sources reported that Libya had abruptly ended its support of radical Palestinian groups and Lebanese factions. Arab diplomats interpreted this development as an apparent move toward moderation by Qaddafi, who was cited as supportive of new Arab diplomatic approaches to the Lebanese problem. The leader of the Lebanese Druse militia accused Qaddafi and Libya of reneging on promises of support. Libya had funded the Druse militia for more than a decade.

References: Paul Wapner, "Problems of U.S. Counter-Terrorism: The Case of Libya," *Alternatives* 13 (April 1988); Philip Jenkins, "Whose Terrorists? Libya and State Criminality," *Contemporary Crises: Law, Crime, and Social Policy* 12 (March 1988); Noam Chomsky, "Libya in U.S. Demonology," in *Pirates and Emperors* (New York: Claremont Press, 1986); John K. Cooley, *Libyan Sandstorm* (New York: Holt, Rinehart, and Winston, 1982).

LIMITED WAR

1. A war in which at least one of the parties refrains from using all of its resources to defeat the enemy. The term is used in strategic discussions to mean virtually anything short of full-scale nuclear war. Limits can be set in two dimensions: the area and number of participants, or the means used to wage the war. A third variable that once would have been important refers to the goals of the opposing sides. In modern times it is more likely that "limited war" refer to a confrontation that does not involve the superpowers or that, if it does include the superpowers, is fought away from Europe and without nuclear weapons.

The problem with the concept of limited war is that war is only ever limited from an external perspective. So, for example, many would regard the Arab–Israeli wars as limited. They only involved second- and third-rank powers, did not use nuclear or chemical weapons, were geographically restricted and were short in duration. The Israeli High Command, however, would not have viewed them as limited, as the very existence of the state of Israel was threatened.

2. State-sponsored terrorism in that this is a relatively cheap way to war against another state; cheap so long as the other side does not escalate to a full-scale war.

References: Stephen Peter Rosen, "Vietnam and the American Theory of Limited War," *International Security* 7 (Fall 1982); Christopher D. Jones, "Just Wars and Limited Wars: Restraints on the Use of the Soviet Armed Forces," *World Politics* 28 (October 1975); William Vincent O'Brien, *The Conduct of Just and Limited War* (New York: Praeger, 1981); Yaacov Bar-Siman-Tov, "Constraints and Limitations in Limited Local War: The Case of the Yom Kippur War," *Jerusalem Journal of International Relations* (1981).

LOD AIRPORT MASSACRE

On May 30, 1972 three members of the JAPANESE RED ARMY attacked Tel Aviv's Lod Airport. The JRA terrorists opened fire on the crowds in the terminal with automatic weapons. Twenty-five people died, and many more were injured, before security personnel killed two of the terrorists and subdued the third. Sixteen of those killed were Puerto Rican pilgrims returning from a tour of the Holy Land.

LONG COMMISSION

A "blue ribbon" panel convened by the U.S. Department of Defense in the aftermath of the October 23, 1983 suicide truck bombing at the U.S. Marine Battalion Landing Team Headquarters at the Beirut International Airport. The findings of the panel have been widely criticized. The report issued by the Commission concluded that even had the truck bomber been intercepted at the Marines' defensive perimeter, the explosion would still have caused severe casualties. Despite having no more than circumstantial evidence, the panel concluded that there had been at least "indirect" involvement in the incident on the part of Syria and Iran.

Reference: Brian Michael Jenkins, *The Lessons of Beirut* (Santa Monica, Calif.: Rand, 1984).

LORENZO ZELAYA POPULAR REVOLUTIONARY FORCES

See FRP-LZ.

LOW-INTENSITY WARFARE

A type of conflict in which one group generally unrestrained by rules and conventions of war wages a struggle against a more formally constituted group that is constrained by institutional and legal restraints. Many conflict theorists argue that the Western powers face a greater threat from guerrilla insurgencies and terrorism than from conventional conflicts, and that the democracies must be prepared to engage in low-intensity warfare to battle non-traditional foes.

References: Lewis B. Ware *et al.*, *Low Intensity Conflict in the Third World* (Maxwell Air Force Base, Ala.: Air University Press, 1988); Donald R. Morelli and Michael M. Ferguson, "Low-Intensity Conflict: An Operational Perspective," *Military Review* (November 1984).

M

M-19 (MOVIMIENTO 19 DE ABRIL)

Spanish, "April 19th Movement." A Colombian leftist urban guerrilla movement, named for the date in 1970 on which ex-dictator Rojas Pinella was defeated in a presidential election rife with accusations and evidence of widespread fraud. M-19's ideology is a mixture of Marxist-Leninism, nationalism and populism. Its rhetoric focuses on the liberation of Colombia from the ruling oligarchy, and it stresses regional solidarity. Its strongest support is in urban areas and from university students.

The group's initial terrorist strike was the theft of Simon Bolivar's sword and spurs from a museum in January 1974. M-19 has a history of bombings, hijackings, and kidnappings, many of which have been directed against U.S. interests. The organization has launched several large-scale military attacks, including amphibious assaults on three Colombian villages in 1981. Its most infamous operation was the siege on November 13–14, 1985 of the Palace of Justice in Bogata, in which more than 100 people lost their lives. The incident ended when the Colombian army staged an assault on the terrorists, killing 24 M-19 gunmen. M-19 has had dealings with the international drug trade as a means of raising funds and has also received support and training from CUBA. Its membership is thought to exceed 1,000.

The group reportedly has ties with many active and dormant Latin American terrorist organizations, including the Uruguayan TUPAMAROS and the Ecuadorean ALFARO VIVE, CARAJO, as well as groups in El Salvador, Costa Rica, Peru, Guatemala and Venezuela. M-19 guerrillas are loosely allied with other Colombian groups and joined the Simon Bolivar Guerrilla Coordinator, the FARC-led alliance formed in 1987. In April 1984, M-19 announced a training and mutual assistance alliance with Spain's ETA. Many guerrillas probably receive basic training at camps in Colombia and reportedly from Cuba, Nicaragua, and Libya as well.

References: Gary Hoskin, "Colombia's Political Crisis," *Current History* (January 1988); Diego Asencio, *Our Man is Inside* (Boston: Little Brown, 1983).

MA'ALOT MASSACRE

An attack on an Israeli school by terrorists of the DEMOCRATIC FRONT FOR THE LIBERATION OF PALESTINE (DFLP) on May 15, 1974. The attack was staged on Israel's Independence Day in an attempt to force the Israeli government to release imprisoned Palestinian terrorists. Gunmen seized a school building in Ma'alot holding more than 100 students and their teachers hostage. Most of the 27 children who died were killed during a flawed rescue operation staged by Israeli anti-terrorist forces.

MACHETEROS

Spanish, "Machete wielders." The popular name for members of Ejercito Borican Popular ("The Popular Army of Borica"). The Macheteros are a violent Puerto Rican separatist organization which has attacked U.S. military targets on the island of Puerto Rico and the Puerto Rican police. The group is tightly organized and is fiercely dedicated to total independence for Puerto Rico. The stated position of the group is that they have "declared war" on the United States.

Two U.S. Navy personnel were killed by the group in December 1979. In January 1981 the Macheteros attacked Muniz Air National Guard Base and destroyed nine U.S. fighter aircraft. Members of the movement staged an attack on a U.S. government building on October 30, 1983, and another in January 1985, using powerful antitank grenade launchers. The Macheteros are thought to have participated in coordinated acts of terrorism with the FALN. Robberies and thefts evidently provide a major source of funds, and the Macheteros may also receive funding from ideological backers.

On August 30, 1985 the FBI arrested several leaders of the group on the island of Puerto Rico in conjunction with the $7.2 million robbery of the Wells Fargo Depot in West Hartford, Connecticut. The Macheteros have been generally quiet since that time.

References: Ronald Fernandez, *Los Macheteros* (Englewood Cliffs, N.J.: Prentice Hall, 1987); Bruce Hoffman, *Terrorism in the United States and the Potential Threat to Nuclear Facilities* (Santa Monica, Calif.: Rand, 1986).

MANDELA, NELSON

The symbol of the South African anti-apartheid movement and leader of the AFRICAN NATIONAL CONGRESS (ANC). Mandela, born in 1918, became a lawyer and joined the ANC in 1944. In 1951–52 he led a "defiance campaign" against apartheid laws. Named deputy national president of the ANC in 1952, he advocated nonviolent resistance and the creation of a nonracial state in South Africa. After the Sharpeville Massacres in 1960 in which 69 unarmed black protesters were killed by the police, Mandela created a paramilitary group to carry out sabotage. Arrested in 1963, he was later convicted of sabotage and sentenced to life imprisonment. Mandela was imprisoned from 1963 to 1990 by the South African government. Mandela consistently refused to accede to government demands that he renounce antiapartheid violence as a precondition to his release. Since his release he has worked with the South African government to peacefully end apartheid.

MANO BLANCO

See WHITE HAND.

MANUEL RODRIGUEZ PATRIOTIC FRONT (MRPF)

In Spanish, "Frente Patriotico Manuel Rodriguez." A left-wing Chilean guerrilla organization which takes its name from a 19th-century Chilean revolutionary executed by Spanish authorities. The MRPF was founded by young members of the Chilean Communist Party in 1983 and has conducted many violent attacks against police and government targets. In early 1985 MRPF spokesman Daniel Huerta said that the purpose of the group was exclusively to conduct urban terrorist operations and that the organization was based on a cellular structure of militants, who would earn their status by demonstrating "selflessness, sacrifice, combat ability, solidarity, and moral and military qualities."

The MRPF has an impressive arsenal that includes remotely-detonated bombs and a variety of small arms, rocket-propelled grenades, and hand grenades. Several caches of weapons have been discovered by authorities, but attacks continue, indicating sufficient sources of supplies. The group's operations have primarily been bombings, although it has also carried out kidnappings and assassinations. The MRPF was responsible for the nearly successful assassination attempt against Chilean president Pinochet in September 1986. Although the MRPF has been most active in Santiago, it has conducted operations in at least eight other cities. It frequently uses the mass media in its campaigns and has on occasion seized radio stations to broadcast its propaganda.

It is thought that CUBA has provided training and material support to the MRPF. The Chilean Communist Party, at its March 1989 Congress, was divided as to the appropriateness of continuing violence against the Pinochet regime as Chile approached its first free elections in more than 15 years. Many Party officials have expressed outrage at the MRPF's continued attacks, which are viewed by many Party members as politically damaging. Now that Chile has a democratically elected government, the MRPF must redefine its tactics and goals.

MARIGHELLA, CARLOS (1912–69)

Brazilian Communist urban guerrilla leader and theorist, and a major influence on guerrilla groups and terrorist organizations around the globe. His most famous work,

The Mini-manual of the Urban Guerrilla, has been translated into many languages and was adopted as a "how-to" instruction book by the Uruguayan TUPAMAROS, who were in turn a major influence on subsequent guerrilla organizations. The manual presented, among other topics, techniques for raising funds (through ransoms and thefts), liquidating the opposition, mastering the art of document forgery and performing emergency surgery on wounded comrades. Marighella founded the Acao Libertadora Nacional (ACN) in 1968 but was killed by police in November 1969.

Reference: Carlos Marighella, *For the Liberation of Brazil* (Middlesex, U.K.: Penguin Books, 1971).

MAROUKA, OSAMU

Japanese terrorist and a leader of the JAPANESE RED ARMY. He was arrested by police in November 1988, and Japanese police used evidence obtained through an investigation of Marouka to uncover a JRA network stretching from Japan to North Korea to Europe.

MARTYRDOM

Self-sacrifice (suicide) for a religious or political cause. This is an ancient ritual that was present in pagan societies prior to the advent of the Judeo-Christian tradition. The best-known early martyrs in the Jewish faith were the zealots of Masada who killed themselves rather than surrender to Roman conquerors. With the rise of Christianity came a second wave of religious martyrs; early Christians in the Roman Empire would literally "go to the lions" in the arena rather than give up their faith. The latest exponents of martyrdom are from the Islamic faith and especially the Shi'ite sect who believe that suicidal acts of aggression against perceived enemies of Islam have a divine sanction.

References: Ronald Ellis Agus, *The Binding of Isaac and Messiah: Law, Martyrdom, and Deliverance in Early Rabbinic Religiosity* (Albany, NY: State University of New York Press, 1988); Robin Wright, *Sacred Rage* (New York: Simon & Schuster, 1985).

MARXIST-LENINIST ARMED PROPAGANDA UNIT (MLAPU)

A Turkish terrorist organization active in the 1970s and early 1980s. The MLAPU was considered to be the most anti-American of all left-wing Turkish groups, killing seven U.S. citizens in 1979 and one in 1980. The group was severely damaged by a government crackdown following the imposition of martial law in Turkey in September 1980. In the crackdown many members were killed or arrested, safehouses were raided and MLAPU members already in prison were executed.

MAS

Spanish, "Death to Kidnappers." A Colombian right-wing organization that is believed to be an umbrella group for paramilitary organizations responsible for numerous attacks against leftists, moderates and government officials. Ironically, one of the leading patrons of MAS has been Pablo ESCOBAR GAVIRIA, the cocaine trafficker who leads the MEDELLIN drug cartel. Kidnapping has long been a key element of Escobar's NARCO-TERRORISM strategy in his war with the Bogota government. Members of the group are suspected in the January 1989 slayings of 12 members of a judicial commission that

was examining DEATH SQUAD violence in Colombia.

MASAWI, HUSSEIN

Former military commander of AMAL, the Lebanese SHI'ITE militia. A disagreement over policy with Amal leader Nabih BERRI led Masawi in 1982 to form his own group, ISLAMIC AMAL, an organization far more extreme in its tactics than Amal. Masawi, who had undergone guerrilla training in IRAN, quickly allied his group with that government. U.S. authorities have considered Masawi to be a prime suspect in the October 23, 1983 bombings of U.S. and French military headquarters in Beirut, a charge which Masawi has denied. By late 1983, Islamic Amal had effectively fallen under the loose umbrella organization of HEZBOLLAH.

MAU MAU

Kenyan anti-colonial guerrilla organization that waged violent anti-British operations during the 1950s. The group was led by Jomo Kenyatta (1893–1978), who later became president of independent Kenya.

MAXIMILIANO HERNANDEZ MARTINEZ ANTI-COMMUNIST ALLIANCE

A Salvadoran right-wing death squad, with strong ties to that country's military and police forces. Roberto D'Aubisson, leader of El Salvador's ARENA party, has been a major force behind the organization. This group is generally believed to be responsible for the March 1980 assassination of Archbishop Oscar ROMERO, as well as for a wide-ranging campaign of violence and repression against leftists, moderates, religious leaders, human rights workers, university students and instructors and labor union members.

MAY 15 GROUP

A Palestinian terrorist organization led by Mohammed al-UMARI, who is considered to be loyal to Yasir ARAFAT. The group is named for the date of Israel's Independence Day. Umari, who is widely known as Abu Ibrahim, is an explosives expert who specializes in aircraft bombings. In April 1986 the group bombed a TWA flight in which four people died. On October 15, 1985, two members of the group were arrested in Rome as they emerged from a flight from Damascus; in their possession was a quantity of the plastic explosive Semtex and an intricate high-altitude triggering device. The May 15 Group is also thought to be responsible for the bombing of a 1982 Pan Am flight en route from Tokyo to Hawaii, in which one person was killed. Very little is known about this organization. Some experts have speculated that it has had past ties to the ABU NIDAL Organization, while others consider it to be no longer operative.

MCKINLEY, WILLIAM (1843–1901)

The 25th president of the United States, a Republican from Ohio. He was shot by Leon Czolgosz, an anarchist, on September 6, 1901 in Buffalo, New York. McKinley died on September 14, 1901. He was succeeded as president by Vice President Theodore Roosevelt.

MEDELLIN CARTEL

The term used to describe the group of Colombian drug barons which controls the majority of South American cocaine trafficking. The Colombian city of Medellin served as the base of operations for Pablo ESCOBAR GAVIRIA and Jose Gonzalo RODRIGUEZ GACHA, whose criminal organizations are said to have been responsible for 80% of the cocaine smuggling into the United States. Until recently the cartel operated in Colombia with complete impunity as the result of a NARCO-TERRORISM campaign that cowed the Bogota government.

References: Anthony P. Maingot, "Laundering Drug Profits," *Journal of InterAmerican Studies and World Affairs* 30 (Summer/Fall 1988); Rensselaer Lee III, "Dimensions of the South American Cocaine Industry," *Journal of InterAmerican Studies and World Affairs* 30 (Summer/Fall 1988).

MEINHOF, ULRIKE (1934–1976)

One of the founding members, with Andreas Baader, of the RED ARMY FACTION, also called the Baader-Meinhof Gang, in West Germany. Meinhof was a left-wing journalist before she turned to terrorism in 1970. After being trained by Palestinians in Jordan, she returned to West Germany to rob banks and bomb symbols of bourgeois society. Captured in 1972, she was found dead by hanging in her prison cell in 1976.

MEXICO

The government of Mexico has been implicated in DEATH SQUAD activities that resulted in the deaths of more than 60 political prisoners during the late 1970s and early 1980s. Suspicions of human rights groups about alleged involvement of the Mexican Army in death squad activity were given strong credence by the testimony of a former Mexican soldier, who confessed to complicity in death squad violence during a February 1989 hearing before a Canadian Immigration Board. In his testimony, the political refugee asserted that the Mexican Ministry of

Defense regularly issued direct orders for clandestine murders during the term of President Luis Lopez Portillo. Mexico categorically denies such charges. The United Nations lists 194 unexplained disappearances in Mexico, while human rights groups have cited more than 540 disappearances linked to political activities.

Reference: Larry Rohter, "Former Mexican Soldier Describes Executions of Political Prisoners," *New York Times* (February 19, 1989).

MIR (MOVIMIENTO DE LA IZQUIERDA REVOLUCIONARIA)

Movement of the Revolutionary Left; a left-wing Chilean organization formed by radical university students in 1965. The group is committed to the establishment of a Marxist state in Chile and has been involved in occasional acts of violence against U.S. and Chilean government targets. The MIR began a close association with the CASTRO regime in CUBA very early in its history, and Cuba continues to support the group's operations. Andres Pascal Allende, the leader of the group, runs the MIR from his headquarters in exile in Havana.

After the 1973 military coup in Chile, the MIR did more to resist the consolidation of the military rule of the Pinochet regime than any other Chilean opposition group and was consequently suppressed by the government. Many MIR leaders, including Miguel Enriquez, the MIR chief, were killed in shoot-outs with the military, while many others fled the country. The political wing of the MIR collapsed, and the group became a purely guerrilla organization, albeit ineffective. After the social unrest of 1983, the MIR rebounded somewhat, both militarily and politically. The political wing is far larger than the group's guerrilla arm. Total MIR membership is estimated at 500.

To help finance its operations, the MIR has relied increasingly on bank robberies. Equipment captured by authorities has included automatic weapons and antitank rockets. The group also has demonstrated the ability to construct a variety of explosive devices.

Reference: William Sater, *The Revolutionary Left and Terrorist Violence in Chile* (Santa Monica, Calif.: Rand, 1986).

MNR (MOZAMBIQUE NATIONAL RESISTANCE)

A right-wing terrorist organization that seeks to undermine the left-wing government of Mozambique. The formation of the MNR in 1975 was fostered by the governments of Rhodesia (now Zimbabwe) and South Africa, which supplied training, weapons and finances to the fledgling organization. The MNR has been quite successful in preventing the government from consolidating control over the former Portuguese colony. The MNR maintains a dominant role in parts of the country and has carried out a fierce campaign of sabotage against government targets. The group is also thought to be responsible for acts of terrorism against the government of Zimbabwe.

MOHTASHEMI, ALI AKBAR

Iranian SHI'ITE militant, a key figure in the IRANIAN HOSTAGE CRISIS and later Interior Minister in the government of the Ayatollah KHOMEINI. Mohtashemi has strong ties to Lebanese Shi'ite terrorists, including HEZBOLLAH. He is presently a leading opposition figure in Iran, having been unseated by Iranian president Mohammad Rafsanjani after the death of Khomeini in 1989.

MOLUCCANS

An east Asian people fighting to resist the absorption of their archipelago into Indonesia. During the 1970s they resorted to terrorism, primarily conducted in Europe, in an attempt to force the Dutch government, the island's former colonial master, to assist them in gaining independence. Among their violent activities of 1975–77 were an attempt to kidnap Queen Juliana of the Netherlands, a bombing at the Indonesian consulate in The Hague and two passenger train hijackings in the Dutch countryside.

MOLLY MAGUIRES

A secret society of Pennsylvania coal miners responsible for hundreds of murders and attacks against representatives of mine owners and mine supervisors during the second half of the 19th century. The Molly Maguires were Irish Catholics, and most of the bosses and owners were English or Welsh, and overwhelmingly Protestant; Hence, the violence transcended the simple explanation of a labor–ownership struggle and included cultural, religious and political elements as well.

The group's name was based on the legend of an Irish heroine who led poverty-stricken farmers in revolt against the despised bailiffs who collected exorbitant rents for absentee English landlords. The Molly Maguires' revolt was manifested in shadowy, clandestine and extremely brutal attacks against individuals perceived to be representing the interests of the absentee owners of eastern Pennsylvania coal mines. In the period between 1862 and 1875 in Schuykill County, Pennsylvania, there were 142 unsolved homicides and 212 felonious attacks, almost all of which were attributable to the miners' group.

In response to the mounting violence, the owners retained service of the famed detective Allan Pinkerton, who assigned James McFarlan to the case as an undercover field agent. McFarlan infiltrated the Molly Maguires, posing for two and a half years as a sympathizer and labor activist; he amassed enough evidence during that time to bring guilty verdicts against many members of the group. Twenty were hanged, including 10 on one day in 1877.

References: Arthur H. Lewis, *Lament for the Molly Maguires* (New York: Harcourt, Brace and World, 1964); Wayne G. Broehl, Jr., *The Molly Maguires* (Cambridge, Mass.: Harvard University Press, 1964).

MONTENEROS

The popular name of the Movimiento Peronista Montenero (MPM), Spanish for "Peronist Montenero Movement." The Monteneros were an Argentine guerrilla organization, founded in 1970 to further the left-wing nationalist policies of Juan Domingo Peron, the former dictator of Argentina. The group was very popular in the early 1970s, with perhaps 10,000 supporters. When Peron returned to power in 1974, the Monteneros were taken aback by his right-wing policies and mounted a campaign of anti-government terrorism. The group was decimated by the DIRTY WAR of the mid-1970s and was unable to return to its former strength or influence.

Reference: Richard Gillespie, *Soldiers of Peron: Argentina's Monteneros* (Oxford, U.K.: Oxford University Press, 1982).

MONTREAL CONVENTION (1971)

The Convention for the Suppression of Unlawful Acts Against the Safety of Civil Aviation, of the United Nations International

Civil Aviation Organization, September 23, 1971. This agreement built on the work of the HAGUE CONVENTION by expanding the agreement to include acts, in addition to hijacking, that "endanger the safety of an aircraft in flight."

MORO, ALDO (1916–78)

Moro was prime minister of Italy and leader of the Christian Democratic Party when he was abducted by the RED BRIGADES in Rome on March 16, 1978. The terrorists killed five bodyguards during the ambush of Moro's escort. Moro was subjected to a Red Brigades "people's court." The Italian government refused to make any concessions to the terrorists, who demanded the release of imprisoned fellow members of their organization. On May 9th the Red Brigades directed police to a car in downtown Rome, the trunk of which contained the bullet-riddled body of Moro.

References: Adrian Lyttelton, "Murder in Rome," *New York Review of Books* 34 (June 25, 1987); Robert Katz, *Days of Wrath: The Ordeal of Aldo Moro* (Garden City, N.J.: Doubleday, 1980).

MORO LIBERATION FRONT (MLF)

A Philippine Muslim guerrilla organization and the primary non-communist separatist organization in the Philippines. The Moros seek Islamic rule on Mindanao and other southern islands of the Philippines and have battled the government since 1972. The MLF was formed in response to rampant anti-Muslim violence of the 1960s, and its name is derived from "Bangsa Moro," the native term for "Islamic self-rule." The group achieved a high degree of success in its guerrilla operations during the period of 1971–76, but it is generally agreed that the

MLF was co-opted by the Marcos regime from 1977 to 1984. In recent years the MLF has been linked to the revolutionary government in Iran, which has provided support and training. President Corazon Aquino signed a truce with the MLF in 1986, and MLF violence has subsided substantially since that time. Also known as the Moro National Liberation Front (MNLF).

References: Lela Garner Noble, "The Philippines: Autonomy for the Muslims," in John L. Esposito, *Islam in Asia* (New York: Oxford University Press, 1987).

MOUNTAIN OFFICERS

A clandestine group of far-right Guatemalan military officers, which claimed responsibility for the 1988 bombing of an office of Mexicana Airlines to protest the airline's transport of leftist leaders. The group made several death threats against civilian president Mario Vinicio Cerezo Arevalo in Spring 1988.

MOUNTBATTEN, LORD LOUIS (1900–79)

Member of the British royal family who was assassinated by terrorists of the PROVISIONAL WING OF THE IRISH REPUBLICAN ARMY (PIRA) off the coast of Ireland on August 27, 1979. A 50-pound bomb exploded aboard Mountbatten's fishing boat shortly after it had left the Irish shore, killing him, his 14-year-old grandson, and a young Irish companion. Four others were seriously wounded including Mountbatten's daughter, Patricia. The assassination of the highly popular Mountbatten, a Royal Navy admiral who had played a major role in World War II and had served as the last viceroy of India, outraged many IRA supporters, especially Irish-Americans. Indignation in the United

States severely curtailed fundraising for the Irish Northern Aid Committee (NORAID) and prompted American authorities to more actively pursue IRA operatives in the United States.

MOVEMENT FOR THE LIBERATION OF BAHRAIN

A secret SHI'ITE Muslim organization established in 1983. Comprised of young militant Shi'ites, this group seeks to establish a revolutionary Islamic government in Bahrain. It is greatly influenced by, and has the full support of, the Iranian government.

MOVIMIENTO DE LA IZQUIERDA REVOLUCIONARIA

See MIR.

MOVIMIENTO DE LIBERACION NACIONAL (MLN)

See TUPAMAROS.

MOVIMIENTO POPULAR DE LIBERACION

See CINCHONEROS.

MRTA (MOVIMIENTO REVOLUCIONARIO TUPAC AMARU)

"Tupac Amaru Revolutionary Movement." A Marxist-Leninist Peruvian guerrilla movement formed in 1983 and named after an 18th-century Peruvian rebel leader. When the MRTA first surfaced in 1984, many thought that it was a cover name for the SENDERO LUMINOSO (SL), Peru's major terrorist/insurgent organization. Available information indicates that the MRTA is an independent group founded by radical university students who espouse a Castroite, Marxist-Leninist ideology. The group seeks to conduct "armed propaganda" to destabilize the Peruvian government and to create a public image that presents MRTA as a militant group aligned with international Marxist revolutionary movements and proponents (in contrast to the xenophobic SL).

Despite its short history, the MRTA has been very active. It has made attacks on U.S. targets a priority policy. In 1983 it bombed a U.S. Embassy Marine Guard residence, and in September 1984 it was responsible for a series of attacks against U.S. and other targets in Lima. Later that September MRTA forced the staff at two American wire services to issue a statement condemning U.S. imperialism. Other anti-American acts include the 1985 burnings of several Kentucky Fried Chicken restaurants. In 1986 MRTA set off a car bomb outside the U.S. Ambassador's residence in Lima. The tactics used and the proficiency demonstrated in MRTA attacks indicate that the group has a relatively high degree of skill.

Some contact apparently exists with other Latin American revolutionary groups, such as Colombia's M-19. Some of the MRTA leadership lived in CUBA and the Soviet Union during the 1970s, after fleeing Peru following a government crackdown on student radicals. The group is led by Ernesto Montes Aliaga.

In Fall 1986, the MRTA announced a merger with the remnants of the earlier Peruvian radical group MIR. The group then conducted a series of bombings in Lima to publicize the new alliance.

A small organization, with an estimated active membership of 500 to 1,500, the MRTA requires relatively little money to support its operations. Through robberies and extortion activities directed at businessmen and narcotics traffickers, the MRTA appears to be capable of attaining sufficient funding for its operations. It is elitist; many of its leaders are from powerful and wealthy families, although there are peasants in the rank and file. This is in contrast to Sendero Luminoso, which is drawn from the country's Indian population. Also distinguishing it is MRTA's announced policy of avoiding harming civilians. Police raids have captured modern weapons, including automatic weapons and a wide variety of commercial and homemade explosives.

References: David Scott Palmer, "Rebellion in Rural Peru: The Origins and Evolution of Sendero Luminoso," *Comparative Politics* 18 (January 1986); Ronald H. Berg, "Sendero Luminoso and Peasants of Andahuaylas," *Journal of InterAmerican Studies and World Affairs* 28 (Winter 1986/87).

MUGHANUJA, IMAD

Arab mastermind of the April 1988 hijacking of a Kuwaiti airliner. Formerly an officer of al-FATAH, Mughanuja is a SHI'ITE extremist with ties to HEZBOLLAH. He has received training in IRAN and is thought to be implicated in Hezbollah's French and American hostage-taking campaign.

MUNICH MASSACRE

The attack on Israeli athletes by terrorists of the BLACK SEPTEMBER group, reportedly sponsored by LIBYA, during the 1972 Olympic Games in Munich, West Germany. Eight Black September terrorists entered the athletes' quarters on September 5, taking nine athletes hostage and murdering two others. They demanded the release of more than 200 Palestinians in Israeli jails, as well as members of the JAPANESE RED ARMY and the Baader-Meinhof Gang (RED ARMY FACTION). In an unsuccessful rescue attempt, all the remaining athlete hostages were killed by a Black September grenade. Five of the terrorists died in a shoot-out with police, and the three remaining terrorists were imprisoned, only to be freed in accordance with terrorist demands made during an October 1972 hijacking of a Lufthansa jetliner.

MUSA, SAED

See ABU MUSA.

MUSLIM BROTHERHOOD

An organization founded in Egypt in 1928 by Hassan al-BANNA to foster a regeneration of Islamic fundamentalism throughout the Arab world. On October 26, 1954 the group failed in an attempt on the life of Gamal Abdel Nasser, president of Egypt. It has drawn considerable support from across the social spectrum and has played an important role in Egyptian politics throughout its existence. In 1981 many members were expelled from the Egyptian armed forces after the assassination of Anwar al-SADAT by Islamic fanatics, but in recent years President Hosni Mubarak appears to look upon the Brotherhood as a favorable alternative to more radical groups such as al-Takfir wal Higra, which was responsible for Sadat's death.

The group has also opposed the ASSAD regime in SYRIA, which responded in 1982 with an attack against the city of HAMAH, whose population forms the core of the Brotherhood's support base. An estimated 25,000 of Hamah's 180,000 citizens died at the hands of the Syrian army.

Reference: Richard Mitchell, *The Society of the Muslim Brothers* (London: Oxford University Press, 1966).

MUSLIM STUDENTS ORGANIZATION

A U.S. pro-Iranian, pro-KHOMEINI group that has been tied to Iranian attempts to squash exiled dissidents in the United States. The MSO is believed to have recruited the Black Muslims who shot Shah Reis, a prominent dissident voice, in July 1980 in Los Angeles.

N

NACCACHE, ANIS

Lebanese SHI'ITE terrorist who in France attempted to assassinate Shahpur Bakhtiar, former prime minister under the Shah of Iran. Naccache killed a policeman and an innocent bystander during a failed attempt to kill Bakhtiar in 1980 and was given a life sentence by a French court. Naccache's freedom is thought to have been a condition of the secret hostage release agreement between French prime minister Jacques Chirac and the government of Ayatollah KHOMEINI in 1988. Naccache and his four fellow conspirators were released in July 1990.

NAR (NUCLEI ARMATI RIVOLUZIONARI)

An Italian FASCIST organization with a history of violent attacks against leftists. The NAR seeks to overthrow the existing Italian system and replace it with a militaristic right-wing government.

NARCO-TERRORISM

1. A concept that attempts to link international terrorism and international drug trafficking as parallel "industries" which interact synergistically. Proponents of this theory find that both of these industries disrupt society through violent means that are outside the accepted norms of war and diplomacy. Dr. Rachel Ehrenfeld suggests that narco-terrorism may be used to "undermine the very foundations of target societies." In addition, the sale of drugs is an oft-utilized and highly profitable source of revenue for terrorist organizations.

2. Acts of terrorism perpetrated by drug kingpins and dealers in order to intimidate and neutralize anti-drug legislation and government and private anti-drug campaigns. Colombian drug cartels, most notably the infamous MEDELLIN group, have been the most active practitioners of narco-terrorism, conducting assassinations of prosecutors and judges, bombings and other physical threats. In the most heinous act in its escalating war against the Colombian government, the Medellin cartel, operating under the name the EXTRADITABLES, on November 27, 1989, exploded an Avianca Airlines passenger plane in mid-flight, killing all 107 people aboard. An anonymous caller later claimed the plane had been bombed in order to kill five police informants among the passengers.

References: Rachel Ehrenfeld, "Narco-terrorism and the Cuban Connection," *Strategic Review* 16 (Summer 1988); Grant Wardlaw, "Linkages Between the Illegal Drugs Traffic and Terrorism," *Conflict Quarterly* 8

(Summer 1988); R. Ehrenfeld and M. Kahan, "The 'Doping' of America: The Ambivalence of the Narco-terrorist Connection and a Search for Solutions," in *Contemporary Research on Terrorism*, edited by Paul Wilkinson and A. M. Stewart (Aberdeen, U.K.: Aberdeen University Press, 1987); Mark S. Steinitz, "Insurgents, Terrorists, and the Drug Trade," *Washington Quarterly* (Fall 1985).

NASSIRI, GENERAL NEMATOLLAH

As the chief of SAVAK, the Shah of Iran's dreaded secret police, Nassiri presided for 15 years (prior to 1978) over a brutal campaign against the regime's opponents. A loyal and close associate of the Shah, he was nonetheless arrested and imprisoned on the Shah's orders during the last months of his rule. Still in prison when KHOMEINI assumed power, he was quickly put on trial and executed, one of the first defendants tried under Islamic justice.

NATIONAL ALLIANCE

One of the three factions of the PLO that emerged after the break between Yasir ARAFAT and his Syrian supporters in 1983–84. This group, based in Damascus, consisted of members of al-FATAH who rejected Arafat's policies of "deviation" from the original military orientation of the PLO, considered Arafat and his bureaucracy to be corrupt, and were incensed over Arafat's handling of the 1982 Israeli invasion of Lebanon.

See DEMOCRATIC ALLIANCE.

NATIONAL ARAB YOUTH FOR THE LIBERATION OF PALESTINE (NAYLP)

See ARAB NATIONALIST YOUTH ORGANIZATION FOR THE LIBERATION OF PALESTINE.

NATIONAL ASSEMBLY

A West German neo-Nazi organization banned by the West German government in February 1989. Subsequent police raids of National Assembly supporters and members uncovered supplies of arms, ammunition, radio communications gear and Nazi paraphernalia. West German Interior Minister Frederick Zimmerman, in announcing the ban, stated that "West Germany will not be a playing field for right-wing extremism." The group's membership was estimated at 170.

Reference: Serge Schmemann, "Bonn Bans Neo-Nazis and Raids Their Homes," *New York Times* (February 10, 1989).

NATIONAL FRONT

A British racist political organization very active in the mid- and late 1970s. Founded in 1967 out of the remains of several fascist groups, the National Front espoused an anti-immigrant policy and was avowedly anti-black, anti-Semitic and anti-Asian. It commonly provoked violent clashes with leftists and with minorities and precipitated racial riots in London.

NATIONAL FRONT FOR THE LIBERATION OF CORSICA (FNLC)

A Corsican separatist organization that directs terrorist actions against French targets, both in France and in Corsica. In 1985 the FNLC was responsible for 96 of the 142 incidents of domestic terrorism in France. The group's attacks generally consist of bombings of property, occurring at night so as to avoid human injury.

NATIONAL LIBERATION ARMY

See ELN.

NATIONAL SALVATION FRONT

An anti-ARAFAT faction of the PALESTINE LIB-ERATION ORGANIZATION (PLO) supported by SYRIA and LIBYA. The NSF is a loose collection of PLO radical groups, which includes the PFLP, the PFLP-GC, the POPULAR STRUGGLE FRONT, SA'IQA, FATAH rebels led by ABU MUSA and the Damascus-based faction of the PALESTINE LIBERATION FRONT.

NATIONAL SOCIALIST LIBERATION FRONT

A U.S. right-wing terrorist organization active during the 1970s. The NSLF was tied to the American Nazi Party and directed bombing attacks against left-wing groups in Southern California.

NATIONALISM

The development of a national consciousness; the totality of the cultural, historical, linguistic, psychological and social forces that pull a people together with a sense of belonging and shared values. This tends to lead to the political belief that this "national" community of people and interests should have their own political order independent from, and equal to, all of the other political communities in the world. The modern nation-state was forged by nationalistic sentiment and most of the wars of the past two centuries have been efforts to find relief for a frustrated nationalism. Much of the terrorism in the world is justified by the perpetrators in terms of nationalist sentiment.

References: James Mayall, "Nationalism and the International Order," *Millennium: Journal of International Studies* 14 (Summer 1985); Ernst B. Haas, "What Is Nationalism and Why Should We Study It?" *International Organization* 40 (Summer 1986).

NAZI

1. The acronym for Nationalsozialistische, "National Socialist." The term "Nazi" referred to members of the fascist National Socialist German Workers' Party. Founded in 1919, this fiercely nationalistic and racist political party evolved into the mechanism of Adolf Hitler's Third Reich. Hitler and the Nazi Party presided over a rule of terror that engulfed most of Europe before their defeat in World War II. The Nazi terror was both physical and psychological and included widespread persecution of minorities (such as Jews, Slavs, gypsies and homosexuals) as well as political dissidents. Nazi Germany's attempted extermination of Europe's Jewish population, which was rounded up and interned in CONCENTRATION CAMPS, has been estimated to have taken six million lives.

2. The term "Nazi," and more recently "NEO-NAZI," is now used to characterize white supremacist, militant right-wing movements such as the U.S. ARYAN NATIONS and the West German HOFFMAN SPORTS GROUP.

See FASCISM; HOLOCAUST.

References: Detlev J. K. Peukert, *Inside Nazi Germany: Conformity, Opposition and Racism in Everyday Life* (London: Batsford, 1987); David A. J. Richards, "Terror and the Law," *Human Rights* 5 (1983); William L. Shirer *The Rise and Fall of the Third Reich* (New York: Simon & Schuster 1959).

NECHAEV, SERGEI G. (1847–1882)

One of the founders of Russian revolutionary thought and an influential proponent of terrorism as a revolutionary tool. Along with Mikhail BAKUNIN, he wrote *The Catechism of the Revolutionary*, which proposed that all which "promotes the success of the revolution is moral, everything which hinders it is immoral." His emphasis on total adherence to the revolution, and the necessity to destroy existing institutions in a "blind campaign of destruction" so as to build anew, was a major influence on Russian revolutionaries.

NECKLACE

A South African slang term for a gasoline-soaked automobile tire hung around a victim's neck and ignited. The necklace is a shockingly common tool of the CHILDREN, organized, militant youths in the townships of South Africa; it is used to execute black collaborators and informers and to discourage future black collaboration with the white regime. The act of burning a person alive through the use of the necklace is called a "Kentucky," after Kentucky Fried Chicken, the international restaurant franchise.

NEO-FASCISM

"New" FASCISM characterized by many of the elements of "classic" fascism as practiced by Germany and Italy prior to and during World War II. The term is most often associated with various post–World War II oppressive regimes in South America. Argentina, Brazil, Chile and Uruguay have all had extended periods of authoritarian rule labeled neo-fascist because the military effectively took control and suspended as well as massively violated traditional civil liberties. Thus neo-fascism is often defined as state terror by right-wing military governments.

References: David Collier, *The New Authoritarianism in Latin America* (Princeton, N.J.: Princeton University Press, 1979); Anthony

James Gregor, *The Ideology of Fascism: The Rationale of Totalitarianism* (New York: Free Press, 1969); Peter G. Snow, "Latin American Violence: The Case of Argentina," in Henry H. Han (ed.) *Terrorism, Political Violence and World Order* (Landham, Md.: University of America Press, 1984).

NEO-NAZIS

"New" nazis; those who accept the racist ideology of World War II Germany. These groups, whether they are SKINHEADS or THE ORDER in the United States or the HOFFMAN MILITARY SPORTS GROUP in Germany, advocate white supremacy. They also support far-right politics, and in some instances call for the overthrow of established governments. In the United States neo-nazi groups tend to be small and splintered. Because of random attacks on non-whites and non-Christians, they are considered dangerous.

References: James Coates, *Armed and Dangerous: The Rise of the Survivalist Right* (New York: Hill and Wang, 1987); Hugh D. Graham and Ted Robert Gurr, *Violence in America: Historical and Comparative Perspectives* (Newbury Park, Calif.: Sage, 1979).

NEW AFRIKAN FREEDOM FIGHTERS (NAFF)

A militant left-wing Afro-American organization and a violent subgroup of the Republic of New Afrika, a black separatist organization that advocates the establishment of a separate black nation within the United States. In August 1985 eight members of the group were convicted on weapons and other charges stemming from an FBI investigation which, in 1984, uncovered numerous weapons and explosives belonging to the NAFF.

NEW CALEDONIA

An overseas French territory in the southwest Pacific, which includes the major island of New Caledonia and other smaller holdings. New Caledonia has been plagued by violence since the early 1980s, both from the pro-independence Kanak National Socialist Liberation Front and from the anti-independence French colonists.

Reference: Jean Guiart, "New Caledonia: Behind the Revolt," *TVI Journal* (Summer 1985).

NEW PEOPLE'S ARMY (NPA)

The guerrilla arm of the Communist Party of the Philippines (CPP), the NPA is Maoist in ideology. It was formed in about 1969 with the aim of overthrowing the government of the Philippines through protracted guerrilla warfare. Since its inception, the group has increased steadily in size and capability, and its insurgent activities have increased commensurately in scope and magnitude. The group has been fairly effective in the rural areas of the Philippines, where it has been able to exert influence and even establish control over village communities.

In the early years of the NPA, the group conducted insurgent operations throughout many of the country's provinces. Operations were often conducted on a local or regional level, usually with the intent of securing weapons and funds and harassing the security forces. Later, as the NPA grew in size and confidence, it increasingly engaged in a campaign of intimidation and terror, targeting local and provincial government officials. Other frequent targets included security personnel, local police units, informants, and members of the media who openly espoused anti-communist rhetoric.

The inability of the Philippine government to curb the growth of the movement was not just a failed effort at COUNTERINSURGENCY. The Marcos regime also failed to institute the necessary political, social and economic reforms, as well as to curb rampant corruption—actions that may have placated critics and popular support.

Although primarily a rural-based guerrilla group, the NPA is building an urban infrastructure to carry out terrorism and now uses city-based assassination units called "SPARROW SQUADS." Urban attacks focus on government officials, police, and military officers in Manila and other major cities. Except for an isolated incident in which three U.S. Navy officers were killed near Subic Bay Naval Base in 1974, the NPA did not attack U.S. targets before October 1987, when it killed two active U.S. servicemen, one retiree and a Filipino bystander at Angeles City, near Clark Airbase. The NPA has vowed to kill U.S. citizens (including civilians) who allegedly are involved in the government's counterinsurgency campaign or the internal affairs of the Philippines.

In recent years, reports of NPA purges have surfaced. The organization's atrocities against its own members suspected of collaborating have become more frequent. Some estimates of the number of NPA members, either held in clandestine NPA detention camps or executed by their own comrades, exceed 1,000. Torture is also said to be an increasingly common tactic.

The group derives most of its funding from the contributions of supporters and "taxes" extorted from local businesses. It is a sizeable organization; the U.S. Department of State estimates that the NPA has 18,000–20,000 active members, with a large support network. The political strength of the NPA has been enhanced through the success of its legal political organization, the National Democratic Front.

References: Richard Vokey, "Eenie, Meenie, Miney, Death," *Newsweek* (June 19, 1989); William Chapman, "A Philippine Laboratory of Revolution," *Washington Post* (May 19, 1985).

NEW WORLD LIBERATION FRONT (NWLF)

A California left-wing group active in the 1970s. In 1974 the group launched a series of bombings against International Telephone and Telegraph to protest that corporation's involvement in the overthrow of the Allende government in CHILE. In the mid-1970s the NWLF directed numerous bombing attacks against public utilities.

NEW WORLD OF ISLAM

An American Black Muslim group that envisions the creation of a separate, black nation in the southern United States. As a means of financing its goal the group has since 1978 staged a series of bank robberies, primarily in the northeastern United States.

NEWTON, HUEY (1942–89)

Cofounder, with Bobby Seale, of the BLACK PANTHERS, a militant U.S. black organization that once supported armed black revolt against the white establishment. Newton was killed in Oakland, California during an argument with a drug dealer.

Reference: Huey Newton, *Revolutionary Suicide* (New York: Harcourt, Brace, Jovanovich, 1973).

NICARAGUA

This Central American country, independent since 1838, has long received a disproportionate amount of attention from the United States. (U.S. Marines first occupied the nation in 1902.) During the presidency of Ronald Reagan the U.S. government supported the CONTRAS, a guerrilla band who were attempting to supplant the Marxist-Leninist regime of the Sandinistas. The Sandinistas themselves had taken power in 1979 with the overthrow of the dictator, Anastasio SOMOZA Debayle. The Sandinista government has received massive shipments of arms and other supplies from the Soviet Union and CUBA and it is believed, in turn, to funnel the supplies to terrorists and communist insurgents throughout Latin America.

NICHOLAS II

Romanov tsar of Russia, executed in Ekaterinburg (now Sverdlovsk) on July 18, 1918 along with the Tsarina Alexandra and their children Olga, Tatiana, Marie, Anastasia and Alexis. Nicholas and his family had been arrested after his abdication in March 1917. Leon TROTSKY, although a supporter of a trial for the imperial family, found an *ex post facto* rationale in the Bolshevik extermination of the Romanovs: "The execution of the tsar's family was needed not only to frighten, horrify, and dishearten the enemy, but also to shore up our own ranks. . . ."

References: Franklin L. Ford, *Political Murder: From Tyrannicide to Terrorism* (Cambridge, Mass.: Harvard University Press, 1985); Leon Trotsky, *Diary in Exile, 1935*, translated by Elena Zarodnaya (Cambridge, Mass.: Harvard University Press, 1958).

NIDAL

See ABU NIDAL.

NIHILISM

1. A philosophy and world view that proposes that nothing is of value.

2. A late 19th-century movement in Russia that supported destruction of all institutions and political structures, advocating terrorism and violence.

See ANARCHISM; NORODNAYA VOLYA.

NKVD

Russian acronym for Norodny Komitet Vnutrennykh Del (People's Commissariat of Internal Affairs). The NKVD was Joseph Stalin's secret police organization during the period of the GREAT TERROR (1935–38), having assumed the authority of the disbanded secret police unit GPU. The NKVD had sweeping authority, operating through a massive network of informers, and conducted its own trials and executions. It inspired terror through ruthless tactics devised to preclude any perceived threat to Stalin's preeminence. Millions were exiled to Siberian GULAGS and to prisons, and hundreds of thousands were executed. The NKVD was Stalin's primary tool for political intimidation and elimination of enemies, real or imaginary.

Reference: Robert Conquest, *Inside Stalin's Secret Police: NKVD Politics, 1936–39* (Berkeley, Calif.: University of California Press, 1985).

NOCS (NUCLEO OPERATIVO CENTRALE DI SICUREZZA)

One of Italy's primary anti-terrorist units, specially trained as a Hostage Rescue Unit (HRU). NOCS is best known for its rescue on January 28, 1982 of U.S. Army General James DOZIER from his RED BRIGADES captors in Padua, Italy. NOCS consists of approximately 50 highly trained individuals, who are often called "leatherheads" because they wear leather headgear in the field.

NOM DE GUERRE

French term for a pseudonym assumed during a time of war. Noms de guerre are common among Palestinian terrorists, many of whom have adopted names linked to the term "Abu," meaning "father of." For example, Abu Jihad, which means "Father of the Holy Struggle," was the nom de guerre of the late Khalil al-WAZIR, an aide to Yasir ARAFAT.

NORAID (IRISH NORTHERN AID COMMITTEE)

A North American fundraising organization for the PROVISIONAL WING OF THE IRISH REPUBLICAN ARMY. NORAID was founded in New York City in 1970 and is now represented by about 100 chapters located throughout the United States (although most are scattered along the East Coast). NORAID has served as a financial conduit to the Provos and has supplied millions of American dollars for supplies, arms and other support.

Reference: James Adams, *The Financing of Terror* (Kent, U.K.: New English Library, 1986).

NORIEGA, MANUEL ANTONIO (1934–   )

A general in the Panamanian Defense Forces who came to power in that country as part of a military triumvirate that succeeded General Omar Torrijos. Although it was not until the very end of the triumvirate's rule that he formally held any office other than his military position, Noriega effectively became the sole leader in August 1983. In rigged elections in 1984 and 1989 he installed figurehead presidents, through whom he ruled. Although Noriega originally was a client and agent of the United States, his greed eventually led him into the drug trade as an associate of the MEDELLIN cartel. In February 1988 he was indicted in Miami by a federal grand jury on charges of drug trafficking. After diplomatic efforts failed to remove him from power in PANAMA, he became overconfident and began to openly challenge the United States.

Noriega escalated tensions between his nation and the United States throughout the latter part of 1989. On December 15th of that year he declared that Panama was in a state of war with the United States. The following day his troops murdered an American marine, and four days after that U.S. president George Bush ordered in American troops, who forcibly removed the Noriega regime from power. Noriega escaped immediate capture and managed to reach the Vatican Embassy in Panama City, where he requested protection. After 10 days in the embassy he surrendered to personnel from the American Drug Enforcement Agency and was immediately transported to the United States to face criminal charges in connection with his drug activities.

References: Frederick Kempe, *Divorcing the Dictator* (New York: Putnam, 1990); John Dinges, *Our Man in Panama* (New York: Random House, 1990).

NORODNAYA VOLYA

Russian, "The Will of the People." A group of violent young Russian intellectuals in pre-Revolutionary Russia. The group was a precursor of many modern terrorist movements. Founded in 1878, Norodnaya Volya launched a NIHILIST campaign of assassination attempts, sometimes successful, against the royal family and major government figures. On March 13, 1881, in its most fateful act, the group assassinated Tsar ALEXANDER II. Police reprisals following the assassination dealt a heavy blow to activities of Norodnaya Volya and other leftist extremists.

Reference: Adam B. Ulam, *In the Name of the People* (New York: Viking, 1977).

NORODNIKI

Young Russian intellectuals, members of NORODNAYA VOLYA, who staged numerous terrorist attacks in pre-Revolutionary Russia.

NORTHERN IRELAND

One of the component countries of the United Kingdom. Northern Ireland's territory, as established in 1921, comprises the six northernmost counties of the island of Ireland. The division of Ireland has been the crux of the dispute between the primarily Protestant North and the primarily Catholic Republic of Ireland in the south. The division underlies the violence and the terror that has plagued Northern Ireland.

Irish nationalists, most visibly in the Irish Republic Army—an anti-British, anti-partition Catholic organization—have waged a bloody and thus far futile campaign of terror against the British and the Protestant majority of Northern Ireland. Protestants in the North and the British security forces have responded in kind. The 1920s and 1930s witnessed the initial wave of IRA violence. The current stage of the violence may be traced to the late 1960s. From 1969 to 1990 about 2,800 have been killed. Since the late 1960s the conflict has typified the ACTION–

REACTION model of violence, with revenge providing justification for both sides. Religious and political strife are intertwined in the Northern Irish situation and are manifest in bombings, shootings and KNEECAPPINGS.

See SINN FEIN, ULSTER DEFENSE ASSOCIATION; ULSTER FREEDOM FIGHTERS; ULSTER VOLUNTEER FORCE.

References: Yonah Alexander and Alan O'Day, eds., *Terrorism in Ireland* (New York: St. Martin's Press, 1984); John Hickey, *Religion and the Northern Ireland Problem* (Totowa, N.J.: Barnes and Noble Books, 1984); Paul Bew and Henry Patterson, "The Protestant-Catholic Conflict in Ulster," *Journal of World Affairs* (Fall–Winter 1982); William Beattie Smith, "Terrorism: The Lessons of Northern Ireland," *Journal of Contemporary Studies* 5 (Winter 1982).

NORTH KOREA

The U.S. Department of State has designated North Korea as a state sponsor of terrorism under Section 6(j) of the Export Administration Act. This action was a direct result of the North Korean government's culpability in the bombing on November 29, 1987 of Korean Air Lines flight 858, in which 115 people were killed. North Korean agent Kim HYUN HEE and a terrorist accomplice took suicide capsules upon their apprehension in Bahrain, but Kim survived to confess her role as a North Korean terrorist agent in the bombing. The government of North Korea has also been implicated in assassination attempts against South Korean officials, including the 1968 "Blue House Raid" against President Park and the 1974 attempt against Park in Seoul, in which his wife was killed. In Rangoon, Burma in 1983, North Korean commandos planted explosives that killed 17 members of the Republic of Korea delegation as well as four Burmese.

NOVEMBER 17

See REVOLUTIONARY ORGANIZATION 17 NOVEMBER.

NUCLEAR TERRORISM

The term applied generally to the threat that would be posed by the use of nuclear materials as a terrorist's weapon. Discussions of nuclear terrorism fall into three primary categories: terrorist access to existing nuclear weapons, terrorist development of nuclear weapons, and terrorist attacks upon nuclear reactors. The level of terror and destruction which the potentiality of nuclear terrorism would inspire has remained a major concern of experts, governments, administrators of nuclear facilities and the public.

References: Bruce Hoffman, *Recent Trends and Future Prospects of Terrorism in the United States* (Santa Monica, Calif.: Rand, 1988); Thomas Schelling, "Thinking About Nuclear Terrorism," *International Security* (Spring 1982); Barbara Salmore and Douglas Simon, "Nuclear Terrorism in Perspective," *Society* (July/August 1980).

NUCLEI ARMATI RIVOLUZIONARI

See NAR.

OAAS

See ORGANIZATION OF THE ARMED ARAB STRUGGLE.

OAS

"Secret Army Organization." An organization of European settlers in Algeria, violent in their opposition to the loss of French sovereignty in that Northern African country. In the early 1960s the OAS launched terrorist attacks against the Muslim Algerian population, both in Algeria and in France. The Mayor of Evian, France, the town in which a negotiated settlement to the Algerian question was being discussed, was killed in an OAS bomb attack. Many members of the French military were active in the OAS. Four French generals, in rebellion against French policy, led the flawed OAS siege of Algiers in April 1961. In the spring of 1962, after the Evian accord had been reached between the French government and the Algerian nationalists, the OAS attempted to thwart enactment of the agreement by conducting a massive campaign of murder and destruction. These acts of terrorism, though tragic, proved ineffectual. They prompted a violent backlash by the Algerian National Liberation Front (FLN) and eventually caused the flight of much of Algeria's European population.

OCCUPIED TERRITORIES

1. Territories under the authority and effective control of a belligerent armed force. The area that comes under the control of the occupying power is often ruled by a military governor who suspends all civil liberties and rules the territory under marshall law. Technically the phrase "occupied territories" is not applicable to territories being administered pursuant to peace terms, a treaty, or other agreement, express or implied, with the civil authority of the area. **2.** The occupied territories of the West Bank, the Gaza Strip and the Golan Heights; territories that came under Israeli control after the 1967 Arab-Israeli War.

References: Raja Shehadeh, *Occupier's Law: Israel and the West Bank*, (Washington, D.C.: Institute for Palestine Studies, 1985); Daniel J. Elazar, *Governing Peoples and Territories* (Philadelphia, Pa: Institute for the Study of Human Issues, 1982).

OKHRANA

"Sections to Guard Security and Order." Russian secret police unit established in 1881 to combat the fledgling but rapidly expanding revolutionary movement in the major cities in imperial Russia. By the early 1900s the Okhrana had a pervasive presence, operating a vast net of informers and double agents in both cities and smaller towns throughout the country. It was abolished in 1917.

OMEGA 7

A right-wing, U.S.-based terrorist organization comprised of anti-CASTRO Cuban exiles. In 1980 it failed in an attempt to assassinate the Cuban ambassador to the United Nations in New York City. This group has directed attacks and physical threats against Cuban-American institutions and individuals which it considers to be sympathetic to the Castro regime. Some analysts have held Omega 7 responsible for the 1976 slaying of Chilean exile Orlando Letelier, though that incident has been properly ascribed to right-wing Chilean agents. Omega 7 ceased to be an active terrorist organization in July 1983, when its leader, Eduardo Arocena, turned FBI informer.

OPEC SIEGE

The siege on December 21–23, 1975 of 11 oil ministers, and almost 60 other hostages, at a conference of the Organization of Oil Exporting Countries (OPEC) in Vienna. The POPULAR FRONT FOR THE LIBERATION OF PALESTINE (PFLP), under the guise of the "Arab Revolution," staged the attack and hostage-taking. The operation was led by the international terrorist CARLOS and also involved operatives from the RED ARMY FACTION. On the morning of December 21, Carlos and his five companions stormed the Vienna headquarters of OPEC, killing three people in the process and barricading themselves and their 70 hostages inside the office building. The terrorists demanded $5 million in ransom, television and radio broadcasts of Palestinian propaganda, and safe passage to Tripoli. After 36 hours, the government

of Austrian Chancellor Bruno Kreisky conceded to the demands; he delivered to the attackers a reported $2 million, broadcast their statement, and arranged for transport to the Vienna Airport. The terrorists flew first to Algiers, then to Tripoli, and once again to Algiers, where some of them surrendered on December 23, without the ransom money. However, millions more were given to associates not directly involved with the attack, so the terrorists soon were able to buy their way to freedom. The main motivation for the siege was the millions in ransom money, and the operation was successful. Carlos is still at large. He has never been arrested and is variously rumored to be living in any number of states supporting terrorism.

OPERATION AJAX

The 1953 CIA covert operation directed by Kermit (Kip) Roosevelt which fomented a successful coup d'état in Iran, unseating Mohammad Mosaddeq and restoring Mohammad Reza Shah Pahlavi to power.

References: Kermit Roosevelt, *Counter-coup: The Struggle for Control of Iran* (New York: McGraw-Hill, 1979); Richard W. Cottam, *Iran & the United States: A Cold War Case Study* (Pittsburgh: University of Pittsburgh Press, 1988).

ORDEN

A right-wing Salvadoran DEATH SQUAD that carries out a campaign of violence against leftists, moderates, religious leaders, labor unionists and human rights workers. Orden was banned in 1979 but still maintains a violent and extensive presence in El Salvador. Most Orden terrorism has been directed against members of the Christian Democratic Party. The group has a history of slaying politically moderate rural mayors. Orden has strong ties to the Salvadoran military and security forces.

THE ORDER

A U.S. white supremacist organization with a neo-NAZI, anti-Semitic, and militaristic orientation. The group is a member of the ARYAN NATIONS, an umbrella organization for white, Christian, racist organizations. The Order was founded in 1983 by 30-year-old Robert Matthews, who was killed in a shoot-out with police in Puget Sound, Washington in December 1984. The group financed its initial operations through a series of armed robberies which included the June 1983 attack on a Brinks armored car outside Ukiah, California. The robbery netted the group $3.6 million and was, at the time, the largest armored car hold-up in U.S. history.

The stated goal of the Order is to overthrow the U.S. government, which it calls Z.O.G. (Zionist Occupied Government), and establish an independent white nation in the northwest United States. Among the terrorist incidents for which members of the Order have been convicted are the firebombing of a Seattle theater; the bombing of a synagogue in Boise, Idaho; and the 1984 murder of Denver radio personality Alan BERG. Successful criminal investigations of the group and its membership by law enforcement agencies, led by the FBI, resulted in a series of arrests and convictions of members in 1987. Since that time the group has been silent.

References: Kevin Flynn and Gary Gerhardt, *The Silent Brotherhood: Inside America's Racist Underground* (New York: Free Press, 1989); Thomas Martinez with John Gunther, *Brotherhood of Murder* (New York: McGraw-Hill, 1988); James Coates, *Armed and Dangerous: The Rise of the Survivalist Right* (New York: Noonday, 1987).

ORGANIZACION REVOLUCIONARIA DEL PUEBLO EN ARMAS (OPRA)

Spanish, "Revolutionary Organization of the People in Arms." A Guatemalan left-wing guerrilla organization, formed in September 1979. It evolved into the most effective of the Guatemalan rebel groups. In August 1984 the group is reported to have killed more than 120 army personnel during one 10-day period. OPRA is believed to have been responsible for the November 1988 massacre of 22 villagers in the tiny hamlet of El Aguacate. The group denies any involvement in the incident and has attempted to shift blame to government DEATH SQUADS, known to have carried out many previous terrorist attacks on villagers. Witnesses and survivors have implicated the guerrillas, however, and the torture and strangulation deaths are consistent with the group's campaign of terror against government collaborators.

ORGANIZATION OF ARAB PALESTINE (OAP)

A radical Palestinian nationalist group, thought to be a splinter group of the PFLP.

ORGANIZATION OF THE ARMED ARAB STRUGGLE (OAAS)

A very small organization which has conducted terrorist operations in support of general Arab revolutionary movements and against Western European nations in retaliation for their Middle East policies. The group was founded in 1978 and is thought to have been led by CARLOS (Ilych Ramirez Sanchez), the Venezuelan master terrorist.

The OAAS came to prominence in 1983 in a series of attacks directed against French interests, probably in retaliation for French military involvement in Beirut. In August 1983 it bombed the French Cultural Center in West Berlin, killing one and wounding 23. Two people died and 45 were wounded in a Marseilles railroad station bombing in December 1983. Later that month, the OAAS exploded a bomb on the high-speed French train line (TGV), killing three and injuring four. This incident may have been conducted in conjunction with ACTION DIRECTE, and the name OAAS may have been the cover name employed by Carlos for this specific series of attacks. Nonetheless, the attacks demonstrated Carlos' ability to attack targets in the Middle East and Europe, indicating an existing network in both regions. Although operations under the OAAS name apparently ceased after the January 1984 bombing of the French Cultural Center in Tripoli, Lebanon, it is possible that the organization still exists.

ORGANIZATION OF THE OPPRESSED ON EARTH

A SHI'ITE Muslim extremist organization thought to be involved with the overarching HEZBOLLAH movement of radical Shi'ites in LEBANON. The group claimed responsibility for the June 1985 skyjacking of a TWA jetliner which resulted in the death of a U.S. Navy diver. It also asserts responsibility for the February 1988 abduction and subsequent murder of U.S. Marine Corps Lieutenant Colonel William HIGGINS, head of the U.N. observer force in Lebanon.

ORGANIZATION OF VOLUNTEERS FOR THE PUERTO RICAN REVOLUTION (OVRP)

A self-described political-military group in Puerto Rico whose objective is to gain independence for Puerto Rico through armed revolution. The group first emerged in 1978, when it joined the MACHETEROS in a theft of explosives. It has participated in acts of terrorism with other Puerto Rican separatist groups, including the ambush on December 3, 1979 of a U.S. Navy bus, which it staged with the Macheteros and the FARP. Two U.S. personnel died in that attack, and nine others were injured. The OVRP has made several serious bombing attacks throughout Puerto Rico. On January 25, 1985 the group claimed joint responsibility with the Macheteros for an attack on a U.S. courthouse in San Juan, and on November 6, 1985 two OVRP members wounded a U.S. Army major.

OTAIBA, JUHAIMAN SAIF AL-

An extremist Sunni Muslim fundamentalist leader who inspired and led the assault on the GRAND MOSQUE of Mecca in November 1979. Juhaiman and 62 of his followers captured when Saudi forces recaptured the Mosque were secretly tried and beheaded in Saudi Arabia in 1980.

OTERO, LUIS

Colombian left-wing guerrilla leader of M-19. He died in the group's attack on the Palace of Justice in November 1985.

P

PALESTINE LIBERATION FRONT (PLF)

A splinter group of the POPULAR FRONT FOR THE LIBERATION OF PALESTINE–GENERAL COMMAND (PFLP-GC) founded in 1977 by ABU ABBAS. The organization was formed in opposition to PFLP-GC leader Ahmed JABRIL's support for the Syrian incursion into Lebanon in June 1976. After unsuccessfully trying to obtain control of the PFLP-GC in September 1976, the PLF was split from that organization officially by PLO Chairman Yasir ARAFAT in April 1977. The PLF, with headquarters in Damascus, was confirmed with Iraqi support. Its existence as an independent group was established when it obtained seats on the PALESTINIAN NATIONAL COUNCIL (PNC) in 1981.

Near the end of 1983, the PLF itself split into factions when Abu Abbas decided that his organization was becoming too close to Syria. Leaving Damascus, along with many supporters, Abu Abbas went to Tunis to ally himself with Arafat and the mainstream al-FATAH organization. After carrying out the hijacking of the *Achille Lauro* cruise ship in October 1985, however, the PLF again relocated, this time to Baghdad, Iraq at the request of the Tunisian Government.

The parts of the PLF that had remained in Damascus split further in January 1984 when Abd al-Fatah Ghanem attempted a takeover of the PLF offices and held Tal'at Yaqub, Secretary General of the PLF, hostage. Through Syrian intervention he was released, and Ghanem formed his own faction with ties to Libya. Yaqub's faction joined the NATIONAL SALVATION FRONT and is generally aligned with Syria.

In its operations, the PLF has often demonstrated creativity and technical acumen. One of its unexpected ploys has been the use of hot air balloons and hang gliders to infiltrate Israel.

Reference: George H. Quester, "Cruise-Ship Terrorism and the Media," *Political Communication and Persuasion* 3 (1986).

PALESTINE LIBERATION ORGANIZATION (PLO)

The umbrella organization for Palestinian nationalist political and guerrilla groups, recognized by the nations of the Arab world as "the sole, legitimate representative of the Palestinian people." The PLO was founded in 1964 by Ahmed al-Shukeiry. In its early years the organization was dominated by traditional Palestinian figures and did not appeal to young, militant Palestinian groups. In February 1969, as a result of the upheavals that followed the resounding defeat of the Arab nations in the 1967 Six-Day War with Irael, the PLO turned to Yasir ARAFAT and his al-FATAH organization for leadership. Arafat has kept the role of chairman since that time, and al-Fatah retains a majority on the powerful Executive Committee of the PALESTINIAN NATIONAL COUNCIL (PNC), the policy-making body for the PLO.

The PLO, through its constituent organizations, carried out numerous raids into Israel in the mid- to late 1960s from its bases in Jordan. In September 1970 King Hussein of Jordan, concerned over the development of a state within his state, expelled the Palestinian guerrilla groups in September 1970, and the PLO shifted its bases from Jordan to Lebanon and Syria.

Dissension in the ranks scarred the PLO following the 1973 Arab-Israeli war, as the "moderate" faction led by Arafat supported PLO participation in peaceful efforts to secure a homeland while the more radical groups dismissed any partial or negotiated approaches to the problem. In 1976 the PLO split when the moderate majority indicated that they would accept a Palestinian state limited to the West Bank and Gaza as part of a negotiated settlement, while those who opposed any compromise with Israel formed the Palestinian Rejection Front.

Since 1974 the mainstream PLO led by Arafat has refused to endorse terrorist activity outside Israel and the occupied territories. The seventh summit of Arab league members, held in Rabat, Morocco, in 1974, declared the PLO to be the sole legitimate representative of the Palestinian people. In October 1974 the United Nations General Assembly also recognized the PLO as the representative of the Palestinians and granted the PLO permanent observer status at the General Assembly. The PLO became a full member of the Arab League in 1976. Arafat addressed the United Nations in 1974, granting the PLO legitimacy in the international arena.

In 1975 and 1976 the PLO became embroiled in the Lebanese civil war, battling the Lebanese Christians. In 1982 the PLO was driven from its camps in Southern Lebanon and its strongholds in Beirut by the Israeli Army's invasion. Following the Israeli siege of Beirut, PLO troops withdrew in September and took refuge in Syria and Tunis. Since 1983, one element of the civil war in Lebanon has been the armed conflict between PLO forces loyal to Arafat and anti-Arafat PLO elements supported by Syria. In November 1984, Arafat and his Fatah majority passed the Amman agreement, by which the PLO and Jordan agreed to seek a political solution to the Arab-Israeli conflict. But King Hussein of Jordan once again ordered a PLO expulsion from his country in July 1986, as he closed down PLO offices and expelled many of the top leaders of the organization.

On August 31, 1988 King Hussein made the surprising move of transferring his claims to the territories occupied by Israel to the PLO, thus putting pressure and responsibility on the PLO to arrive at some political approach to the Palestinian question. In Algiers on November 15, 1988 the Palestinian National Council declared an independent Palestinian state in the West Bank and the Gaza Strip and accepted the United Nations' RESOLUTION 242 and RESOLUTION 338, which implicitly recognize the existence of Israel. December 1988 marked a political watershed for the PLO. Arafat explicitly stated on December 7 in Stockholm that the PLO accepted Israel's right to exist. On December 13 Arafat repeated his new position when he addressed the U.N. General Assembly, sitting in Geneva, after the U.S. had refused to grant him a visa to travel to New York. On December 14 President Ronald Reagan, after being satisfied with the PLO's renunciation of terrorism and its acceptance of Israel, authorized a dialogue between U.S. diplomats in Tunis and PLO representatives.

See BLACK SEPTEMBER.

References: Neil C. Livingstone and David Halevy, *Inside the PLO* (New York: William Morrow, 1990); Arthur Day, *East Bank/West Bank* (New York: Council on Foreign Relations, 1986); Emil Sahliyeh, *The PLO After the Lebanon War* (Boulder, Colo: Westview Press, 1985); Eytan Gilboa, ''Trends in American Attitudes toward the PLO and the Palestinians,'' *Political Communication and Persuasion* 3 (1985); Helena Cobban, *The Palestinian Liberation Organization* (Cambridge: Cambridge University Press, 1984).

PALESTINIAN NATIONAL COUNCIL (PNC)

The policy-making body that acts as a Palestinian parliament-in-exile and sets the policy for the PALESTINE LIBERATION ORGANIZATION. The council meets approximately once a year. It is dominated by an Executive Committee of about 15 members, elected by the council. This committee is chaired by Yasir ARAFAT, whose al-FATAH organization has the largest number of committee seats among the Palestinian groups represented. On November 15, 1988 the PNC declared an independent Palestinian state in the occupied territories of the West Bank and the Gaza Strip.

PALESTINIAN REJECTION FRONT

See REJECTIONIST FRONT.

PAN AM 103

On December 21, 1988, while en route from London to New York, this Pan Am Boeing 747 exploded in midair killing all 259 persons on board. The wreckage of the plane rained down over a large area of southwest Scotland, but was most concentrated in the village of Lockerbie where 11 more people were killed when a large piece of the 747's fuselage tore through a row of houses setting fires and causing secondary explosions. Although the investigation continues, investigators feel certain the bombing was the work of Ahmed Jabril's POPULAR FRONT FOR THE LIBERATION OF PALESTINE-GENERAL COMMAND. The PFLP-GC is believed to have been operating on behalf of Iran and with the assistance of Syria.

Made using SEMTEX, the bomb, which had been concealed in a Toshiba radio-cassette player packed inside a Samsonite suitcase, and stowed in the aircraft's forward baggage compartment, was detonated by a delayed timer. The terrorists' intention was that Pan Am 103 disintegrate over the Atlantic Ocean, leaving no clues, but the plane took off from London's Heathrow Airport 25 minutes late and thus exploded before it had cleared the English coast. It has been the large volume of physical evidence that investigators have been able to recover that has allowed them to piece together the crime.

Reference: Steven Emerson and Brian Duffy, *The Fall of Pan Am 103* (New York: G. P. Putnam, 1990).

PANAMA

This small Central American nation of barely more than 2,000,000 people has frequently drawn international attention due to its location astride the Panama Canal. More than 20,000 U.S. troops are stationed there to safeguard the Canal, which is jointly administered by the United States and Panama. The United States has exercised sovereignty over the Canal since 1903 and it was only in 1978 that the U.S. Senate ratified the Panama Canal Treaty, which stipulates that the Canal be transferred to full Panamanian control on December 31, 1999.

The strategic significance of the Canal had led the U.S. government to ignore the succession of right-wing military dictators who have controlled the country since 1968. The last of these Latin strongmen was General Manuel Antonio NORIEGA, who ruled the country from August 1983 to December 1989, when U.S. President George Bush used American combat troops to forcibly remove the general from power. Bush's action came as the result of increasing evidence that Noriega was in league with Colombia's druglords, the MEDELLIN cartel; of his indictment on drug charges by a Miami grand jury; and of his use of terrorist violence against the Panamanian people.

On May 10, 1989 television news cameras captured the horror of Panamanian repression when they filmed the brutal beatings of Panama's duly elected president and vice presidents. The beatings took place in broad daylight and in full view of Panamanian Defense Force troops and police, who did nothing to intervene. Only three days earlier, Noriega had voided the election results in which these men had been selected. In December a U.S. Marine became a victim of the escalating anti-U.S. campaign and another U.S. serviceman and his wife were captured and terrorized; this proved to be the final straw for President Bush, who ordered the invasion on December 20, 1989.

References: Steve C. Ropp, Ratification of the Panama Canal treaties: The muted debate, *World Affairs* 141 (Spring 1979); James M. McCormick and Michael Black, Ideology and Senate voting on the Panama Canal treaties, *Legislative Studies Quarterly* 8 (February 1983); Craig Allen Smith, "Leadership, Orientation, and Rhetorical Vision: Jimmy Carter, the 'New Right,' and the

Panama Canal," *Presidential Studies Quarterly* 16 (Spring 1986).

PARAMILITARY ORGANIZATION

1. An organization that operates with or in place of a regular military organization. In this capacity, it is often clandestine and semi-official. For example, private paramilitary organizations called DEATH SQUADS have been used by some Latin American governments to influence left-wing and liberal elements through extralegal means, such as torture and kidnapping, with which official government forces do not wish to be associated. In this way, paramilitary organizations have often been used to buffer governments from accusations of state-sponsored terrorism.

See AAA; ORDEN.

2. An illegal non-governmental organization that adopts the structure, discipline and orientation of a regular military organization, to the dismay of governmental authorities.

See HOFFMAN SPORTS GROUP.

PARTIYA KARKEREN KURDISTAN (PKK)

See KURDISH WORKERS' PARTY.

PATRIOTIC PEOPLE'S MOVEMENT

A Sri Lankan left-wing radical Sinhalese organization. Along with the PEOPLE'S LIBERATION FRONT, it has waged a campaign of terror against Sri Lankans whom it deems to be supporters of the India-Sri Lanka military accord, which has brought Indian troops into the Sri Lankan battle against Tamil separatists. The PPM threatened and intimidated voters during the presidential election of December 1988. Anti-voter terrorism is considered to be one of the reasons that Ranasinghe Premadasa triumphed in the balloting and became president in 1989.

PEACE CONQUERORS

The name used by terrorists involved in the June 1985 bombing at the Frankfurt airport, in which three people died. The terrorists, who claimed to be hard-line environmentalists, are actually believed to have been operatives of the ABU NIDAL organization.

PEOPLE'S LIBERATION FRONT

See PATRIOTIC PEOPLE'S MOVEMENT.

PEOPLE'S LIBERATION ORGANIZATION OF TAMIL EELAM (PLOTE)

A TAMIL separatist movement, second only in size and power to the LIBERATION TIGERS.

PEOPLE'S RESISTANCE FRONT

An Argentine group that claimed responsibility for the leftist guerrilla attack on La Tablada army base outside of Buenos Aires on January 23, 1989. The Argentine government declared that the assault, in which 39 people were killed, was led by Enrique Haroldo Gorriaran, the former deputy commander of ERP.

PHALANGE

See CHRISTIAN PHALANGE.

PHOENIX PROGRAM

A campaign of counterinsurgency terrorism during the Vietnam War mounted by the South Vietnamese military, the CENTRAL INTELLIGENCE AGENCY and the U.S. Army Special Forces (Green Berets). The Phoenix program ran from 1968 to 1971 and was an effort to use Viet Cong tactics, assassinations, kidnappings and intimidation against the enemy. A U.S. House of Representatives subcommittee report in 1971 found that "many of the 20,000 suspected VC [Viet Cong] killed under the program were actually innocent civilians who were victims of faulty intelligence". According to Neil Sheehan in *A Bright Shining Lie* (1988), "the English name Phoenix [was] a compromise translation for the Vietnamese name Phung Hoang, a mythical bird that could fly anywhere." Frances FitzGerald wrote in *Fire in the Lake* (1972) that the Phoenix "program in effect eliminated the cumbersome category of 'civilian'; it gave . . . license and justification for the arrest, torture, or killing of anyone in the country, whether or not the person was carrying a gun. And many officials took advantage of that license."

PKK

See KURDISH WORKERS' PARTY.

PLASTIC EXPLOSIVES

A lightweight explosive material that is malleable at room temperature, used mainly for demolition or by terrorists to produce bombs. Plastic explosives are uniquely suited to aircraft bombings. Their malleability allows the explosive substance to be shaped into innocuous forms that are likely to elude X-ray detection. In addition, they will not set off airport metal detectors, and they yield immense explosive power from a comparatively small package. Plastic explosives are often referred to as "plastique." The most well-known are C-4 and SEMTEX. Though developed for conventional military applications, quantities of both explosives have found their way into terrorist hands and have been used in some of the most vile terrorist attacks in recent history.

PLO

See PALESTINE LIBERATION ORGANIZATION.

PLOTE

See PEOPLE'S LIBERATION ORGANIZATION OF TAMIL EELAM.

POGROMS

Attacks against Russian Jews by armed mobs, sponsored in party by the Russian government, between 1881 and the revolution of 1917. This same state-condoned and abetted violent anti-Semitism was later undertaken by NAZI Germany against Jewish communities in Germany and the rest of Europe before and during World War II.

POL POT

The name taken by Saloth Sar, prime minister and strongman of Cambodia from 1975 to 1978. Pol Pot, as head of the KHMER ROUGE, attempted to remake Cambodia according to his own communist vision, and in the process more than one million Cambodians were killed. He was deposed in 1978 by the invading Vietnamese Army and went into hiding. His troops still inspire fear among Cambodians as they continue to conduct guerrilla operations out of refugee camps along the Thai–Cambodian border. Negotiations on the establishment of a successor government after completion of the withdrawal of Vietnam's occupation army have broken down over the issue of including the Khmer Rouge. Although Khmer

Rouge leaders deny that Pol Pot would lead any potential Khmer Rouge government, it is assumed by most observers that Pol Pot would emerge as the de facto power in any such regime.

References: Ben Kiernan, *How Pol Pot Came to Power: A History of Communism in Kampuchea, 1930–1975* (London: Verso, 1985); John Barron and Anthony Paul, *Murder of a Gentle Land: The Untold Story of Communist Genocide in Cambodia* (New York: Reader's Digest Press, 1977); William Shawcross, *Sideshow: Kissinger, Nixon and the Destruction of Cambodia* (New York: Simon and Schuster, 1979).

POLITICAL RISK

In foreign investment, the risk of loss due to such causes as currency inconvertibility, government action preventing entry of goods, expropriation or confiscations, war and terrorism.

References: David L. Lewis and David L. Bodde, "Understanding Political Risk in Investment Planning," *Journal of Policy Analysis and Management* 3 (Summer 1984); Robert Meadow, Gerald T. West, and Dan Haendel, "The Measurement of Political Risk and Foreign Investment Strategy: A Conference Report," *Orbis* 19 (Summer 1975).

POPULAR FORCES OF 25 APRIL (FP-25)

A Portuguese communist terror group, named for the month in 1974 in which the nation's military dictatorship was overthrown. The organization's stated goal is the ousting of the present regime by a revolutionary workers' army. Domestic businessmen and landed interests were FP-25's targets in the early 1980s, but in recent years the group has included U.S. and NATO interests in its attacks. In 1984 it launched a mortar attack against the U.S. Embassy in Lisbon, and it again used a mortar assault in its shelling of NATO and U.S. targets in 1985 and 1986. The FP-25 are thought to have cooperated with both the ETA and the RED ARMY FACTION.

POPULAR FRONT FOR THE LIBERATION OF PALESTINE (PFLP)

Created in 1967 by George HABASH as a Marxist-Leninist guerrilla organization and an ideologically-based alternative to al-FATAH. The early days of the PFLP also known as "Arab Revolution" were marked by violent incursions into Israel from its bases in Jordan. In July 1968 the group began a series of hijackings of airplanes flown by EL AL, the Israeli airline, as a way to publicize their cause. The PFLP staged perhaps the most spectacular hijacking incident in history in September 1970, when it directed three jetliners to land in DAWSON'S FIELD in Jordan, where it subsequently blew them up. In May 1972 the group organized a JAPANESE RED ARMY attack at LOD AIRPORT in Tel Aviv in which twenty-five people were killed. On June 27, 1976 it staged the hijacking of an Air France jetliner which ended with the Israeli raid at Entebbe, Uganda. Members hijacked a Lufthansa plane on October 13, 1977 and directed it to Mogadishu, Somalia, where West German commandos conducted a successful rescue operation on October 17.

The PFLP is noted for its recruitment of and working relationship with Ilyich Ramirez Sanchez, better known as CARLOS. Operations with Carlos include the OPEC Siege in 1975.

The PFLP is opposed to any compromise on the Palestinian issue and has criticized the PLO leadership for pursuing what it calls "partial" solutions. The PFLP was the leading organization in the formation of the REJECTIONIST FRONT.

References: Abu Khalil As'ad, "Internal Contradiction in the PFLP: Decision Making and Policy Determination," *Middle East Journal* 4 (Summer 1987); Walid W. Kazziha, *Revolutionary Transformation: Habash and his Comrades from Nationalism to Marxism* (New York: St. Martin's Press, 1975).

POPULAR FRONT FOR THE LIBERATION OF PALESTINE– GENERAL COMMAND (PFLP-GC)

A splinter group of the PFLP established in 1968 by Ahmed JABRIL. The organization stresses militant action versus political maneuvering. The PFLP-GC is committed to the destruction of Israel and the establishment of an independent Palestinian state in its place. Many of its attacks are designed to terrorize Israeli citizens, especially those in border regions and the occupied territories. Group operations include using letter bombs and conducting many cross-border operations. The PFLP-GC also has shared its terrorist expertise with other international groups, such as the ARMENIAN SECRET ARMY FOR THE LIBERATION OF ARMENIA (ASALA), as well as European groups who have sent members to Lebanon for training. The PFLP-GC arsenal includes many sophisticated weapons such as Soviet SA-7 antiaircraft missiles, heavy artillery and light aircraft such as motorized hang gliders and ultralights. It has launched many unusual attacks, including anti-Israeli strikes from hot air balloons and hang gliders. The Communist bloc countries have provided small arms such as Kalashnikov assault rifles and antitank rockets; Syrian and Libya may serve as the conduits for such support.

Major PFLP-GC terrorist operations began in July 1968, when it hijacked an EL AL airliner and staged a lengthy hostage incident. In February 1970 the group bombed a Swiss airliner and killed 47 people. In May of that year the group attacked an Israeli school bus, killing 12 children and several adults. It was responsible for a bombing in Jerusalem on July 4, 1975 in which 13 people died and more than 70 were injured. The PFLP-GC has actively participated in the Lebanese conflict, including sniping attacks which injured U.S. Marines serving as a peacekeeping force in Beirut during 1982–83. In May 1985 the group engineered the exchange of three Israeli prisoners, captured near Beirut in September 1982, for 1,150 Palestinian prisoners held in Israel. In 1987 the group broke out of a period of relative dormancy with the spectacular hang glider attack near QIRYAT SHEMONA in November. In the fall of 1988 West German officials arrested 14 PFLP-GC operatives and in the process located a huge PFLP-GC cache of weapons in Stockholm, including 11 pounds of the plastic explosive SEMTEX and sophisticated high-altitude detonators. The group is considered by some to be the most likely suspect in the bombing in December 1988 of Pan Am Flight 103.

The PFLP-GC opposes any compromise with Israel and is part of the REJECTIONIST FRONT of the PLO. The PFLP-GC has close ties to Syria and maintains its headquarters in Damascus. In the summer of 1989 it was reported that the PFLP-GC had ended its long association with Libya and had shifted its allegiance to Iran. It is believed that the group has been involved with the radical and shadowy HEZBOLLAH.

Ahmed Jabril has maintained control of the group since its inception. The membership of the PFLP-GC is thought to number approximately 500.

References: Abu Khalil As'ad, "Internal Contradiction in the PFLP: Decision Making and Policy Determination," *Middle East Journal* 4 (Summer 1987); Walid W. Kazziha, *Revolutionary Transformation: Habash and his Comrades from Nationalism to Marxism* (New York: St. Martin's Press, 1975).

POPULAR FRONT FOR THE LIBERATION OF PALESTINE– SPECIAL COMMAND (PFLP-SC)

Formed in 1979 by Salim Abu Salim as a splinter of the PFLP–Special Operations group, which no longer exists. In April 1985 the PFLP-SC bombed a restaurant in Torrejon, Spain frequented by U.S. servicemen, killing 18 Spanish civilians. The group is reportedly funded by Libya and Syria and is believed to have ties to the ARMENIAN SECRET ARMY FOR THE LIBERATION OF ARMENIA (ASALA), the ABU NIDAL Organization, and the FARL.

POPULAR STRUGGLE FRONT

A radical Palestinian organization, led by Samir GOSHEH, which directs terrorist operations against Israelis, moderate Arabs and members of the PALESTINE LIBERATION ORGANIZATION (PLO). The PSF is primarily funded by Syria and is involved in the Palestinian National Salvation Front. A veteran Palestinian activist, Bahjat Abu Gharbiyah, founded the PSF in 1967 in cooperation with Major Fayez Hamden of the Palestine Liberation Army. Gharbiyah was involved with the first PLO leadership after 1964 but suspended PSF activities and participation on the PLO Executive Committee after the Jordanian suppression of 1970. The PSF was revived after the October 1973 War. In 1974 Gharbiyah resigned and was succeeded by

Gosheh. At that point, the PSF joined the REJECTIONIST FRONT, adopting its stance against a Palestinian state in the West Bank and Gaza and advocating closer cooperation with various other guerrilla and leftist movements.

Since the Israeli invasion of Lebanon in 1982, the PSF has come under stronger Syrian influence. The PSF joined the Palestine National Salvation Front in opposition to the Arafat–Hussein accord of February 1985, which called for a political settlement of the Arab-Israeli conflict. The group is currently headquartered in Damascus and is primarily based in Lebanon's Bekaa Valley. The Israeli Air Force claimed in 1985 to have attacked PSF bases near Bar Elias in the Bekaa Valley and in Shamlam, near Beirut. The PSF has undertaken several rocket attacks and cross-border operations into Israel and has claimed responsibility for many actions that were never confirmed.

POSSE COMITATUS

A radical U.S. right-wing organization opposed to the U.S. federal system, including state and federal income taxes, the primacy of federal courts and the Federal Reserve Bank. It was founded by American neo-Nazi Mike Beach in 1969. The group is anti-Semitic and white supremacist. The name of the organization translates from Latin as "The power of the county."

Reference: Phillip Finch, "Renegade Justice," *The New Republic* (April 25, 1983).

PRIMIA LINEA

Italian, "Front Line." A left-wing Italian terrorist group that first surfaced in 1976. The group has directed many of its attacks against large capitalist enterprises, including the assault on November 29, 1976 on a Fiat plant in Turin. In the summer of 1977 Primia Linea damaged Milan's public transit system. Primea Linea has been responsible for a number of shooting attacks against politicians, judges, police and business executives. It has conducted several joint terrorist operations with the French organization ACTION DIRECTE and the Italian RED BRIGADES. The group was badly damaged during the Italian police crackdown on terrorist organizations following the murder of former Prime Minister Aldo MORO.

PRINCIP, GAVRILO (1894–1918)

The assassin of Archduke FRANZ FERDINAND of Austria and his wife, Countess Sophie. Princip was the only successful marksman in the group of five young Serbian nationalist members of "Young Serbia" who attacked the royal motorcade in Sarajevo on June 28, 1914. All five were arrested and found guilty in an Austrian court but were spared execution because of their ages. Princip died of tuberculosis while in prison.

PROUDHON, PIERRE (1809–65)

French social and political theorist, and one of the intellectual fathers of ANARCHISM.

Reference: George Woodock, *Proudhon* (New York: Black Rose, 1987).

PROVISIONAL WING OF THE IRISH REPUBLICAN ARMY (PIRA)

Called Provos. The militant and violent nationalist Irish Catholic terrorist organization, formed in 1969 when the dormant IRISH REPUBLICAN ARMY (IRA) split into two wings, the Official wing and the Provisional. Initially both wings were aggressively militant, but in 1972 the Officials renounced terrorism. Other Northern Irish extremist groups have emerged, but the PIRA has maintained its dominant status.

Most PIRA adherents, particularly in the rural areas, are traditional Irish nationalists ("Republicans"), as are older veterans of the movement. A group of younger leaders, however, primarily from Northern Ireland, have radical leftist tendencies and now dominate the more traditional and conservative Republicans. These younger forces sponsored the PIRA's dual "Armalite and Ballot Box" strategy, according to which the PIRA has pursued both terrorism and political activism promoting the efforts of its political wing, SINN FEIN, as it seeks to become a legitimate political force in both Northern Ireland and the Republic of Ireland. In 1984–85 some members split from the Provisional Sinn Fein in response to its sponsorship of more political activity. Many traditional PIRA members reportedly are suspicious of the socialist inclinations and political aspirations of the new leadership. They fear that the PIRA will be drawn toward political activity, thereby forsaking violence and terrorism, which in their view are the only effective weapons in the struggle to achieve the group's goals.

PIRA terrorism is designed to move the people of Northern Ireland and Britain to pressure the British Government to withdraw from Northern Ireland and let the Catholic and Protestant Irish settle the conflict without British interference. By using violence, the Provos also hope to focus worldwide attention on the struggle against British "oppression" and thereby generate broader international pressure on the British government. PIRA leaders have settled in for a long war of attrition in the hope that the prohibitive economic costs and international stigma attached to Britain's presence in Northern Ireland will drive the British Army out of Ulster. The PIRA admits that a military victory is unlikely.

From the inception of the PIRA, the group has focused its energy on causing casualties. The more than 1,000 who have died, and the many more who have been injured, are grim testimony to the PIRA's determination to "wash the British out of Ireland on a wave of blood." Favored PIRA targets include the British Army, Ulster security forces, prison and judicial officials and Loyalist political party members. Most attacks have occurred in Northern Ireland, but occasionally actions have been carried out in the Republic of Ireland, Great Britain and various West European nations. PIRA methods include shootings, bombings and mortar attacks. The PIRA arsenal is large and varied.

In the early 1970s the police were especially effective in using information gathered from informers to round up large numbers of PIRA radicals. As a result, beginning in 1977, the PIRA was reorganized. Cells, called "Active Service Units" or "ASUs," are compartmentalized, with members knowing only each other and the person issuing orders from above. The ASUs specialize in such activities as intelligence, snipings, executions, bombings and robberies. They are subordinate to local commands or brigades and are ultimately responsible to a new "Northern Command," the primary PIRA operational authority.

Beginning in 1982, the British government succeeded in convincing many former PIRA terrorists to inform on their comrades-in-arms. These informers, referred to as SUPERGRASSES, have helped the British to arrest many PIRA activists. Nevertheless, PIRA actions, such as the 1984 BRIGHTON BOMBING, indicate that the group remains a potent terrorist force.

Financial backing for the PIRA has come from a variety of sources. It has a solid civilian base of support. Robberies of banks, post offices and corporate payrolls also are used routinely. Private U.S. citizens have been a significant source of funds (*see* NO-RAID). The PIRA has also received large amounts of money from the government of Libya, as well as arms and perhaps training. In 1973 five tons of Libyan weapons were intercepted off the coast of Ireland, in a ship that carried PIRA leader Joe Cahill. In April 1986 the British Secretary of State for Northern Ireland stated publicly that substantial support in arms and cash had been provided to the PIRA by Libya since 1982. In 1987 150 tons of Libyan munitions were discovered when the trawler EKSUND was seized off the coast of Brittany.

In addition to the Libyan connection, the PIRA is reported to have links with other terrorist organizations. The PIRA's closest ally among European terrorist groups is reportedly the Basque ETA. Close links between these groups are thought to date back to the early 1970s. The PIRA allegedly also has had contacts with the West German REVOLUTIONARY CELLS.

References: Paul Arthur, *Government and Politics in Northern Ireland*, 2nd edition (Essex, U.K.: Longman, 1984); Conor Cruise O'Brien, "Terrorism Under Democratic Conditions," in Martha Crenshaw, *Terrorism, Legitimacy, and Power* (Middletown, Conn.: Wesleyan University Press, 1983); Alfred McClung Lee, *Terrorism in Northern Ireland* (New York: General Hall, 1983).

PROVOS

See PROVISIONAL WING OF THE IRISH REPUBLICAN ARMY.

PRTC (PARTIDO REVOLUCIONARIO DE LOS TRABAJADORES CENTROAMERICANOS)

(Revolutionary Party of Central American Workers.) A left-wing Salvadoran guerrilla group and a constituent member of the FMLN umbrella organization.

PUERTO RICAN TERRORISM

Puerto Rican radical separatists constitute one of the primary and most dangerous domestic U.S. terrorist movements. Since 1898, when the United States acquired the island of Puerto Rico as a result of the Spanish-American War, violence has been directed against the U.S. government and the private sector on the island and against private corporations and other targets on the U.S. mainland. In the 1980s more than a third of terrorist incidents perpetrated in the United States and Puerto Rico were committed by Puerto Rican separatists.

At least nine clandestine Puerto Rico-based groups have been waging an armed struggle for independence from the United States. The largest of these groups is the MACHETEROS. Others include the ORGANIZATION OF VOLUNTEERS FOR THE PUERTO RICAN REVOLUTION (OVRP), the Armed Forces of Popular Resistance (FARP), the People's Revolutionary Commandos (CRP) and the Armed Commandos for National Liberation (CALN).

On the U.S. mainland, the Puerto Rican Armed Forces of National Liberation, known as the FALN, has been most active in New York and Chicago. This group has been responsible for more than 150 acts of violence since it first emerged in 1974.

References: William Sater, *Puerto Rican Terrorists: A Possible Threat to U.S. Energy Installations?* (Santa Monica, Calif.: Rand, 1981); Rueben Berrios Martinez, "Independence for Puerto Rico: The Only Solution, *Foreign Affairs* 55 (April 1977).

QADDAFI, MUAMMAR AL-

The Libyan head of state and one of the foremost proponents of international STATE-SPONSORED TERRORISM. "Brother Colonel," as he prefers to be called, rose to power in a bloodless coup on September 1, 1969 while King Idris and his wife Queen Fatimah were vacationing in Turkey. Qaddafi's early rule of Libya was characterized by an emphasis on Islamic law and a wave of revolutionary populism. His government was looked favorably upon by the United States and most Western nations, for Qaddafi initially assumed a vocal anti-Communist stance, and he kept Libya's oil exports high. Today it seems ironic that in the early 1970s the Soviets called Qaddafi an "ignorant anti-Soviet," while the CIA protected him and considered him to be America's primary strategic buffer against coups in northern Africa.

In 1972, following its falling out with Egypt when President Sadat expelled all Soviet advisors, the Soviet Union initiated the first of many significant arms shipments to Qaddafi, thus establishing a firm Soviet–Libyan relationship. This relationship has not been without difficulties, for Qaddafi's rantings and excessive demands have made the Soviets justifiably cautious and calculating in their dealings with Libya. The Soviets have maintained and nurtured close relations with Qaddafi in spite of his unpredictability; however, for in Libya the Soviets have found both a northern African military outpost and a useful surrogate for anti-Western activities.

Qaddafi is thought to have been the financier of many BLACK SEPTEMBER operations, including the 1972 MUNICH MASSACRE and the killing of five TWA passengers in the terminal at Athens airport on August 5, 1973. On December 17, 1973 two Arab terrorists under Qaddafi's sponsorship attacked an American airliner at Rome airport, leaving 33 people dead. Qaddafi gave his support to the December 1975 OPEC SIEGE. In 1975 he severed ties with Yasir ARAFAT and the PLO. He has been a generous sponsor to the more radical Palestinian organizations such as the POPULAR FRONT FOR THE LIBERATION OF PALESTINE and its leader George HABASH and to the terrorist ABU NIDAL.

In 1985 the U.S. Government imposed sanctions against Libya, accusing Qaddafi of complicity with the Abu Nidal Organization in the Vienna airport attack on December 27, 1985, in which two people were killed, and the Rome airport attack on the same day which left 16 dead. Libya was again implicated in state-sponsored terrorism in connection with the bombing of La

Belle Disco in West Berlin on April 5, 1986. Qaddafi has denied any responsibility for these attacks. Nonetheless, the United States took military action against Libya in April 1986, attacking the cities of Tripoli and Benghazi and destroying Libyan ships in the Gulf of Sitre. Reports say that Qaddafi narrowly escaped death when American pilots targeted his quarters; his four-year-old adopted daughter died in the U.S. attack. Since that time Qaddafi has uncharacteristically reined in his direct involvement in international terrorism.

See WILSON, EDWIN.

References: David Blundy and Andrew Lycett, *Qaddafi and the Libyan Revolution* (London: Weidenfeld and Nicolson, 1987); Seymour Hersh, "Target Qaddafi," *The New York Times Magazine* (February 22, 1987); Mahmoud G. El Warfally, *Imagery and Ideology in U.S. Policy Toward Libya, 1969–1982* (Pittsburgh: University of Pittsburgh Press, 1988).

QIRYAT SHEMONA

Town in northwestern Israel that was the site of a November 25, 1987 attack by a lone terrorist of the POPULAR FRONT FOR THE LIBERATION OF PALESTINE–GENERAL COMMAND. The terrorist penetrated Israel by flying in a hang glider launched from across the border in Lebanon. Six Israelis were killed. Earlier on April 11, 1974 three members of the same terrorist group killed 18 Israelis at this same place.

QUEBECOIS TERRORISM

Acts of terrorism by members of Quebec's French Canadian separatists, especially by members of the group FLQ.

QUEBEC LIBERATION FRONT

See FLQ.

QUTBIYAN

The followers of Sayyid Qutb, the leader of the MUSLIM BROTHERHOOD who was executed in 1965 for his organization's plot to assassinate President Gamel Abdel Nasser of Egypt. In the late 1970s several Qutbiyan revolutionary splinter groups were formed, including TAKFIR WAL HIGRA, TANZIM AL-JIHAD and TAHRIR AL-ISLAMI.

R

RABBO, YASIR ABD AL-

A leader of the DEMOCRATIC FRONT FOR THE LIBERATION OF PALESTINE (DFLP) and a member of the PLO Executive Committee. Rabbo led the first PLO delegation to meet officially with U.S. envoys after President Ronald Reagan's decision in December 1988 to authorize a dialogue.

RAINBOW WARRIOR

A ship, operated by the Greenpeace organization, that was destroyed on July 10, 1985 while at port in Auckland, New Zealand. Intelligence agents of the French government were responsible. The vessel had been engaged in Greenpeace's efforts to interfere with French testing of nuclear weapons in the Pacific. One of the crew members was killed during the incident. The French government later apologized for the attack and agreed to assume some financial responsibility for the death of the crewman. Two French agents were convicted and sentenced to 10 years in jail for their part in the sabotage.

References: Michael King, *Death of the Rainbow Warrior* (New York: Penguin Books, 1986); John Dyson, *Sink the Rainbow!: An Inquiry into the "Greenpeace Affair"* (London: V. Gollancz, 1986).

RAISON D'ÉTAT

An overwhelmingly important social motive for an action taken to benefit a social group or nation or state *(état)*. There may be, it is argued, problems of such utter importance to the entire well-being of a state, or interests so vital to the population as a whole, that all ordinary moral or political restrictions on government actions must be dropped. (Thus raison d'état is sometimes used to justify terrorism.)

RAISON DE GUERRE

A doctrine, akin to the conception of RAISON D'ÉTAT, justifying certain actions in war *(guerre)*. While raison d'état argues that when the safety of an entire state is at stake, the state can do anything necessary to protect itself—regardless of ordinary moral or legal restriction—raison de guerre, by analogy, is the doctrine that the vital necessity of winning a battle may, at times, justify behavior, such as terrorism, that would not normally be acceptable even in the context of the already less-constrained standards of morality that exist in war. While raison d'état has long been recognized in international law, raison de guerre is not so well established.

RASHID, MOHAMMED

Palestinian terrorist and member of the MAY 15 GROUP. Rashid, wanted by the United States for his role in a number of airplane bombings—including the 1982 bombing of a Pan Am flight from Tokyo to Honolulu in which one person died—is at the center of an EXTRADITION dispute between the United States and Greece. He was arrested in May 1988 at the Athens Airport carrying a Syrian passport. The Rashid case is viewed by many as a test of Greek anti-terrorist resolve; the Greek government has bowed to pressure from domestic terrorist organizations, including the REVOLUTIONARY ORGANIZATION 1 MAY, seeking to prevent Rashid's extradition.

REBEL ARMED FORCES

See GUATEMALAN NATIONAL REVOLUTIONARY UNITY (URNA).

RED ARMY FACTION (RAF)

In German, "Rote Armee Fraktion." A German terrorist organization with its origins in the student unrest of the late 1960s. The group, founded by Andreas BAADER, Ulrike MEINHOF, and Gudrun ENSSLIN, was known as the Baader-Meinhof Gang in its early years; it mounted a campaign of "armed resistance to U.S. imperialism and West German complicity." Although the group's leadership has periodically been captured by German authorities, it has been able to resurface with renewed and vicious attacks. The RAF sees itself as part of an international movement aimed at bringing about a worldwide revolution that would topple the existing power structures in the capitalist world.

The RAF has perpetrated a variety of bombing and assassination attacks over the years. Its first attacks were in 1968 against West German business targets. In the 1970s it was a major component in an international terrorist network which included several Palestinian groups. Members were trained by Palestinian terrorists and brought their newly-gained expertise in violence to bear upon military bases and government offices. Baader, Meinhof and Ensslin were arrested by West German authorities in 1972, along with a number of other RAF members. In December 1975 members of the gang were involved in the OPEC SIEGE in Vienna. Members of the group were also implicated in the June 1976 hijacking of an Air France jetliner which culminated in the Israeli raid at ENTEBBE. In April 1977 the RAF assassinated West German Federal Prosecutor Siegfried Buback. In October 1977 efforts to force the release of the group's imprisoned leadership culminated in a commando operation at Mogadishu, Somalia, after which Baader, Ensslin and another jailed RAF operative committed suicide in prison.

The late 1970s saw the RAF swing toward West German capitalist targets, including the 1977 kidnapping and murder of Hans-Martin Schleyer, a German industrialist. In the mid-1980s the group once again appeared to shift its emphasis and displayed a high level of sophistication in its attacks on U.S., NATO and West German political and military targets. These targets have included U.S. military bases in Frankfurt, Heidelberg and Ramstein. In one attack six U.S. servicemen were killed, while assassination attempts against generals Alexander Haig and Frederic Kroessen were foiled. In August 1985 the RAF murdered a U.S. serviceman and used his military identification to gain access to Rhein-Main Air Force Base, where they detonated a car bomb. On February 1, 1985 RAF assassins had killed Ernst Zimmerman, a West

German businessman, near his Munich home.

The RAF subgroup "Action Christian Klar" bombed a Dortmund department store in March of 1985. In October 1986 the group murdered West German Foreign Ministry official Gerold von Braunmuhl, and in late 1988 they attempted the assassination of Finance Ministry State Secretary Hans Tietmeyer.

The RAF leadership, which has undergone many transformations in the two-decade history of the group, is well educated and is collective in nature. Many of the leaders have medical, legal or technical training. Each major RAF operation is the subject of detailed planning and generally is executed in a "professional" manner. The RAF organizational concept calls for a multilevel structure. The "hard core" consists of perhaps 20–30 combatants who live underground and conduct most of the lethal terrorist activities. West German authorities say that the hard-core command level also directs the operations of "illegal militants," who carry out bombings and lower-level attacks. The "periphery," which consists of perhaps as many as several hundred people, forms the vital support base that provides necessary funding, shelter and communications for the operatives. A larger number of legal sympathizers assist in propaganda activities.

In 1990 with the demise of East Germany it came to light that the RAF was trained, operated and controlled by the Interior Ministry of East Germany. The question remains: does the end of East Germany also mean the end of the RAF?

References: Hans Josef Horchem, "Terrorism in West Germany," *Conflict Studies* 186 (1986); Gerhard Falj, "Terror as Politics: The German Case," *International Review of Politics and Political Science* 20 (1983); "The Future of Terrorism in West Germany," *TVI Journal* 4 (1983).

RED ARMY FOR THE LIBERATION OF CATALONIA (ERCA)

A Marxist-Leninist organization operating in the Spanish province of Catalonia. The U.S. Department of State believes that the group may be a radical offshoot of the TERRA LLIURE, another Catalonian separatist group. The ERCA launched a series of 1987 bombings against U.S. targets, including an attack on a Barcelona USO facility in which one serviceman was killed.

RED BERETS

A former unit of the Czechoslovak secret police that was purportedly designed to fight terrorists. According to *U.S. News and World Report* (December 18, 1989), however, the Red Berets provided Middle Eastern terrorist gangs with training, safe havens and technical assistance as well as with arms, including quantities of the explosive Semtex.

RED BRIGADES (BR)

In Italian, "Brigate Rosse" (BR). A violent Italian terrorist organization that developed out of the student unrest of the late 1960s and the ultra-radical wing of the Italian labor movement. The group was founded by a number of young Italian communists in 1970.

The BR has been one of the most lethal of the major European terrorist groups. It has conducted an extensive number of violent attacks, with murder, KNEECAPPING and kidnapping as its favored tactics. Preferred targets have been representatives of the Italian establishment whom it considers to be the "oppressors of society." The group initiated its campaign of kidnappings and violence in the mid 1970s, much of it directed against Italian judges, politicians and policemen. This campaign reached its zenith with the kidnapping and murder of former Italian Prime Minister Aldo MORO in 1978.

Although the BR began with a clear focus on destroying the Italian establishment, it expanded its horizons in late 1981 when it "declared war" on NATO and in early 1984 when it expressed solidarity with Middle Eastern terrorist groups. In December 1981 the Red Brigades kidnapped Brigadier General James DOZIER, the American deputy commander of NATO. (He was released the next month.) Recently, the group's propaganda has supported the idea of increasing contacts and cooperation among West European terrorist groups and of targeting individuals and institutions involved in the U.S. Strategic Defense Initiative (SDI).

The BR organizational structure is thought to be highly cellular and strictly compartmentalized, helping to ensure security and independent action by the various units. In the late 1970s and early 1980s the Italian police succeeded in arresting many BR leaders and confiscated large amounts of arms and explosives. After the Dozier incident the Italian police arrested hundreds of members and supporters. In 1987, with the cooperation of French and Spanish authorities, the Italians succeeded in apprehending numerous BR terrorists, including those responsible for the assassination of Italian Air Force General Lucio Giorgieri. While the operational capacity of the BR has been drastically reduced, police action has not destroyed the organization.

Two separate factions appear to have developed within the BR since 1984. One faction, the Militarists or the Fighting Communist Party (PCC), constitutes the majority and usually follows a strict Leninist view that only violent terrorist acts can pave the way for revolution. The other faction, the Movementalists or Union of Fighting Communists (UCC), is the minority (or splinter) group. It does not believe that a revolution is possible until the proletariat has been sufficiently politicized to support revolutionary action. Regardless of their differences in ideology and rhetoric, the two groups show little difference in either method of operation or targeting.

The BR has had contacts with the West German RED ARMY FACTION (RAF) and the French ACTION DIRECTE (AD). BR members have been arrested in France in the company of AD militants. Large numbers of BR militants enjoy safe haven in France, and evidence points to the existence of a BR "external column" whose task is to protect fugitives and recruit new militants. Recent arrests indicate a BR presence in Spain, and the BR may also have ties to Palestinian terrorist groups. In the late 1970s BR members smuggled into Italy at least two shipments of weapons provided by Palestinian elements. Training of BR members in Palestinian camps in Lebanon has also been alleged. Moreover, the BR is suspected of involvement with the FARL in the 1984 assassination of Leamon Hunt, Director General of the Multinational Peacekeeping Force in the Sinai.

References: Alison Jamieson, "Political Kidnapping in Italy," *Conflict* 8 (1988); Daniela Salvioni and Anders Stephanson, "Reflections on the Red Brigades," *Orbis* 29 (Fall 1985); S. Romano, "Roots of Italian Terrorism," *Policy Review* 25 (Summer 1983); Vittorfranco Pisano, "Terrorism in Italy: the 'Dozier Affair'," *Police Chief* 49 (April 1982).

RED GUERRILLA RESISTANCE (RGR)

A U.S. terrorist group opposed to U.S. and Israeli imperialism, militarism around the world, and the apartheid policies of South Africa. On April 5, 1984 the group claimed credit for a bombing attack on Israeli Aircraft Industries in New York City. On February 23, 1985 the group bombed a room adjacent to a New York City police association.

RED HAND COMMANDOS

A Northern Irish Protestant terrorist organization active in the turbulent Ulster scene of the early 1970s. The RHC coordinated many of its operations with the ULSTER VOLUNTEER FORCE, another loyalist gang of the time. Both of these groups were outlawed by the British government in 1973.

REJECTIONIST FRONT

Those groups that in 1982 broke from the PLO mainstream to oppose what they considered to be the defeatist policies of Yasir ARAFAT. The Front's groups include the POPULAR FRONT FOR THE LIBERATION OF PALESTINE, the POPULAR FRONT FOR THE LIBERATION OF PALESTINE-GENERAL COMMAND; the ARAB LIBERATION FRONT, the POPULAR STRUGGLE FRONT and the PALESTINE LIBERATION FRONT. The Rejectionist Front was encouraged by Libya, Iraq and Syria and stood against any negotiated settlement of the Palestinian question.

Reference: Muhammad Y. Muslik, "Moderates and Rejectionists Within the PLO," *Middle East Journal* 30 (Spring 1976).

RENAMO (RESISTENCIA NACIONAL MOCAMBICANA)

"Mozambican National Resistance." A guerrilla insurgency against the Marxist government of Mozambique. RENAMO, originally known as the National Resistance Movement, was established in 1976 under the sponsorship of Rhodesia's security forces, who recruited Mozambicans opposed to the communist regime set up by FRELIMO (Front for the Liberation of Mozambique). In 1982 the group changed its name to RENAMO. It operates against government and civilian targets and frequently and increasingly runs cross-border operations into Zimbabwe, Malawi and Zambia, where it has murdered and kidnapped numerous civilians and destroyed private property.

RESOLUTION 242

The United Nations resolution adopted after the 1967 Arab–Israeli war that calls for Israeli withdrawal from its occupied territories and respect for "the sovereignty, territorial integrity and political independence of every state in the area."

RESOLUTION 338

The United Nations resolution adopted in 1973, which supplements RESOLUTION 242 and explicitly recognizes Israel's right to exist.

REVOLUTIONARY ARMED FORCES OF COLOMBIA (FARC)

In Spanish, "Fuerzas Armadas Revolucionarias de Colombia." Founded in April 1966 as the guerrilla wing of the Colombian Communist Party. The FARC is the largest of Colombia's anti-government guerrilla movements, with an estimated strength of 10,000 members. The group has stated its anti-American and anti-bourgeoise policies. It kidnapped a U.S. Peace Corps worker in February 1977, holding him until February 1980, when a $250,000 ransom was paid. In 1983 the FARC joined forces with M-19 and the NATIONAL LIBERATION ARMY in a political alliance. In recent years the group has seemed to move toward more nonviolent, political approaches to its goals, although its cease-fires and truces with the government have been only partially successful at best. The U.S. Department of State believes that the FARC "has well-documented ties to drug traffickers."

REVOLUTIONARY CELLS (RZ)

"Revolutionaere Zellen." A left-wing West German terrorist group. The RZ sums up its organizational goals with these words: "We will not hesitate from shooting, bombing, extortion, and taking hostages. The whole ruling class will be made to feel insecure." The RZ was formed in 1973 and is headquartered in West Berlin and Frankfurt. It conducts "urban guerrilla" terrorist activity in support of "anti-fascism," "anti-imperialism," "anti-Zionism" and "anti-militarism."

The RZ occasionally has been linked with the RED ARMY FACTION (RAF) but normally tries to keep its distance. The RZ believes in a decentralized form of terrorism, directed at targets within the immediate vicinity of each cell. To achieve maximum security, the cells typically are composed of less than ten members with minimal contact between cells.

The group is believed to have picked up members from other small, defunct anti-establishment radical groups of the early 1970s. In addition, one former terrorist-turned-police-informer claimed that the RZ has ties to Palestinian terrorist organizations. The RZ is believed to have contacts with the IRISH NATIONAL LIBERATION ARMY (INLA) and the PROVISIONAL WING OF THE IRISH REPUBLICAN ARMY (PIRA), as well as other European anarchist groups.

In its publication *Revolutionaere Zorn* ("Revolutionary Wrath"), the RZ declared its intent to "immediately and everywhere begin the armed struggle." In the same publication, it further contends that the situation demands a "struggle of workers, youth, and women." Within the RZ is an autonomous women's group, Rote Zora, that professes a doctrine of struggle against exploitation of the Third World, repression of women, sexism and racism.

The RZ seeks to establish a pool of semi-independent strike teams to be spread across Germany, carefully "covered" by the appearance of normal civilian lifestyles. From this position, they can strike quickly and without warning, from a variety of locations and without the need to set up elaborate chains of support. West German authorities report that the RZ has significant caches of weapons in rural forest areas.

RZ members have evidenced their mastery of a wide variety of terrorist skills. They are not only competent with standard military weapons but can also make their own explosives and sophisticated timing devices. The group's favorite form of attack has been the time-delayed bomb.

The group has targeted U.S. military facilities in West Germany to oppose America's "neocolonial" presence in that country. In 1986–87 the RZ embarked upon a terror campaign protesting West German "anti-immigration" policies.

Reference: David Schiller, "Germany's Other Terrorists," *Terrorism* 9 (1987).

REVOLUTIONARY GUARDS

The strongmen of the Ayatollah KHOMEINI and the Iranian Revolution. The Guards were established in 1979 as a militia to monitor and police the revolution. One of the group's founders was Mustafa Chamron, a U.S.-educated member of the Muslim AMAL organization. The Guards have a history of brutally enforcing the Ayatollah's interpretation of Islamic law. They have also been very active in the export of the revolution, providing both indigenous and foreign "volunteers for martyrdom" with explosives and weapons training. U.S. intelligence sources have implicated the Guards in the 1983 bombing of the U.S. Marine barracks in Beirut and the 1988 bombing of Pan Am flight 103 over Lockerbie, Scotland.

REVOLUTIONARY ORGANIZATION OF SOCIALIST MUSLIMS

One of the covers used by the ABU NIDAL Organization in attacks against British targets. Among the Abu Nidal operations carried out under this guise are the attack on the London Hotel in Athens in August 1985; the violence at the Glyfad Hotel in Athens in September 1985; and the bombings of the Cafe de Paris and the British Airways office in Rome in September 1985.

REVOLUTIONARY ORGANIZATION 1 MAY

A Greek left-wing terrorist organization that was implicated in a rash of shootings in early 1989 which left three state prosecutors dead. The urban guerrilla tactics of the group have contributed to the pervasive fear of violent retribution which plagues the Greek legal system. Two Greek Supreme Court justices resigned after the shootings, and the Supreme Court's refusal to extradite Palestinian terrorist Mohammed RASHID is considered to be further evidence of the success of Greek terrorist intimidation tactics.

REVOLUTIONARY ORGANIZATION 17 NOVEMBER

In Greek, "Epanastaiki Organosi 17 Noemvri." An ethnocentric Greek terrorist organization, named in commemoration of the date on which a young Greek radical was killed during an Athens Polytechnic demonstration in 1973. Headquartered in Athens, the group's membership is thought to number fewer than 25. The group surfaced in December 1975 as it claimed responsibility for the murder of Athens CIA chief Richard Welch. Since that time it has established itself as one of the most proficient and lethal terrorist groups in Europe. The group is reported to be Marxist in orientation, and much of its rhetoric and terrorist activity have been directed against U.S. and NATO targets and against Greek targets which it considers to be opposed to the "revolution." The group is dedicated to the severance of Greek ties to NATO. It is also anti-Soviet and anti-Turkish.

The group's attacks have been almost exclusively ambush-style assassinations by teams of two and three members. Victims usually are attacked near their homes or offices. A trademark of 17 November has been to use the same pistol in several of its attacks, including the assassinations of two Americans. This could indicate that the group has limited resources, or it may be a way to "authenticate" its responsibility for attacks. In any case, using the same weapon indicates that the group is confident of its ability to elude the police. Not a single 17 November member has been arrested in more than 13 years of attacks.

The 17 November organization has been responsible for several bombings since 1985, including an attack against a bus transporting U.S. military personnel in April 1987, which injured 18. The group also claimed responsibility for an August 1987 bomb attack against another U.S. military bus, in which 12 people were injured. Since the beginning of 1988 the frequency of the group's attacks has increased considerably.

Little is known about the group's membership, organization or relationships (if any) to other Greek terrorist groups. Following an October 1987 shootout between police and members of the REVOLUTIONARY POPULAR STRUGGLE (ELA), however, and a subsequent search of ELA hideouts, Greek police believed that they had established a linkage between the two organizations. There is no evidence that 17 November maintains ties to foreign terrorist groups.

REVOLUTIONARY POPULAR STRUGGLE (ELA)

An extreme leftist group operating in Greece since 1973. Little is known of the group's structure or membership. The ELA has expressed solidarity with other terror organizations such as ACTION DIRECTE and the RED ARMY FACTION though there is no evidence of any formal links between the groups. The ELA opposed the military dictatorship of Greece before it ended in 1974 and remains strongly opposed to the United States.

RHEIN-MAIN INCIDENT

On August 8, 1985 a car bomb exploded at the U.S. Air Force Base at Rhein-Main, West Germany, killing two and injuring 17. The attack was a joint effort of the RED ARMY FACTION and ACTION DIRECTE.

RICARDO FRANCO FRONT (RFF)

Spanish, "Frente Ricardo Franco." A splinter group of Colombia's FARC. Like its parent organization, the RFF seeks to overthrow the established Colombian political and social order and form a "people's government." The group opposes U.S. involvement in Colombia and has demonstrated the strongest anti-American sentiments of any of that country's guerrilla groups. During 1984 and 1985 the RFF frequently targeted U.S. official and commercial installations, though the group has been relatively inactive since that time.

The RFF grew out of the dissention within the FARC over that organization's agreement to a government truce in 1984. RFF and FARC guerrillas have attacked each other on several occasions since the split. The RFF increased terrorist activities in 1985, at a time when the FARC was trying to pursue political objectives and to abide by the truce. The FARC has been blamed for many RFF actions, and its credibility has been damaged because of the former close relationship with the membership of the RFF.

In 1985 the RFF decided to cooperate with some of Colombia's other guerrilla organizations and formalized an agreement to undertake joint actions with the ELN (National Liberation Army), the only other major movement which was at that time opposing the government truce. The RFF also apparently allied itself with M-19 and on one occasion fought alongside M-19 for 10 days in the Tolima Department (a Colombian province).

In December 1985 a bloody purge occurred within the RFF and as many as 100

RFF members were killed and buried in mass graves, which were later uncovered by Colombian security forces. When news of the purge became public, other members of the NATIONAL GUERRILLA COORDINATOR (CNG), such as M-19, issued public statements breaking off relations with the RFF. The incident caused serious factionalization within the RFF, and the group has been fairly inactive since that time. At present, the RFF might be more accurately described as a group of bandits rather than a guerrilla organization.

Reference: Bruce Michael Bagley, "Colombian Politics: Crisis or Continuity?," *Current History* (January 1987).

RODERIGO FRANCO COMMAND

A Peruvian paramilitary organization reportedly sponsored by extremists within the American Popular Revolutionary Alliance (APRA), the party of Peruvian President Alan Garcia. Its name is derived from an APRA leader killed by terrorists in 1987. The group was originally organized to carry out acts of reprisal against the Peruvian Indian group SENDERO LUMINOSO but has also been responsible for terrorist acts against conservative critics of APRA. It claimed responsibility for the murder on July 28, 1988 of a Sendero Luminoso defense attorney. In November 1988 the group started a campaign of bombings and death threats in Lima. Two journalists were ambushed while investigating a DEATH SQUAD incident in late November; one of the reporters survived the attack and has expressed certainty that his assailants were from the Roderigo Franco Command.

Reference: "Death Squad Is Linked to Peruvian Ruling Party," *New York Times* (December 4, 1988).

RODRIGUEZ GACHA, JOSE GONZALO (1947–89)

Cocaine trafficker and leader, along with Pablo ESCOBAR GAVIRIA, of Colombia's infamous MEDELLIN drug cartel. By the time of his death in a police shootout in December 1989, Rodriguez Gacha, a former pig farmer with a grade school education, had amassed an illegal fortune believed to be in the billions of dollars. Together with Escobar, Rodriguez Gacha was responsible for scores, if not hundreds, of assassinations and other acts of NARCO-TERRORISM. It was the cartel's murder of Luis Carlos Galan, a candidate for the presidency, which spurred the Bogota government to launch a war against the drug lords. The government seized dozens of homes, ranches, airplanes, helicopters and other expensive possessions belonging to the drug runners and drove the criminals into hiding. Throughout the latter months of 1989 the cartel leaders were kept constantly on the run by the Colombian police and army. The cartel leaders countered, forming an organization known as the EXTRADITABLES, to conduct a stepped-up terror campaign throughout Colombia. They murdered more than 100 people when they destroyed an Avianca jet in flight, and they killed almost as many again with a truck bomb planted in front of a Bogota police building. Finally, on December 15, 1989 government forces closed in on Rodriguez Gacha near the coastal city of Cartagena, killing him, his son Freddy, and 15 of their gunmen in a shootout.

ROMERO Y GALDAMES, OSCAR (1917–80)

Archbishop of San Salvador, El Salvador, assassinated while celebrating Mass on

March 24, 1980. His assassins are generally believed to have been members of the MAXIMILIANO HERNANDEZ MARTINEZ ANTI-COMMUNIST ALLIANCE. Archbishop Romero, a Nobel Peace Prize nominee, was an internationally respected opponent of the regime in El Salvador and an outspoken critic of that country's right-wing DEATH SQUADS. Government troops opened fire on the huge crowds at the Archbishop's funeral on March 30, killing 40 mourners and wounding many others.

Reference: Placido Endozain, *Archbishop Romero: Martyr of Salvador* (Guildford, U.K.: Lutterworth Press, 1981).

ROYAL ULSTER CONSTABULARY (RUC)

The civilian police force of NORTHERN IRELAND. The RUC, with 13,000 members, has suffered more than 270 deaths since 1969. It is largely a Protestant institution and has been attacked by Irish Catholics as a symbol of British occupation and anti-Catholic authority.

Reference: Robert M. Pockrass, "The Police Response to Terrorism: The Royal Ulster Constabulary," *Conflict* 6 (1986).

RUKNS, EL

A Chicago-based criminal organization. In November 1987 five members of the organization were convicted on numerous weapons and conspiracy charges after a successful FBI undercover investigation, begun in 1986, exposed their scheme to commit terrorist acts for a fee. El Rukns' members had negotiated an agreement with a Libyan representative to conduct terrorism in the United States in exchange for money from Libya.

RULES OF ENGAGEMENT

1. Military or paramilitary directives that delineate the circumstances and limitations under which force can be used. For example, soldiers might be told to shoot only if they are fired upon first or police might be told only to use deadly force when lives (as opposed to property) are in immediate danger.

2. Directives from a military headquarters that delineate the circumstances and limitations under which troops will initiate or continue combat engagement with other opposition.

RUSHDIE, SALMAN

Indian-born British novelist who wrote the controversial novel *The Satanic Verses* (1988). Rushdie became the target of death threats when fundamentalist Muslims accused him of blasphemy in the novel. In February 1989 Iran's Ayatollah Ruhollah KHOMEINI called on Muslims to kill Rushdie for having defamed Islam, the Prophet Mohammed and the Prophet's wives. The Ayatollah's death threats, accompanied by the promise of a huge financial reward for the successful assassin, triggered a sweeping international reaction. In March 1989 Britain and Iran broke off diplomatic relations as a result of the Rushdie controversy. Naguib Mahfouz of Egypt, the winner of the 1988 Nobel Prize for Literature, called Khomeini's actions "intellectual terrorism," and Western commentators debated the appropriateness of proposed responses to what was widely considered to be a terroristic attack on free speech and civil liberties. Bookstores in the United States which pulled the embattled book from the shelves were criticized for bowing to terrorist-inspired fear. The basis of these fears was confirmed by the bombing of two bookstores in California on February 28, 1989. Starting in December 1990 Rushdie began making limited public appearances in an effort to calm Islamic sensibilities. However, the Iranians would have none of his publicly proclaimed contrition and refused to lift the death sentence as of the end of 1990.

Reference: Malise Ruthven, *A Satanic Affair: Salman Rushdie and the Rage of Islam* (London: Chatto, 1988).

SABRA AND SHATILA

Palestinian refugee camps in Beirut, Lebanon in which refugees were slaughtered by members of the Christian Phalangist militia on September 16–17, 1982. No accurate death toll is known, but the victims are thought to number from 800 to a thousand. The Israeli Minister of Defense Ariel Sharon was seriously criticized for allowing the Phalangists into the camps while his troops remained outside. Sharon's intent was to frighten the Palestinian residents of Lebanon enough to make them leave Lebanon, so that the country would be free of all non-Lebanese. Sharon resigned when an Israeli government investigative panel, the Kahane Commission, found him partially responsible for the bloodshed.

References: Jonathan C. Randall, *Going All the Way: Christian Warlords, Israeli Adventurers, and the War in Lebanon* (New York: Viking Press, 1983); Yezid Sayigh, "Reflections on the Fall of Shatilla," *Middle East International* 335 (October 7th, 1988).

SADAT, ANWAR ÀL- (1918–81)

President of Egypt, assassinated on October 6, 1981 as he sat in review of a military parade commemorating the Arab-Israeli War of 1973. As the army vehicles passed the reviewing stand, one halted and four men in military fatigues leapt out of the back and stormed the presidential dais, brandishing automatic rifles and hand grenades. As a young Egyptian army officer during World War II, Sadat was court-martialed and imprisoned by the British (who then controlled Egypt) for collaborating with the Nazis. After the war he took part in the 1952 coup that deposed King Farouk. Thereafter he served as Egyptian president Gamal Abdel Nasser's loyal aide. As vice president of Egypt under Nasser (1964–66; 1969–70) he succeeded to the presidency upon Nasser's death in 1970. After the 1973 Arab-Israeli war he sought a rapprochement with the United States and Israel. In a dramatic gesture he visited Jerusalem in 1977 and addressed the Israeli parliament. This led to the Camp David Accords, the agreements negotiated and signed by Sadat and Israeli prime minister Menachem BEGIN in September 1978 at Camp David, the United States president's private resort in the Catoctin Mountains in Maryland. These agreements led to the formal Egyptian-Israeli peace treaty of March 1979. For this Sadat shared the 1978 Nobel Peace Prize with Begin. These efforts for peace led to his death. His assassins were members of TANZIM AL-JIHAD an Islamic group that considered Sadat to be overly influenced by Western powers and a traitor to the Arab cause. These sentiments had been exacerbated by Sadat's participation in the Camp David Accords.

References: Anwar el-Sadat, *In Search of Identity: An Autobiography* (New York: Harper & Row, 1978); Majid Khadduri, *Arab Personalities in Politics* (Washington, D.C.: The Middle East Institute, 1981).

SADR, IMAM MUSA AL-

The Iranian-born mullah (Islamic holy man) who emigrated to Lebanon in the 1950s and engaged the downtrodden Lebanese SHI'ITE Muslims in the struggle for power in the Lebanese state. He founded the grassroots Shi'ite organization Harakat al-Mahurmeen, "The Movement of the Disinherited," and its militant wing AMAL. Al-Sadr disappeared and is believed to have been assassinated, along with two aides, by Muammar QADDAFI during a 1978 visit to Libya. Several acts of terrorism have been committed by his followers in efforts to ascertain the whereabouts of their spiritual father.

See HAMZA.

Reference: Fouad Ajami, *The Vanished Imam: Musa al Sadr and the Shia of Lebanon* (Ithaca, N.Y.: Cornell University Press, 1986).

SAFE HOUSE

A house or premises established by an organization for the purpose of conducting clandestine or covert activity in relative security.

SA'IQA, AL-

Arabic, "The Thunderbolt." A Palestinian group formed in 1968 to represent Syrian interests in the Palestinian struggle. It is the Palestinian wing of the Syrian Ba'ath party. Though generally considered to be one of the "moderate" factions of the PLO, with a history of alliances with al-FATAH, al-Sa'iqa has in recent years been associated with the REJECTIONIST FRONT of the PLO. Al-Sa'iqa's role in the PLO is not as important as its role as a Syrian surrogate. Al-Sa'iqa is integrated into the Syrian armed forces, and its support of Syrian intervention in Lebanon in 1976 undermined its standing in the Palestinian movement.

The strength of al-Sa'iqa within the PLO movement has historically been dependent on perceptions of Syrian strength in the region and in the Palestinian cause. It is not an organization with a strong ideological base (such as the POPULAR FRONT FOR THE LIBERATION OF PALESTINE) or a deep grassroots following in the Palestinian community (such as al-Fatah).

The most visible terrorist operations carried out by the group have been conducted under its "Eagles of the Palestinian Revolution" guise, including the assault on the Egyptian Embassy in Ankara in July 1979 and a Austrian hostage-taking incident in Austria in September 1973. In this episode, Austrian Chancellor Bruno Kreisky met al-Sa'iqa's demands and closed down a refugee camp for Jewish Soviet emigres in exchange for the release of three hostages (two of whom were Jewish). This compromise with al-Sa'iqa terrorists drew the sharp derision of Israeli Prime Minister Golda Meir. Al-Sa'iqa terrorist activity increased following the 1979–80 Israeli–Egyptian accords, as the group targeted both Israeli and Egyptian interests. Al-Sa'iqa's membership is thought to number approximately 2,000.

References: Laurie Brand, "Palestinians in Syria: The Politics of Integration," *Middle East Journal* 42 (August 1988); Helena Cobban, *The Palestine Liberation Organization: People, Power, and Politics* (New York: Cambridge University Press, 1983).

SALEMEH, ABU HASSAN

Member of BLACK SEPTEMBER and one of the leaders of the September 1972 MUNICH MASSACRE at the Olympic Games. Although he was not one of the guerrillas who took part in the attack, Salameh is thought to have been responsible for much of the planning of the incident. Born to a wealthy Palestinian family, he was educated in Egypt and Europe. A strong and loyal supporter of Yasir ARAFAT, Salameh was appointed by Arafat's FORCE 17. He was assassinated by Israeli agents in a car bombing in Beirut in January 1979.

Reference: James Adams, *The Financing of Terror* (London: New English Library, 1986).

SALEH, FOUAD ALI

A Tunisian-born Frenchman, also known as Ali al-Tunsi (or Ali the Tunisian). He was arrested by French police for being the mastermind behind 15 bombings and attempted bombings that killed 13 people and wounded more than 200 in Paris in 1985 and 1986. His motive was to discourage France from sending arms to Iraq during its 1980–1988 war with Iran. In 1990 he was put on trial in France; the results are pending.

SAM MELVILLE-JONATHON JACKSON UNIT

A left-wing militant U.S. organization that staged bomb attacks in Massachusetts in the late 1970s. Members of the group surfaced as members of the UNITED FREEDOM FRONT in the early 1980s.

SANDS, BOBBY

Member of the Irish Republican Army who died as a result of a highly publicized hunger strike in March 1981 while imprisoned at Maze Prison in Northern Ireland. During the hunger strike, Sands was elected to the British Parliament as a SINN FEIN candidate.

Reference: John M. Feehan, *Bobby Sands and the Tragedy of Northern Ireland* (London: Permanent Press, 1986).

SAR, SALOTH

See POL POT.

SAS (SPECIAL AIR SERVICE)

An elite British army regiment created during World War II to conduct penetration missions behind enemy lines and to engage in irregular warfare. The SAS has been used extensively in Northern Ireland as an anti-terrorist force and is considered to be one of the most effective units of its kind. The members of the SAS are drawn from troops and officers in the army, with long-term careers in their own regiments. They are seconded to the SAS for periods of a few years and then returned to regimental service. They are organized into four-man "bricks," making up 20-man "troops," and the whole regiment consists of no more than a few hundred men in three "squadrons." Its best known operation was Operation Nimrod at the Iranian Embassy in London. On May 5, 1980 the SAS stormed the building where anti-Khomeini Iranians were holding 21 hostages. Five of the six terrorists and two hostages were killed during the raid.

Reference: James Ladd, *SAS Operations* (London: Hale, 1986).

SAVAK

The acronym, in Farsi, for the National Security and Information Organization, the

Iranian government's secret police during the reign of the Shah. Under the command of General Nassiri Nematollah, SAVAK systematically attempted to eliminate the Shah's political enemies through violence and physical intimidation. During the 1970s the organization began to pursue the regime's opponents outside Iran, including Iranian students studying in the United States. SAVAK is believed to have been responsible for the 1977 death of the Ayatollah Khomeini's son, one of the events which sparked the Iranian Revolution.

SCHLEYER, HANS-MARTIN (1915–77)

West German industrialist who was kidnapped outside Cologne by the RED ARMY FACTION (RAF) on September 5, 1977. His body was found October 19 in Paris after the terrorists' demands were not met. These demands included the release of 10 RAF prisoners, among them its leader, Andreas BAADER.

SEA-AIR-LAND TEAM (SEAL)

A U.S. Navy commando-type force especially trained and equipped for conducting unconventional and paramilitary operations. SEALS also train personnel of allied nations in such operations, including surveillance and reconnaissance in and from restricted waters, rivers and coastal areas. SEALs teams are especially skilled at infiltrating enemy territory by sea in small boats or as frogmen, by air from helicopters or by parachute, and by land in ranger patrols. They have, by mid-1990, only been used against terrorists in a 1990 film, *Navy Seals*.

SEA-AIR-LAND TEAM SIX

The U.S. Navy's elite counterterrorism unit. It is not generally known if this group has ever been used in an actual antiterrorist operation.

The SEAL Team Six is a subgroup of the Navy's SEAL TEAM (see above).

SEMTEX

A type of plastic explosives manufactured by Soviet-bloc nations. Like most plastic explosives, Semtex is very pliable and malleable. It is metallic, but when formed into innocuous shapes it is very difficult to detect. It is also generally impervious to vapor-sniffing detection devices. In 1990 the new democratically elected government of Czechoslovakia admitted that it had sold over 1,000 tons of Semtex to Libya over the last two decades. Along with this admission was the announcement that Czechoslovakia would no longer manufacture Semtex. Nevertheless, because such vast quantities of it had been distributed by Libya to terrorist groups all over the world, Semtex has become and seems likely to remain a popular plastic explosive for many terrorists. Semtex is the brand name for the Eastern European manufactured version of C-4 plastic explosive, which is manufactured in the United States.

SENDERO LUMINOSO (SL)

"The Shining Path" formed in 1969 by Abimael GUZMAN as a Peruvian Indian left-wing guerrilla group. This organization has been cited as the most dangerous and unpredictable terrorist and insurgency group in Latin America, and its operations have left an estimated 15,000 dead since 1980. The group's name is taken from an early Peruvian communist's statement which hailed Marxism as the "shining path to the future." It is dedicated to the violent overthrow of the government of Peru and its replacement with a revolutionary Marxist peasant regime by the year 2000. This strategy is based on a rural insurgency which the Sendero Luminoso hopes will sweep into the cities, destroying the current system of government. The group feels that the "old, heroic traditions of the Quechua Indians" are the proper elements for a new socio-political system. By using names and drawing upon symbols from the Indian heritage of the rural regions, the SL has been able to attract some support that might not have been drawn to a purely Marxist ideology.

The SL is organized to conduct urban terrorism and rural guerrilla warfare simultaneously. Although it is large and adequately equipped and trained, the group tends to avoid direct conflict with the military unless it can attack with overwhelming force. Its forces are thought to number between four and six thousand. Unlike most other Latin American subversive groups, the SL is not believed to have obvious or extensive ties to Cuba or other sponsors. Bank robberies and extortion are the primary sources of funding. The SL has imposed a "war tax" that apparently provides a substantial source of income, as well as a "people's tax" on much of Peru's illicit and immensely profitable cocaine industry.

The SL conducts very aggressive indoctrination programs in its rural bases. Its recruiting practices frequently target 12- to 15-year olds who can be molded into highly motivated activists. Though a radical Maoist-Marxist organization, the Sendero Luminoso has included attacks upon Soviet and Communist Chinese diplomatic missions among its targets. Foreign businessmen and Peruvian institutionalism in both the public and private sectors have also been frequent victims of its terrorist violence. The majority of Sendero Luminoso terrorism is directed against the peasant population of Peru, most of whom are destitute Indians, as a means of limiting peasant collaboration with government forces. SL guerrilla actions in 1988–89 were viewed as attempts to ignite a military coup and unseat the troubled government of President Alan Garcia, thereby polarizing the country. In July 1988 Peruvian police arrested three members of the ABU NIDAL Organization who were suspected of planning joint terrorist operations with the SL.

See ENFORCEMENT TERRORISM.

References: David Scott Palmer, "Rebellion in Rural Peru: The Origins and Evolution of Sendero Luminoso," *Comparative Politics* 18 (January 1986); Robert B. Ash, "Sendero Luminoso and the Peruvian Crisis," *Confict Quarterly* (Summer 1985); J. McGuire, "The Challenge of Shining Path,". *Nation* (December 8, 1984); Cynthia McClintock, "Why Peasants Rebel: The Case of Peru's Sendero Luminoso," *World Politics* (October 1984); Phillip Bennett, "Peru: Corner of the Dead," *Atlantic* (May 1984).

SENDIC ANTONACCIO, RAUL (1925–89)

Founder and leader of TUPAMAROS, a Uruguayan Marxist guerrilla organization. A former law student and labor organizer, Sendic founded the Tupamaros in 1963 and directed the group's anti-government insurgency until its defeat in 1972. Sendic was imprisoned in 1970 but led a massive Tupamaros escape in 1971, in which more than 100 jailed guerrillas were freed. Sendic was jailed again in 1972 and remained imprisoned throughout the period of military rule in Uruguay. As a result of the amnesty declared after the restoration of civilian rule, he was released in 1985. He then converted the Tupamaros into a legal political party. Sendic died in April 1989 after an extended illness.

SEPARATIST MOVEMENT

An attempt by a group or population to secede from a given state either to form a new state or to attach the group's territory to a neighboring state to which it feels strongly tied. A separatists group's motivation is often a belief that it is culturally distinct from the majority of the population with which it lives.

Reference: Vittofranco S. Pisano, "Terrorist Ethnic Separation in France and Italy," *Conflict*, 8 (1988).

SEPTEMBER, DULCIE (1943–88)

The Paris representative of the AFRICAN NATIONAL CONGRESS (ANC) who was assassinated at her office on March 29, 1988 by attackers believed to be agents of the government of South Africa. South African government sources denied responsibility and suggested that dissension among the ANC ranks may have led to the shooting.

SHABIBA

A youth movement operating among the Palestinian refugee camps of the Israeli-occupied territories. The group is ostensibly a volunteer community service organization, but it has proven to be a strong Palestinian nationalist recruitment device for al-FATAH.

SHARIF, BASSAM ABU

See ABU SHARIF, BASSAM.

SHARPEVILLE INCIDENT

On March 20, 1960, 69 blacks were killed and more than 200 were wounded when South African police opened fire with automatic weapons in Sharpeville township near Johannesburg. The incident led the AFRICAN NATIONAL CONGRESS (ANC) to abandon its policy of nonviolence in its struggle for civil rights.

SHEIKHOLESLAM, HUSSEIN

One of the key Iranian government officials involved in the exporting of the Iranian revolution. While educated at the University of California-Berkeley, he adopted an anti–United States stance upon returning to Iran and became one of the key figures in the IRANIAN HOSTAGE CRISIS. He was also reportedly involved in the October 23, 1983 bombing of the U.S. Marine headquarters in Beirut on October 23, 1983.

SHI'ITES

A sect of Islam that split from the mainstream SUNNI sect during the seventh century in a dispute over leadership of the faith. Shi'ites believe that the mantle of leadership belongs to the descendants of Ali, cousin and son-in-law of the Prophet Mohammed. Ali's son Hussein is the forefather of today's Shi'ites, having died in battle to maintain leadership of Islam within the family of the Prophet. Shi'ites see in Hussein the virtues of righteous rebellion, militancy and martyrdom.

Shi'ites comprise perhaps one-tenth of the world's Islamic population, and their minority status and theological differences with the majority have brought them much persecution in the Sunni-controlled states of Saudi Arabia, Kuwait and Iraq. Only in IRAN, where they form a majority population, have Shi'ites seized power and instituted a government according to the precepts of their faith. Since the rise of revolutionary Iran in 1979, fundamentalist Shi'ites have attempted to spread their revolutionary religious fervor through widespread acts of terror by such groups as AMAL, HEZBOLLAH, and the ORGANIZATION OF THE OPPRESSED ON EARTH.

See FADLALLAH; JIHAD; KHOMEINI.

SHINING PATH

See SENDERO LUMINOSO.

SHUKEIRY, AHMED AL-

Founder of the PLO PALESTINE LIBERATION ORGANIZATION in 1964. The PLO was initially an umbrella group for various guerrilla movements opposed to any settlement with Israel. In 1969, one of these guerrilla groups, al-FATAH, under Yasir ARAFAT, grew so strong that it took over the PLO. Thus Al-Shukeiry faded into obscurity.

SHULTZ DOCTRINE

As stated by U.S. Secretary of State George Shultz in October 1984, the U.S. policy toward terrorism ''should go beyond passive defense to consider means of active prevention, preemption, and retaliation.''

SIKHS

Sikhs are a religious minority in Northern India, historically in conflict with Hindus and the Hindu-dominated Indian government. This conflict has in recent years been marked by rampant acts of terrorism by radical Sikhs.

The Sikh religious tradition is traced back to the founder of the sect, Guru Nanak (1469–1539), who preached a pacifist spirituality drawn from Hindu doctrine. This tradition is in stark contrast to the militant religion that is modern Sikhdom.

Sikh terrorism is supported by a number of groups both within India and internationally, though information concerning the culpability of specific Sikh groups for specific operations or even on the infrastructure of Sikh elements is sparse. Sikh extremism is especially prevalent in the northern state of Punjab, where desecration of Hindu shrines, murders and bombings frequently occur.

A small but violent movement emerged in 1981 when Sant Jarnail Singh BHINDRANWALE began preaching Sikh fundamentalism and urging the Sikh community in India to pressure the government for an independent Sikh state. Bhindranwale's followers and supporters adopted terrorism as one of their tactics. An upswing in the level of Sikh violence has followed the Indian government's 1984 attack on the GOLDEN TEMPLE OF AMRITSAR, the most revered of Sikh holy places and the site of Bhindranwale's headquarters. In response to the assault of the Golden Temple, Sikhs assassinated Indian Prime Minister Indira GANDHI in October 1984. One of the most tragic episodes of Sikh terrorism was the bombing of an Air India jetliner in June of 1985, in which 329 people perished. Sikhs have denied responsibility for the incident, but most experts believe otherwise. Groups that carry out Sikh terrorism include DASHMESH, DAL KHALSA, Babbar Khalsa and the All-India Sikh Students Federation. These organizations support the formation of an independent Sikh state of Khalistan and have escalated Hindu–Sikh tensions, thereby exacerbating communal animosities and weakening the position of moderates.

References: W. H. McLeod, *The Sikhs: History, Religion, and Society* (New York: Columbia University Press, 1989); James Manor, ''Collective Conflict in India,'' *Conflict Studies* 212 (1988); Surjit Singh Gandhi, *The Struggle of the Sikhs for Sovereignty* (New Delhi: Gur Das Kapur, 1980).

SINN FEIN

The legal Northern Irish political wing (founded in 1905) of the outlawed paramilitary IRISH REPUBLICAN ARMY. The organization is led by president Gerry Adams, an elected member of the British Parliament, who denies any involvement with the IRA. Adams is considered to be the foremost advocate of political approaches to the Republican goal of a united Ireland. Adams and Sinn Fein espouse a left-wing political ideology which decries foreign economic investment in Ireland, supports the withdrawal of Ireland from the European Community, and envisions nationalization of industry and collectivization of farms. In Northern Ireland the organization's candidates have fared well in both local and national elections, regularly garnering more than 10% of the total vote.

Many Sinn Fein members have been implicated in IRA acts of terrorism, and the group's leadership has often voiced support for the actions of the PROVISIONAL WING OF THE IRA (PIRA). However, Adams publicly distanced himself and his organization from several indiscriminate PIRA acts of violence in late 1988 and early 1989 and chastised the PIRA for its recklessness. Sinn Fein, which means "we ourselves" in Gaelic, is headquartered in Belfast.

References: Liam Clarke, *Broadening the Battlefield* (Dublin: Gill and Macmillan, 1987); Jack Holland, *Too Long a Sacrifice* (New York: Dodd, Mead, and Co., 1981).

SIRHAN SIRHAN

The assassin of Robert F. Kennedy, U.S. Senator and candidate for president of the United States. On June 5, 1968 Sirhan shot Kennedy in the kitchen of a Los Angeles hotel. Sirhan, who was born in Jordan, believed that Kennedy, a strong supporter of Israel, posed a threat to Arab interests. Sirhan's repeated requests for parole from prison have been denied by the state of California.

SKINHEADS

Violent young white males, characteristically with shaved heads or very closely cropped hair, often responsible for racially motivated gang violence. Skinhead movements have become major problems in many U.S. cities, where the youths have, in the words of a 1989 report of the Southern Poverty Law Center (SPLC), become the white supremacist movement "most obsessed with violence."

Many skinheads espouse NEO-NAZI philosophy and sport neo-Nazi attire and insignia. Skinheads were linked to about 60% of the U.S. racial violence documented by the SPLC in 1988, including four murders. The youths have also been tied to attacks and burnings of churches and synagogues. Skinhead racial violence has been directed against blacks, Asians, hispanics, Jews and homosexuals. The majority of skinhead activity is centered on the West coast. Skinheads have also become involved with the KU KLUX KLAN and the ARYAN NATIONS. Skinheads have also plagued European nations, especially the United Kingdom and West Germany. In Hungary in 1988 there were widespread reports of skinhead violence against the gypsy population.

SKYJACKING

The act of taking an airliner and its passengers hostage for personal or political motives. Modern skyjacking dates from 1961 when the first U.S. airliner was hijacked to CUBA. Elaborate airport security procedures implemented since have dramatically cut the number of skyjackings. In the early seventies skyjacking became the modus operandi of the POPULAR FRONT FOR THE LIBERATION OF PALESTINE (PFLP) to publicize the Palestinian cause. Some of the most celebrated cases are the skyjacking of an Air France airliner to ENTEBBE in July of 1976 and the diverting of a number of European airliners to DAWSON'S FIELD in Jordan in 1970.

See also HAGUE CONVENTION, THE.

References: Nancy D. Joyner, *Aerial Hijacking as an International Crime* (Dobbs Ferry, NY: Oceana Publications, 1974); David Phillips, *Skyjacking: The Story of Air Piracy* (London: Harrap, 1973).

SLEEPERS

Terrorist agents who maintain a low profile so as to be in a position to provide aid to their more active terrorist brethren. Sleepers may provide safe houses, forged identification and documents, weapons, vehicles and transport, money, information and other valuable forms of assistance.

SNOOPE (SYSTEM FOR NUCLEAR OBSERVATION OF POSSIBLE EXPLOSIVES)

An advanced system for the detection of PLASTIC EXPLOSIVES. A cloud of neutrons chemically reacts with concealed explosives, causing emissions that are then detected by the SNOOPE computer. The system was developed by the Science Applications International Corporation of San Diego, California, which has received several orders from the Federal Aviation Administration for the new technology.

SOLDIERS OF JUSTICE

A pro-Iranian SHI'ITE extremist organization based in Lebanon. The group has claimed responsibility for a number of attacks upon Saudi diplomats, including the January 1989 assassination of a diplomat in Bangkok, Thailand and the December 1988 wounding of an official at the Saudi Embassy in Karachi, Pakistan. The Soldiers of Justice are believed to be comprised of both Lebanese and Saudi Shi'ite Muslims. The revolutionary government of Iran, a professed enemy of the Sunni royal family and the government of Saudi Arabia, is thought to have been instrumental in the group's formation.

SOMOZA DEBAYLE, ANASTASIO (1925–80)

The dictator of Nicaragua from 1967 until his overthrow by the Sandinistas in July 1979. Somoza directed a violent and repressive regime through his brutal National Guards. Somoza was himself the victim of political violence when he was gunned down in Paraguay on September 17, 1980 by members of the Argentinian ERP.

SOUTH MOLUCCANS

See MOLUCCANS.

SPARROW SQUADS

Assassination squads of the Filipino NEW PEOPLE'S ARMY.

SPECIAL AIR SERVICE

See SAS.

SPETSNAZ

Russian special forces trained by the KGB to land by parachute or submarine behind NATO lines and attack Western military sites at the onset of war.

Reference: Viktor Suvorov, "Spetsnaz: The Soviet Union's Special Forces," *Military Review* (March 1984).

SPILLOVER TERRORISM

The term applied to the "spilling over" of regional conflict into other, geographically removed areas, in the form of terrorist episodes. This concept is presented by D. A. Pluchinsky, a European analyst for the U.S. Department of State's Bureau of Diplomatic Security, in "Middle Eastern Terrorist Activity in Western Europe in 1985: A Diagnosis and Prognosis," in William Gutteridge's *Contemporary Research in Terrorism* (New York: Facts On File, 1986). Pluchinsky discusses the attractiveness of Western Europe as a site for spillover terrorism: its proximity to troubled regions, its available sources of manpower, its easy terrorist targets and its heavy concentration of media sources.

SRI LANKAN TERRORISM

The small Indian Ocean island nation of Sri Lanka has been plagued by rampant ethnic terrorism since 1983. Violence between the majority Sinhalese and the Tamil minority has resulted in enormous casualties. Terrorism has disrupted the political system of the nation and has led to the introduction of Indian Army "peacekeeping" troops to neutralize Tamil separatists rebels in the east and north of the island. The Indian Army is viewed by many as an occupation force.

An Indian–Sri Lankan political settlement, which meets many of the Tamil separatist demands, was signed in July 1987. This agreement includes the establishment of a new Northeast Province, which approximates the embattled Tamil homeland. The agreement also makes Tamil an official language of Sri Lanka. Despite such political momentum, ethnic violence has continued to plague the nation. Sinhalese anti-government violence during the parliamentary elections in February 1989 left at least 56 people dead. The terror continues and no real and lasting political settlement is in sight.

See also LIBERATION TIGERS OF TAMIL EELAM; PEOPLE'S LIBERATION FRONT.

References: Kumar Rupesinghe, "Ethnic Conflicts in South Asia: The Case of Sri Lanka and the Indian Peace-Keeping Force," *Journal of Peace Research* 25 (December 1988); M. L. Marasinghe, "Ethnic Politics and Constitutional Reform: The Indo-Sri Lankan Accord," *International and Comparative Law Quarterly* 37 (July 1988).

STATE-SPONSORED TERRORISM

Also called state terrorism. The purposive acts of a nation intended to strike fear into groups or individuals so as to achieve state policies, or the deliberate acts of violence directed against individuals or groups by a nation so as to achieve the ends of the state.

State-sponsored terrorism may be a domestic or an international phenomenon. The regimes of Joseph Stalin and Adolph Hitler provide recent historical benchmarks in 20th-century state terrorism. More recent examples include the brutal Cambodian rule of POL POT and LIBYA under the leadership of Muammar QADDAFI. Although these examples are easily accommodated within almost all definitions of state terrorism, political violence in and by many governments does not facilitate easy categorization as state-sponsored terrorism. Martin Slann presents a simple yet accurate assessment of this definitional problem: ". . . governments can get away with more violence than can any other institution in society, because of unrivaled resources, and because there is usually either some popular support for even the most brutal political regime, or legitimization of the government from outside by the recognition of international law."

See ARGENTINA; GUATEMALA; IRAN; IRAQ; NORTH KOREA; SYRIA.

References: Michael Stohl, *Terrible Beyond Endurance? The Foreign Policy of State Terrorism* (New York: Greenwood Press, 1988); Martin Slann and Bernard Schechterman (London: Lynne Rienner Publishers, 1987); James Petras, "The Anatomy of State Terror: Chile, El Salvador, and Brazil," *Science and Society* 51 (Fall 1987); Frank Brenchly, "Diplomatic Immunities and State-sponsored Terrorism," *Conflict Studies* 164 (1984); Paul Wilkinson, "State-Sponsored International Terrorism: The Problems of Response," *World Today* 40 (July 1984).

STERN GANG

A Zionist terrorist organization comprised of the followers of Abraham Stern, who directed terrorist activities against British targets in Palestine during the early 1940s. Stern died in 1942 and his group then called itself "Lehi." Lehi's leadership was a triumvirate that included Yitzhak SHAMIR and Menahem BEGIN, both of whom later became prime ministers of Israel. The organization is best known for its 1948 assassination of the U.N. mediator for Palestine, Count Folke BERNADOTTE, whom Lehi considered to be an enemy of Zionism. Lehi also participated in the massacre of Palestinian civilians at DEIR YASSIN, where more than 200 people were slaughtered.

References: Y.S. Brenner, "The 'Stern Gang,' 1940–1948," *Middle East Studies 2* (October 1965); J. Bowyer Bell, *Terror Out of Zion: Irgun Zvai Leumi, LEHI and the Palestine Underground, 1929–1949* (New York: St. Martin's Press, 1976).

STETHEM, ROBERT DEAN (1962–85)

U.S. Navy enlisted man who was beaten and murdered on June 15, 1985 at Beirut during the hijacking of TWA Flight 847. Terrorists of the Hezbollah organization were responsible.

STINGER

A light-weight, man-portable, shoulder-fired air defense artillery missile weapon for low-altitude air defense of forward-area combat troops. The Stinger is that rare example of a tactical weapon that has had strategic significance. Supplied to the Afghan resistance fighters indirectly by the United States after the 1979 Soviet invasion of Afghanistan, this weapon allowed the Afghans, without any air force of their own, to gain the local air superiority necessary for success on the ground. Unfortunately, the Stinger can be equally useful as a terrorist weapon, and there is a great concern that it may be used against civilian airlines.

STOCKHOLM SYNDROME

The term used to describe the ironic psychological phenomenon of aggressor identification: a tendency for some victims of aggression to identify and sympathize with those who have abused them. It is derived from the experiences of four Swedish hostages who, after being subjected to a week of extreme physical and mental duress inside a Stockholm bank vault, put themselves between their rescuers and the men who had taken them hostage, so as to prevent the police from harming the terrorists.

Reference: Frank Ochberg and David Soskis, eds., *Victims of Terrorism* (Boulder, Colo.: Westview Press, 1982).

SUDANESE PEOPLE'S LIBERATION ARMY (SPLA)

A left-wing insurgent organization in Southern Sudan. Prior to 1985 the group was supported heavily by Muammar QADDAFI and led a terrorist campaign that included kidnappings and armed attacks on Sudanese civilians and foreigners. The SPLA is a Christian organization and has carried out attacks in protest of the institution of Islamic rule in the Sudan in 1983. Non-Muslims (Christians and animists) comprise approximately one-third of the Sudanese population and occupy much of the southern regions of the country. The SPLA has had a devastating effect on the economy of the Sudan.

SULLIVAN PRINCIPLES

A set of principles for fair employment practice, drafted by Leon H. Sullivan, a black minister in Philadelphia, in 1977. An agreement to adopt the principles was subsequently signed on a voluntary basis by many U.S. corporations doing business in South Africa. This was seen as a means of reducing some of the effects of apartheid and reducing the need for blacks to resort to terrorism.

SUNNI

From the Arabic *sunna*, meaning "the traditional way." The name given to the orthodox Islamic majority sect. Most Arab states are dominated by Sunnis, and this domination has given rise to political as well as religious rivalry with the SHI'ITE minority.

SUPERGRASS

The term, derived from "snake in the grass," applied to Irish militants (usually from the IRISH NATIONAL LIBERATION ARMY and the PROVISIONAL WING OF THE IRISH REPUBLICAN ARMY) who provide information to the authorities about their colleagues and organizations. The supergrass system has been exploited by Northern Irish authorities with a high degree of success. The most famous of IRA supergrass informants was Christopher Black, who in 1981 and 1982 provided authorities with evidence that led to the conviction of 35 fellow IRA members. The total number of arrests made possible by the testimony of Irish supergrass informers numbers in the hundreds.

Reference: Tony Gifford, *Supergrasses: The Use of Accomplice Evidence in Northern Ireland* (London: Cobden Trust, 1984).

SURGICAL STRIKE

A euphemistic term that describes plans to destroy vital targets by means of carefully controlled force, so as to minimize collateral damage. It can refer to the use of conventional force, such as a precisely planned bombing raid on a terrorist headquarters intended to spare all innocent civilians nearby. It can also be used in nuclear strategy, where a surgical strike might be considered as a limited nuclear option against a command, control, communications and intelligence bunker or a set of missile silos. Surgical strikes can rarely be as clean and discriminating in their destruction as planned, however, and the idea of such an attack using nuclear weapons is patently absurd by any normal standards.

SWAPO (SOUTH-WEST AFRICAN PEOPLES ORGANIZATION)

A left-wing organization committed to the independence of Namibia from South Africa. Supported by the Soviet Union, Cuba, and a number of African states, SWAPO sought to maintain a low-intensity conflict against South African forces, previous to the negotiated settlement of 1988. In April 1989 the group stood accused of breaking the negotiated truce. In late 1989 SWAPO emerged from the United Nations-monitored elections as the legitimate spokesman for Namibian nationalism.

SYMBIONESE LIBERATION ARMY (SLA)

A small California left-wing organization that captured the national spotlight when it kidnapped media heiress Patricia HEARST on February 4, 1974. After an extended period of brainwashing indoctrination, Hearst was converted into an active member of the SLA, the primary terrorist activities of which consisted of bank robberies and bombings in California cities. On May 17, 1974 six members of the group perished in a gunfight with Los Angeles police, effectively spelling the end of the SLA. Hearst was arrested in September 1975 for her role in an April 1974 San Francisco bank robbery.

SYRIA

The Middle Eastern state about the size of North Dakota located south of Turkey, east of Iraq and north of Jordan. To its west are Lebanon and Israel. While technically a republic, Hafez al-ASSAD, elected president in 1971, has dictatorial control. Syria was an active belligerent in the 1967 Arab-Israeli war, which resulted in Israel's occupation of the Golan Heights and the city of Qunaytrah. Following the October 1973 war, Israel occupied additional Syrian territory. As a result of the mediation efforts of former U.S. Secretary of State Henry Kissinger in May 1974, a Syrian-Israeli disengagement agreement was reached, enabling Syria to recover some territory lost in the October war and part of the Golan Heights occupied by Israel since 1967.

The Syrian elite (including President Assad) is a sectarian minority known as the Alawites, who rule the country through the use of terror and a large security force. The SUNNI majority opposes their rule and carried out several attacks against the regime, mainly in the early 1980s. The Syrian regime used excessive force to crush any opposition, however, resulting in the massacre of about 25,000 civilians in the city of HAMAH alone in 1982.

According to the U.S. Department of State, Syrian personnel were directly involved in terrorist operations from the mid-1970s until 1983. These operations were primarily directed against other Arabs, such as Syrian dissidents, "moderate" Arab states such as Jordan, and pro-ARAFAT Palestinians. Israeli and Jewish interests were also major targets. In 1982 a car bomb exploded in front of a pro-Iraqi, Lebanese-owned newspaper in downtown Paris, killing one person and injuring scores of others. Syrian government complicity led to France's expulsion of two Syrian diplomats.

By late 1983 the Syrian government had begun to rely on terrorist groups made up primarily of non-Syrians who were supported and trained in Syria and in Syrian-controlled regions of Lebanon. The most notorious of these is the ABU NIDAL Organization. Other terrorist organizations that are supported in varying degrees by the Syrian government include the PFLP, the PFLP-GC, and SA'IQA. Non-Palestinian groups that have been major beneficiaries of Syrian support include the JAPANESE RED ARMY and the ASALA.

Despite its preference for indirect involvement, the Syrian government was directly involved in the foiled attempt by Nizar HINDAWI on April 17, 1986 to use his pregnant girlfriend as an unwitting suicide bomber on an EL AL flight and in the bombing on March 29, 1986 of the West Berlin German-Arab Friendship Union.

References: Raymond A. Hinnebusch, "Revisionist Dreams, Realist Strategies, The Foreign Policy of Syria," in Bahgat Korany and Ali E. Hillal Dessouki, *The Foreign Policies of Arab States* (Boulder, Colo.: Westview Press, 1985); Diane Tueller Pritchett, "The Syrian Strategy on Terrorism: 1971–1977," *Conflict Quarterly* 8 (Summer 1988); Moshe Ma'oz, "State-Run Terrorism in the Middle East: The Case of Syria," *Middle East Review* 19 (Spring 1987); Patrick Seale, *Asad of Syria: The Struggle for the Middle East* (Berkeley: University of California Press, 1989).

SYRIAN SOCIALIST NATIONALIST PARTY (SSNP)

An organization dedicated to the establishment of the state of Greater Syria, incorporating the land between the Euphrates and Nile rivers, as well as the island of Cyprus. The SSNP has a history of more than 50 years of terrorist activity, making it perhaps the oldest active terrorist organization in the world. Its activities have emphasized political assassination, including the murder of Lebanese president-elect Bashir Gemayel in 1982. Recent years have seen the shocking rise of SSNP suicide car bombings, which have often been staged by young women and have been directed primarily against Israeli targets. In April 1982 four people died during a SSNP explosion aboard a TWA flight to Athens.

The organization was founded by and is today comprised mainly of Christians and traces its lineage to Antun Sa'aseh, a Lebanese Greek Orthodox Christian. The group has a strong fascist element.

References: Ehud Ya'ari, "Behind the Terror," *Atlantic* 259 (June 1987); Patrick Seale, *The Struggle for Syria: A Study of Post-War Arab Politics, 1945–1958* (London: Oxford University Press, 1965).

TABLADA, LA

An Argentine Army base attacked on January 23, 1989 by members of the left-wing New Argentine Army. Fifty guerrillas stormed the base, leaving 21 dead and 30 injured.

TAHRIR AL-ISLAMI, AL-

Arabic, "Islamic Liberation." An Egyptian Islamic fundamentalist offshoot of the MUSLIM BROTHERHOOD that was very active in Egypt throughout the 1970s. The group participated in an attempted coup in April 1974; members attacked the Technical Military Academy near Cairo, and in the ensuing battle with Egyptian security forces 11 people were killed and 27 were wounded.

AL-TAKFIR WAL HIGRA

Arabic, "Atonement and Holy Flight." An Egyptian offshoot of the MUSLIM BROTHERHOOD. The organization seeks to rekindle Islamic fundamentalism in Egypt. In March 1978 the group executed a former Egyptian minister of religious endowments whom it had earlier kidnapped. Egyptian security forces responded to the incident by arresting 400 people and executing five of the leaders of the organization. Members of this

organization are often cited as the assassins of Anwar al-SADAT, a claim to infamy more properly attributed to TANZIM AL-JIHAD.

TAL, WASFI AL- (1920–71)

Prime Minister of Jordan who was assassinated by BLACK SEPTEMBER gunmen on November 28, 1971. Al-Tal was considered by radical Palestinians to be a mortal enemy for his role in the September 1970 expulsion of the Palestinian guerrilla forces from Jordan.

TALEGHANI CENTER

The name used by Western intelligence agencies for the Teheran building from which Iran coordinates its export of revolution. Many terrorist acts have been conceived, planned and financed there, and many individuals and organizations have been trained in the use of violence as a tool for spreading the Islamic fundamentalist revolution. Taleghani Center serves as a communications and organizational base for foreign groups. Its clientele is primarily SHI'ITE, with a small complement of SUNNI fundamentalists, and is comprised of both clerics and laymen. Advisors from Syria and Libya assist the Iranian hosts in their indoctrination and training of contingents from the

Philippines, Saudi Arabia, Kuwait, Lebanon and many other countries. These organizations fall under the control of the "Council for the Islamic Revolution" established by the late Ayatollah KHOMEINI as a tool to export the Iranian brand of Islamic militancy.

TAMIL TIGERS

See LIBERATION TIGERS OF TAMIL EELAM.

TANIA

The revolutionary name used by kidnap victim Patricia HEARST when she participated with her captors, members of the Symbionese Liberation Army, in the robbery of a bank in 1974.

TANZIM AL-JIHAD

Arabic, "The Holy War Organization." An Egyptian fundamentalist organization sometimes simply referred to as "al-Jihad." It is an offshoot of al-TAHRIR AL-ISLAMI. Four members of this group staged the daring and successful assassination on October 6, 1981 of President Anwar al-SADAT of Egypt, who was targeted as a symbol of modern secular Egypt and because he was considered to have compromised Arab and Islamic ideals in his relations with Israel and the United States. The assassins were eventually executed and the Egyptian government has supressed this group as much as it is has been able.

TASK FORCE 160

The U.S. Army's transportation and support unit for counterterrorist operations. Its helicopters, equipped for night operations, can move members of its strike team, DELTA FORCE, up to 200 miles in pitch-black conditions. For longer-distance counterterrorism operations, the U.S. Air Force has a Special Operations Wing with similar capabilities.

TCHARKUTCHIAN, VICKEN

Armenian terrorist and member of ASALA. He was responsible for a number of bombings in the Los Angeles area in 1981 and 1982. He was arrested by the FBI in Los Angeles on September 7, 1987, and was sentenced to a 12-year prison term on December 14, 1987.

TERPIL, FRANK

Former U.S. CIA agent hired, along with fellow former CIA man Edwin WILSON, by Muammar al-QADDAFI to train and equip Libyan military special forces during the 1970s. Terpil was dismissed from his CIA position in 1971. Among the former agents' most infamous dealings were sales to Libya of enormous quantities of the plastic explosive Semtex, portions of which have turned up in terrorist attacks by various groups around the world. It is believed that Terpil and Wilson sold as much as 20 tons of Semtex to the Libyans. Terpil has also been implicated in several assassinations in Africa and an unsuccessful coup attempt in Chad in 1978. He remains at large.

Reference: Richard Lloyd, *Beyond the CIA: The Frank Terpil Story* (New York: Seaver Books, 1983).

TERRA LLIURE

"Free Land." A left-wing Catalonian terrorist organization formed in the 1970s to seek the ultimate goal of an independent Marxist state in the Spanish provinces of Catalonia and Valencia. Its primary terrorist activities have been bombings in northeastern Spain against targets which include travel agencies and foreign banks. In May 1988 11 people were injured when Terra Lliure bombed a bank in Barcelona.

TERRORISM

1. Highly visible violence directed against randomly selected civilians in an effort to generate a pervasive sense of fear and thus affect government policies.

2. Violence against representatives (such as police, politicians or diplomats) of a state by those who wish to overthrow its government; in this sense terrorism is revolution, hence the cliché that one man's terrorist is another man's freedom fighter.

3. Covert warfare by one state against another; in effect, STATE-SPONSORED TERRORISM.

4. The acts of a regime that maintains itself in power by random or calculated abuse of its own citizens; in this sense, all oppression and dictatorial regimes are terrorist.

References: Christopher Hitchens, "Wanton Acts of Usage: Terrorism: A Cliche in Search of a Meaning," *Harpers* 273 (September 1986); Donald B. Vought and James H. Fraser Jr., "Terrorism: The Search for Working Definitions," *Military Review* 66 (July 1986).

TERRORISM, COUNTER

See COUNTERTERRORISM.

TIGER (TERRORIST INTELLIGENCE GATHERING EVALUATION AND REVIEW)

A British government organization which seeks to centralize and coordinate anti-terrorism operations in Great Britain. TIGER was established by Prime Minister Margaret Thatcher following the BRIGHTON BOMBING in October 1984 and focuses on intelligence initiatives against the IRISH REPUBLICAN ARMY.

TONTON MACOUTE

Haitian Creole, "Uncle Knapsack." The popular nickname of the feared and sinister Volunteers for National Security of Haiti. The Tonton Macoutes were established by Haitian strongman François "Papa Doc" Duvalier upon his ascent to power in 1957. They were originally formed to provide an alternative source of armed power to the traditionally strong Haitian army, and it was not long before the Tonton Macoutes became more powerful than the regular military forces. The organization was a source of terror to the Haitian people under the dictatorships of the Duvalier family, who freely utilized the brutally violent Tonton Macoutes to keep both the military and political opposition in check. Torture, beatings and murder of government critics were common, and freedom of the press was nonexistent.

The organization was officially disbanded after Jean-Claude "Baby Doc" Duvalier was deposed in 1985. However, large-scale Tonton Macoute violence on election day in November 1987 indicated that President Henri Namphy was prepared to use the terroristic methods of the Duvalier era to further his own ends. Though not officially recognized, the organization still exists in secret groups, emerging intermittently to commit heinous acts of terrorism. In August 1988 a group identified as Tonton Macoute stormed a Roman Catholic mass in Port-au-Prince, killing 12, wounding 77 and setting the church on fire. Namphy was overthrown in September 1988 by Army officers who cited his support of the Tonton Macoutes as the underlying motivation of their coup. The Tonton Macoutes have since been hunted down and murdered by the Haitian citizens whom they had brutalized for so many years. However, the brief government of former Namphy associate General Prosper Avril, which took power in September 1988 and ended in Avril's resignation on March 10, 1990, had also been criticized as being yet another Haitian government unwilling to bring the Tonton Macoutes to justice. President-elect Jean-Bertrand Aristide (December 16, 1990) has promised to prosecute Tonton Macoute terrorists.

References: Americas Watch, the National Coalition for Haitian Refugees, and Caribbean Rights, *The More Things Change . . .* (New York, 1989); "Haitian Terrorists Form in Secret in New Groups," *New York Times* (September 23, 1988).

TOWER COMMISSION

The Presidential Commission set up by Ronald Reagan in 1987 to investigate the IRAN-CONTRA AFFAIR. The Commission was comprised of John Tower, a former U.S. Senator from Texas and a Republican; Brent Scowcroft, a former advisor to the National Security Council and a Republican; and Edmund Muskie, a former Secretary of State and U.S. Senator from Maine and a Democrat. Its report contained a review of the affair and recommendations for preventing future incidence of such operations. Included was a criticism of President Reagan's management style, a mandate for reform of the National Security Council, and a rebuke of the "critical role" played by dubious intermediaries in the implementation of U.S. foreign policy.

Reference: New York Times Special, *The Tower Commission Report* (New York: Times Books/Bantam, 1987).

TRAC (TERRORIST RESEARCH AND ANALYTICAL CENTER)

The anti-terrorist unit of the U.S. Federal Bureau of Investigation, founded in 1981. TRAC collects and utilizes intelligence in the interest of preventing terrorism and of mounting an effective investigative response.

TRANSNATIONAL TERRORISM

International terrorism; terrorism created by citizens of one state in another state; or terrorism that crosses borders without the help of governments. If a government helps the terrorists, the action is defined as state-controlled or STATE-SPONSORED TERRORISM.

References: Kent Layne Oots, *A Political Approach to Transnational Terrorism* (New York: Greenwood Press, 1987); Todd Sandler, John T. Tschirhart, and Jon Cauley, "A Theoretical Analysis of Transnational Terrorism," *American Political Science Review* 77 (March 1983).

TREVI GROUP

The popular name of the European Community's anti-terrorism group, the European Convention for the Prevention of Terrorism. It was formed at the suggestion of former British Prime Minister Harold Wilson in Rome in 1975 at the European Council of Trevi. The Trevi group first met in 1976 and now includes the Interior Ministers of the European Community nations and a delegation from the United States. The group has not successfully dealt with questions of extradition, and this failure has been a major stumbling block to its effectiveness. Other efforts of the Trevi group include the sharing of intelligence and mutual assistance agreements.

Reference: "Anti-Terror Unit to Talk Strategy," *New York Times* (December 9, 1988).

TROTSKY, LEON (1879–1940)

A Russian revolutionary, a BOLSHEVIK, and one of the founders of the Soviet Union. After the death of LENIN, Trotsky lost his bid to become leader of the Soviet Union to Joseph STALIN. Trotsky was an influential proponent of world revolution and advocated terrorism in the name of organized revolution. However, he was an outspoken critic of ANARCHIST terrorism. He was assassinated by Stalinist agents in Mexico City in 1940.

References: Leon Trotsky, *Against Individual Terrorism* (New York: Pathfinder, 1974); Leon Trotsky, *Terrorism and Communism: A Reply to Karl Kautsky* (London: New Park, 1920; 1975).

TUPAC AMARU REVOLUTIONARY MOVEMENT

See MRTA.

TUPAMAROS

The popular name of the Movimiento de Liberacion Nacional (MLN), a left-wing Uruguayan group founded in the early 1960s by Raul SENDIC Antonaccio. The name "Tupamaros" is derived from the name of an 18th-century Peruvian Indian chieftain, Tupac Amaru, who battled Spanish invaders.

Early actions by Tupamaros revolved around bank robberies and bombings of institutional targets. Beginning in 1966 the group turned to URBAN GUERRILLA tactics in the capital of Montevideo. It carried out an agenda of exposing institutional corruption in both the private and public sectors and vied for mass support through such "Robin Hood" tactics as turning over loot from Tupamaros robberies to the poor of the capital city. The MLN also broadcast regularly from an underground radio station.

Frequent targets of violence included the offices of multinational corporations and members of the Uruguayan security forces. An employee of U.S. AID, Daniel A. Mitrione, was kidnapped and later murdered in 1970 by Tupamaros, who claimed that he was a CIA agent. The kidnapping of Mitrione and the story of his ordeal is depicted in "State of Siege," a film by Costa-Gravas. In 1971 the group abducted the British Ambassador and held him for eight months.

The Uruguayan government unleashed an all-out campaign against the group in 1972 and arrested more than 2,500 people, a blow from which the MLN never recovered. The efforts of the Tupamaros had so weakened the democratic government of Uruguay, however, that the military assumed power in 1973 and maintained control of the state until the resumption of civilian rule in 1984. Members of the MLN were released in a general amnesty declared by the government in 1985. Sendic, upon release, converted the old Tupamaros into a legal political party.

References: J. Kohl and J. Litt, eds., *Urban Guerrilla Warfare in Latin America* (Cambridge, Mass.: MIT Press, 1974); Arturo Porzecanski, "Uruguay's Continuing Dilemma," *Current History* 66 (January 1974); Alain Labrosse, *The Tupamaros: Urban Guerrillas in Uruguay* (Harmondsworth, U.K.: Penguin, 1973); John Litt, "The Guerrillas of Montevideo," *Nation* 214 (February 28, 1972).

TURKISH PEOPLE'S LIBERATION ARMY (TPLA)

One of the two primary Turkish urban guerrilla organizations to emerge from the well-spring of left-wing radicalism in the late 1960s and early 1970s. Comprised primarily of university students who had become disenchanted with what they considered to be the plodding nature of the established Turkish leftist organizations, the TPLA was fervently anti-American and anti-NATO and was violently opposed to the radical Turkish right wing. Deniz Gemiz, a TPLA leader of Kurdish extraction, trained in a PLO camp in Jordan in 1969. Upon his return he directed a campaign of terrorism that included the abduction of U.S. servicemen stationed in Turkey. He was executed in 1972 and subsequently became a martyr for the radical left. The TPLA went into decline after the institution of military rule in 1971 brought strong and pervasive anti-terrorist measures to bear on terrorists and their organizations throughout the country.

Reference: Sabri Sayeri, *Generation Changes in Terrorist Movements: The Turkish Case* (Santa Monica, Calif.: Rand, 1985).

TURKISH PEOPLE'S LIBERATION FRONT (TPLF)

Along with the TURKISH PEOPLE'S LIBERATION ARMY, one of the two main urban guerrilla movements to arise out of the Turkish student unrest of the late 1960s and early 1970s. The organization was led by Mahir Cayan, a violent revolutionary who was killed in a shoot-out with police during a hostage-taking incident in May 1972. Cayan's fate brought him a martyr status among Turkish radicals. The rise of the military in Turkish politics in March 1971 brought anti-terrorist measures, which resulted in the death or imprisonment of many primary TPLF leaders.

TWA FLIGHT 847

Trans World Airlines Flight 847, with 145 passengers on board, was hijacked by two Lebanese SHI'ITE gunmen while en route to Athens from Rome on June 14, 1985. In the process of making two round trips from Beirut to Algiers during the next three days, the hijackers demanded the release of all Shi'ite Muslims imprisoned in Israel, allowed all but 39 of the hostages to be freed and boarded an additional terrorist. A passenger, a U.S. Navy diver named Robert Stethem, was murdered and his body was dumped onto the tarmac on June 15th, in full view of the international media. On June 17th the remaining hostages were taken off the plane and dispersed to a number of Shi'ite strongholds in Beirut for safekeeping. Extensive negotiations were brokered by Nabih BERRI, the leader of the AMAL militia, although the terrorists were believed to be affiliated with the HEZBOLLAH movement.

The plane's captain, John Testrake, became a central figure in the media coverage and gained world-wide respect for his disciplined and cool-headed handling of the hostage drama. After much effort a complex set of exchanges was arranged, including the release of prisoners in Israeli jails. The terrorists held the aircraft and the remaining hostages for 17 days before they were released unharmed.

References: Tony Atwater, "Terrorism on the Evening News: An Analysis of Coverage of the TWA Hostage Crisis on 'NBC Nightly News,'" *Political Communication and Persuasion* 4, no. 2 (1987); Ferdinand A. Ermlich, "Terrorism and the Media: Strategy, Coverage, and Responses," *Political Communication and Persuasion* 4 (1987).

U

UGB (UNION DE GUERREROS BLANCOS)

White Warrior's Union. A Salvadoran right-wing DEATH SQUAD with strong ties to the country's security forces. The group is considered to be responsible for the assassination on February 23, 1980 of Mario Zamora Rivas, Attorney General of El Salvador and a leading member of the Christian Democrat Party.

ULSTER DEFENSE ASSOCIATION (UDA)

An illegal Northern Irish Protestant "defense" organization, formed in the early 1970s as a paramilitary vigilante group in response to the growth of IRISH REPUBLICAN ARMY activism. The UDA is very large, and its membership is thought to exceed 40,000. The group claims an active membership of 85,000 but this figure is believed to be greatly exaggerated.

The UDA adamantly supports the continuance of British rule in Ulster and stands in violent opposition to any political compromise. The group is the most powerful of Ulster Protestant organizations and has ties to the police and the ROYAL ULSTER CONSTABULARY. The Ulster Defense Association has a history of assassinations and beatings of Catholics, and its members have been convicted of kidnapping, murder and firearms violations. In April 1989 three UDA members were arrested by French police in connection with a suspected arms deal between the UDA and the South African Government, in which the UDA was to have exchanged British Blowpipe anti-aircraft artillery for a supply of weapons from South Africa.

Reference: Geoffrey Bell, *The Protestants of Ulster* (London: Pluto, 1976).

ULSTER FREEDOM FIGHTERS (UFF)

A Northern Irish Protestant organization, outlawed by the government of Northern Ireland for its anti-Catholic violence. The UFF was formed in 1973 as a radical splinter group of the ULSTER DEFENSE ASSOCIATION (UDA) and is far more prone to violence than its parent group. The UDA appears to be the primary source of anti-Catholic violence in Ulster. In February 1989 the UFF murdered a prominent Catholic lawyer whom it accused of belonging to the IRISH REPUBLICAN ARMY.

ULSTER VOLUNTEER FORCE (UVF)

Formed in 1966 as "a secret Protestant private army" of Ulster nationalists. It takes its name from a popular home-rule organization of the early 20th century, which amassed a membership of 100,000 during 1911–12. The UVF supported and carried out violent reprisals against IRISH REPUBLICAN ARMY members and sympathizers until 1976, when it publicly renounced terrorist violence. Its massive bombing campaign in 1969 helped to lead to the resignation of Prime Minister Terence O'Neill. The contemporary UVF was banned soon after its founding under the Special Powers Act, only to be legalized again in 1973. Many of the group's critics doubt the sincerity of the UVF's 1976 pledge and voice the contention that the group still carries out the vast majority of organized anti-Catholic violence and crime.

Reference: David Boulton, *The Ulster Volunteer Force 1966–73* (Dublin: Gill and McMillan, 1973).

UMARI, MOHAMMED AL-

Palestinian terrorist and leader of the MAY 15 GROUP. Umari is considered to be among the most technically proficient and dangerous of terrorist bomb-makers and is expert in the use of barometric detonators and PLASTIC EXPLOSIVES. Formerly affiliated with the POPULAR FRONT FOR THE LIBERATION OF PALESTINE (PFLP), he is also known by his nom de guerre, Abu Ibrahim.

UNITED FREEDOM FRONT (UFF)

A radical, left-wing U.S. organization dedicated to the violent protest of American imperialism, especially the U.S. role in Central America. The UFF was the most active domestic U.S. terrorist organization in the early 1980s. The group's terrorist acts have primarily taken the form of bombings against military or industrial targets in the New York metropolitan area. Among these bombings was the attack on an Army Reserve facility in Uniondale, New York on May 12, 1983. Through 1985 10 similar attacks were staged against such targets as IBM, Honeywell, and the U.S. National Guard.

All known members of the group have been arrested and sentenced to lengthy prison terms for their criminal activities. This case represents one of the greatest successes by law enforcement agencies against a domestic left-wing terrorist group. Federal, state and local agencies cooperated to bring these cases to a successful conclusion.

UNITED LIBERATION FRONT OF ASSAM (ULFA)

The indigenous separatist movement operating in India's northeast province of Assam. ULFA, with about 600 armed guerrillas, frequently engages in kidnappings. Another favorite tactic is to extort protection money from the regions many foreign-owned tea plantations.

UNITED NATIONS

From its creation in 1945 until 1972 the United Nations gave little attention to the problem of terrorism. After the MUNICH MASSACRE at the 1972 Olympic games, however, that began to change slowly. The desire of some UN members to draft conventions against terrorism is tempered by the need to couch any condemnation of terrorism in terms that do not potentially embrace wars of liberation. Efforts have been made to adopt treaties obligating signatories to punish airplane hijackers and hostage takers. Much stronger international sanctions are needed, however, against both the individual perpetrators of terrorism and the states that support or harbor them.

Reference: Seymour Maxwell Finger, "The United Nations and International Terrorism," *The Jerusalem Journal of International Relations*, 10 (1988).

UNRG

See GUATEMALAN NATIONAL REVOLUTIONARY UNITY.

UPC (UNIONE DI U POPULO CORSCO)

A Corsican nationalist political party which has been responsible for anti-French terrorist acts, including the 1980 siege of a hotel in Ajaccio in which three people died in a shoot-out with police.

URUGUAY

Counterinsurgency excesses by Uruguayan military authorities during the 1960s and 1970s raised many charges of STATE-SPONSORED TERRORISM. It is estimated that 200 people died in detention or disappeared during the government's anti-leftist campaigns (*see* DISAPPEARED). Thousands of citizens were tortured. The brutal tactics were Uruguay's response to the left-wing guerrilla movements of the TUPAMAROS and the ELN. These Marxist insurgencies shook the long-standing democracy of Uruguay to its core and eventually brought it down, as the military assumed power in 1973. Shortly after civilian government returned to power in 1984, Uruguay granted amnesty to leftists and other political prisoners and began to prosecute members of the military for abuses of human rights. After the military began to protest these prosecutions, however, the government opted in 1986 to extend amnesty to police and military personnel. In a national referendum held in April 1989 the voters of Uruguay elected to uphold the amnesty for police and members of the armed forces.

USTACHI

A right-wing Croatian nationalist terrorist group. In 1971 the group attempted a siege of the Yugoslavian Embassy in Stockholm.

V

VIET CONG

The communist insurgents in South Vietnam, formally the National Liberation Front of Vietnamese Communists (Viet Nam Cong San). In the early 1960s, with the support of the government of communist North Vietnam, the Viet Cong initiated a major effort to overthrow the American-supported government of South Vietnam. After failing to succeed by using traditional guerrilla and terror tactics, they launched a traditional offensive during the Tet holiday in 1968 and were virtually wiped out by South Vietnamese and American forces. Thereafter, most of the fighting by the communists was done by military units of North Vietnam. The Tet offensive was significant for the Viet Cong, however, in that it helped to break the American will to continue with the war.

References: Stanley Karnow, *Vietnam* (New York: Penguin, 1983); Don Oberdorfer, *Tet!* (Garden City, N.Y.: Doubleday, 1971).

VIETT, INGE

West German terrorist, member and leader of the RED ARMY FACTION (RAF). A former school teacher, Viett is known for forging ties between the RAF and the French terrorist group ACTION DIRECTE (AD).

VIGILANTISM

The actions and underlying beliefs of vigilantes, private citizens who undertake to redress through extralegal violent action the perceived or actual failure of legal law enforcement authorities. Vigilante groups have commonly been active in nations where police and government authorities have been unable to prevent or control terrorism arising out of frustration with the state's ineffectiveness and the desire to exact revenge. The ULSTER DEFENSE ASSOCIATION in Northern Ireland and Latin American DEATH SQUADS such as AAA and ORDEN are well-known examples of vigilante groups which, through illegal and extremely violent means, have utilized terrorism in their own right.

Vigilante terrorist groups are often identified with the political status quo and have often included members of the established order in their ranks. For example, off-duty policemen were very active in Argentinian death squads, with the tacit approval of the government. In such state-condoned cases, vigilante groups may be seen as elements of covert STATE-SPONSORED TERRORISM, in which "independent" vigilante groups are encouraged to carry out illicit operations with which the state does not wish to be publicly associated.

Reference: H. Jon Rosenbaum and Peter C. Sederberg, eds., *Vigilante Politics* (Philadelphia: University of Pennsylvania Press, 1976).

VIOLENCIA, LA

The period of extreme domestic violence, essentially a civil war, in Colombia that extended approximately from 1946 to 1966, during which more than 200,000 people were killed. From 1946 to 1950 alone, it is estimated that 112,000 people died. Most of the deaths of la violencia were attributable to civilian violence and there has been much debate about its underlying causes. While it was primarily a rural conflict between conservatives and would-be reformers, it was made all the more intense by banditry and personal feuds.

Reference: Paul Oquist, *Violence, Conflict, and Politics in Colombia* (New York: Academic Press, 1980).

W

WAR CRIME

1. An act that retains its essential criminality even though it is committed during war and under orders. Thus, many German and Japanese officers were convicted of war crimes after World War II because their conduct had gone beyond what was considered to be allowable in war—especially when it involved the murder of prisoners of war or the systematic killing of whole populations of innocent, noncombatant civilians.

2. An act that the victor determines to be illegal after a war is over. As Winston Churchill once told his generals apropos the Nuremberg trials of NAZI war criminals after World War II: "You and I must take care not to lose the next war."

References: Kenneth A. Woeard, "Command Responsibility for War Crimes," *Journal of Public Law* 21 (1972); Kurt Steiner, "War Crimes and Command Responsibility: From the Bataan Death March to the MyLai Massacre," *Pacific Affairs* 58 (Summer 1985); Jonathan P. Tomes, "Indirect Responsibility for War Crimes," *Military Review* 66 (November 1986).

WATCH LISTS

Information and descriptions of terrorists developed and circulated by the U.S. Department of State among border police in many nations. Watch lists have proven to be successful tools in the fight against international terrorism. Among the success stories are the January 1987 arrests of two Lebanese terrorists, on two successive days, who were attempting to smuggle explosives across the borders of Italy and West Germany.

WAZIR, KHALIL AL- (1936–88)

Also known as Abu Jihad ("Father of the Holy War"). The PLO military chief who was assassinated on April 16, 1988 when a nine-man commando team stormed his headquarters in Tunis. The Israeli government is believed to have organized the attack on Wazir, who was thought to have been leading the PLO's supporting effort in the INTIFADA. Israel had long considered Abu Jihad to be an "arch-terrorist steeped in blood."

References: "Abu Jihad: A Message from Mossad," *The Economist* (April 23, 1988); "Assignment Murder: How Israel Planned the Killing of Arafat's Right-hand Man," *Time* (April 25, 1988).

WEATHER UNDERGROUND

Popularly known as the "Weathermen." A violent U.S. Marxist, subversive organization active in the late 1960s and early 1970s. The group was formed in 1969 by radical members of the Students for a Democratic Society (SDS), who advocated a more forceful revolutionary stance. The first year of Weatherman activities was marked by a series of more than 400 arson and bombing incidents. These included attacks on the U.S. Capitol building and the Pentagon.

The Weathermen were dealt a crushing blow in March 1970, when a cache of their explosives detonated accidentally in a townhouse in Greenwich Village, New York, killing seven of the group's top leaders. The sole surviving leader of the group lived in hiding until he surrendered himself to New York police in 1977.

In October 1981 Kathy BOUDIN, a member of the Weather Underground who had been living in hiding, led a bloody robbery in Nyack, New York. Two policemen and a security guard were killed in the raid, and Boudin was later arrested. FBI investigators drew a connection between Boudin and her Weather Underground colleagues, the BLACK LIBERATION ARMY, and the Puerto Rican separatist terrorist organization FALN. With the arrest of Boudin the Weather Underground dissipated.

References: Peter Collier and David Horowitz, "Doing It: The Inside Story of the Rise and the Fall of the Weather Underground," *Rolling Stone* (September 30, 1982); Peter Shaw, "The End of the Seventies," *New Republic* 185 (December 23, 1981); Todd Gitlin, "White Heat Underground," *Nation* 233 (December 19, 1981); Lucinda Franks, "The Seeds of Terror," *New York Times Magazine* (November 22, 1981).

WEHRSPORTGRUPPE HOFFMAN

See HOFFMAN MILITARY SPORTS GROUP.

WELCH, RICHARD (1929–75)

CIA station chief in Athens, Greece who was murdered in 1975 by members of the REVOLUTIONARY ORGANIZATION NOVEMBER 17.

WEST BANK

Those lands on the West Bank of the Jordan River occupied by Israel since the Six-Day War of 1967. The West Bank is a focus of the Israeli–Palestinian struggle and in recent times has been embroiled in the youth uprising known as the INTIFADA. In November 1988 the West Bank was declared part of an independent Palestinian state by the PALESTINIAN NATIONAL COUNCIL (PNC).

References: Don Peretz, *The West Bank: History, Politics, Society, and Economy* (Boulder, Colo.: Westview Press, 1986); Emile Sahliyeh, *In Search of Leadership: West Bank Politics Since 1967* (Washington, DC: Brookings Institution, 1988).

WHITE HAND

A right-wing Guatemalan DEATH SQUAD with strong ties to the Guatemalan military and police, which emerged in the mid-1960s. White Hand was reputedly founded by Guatemalan military leader Colonel Enrique Trinadad Oliva and was later reportedly led by the national chief of police. White Hand played a major role in the right-wing, government-condoned violence that plagued Guatemala for two decades.

Reference: George Black, *Garrison Guatemala* (London: Zed Press, 1984).

WHITE PATRIOT PARTY (WPP)

Right-wing U.S. paramilitary white supremacist organization, originally known as the Carolina Knights of the KU KLUX KLAN. The

WPP was formed and led by Glenn Miller and appears to have ceased to exist after the arrest of Miller and three other WPP members in April 1987. Miller had earlier declared "war" against the U.S. government (called ZOG—Zionist Occupation Government—by the group). He was arrested for failure to abide by the terms of probation from an earlier conviction. After his arrest, an FBI search of his mobile home and van in the Springfield, Missouri area uncovered numerous weapons and explosives.

WILSON, EDWIN

Former CIA agent who was hired, along with another former CIA gent, Frank TER-PIL, by Muammar al-QADDAFI to train and equip Libyan military special forces. Wilson's most infamous dealings with Qaddafi were his sales to Libya of enormous quantities of the plastic explosive C-4, portions of which have turned up in terrorist attacks by various groups around the world. Wilson also supplied Libya with highly sophisticated detonators and other related hardware. Wilson was captured by U.S. agents in the Dominican Republic in 1982 and is now serving a 25-year sentence in a U.S. federal penitentiary.

References: Peter Maas, *Manhunt* (New York: Random House, 1986); Peter Maas, "Selling Out: How an Ex-CIA Agent Made Millions Working for Qaddafi," *New York Times Magazine* (April 13, 1986); Joseph C. Goulden, *The Death Merchant: The Rise and Fall of Edwin P. Wilson* (New York: Simon and Schuster, 1984).

WRATH OF GOD

A clandestine Israeli military commando team that targets PLO leaders and other Palestinian guerrilla leaders for assassination. Wrath of God was born in the aftermath of the MUNICH MASSACRE in 1972 when the Israelis sought out and killed most of those it thought responsible.

XYZ

YANIKIAN, GURGEN (1900–84)

Yanikian, a retired Armenian engineer living in California, is credited with sparking the beginning of contemporary ARMENIAN TERRORISM in 1975. Yanikian invited two representatives of the Turkish mission in Los Angeles out to lunch, and after dining he pulled out a handgun and shot them to death. At his trial he stated that the shootings were in revenge for the sufferings of his family during the Armenian genocide of 1915–22. Since these murders, more than 50 Turkish diplomats around the world have been killed by Armenian terrorists, many of whom look to Yanikian as the unwitting father of their movement.

YUNGANTAR GROUP

An early 20th-century Indian terrorist organization responsible for a series of assassinations in India beginning in 1917.

YUNIS, FAWAZ

The Palestinian-born Yunis, a member of the Shi'ite AMAL militia, hijacked a Royal Jordanian airliner on June 11, 1985. He was captured by FBI agents in September 1988 in an elaborate conterterrorist sting that involved several U.S. government organiza-tions. He was lured onto a yacht in the Mediterranean, where he was seized by FBI agents, and was flown to the United States by Navy fighter aircraft. Yunis was the first accused terrorist to be captured and tried under a 1984 U.S. statute that facilitates the prosecution of foreign terrorists who commit crimes against American nationals. He was found guilty and sentenced to prison on March 14, 1989. He remains in federal prison.

Reference: G. Gregory Schuetz, "Approaching Terrorists Overseas Under United States and International Law: A Case Study of the Fawaz Younis Arrest," *Harvard International Law Journal* 29 (Spring 1988).

ZANU

The Zimbabwe African National Union, founded in 1963, a native Zimbabwean liberation movement that operated in the white-ruled southern African state of Rhodesia in the 1970s. Although ZANU, led by Robert Mugabe and with its ranks dominated by members of the Shona tribe, was an offshoot of ZAPU, it eventually grew to be much more powerful than its guerrilla rival. ZANU espoused a strict Marxist-Leninist ideology. The group's paramilitary wing, known as the Zimbabwe National Liberation Army (ZANLA), waged a guerrilla campaign against the government of Rhodesia. ZANLA received its weapons from the People's Republic of China.

In the decade of the 1970s the guerrilla struggle in Rhodesia intensified, both between the rebels and the white Rhodesian government and between ZANU and ZAPU forces. During 1978–79 the United States and the United Kingdom intervened diplomatically to bring about a cease-fire and arrange for the holding of democratic elections—the first in which all black Zimbabweans would be allowed to vote—in February 1980. ZANU was the overwhelming victor in those elections and Robert Mugabe became the first president of the new nation of Zimbabwe.

See ZAPU.

ZAPU

The Zimbabwe African People's Union, founded in 1961, the older of the two principal native Zimbabwean liberation movements (the other being ZANU) that operated in the white-ruled southern African state of Rhodesia in the 1970s. ZAPU was led by Joshua Nkomo and consisted primarily of members of the Ndebele tribe. The Zimbabwe People's Revolutionary Army (ZIPRA), ZAPU's military arm, received support from the Soviet Union. ZAPU's guerrilla campaign frequently involved terrorism against Rhodesia's white settlers and black government collaborators.

See ZANU.

ZIMMERMAN, ERNST (1930–85)

A leading West German industrialist who was murdered near his Munich home on February 1, 1985 by members of the RED ARMY FACTION. Zimmerman's business interests were centered on the armaments industry and his company produced engines used in both military aircraft and tanks.

ZOG ("ZIONIST OCCUPATION GOVERNMENT")

The derisive term applied to the United States of America by members of the ARYAN NATIONS and other right-wing racists, in reference to the erroneous notion that U.S. commercial, social and political institutions are controlled by Jews.

ZOMAR, OSCAMA ABDEL AL-

Palestinian jailed in Greece whose requested extradition to Italy was denied by the Greek government. Zomar is believed to have been involved in the massacre of worshippers at a synagogue in Rome in 1982. Greek Justice Minister Vassos Rotis was quoted as finding Zomar's involvement "an action for gaining his country's independence and therefore freedom." The released terrorist was reportedly given his choice of nations to be sent to; it is believed that he went to Libya.

ZUTIK

Basque, "Stand up." The official publication of the Basque separatist organization ETA.

Part III

---

quotations
on
terrorism

He was that extraordinary product—a terrorist for moderate aims. A reasonable and enlightened policy—the Parliamentary system of England . . . freedom, toleration and good will—to be achieved wherever necessary by dynamite at the risk of death.

> —Winston Churchill, on Boris Savinkov (the Russian Vice Minister of War in the 1917 government of Alexander Kerensky) in Churchill's *Great Contemporaries* (New York: G. P. Putnam, 1937).

The success of a terrorist operation depends almost entirely on the amount of publicity it receives. This was one of the main reasons for the shift from rural guerrilla to urban terror in the 1960s; in the cities the terrorist could always count on the presence of journalists and TV cameras.

> —Walter Laqueur, *Terrorism* (Boston: Little, Brown, 1977).

Terrorism has received so much coverage from the media that it has been a spectator sport for the public . . . modern terrorism is theatre.

> —Robert H. Kupperman, *U.S. News and World Report*, March 6, 1978.

Let terrorists beware that when the rules of international behavior are violated, our policy will be one of swift and effective retribution.

> —President Ronald Reagan, speaking in Washington, D.C., January 27, 1981.

A certain amount of political violence is a price paid for a free and open society. Terrorism, or at least public knowledge of it, is absent only in totalitarian states.

> —Brian Jenkins of the Rand Corporation, *The Washington Post*, February 1, 1981.

Our rate of casual, day-to-day terrorism in almost any large city exceeds the casualties of all reported "international terrorists" in any given year. Why do we show such indignation over alien terrorists and such tolerance for the domestic variety?

> —Warren E. Burger, Chief Justice of the United States, *Los Angeles Times*, February 9, 1981.

We put the production of nuclear weapons at the top of the list of terrorist activities. As long as the big powers continue to manufacture atomic weap-

ons, it means they are continuing to terrorize the world. . . . This is one reason why the U.S. is a top terrorist force in the world.
> —Muammar al-Qaddafi, *Time*, June 8, 1981.

No person employed by or acting on behalf of the United States Government shall engage in, or conspire to engage in, assassination.
> —President Ronald Reagan, Executive Order 12333, December 4, 1981.

Italian terrorism is about to be defeated. . . . The reason is this: the terrorists are talking. Before, they didn't. . . . From what I have been told, over 300 jailed terrorists are talking. If these terrorists are talking, it means first of all that they are not guided by any true political belief. Second, it indicates that they are feeling the ground eroded out from their feet. . . . If they are talking, it's because they are all puppets.
> —Sandro Pertini, President of Italy, *The New York Times*, April 3, 1982.

At the wheel was a young man on a suicide mission. The truck carried some 2,000 pounds of explosives, but there was no way our marine guard could know this. Their first warning that something was wrong came when the truck crashed through a series of barriers, including a chain link fence and barbed wire entanglements. The guards opened fire but it was too late.

The truck smashed through the doors of the headquarters building in which our marines were sleeping and instantly exploded. The four-story concrete building collapsed in a pile of rubble.

More than 200 of the sleeping men were killed in that one hideous insane attack.
> —President Ronald Reagan, speech to the nation on Lebanon and Grenada, October 27, 1983.

We also must recognize that although we may make moral distinctions between dropping bombs on a city from 20,000 feet and car bombs driven into embassies by suicidal terrorists, the world may not share that fine distinction.
> —Brian Jenkins, *U.S. News and World Report*, July 1, 1985.

We have an obligation to punish murder of American citizens in places where courts of law cannot reach. My conviction is that we will save a lot more lives in the long run by being tough and steady.
> —Lawrence S. Eagleburger, *U.S. News and World Report*, July 1, 1985.

International publicity is the mother's milk of terrorism.
> —U.S. Senator John Glenn, *U.S. News
> and World Report*, July 8, 1985.

*The American people are not—I repeat, not—going to tolerate intimidation,
terror and outright acts of war against this nation and its people. And we
are especially not going to tolerate these attacks from outlaw states run by
the strangest collection of misfits, Looney Tunes and squalid criminals since
the advent of the Third Reich.*
> —President Ronald Reagan, speaking in
> Washington, July 8, 1985.

*[We] must try to find ways to starve the terrorist and the hijacker of the
oxygen of publicity on which they depend.*
> —Margaret Thatcher, Prime Minister of
> Great Britain, speaking to the
> American Bar Association in London,
> July 15, 1985.

*If I should ever be captured, I want no negotiation—and if I should request
a negotiation from captivity they should consider that a sign of duress.*
> —Henry Kissinger, *U.S. News and World
> Report*, October 7, 1985.

*These young Americans [U.S. forces that captured in midair a plane carry-
ing five terrorists] sent a message to terrorists everywhere. The message:
You can run but you can't hide.*
> —President Ronald Reagan, press
> conference, October 11, 1985.

*We know that this mad dog of the Middle East [Muammar al-Qaddafi of
Libya] has a goal of a world revolution.*
> —President Ronald Reagan, press
> conference, April 9, 1986.

*I'm a participant in the doctrine of constructive ambiguity. I don't think we
should tell them [terrorists] what we're going to do in advance. Let them
think. Worry. Wonder. Uncertainty is the most chilling thing of all.*
> —General Vernon Walters, on dealing
> with terrorists, *Christian Science
> Monitor*, April 18, 1986.

*For us to ignore, by inaction, the slaughter of American civilians and Amer-
ican soldiers, whether in nightclubs or airline terminals, is simply not in
the American tradition. When our citizens are abused or attacked anywhere*

in the world, on the direct orders of a hostile regime, we will respond, so long as I'm in this Oval Office. Self-defense is not only our right, it is our duty.

> —President Ronald Reagan, address to the nation on the bombing of Libya in reprisal for terrorist acts, April 14, 1986.

Terrorism [takes] us back to ages we thought were long gone if we allow it a free hand to corrupt democratic societies and destroy the basic rules of international life.

> —Jacques Chirac, Premier of France, speech to the U.N. General Assembly, September 24, 1986.

One difference between French appeasement and American appeasement is that France pays ransom in cash and gets its hostages back while the United States pays ransom in arms and gets additional hostages taken.

> —William Safire, *New York Times,* November 13, 1986.

In 1984, Edgar Chamorro . . . leaked a CIA contra training manual to the American press. The manual, Psychological Operations in Guerrilla Warfare, *clearly advocated a strategy of terror as the means to victory over the hearts and minds of Nicaraguans. . . . The contra pupils whom it was intended to instruct were told of the most effective use of assassinations, preferably in the form of public executions, to impress Nicaraguan villagers. "Neutralize" was the actual euphemism employed, but its meaning left nothing to the imagination. The little booklet thus violated President Reagan's own Presidential Directive 12333, signed in December 1981, which prohibited any U.S. government employee—including the CIA—from having anything to do with assassinations.*

> —Leslie Cockburn, *Out of Control* (New York: Simon & Schuster, 1987).

The idea that one person's terrorist is another's freedom fighter cannot be sanctioned. Freedom fighters or revolutionaries don't blow up buses containing non-combatants; terrorist murderers do. Freedom fighters don't set out to capture and slaughter school children; terrorist murderers do. Freedom fighters don't assassinate innocent businessmen, or hijack and hold hostage innocent men, women, and children; terrorist murderers do. It is a disgrace that democracies should allow the treasured word "freedom" to be associated with acts of terrorists.

> —Senator Henry "Scoop" Jackson quoted in Stephen Segaller, *Invisible Armies* (1987).

Whoever thinks of stopping the intifadeh *before it achieves its goals, I will give him ten bullets in the chest.*

> —Yasir Arafat, speaking on January 1,
> 1989, quoted in *Time*, August 7, 1989.

You have to know for certain whom you are retaliating against [for terrorism] and you have to limit the number of innocent people you kill. An indiscriminate, unfocused response does little good. If you just drop a stick of bombs on Teheran, the loss of life would be awful and would be an excuse for the Iranian government to do anything they can think of in the way of further beastliness.

> —Caspar W. Weinberger, former
> Secretary of Defense, *The New York
> Times*, August 9, 1989.

The hostage holder of Terry Anderson found his village shelled by the battleship New Jersey, *during which he lost his entire family, including his wife, children, grandparents, aunts and uncles.*

When I asked the kidnappers, in the name of Islam, to release their hostages because they are innocent, one captor replied, "But my wife, children and grandparents who were killed by Americans were also innocent!"

> —M. T. Mehdi, President of the
> American-Arab Relations Committee,
> *The New York Times*, August 27, 1989.

All terrorists believe if they just keep bombing, if you just injure enough people, you will win.

> —Paul Wilkinson, Research Foundation
> for the Study of Terrorism, quoted in
> *The New York Times*, February 20, 1991.

It seems that so long as there are British soldiers in the north of Ireland so there will be an IRA.

> —Tim Pat Coogan, testimony at the trial
> of the crew of the *Eksund*, January 8,
> 1991.

Part IV

definitions of terrorism

Terrorism is a term used to describe the method or the theory behind the method whereby an organized group or party seeks to achieve its avowed aims chiefly through the systematic use of violence. Terroristic acts are directed against persons who as individuals, agents or representatives of authority interfere with the consummation of the objectives of such a group. J. S. B. Hardman, "Terrorism," *Encyclopedia of the Social Sciences*, vol. 14 (New York: Macmillan, 1936).

The threat or the use of violence for political ends. As a weapon, it may be wielded by rebels or their opponents; in the second case, however, it becomes counter-terrorism. B. Crozier, *The Rebels: A Study of Post-War Insurrections* (London: Chatto and Windus, 1960)

A symbolic act designed to influence political behavior by extranormal means, entailing the use or threat of violence. Terrorism may gain political ends in one of two ways—whether by mobilizing forces or by immobilizing forces and reserves sympathetic to the cause of the insurgents or by immobilizing forces and reserves that would normally be available to the incumbents. T. P. Thornton, "Terror as a Weapon of Political Agitation," *Internal War* ed. by H. Eckstein (New York: Free Press, 1964)

An action of violence is labelled "terrorist" when its psychological effects are out of proportion to its purely physical result. In this sense, the so-called indiscriminate acts of revolutionaries are terrorist, as were the Anglo-American zone bombings. The lack of discrimination helps to spread *fear*, for if not one in particular is a target, no one can be safe. E. V. Walter, "Violence and the Process of Terror," *American Sociological Review* 29 (Spring 1964)

Terrorism is the systematic use of intimidation for political ends. R. Moss, *Urban Guerrillas* (London: Temple Smith, 1972)

Events involving relatively highly organized and planned activity, on the part of small but cohesive groups, in which the aim of the activity is to damage, injure, or eliminate government property or personnel. These activities include bomb plants, sabotage of electrical and transportation facilities, assassinations (attempted and successful), and isolated guerrilla activities. D. G. Morrison et al., *Black Africa* (New York: Free Press, 1972)

What is usually referred to as terrorism is unsponsored and unsanctioned violence against the body or bodies of others. I. L. Horowitz, "Political Terrorism and State Power," *Journal of Political and Military Sociology* 1 (1973)

"Motivated violence for political ends" (a definition that distinguishes terrorism from both vandalism and non-political crime). Measures of extreme repression, including torture, used by states to oppress the population or to repress political dissenters, who may or may not be terrorists or guerrillas, are termed "terror." B. Crozier, "Aid for Terrorism," *Annual of Power and Conflict, 1973–1974* (London: Institute for the Study of Conflict, 1974)

The use of violence for political ends, and includes any use of violence for the purpose of putting the public or any section of the public in fear. United Kingdom Prevention of Terrorism Act of 1974 quoted in E. F. Mickolus, *The Literature of Terrorism* (Westport, CT: Greenwood Press, 1980)

The threat of violence, individual acts of violence, or a campaign of violence designed primarily to instill fear—to terrorize—may be called terrorism. B. Jenkins. *International Terrorism* (Los Angeles: Crescent Publications, 1975)

The selective use of fear, subjugation, and intimidation to disrupt the normal operations of a society. I. L. Horowitz, "Transnational Terrorism," *Terrorism*, ed. by Y. Alexander and S. Finger (New York: John Jay Press, 1977)

Political terrorism is the threat and/or use of extra-normal forms of political violence, in varying degrees, with the objective of achieving political objectives and goals. R. Shultz, "Conceptualizing Political Terrorism," *Journal of International Affairs* 32 (1978)

The term terrorism has come to be applied mainly to "retail terrorism" by individuals or groups. Whereas the term was once applied to Emperors who molest their own subjects and the world, now it is restricted to thieves who molest the powerful. Extricating ourselves from the system of indoctrination, we will use the term "terrorism" to refer to the threat or use of violence to intimidate or coerce (generally for political ends), whether it is the wholesale terrorism of the Emperor or the retail terrorism of the thief. N. Chomsky, *The Culture of Terrorism* (Boston: South End Press, 1988)

It is the unlawful use or threat of violence against persons or property to further political or social objectives. It is generally intended to intimidate or coerce a government, individuals, or groups to modify their behavior or policies. Vice President's Task Force on Combatting Terrorism, *Public Report of the Vice-President's Task on Combatting Terrorism* (Washington, D.C.: Government Printing Office, 1986)

The use of covert violence by a group for political ends . . . usually directed against a government, but it is also used against other ethnic groups, classes or parties. The ends may vary from the redress of specific grievances to the overthrow of a government and the seizure of power, or to the liberation of a country from foreign rule. Terrorists seek to cause political, social and economic disruption, and for this purpose frequently engage in planned or indiscriminate murder . . . Any definition of political terrorism venturing beyond noting the systematic use of murder, injury, and destruction or the threats of such acts towards achieving political ends is bound to lead to endless controversies. W. Laqueur, *The Age of Terrorism* (Boston: Little, Brown and Co., 1987)

Politically motivated violence by small groups claiming to represent the masses. R. Rubenstein, *Alchemists of Revolution* (New York: Basic Books, 1987)

Note: Some of the definitions in this listing were first compiled by Alex Schmid and others in their excellent resource book, *Political Terrorism* (Amsterdam: SWIDOC, 1983).

SUGGESTED FURTHER READING

BOOKS:

Adams, James. *The Financing of Terror*. London: New English Library, 1986.

Alexander, Yonah, and Alan O'Day, eds. *Terrorism in Ireland*. New York: St. Martin's Press, 1984.

Alexander, Yonah, and Robert A. Kilmarx, eds. *Political Terrorism and Business: The Threat and Response*. New York: Praeger Publishers, 1979.

Alexander, Yonah, and Kenneth Myers, eds. *Terrorism in Europe*. London: Croom Helm, 1982.

Avrich, Paul. *Anarchist Portraits*. Princeton, N.J.: Princeton University Press, 1988.

Baldy, Tom F. *Battle for Ulster*. Washington, D.C.: National Defense University Press, 1987.

Becker, Jillian. *Hitler's Children: The Baader-Meinhof Terrorist Gang*. Philadelphia: J.B. Lippincott Co., 1978.

Bell, J. Bowyer. *Assassin!* New York: St. Martin's Press, 1979.

——. *A Time of Terror*. New York: Basic Books Inc., 1978.

——. *Transnational Terror*. Washington, D.C.: American Enterprise Institute, 1975.

Boulton, David. *The Ulster Volunteer Force, 1966–1973*. Dublin: Gill and McMillan, 1973.

Burton, Anthony M. *Urban Terrorism: Theory, Practice and Response*. New York: The Free Press, 1975.

Carr, Gordon. *The Angry Brigade: The Cause and the Case*. London: Gollanz, 1975.

Cassese, Antonio. *Terrorism, Politics, and Law: The Achille Lauro Affair*. London: Basil Blackwell, 1989.

Celmer, Marc A. *Terrorism, U.S. Strategy, and Reagan Policies*. Westport, Conn.: Greenwood Press, 1987.

Chomsky, Noam. *The Culture of Terrorism.* Boston, Mass.: South End Press, 1988.

Clark, Robert P. *The Basque Insurgents.* Madison: University of Wisconsin Press, 1984.

Cline, Ray, and Yonah Alexander. *Terrorism as State-sponsored Covert Warfare.* Fairfax, Va.: Herobook, 1986.

Clutterback, Richard. *Guerrillas and Terrorists.* London: Faber and Faber, 1977.

————. *Kidnap and Ransom: The Response.* London: Faber and Faber, 1978.

Coates, James. *Armed and Dangerous: The Rise of the Survivalist Right* New York: Noonday, 1987.

————. *Pirates and Emperors: International Terrorism in the Real World.* New York: Claremont Research and Publication, 1986.

Cobban, Helena. *The Palestinian Liberation Organization.* Cambridge: Cambridge University Press, 1984.

Demaris, Ovid. *Brothers in Blood: The International Terrorist Network.* New York: Charles Scribner's Sons, 1977.

Dobson, Christopher, and Ronald Payne. *The Carlos Complex: A Study in Terror.* New York: G.P. Putnam's Sons, 1977.

————. *War Without End.* London: Harrap, 1986.

Drake, Richard. *The Revolutionary Mystique and Terrorism in Contemporary Italy.* Bloomington: Indiana University Press, 1989.

Duvall, Raymond and Michael Stohl. *The Politics of Terrorism,* 3rd ed. New York: Marcel Dekker, 1988.

Evans, Ernest. *Calling A Truce to Terror.* Westport, Conn.: Greenwood Press, 1979.

Falk, Richard. *Revolutionaries and Functionaries: The Dual Face of Terrorism.* New York: E.P. Dutton, 1988.

Fontaine, Roger W. *Terrorism: The Cuban Connections.* New York: Crane, Russak & Co., 1988.

Ford, Franklin L. *Political Murder: From Tyrannicide to Terrorism.* Cambridge, Mass.: Harvard University Press, 1985.

Freedman, Lawrence Zelic, and Yonah Alexander, eds. *Perspectives on Terrorism.* Wilmington, Del.: Scholarly Resources Inc., 1983.

Freedman, Lawrence Zelic, *et al. Terrorism and International Order.* London: Routledge and Keegan Paul, for the Royal Institute of International Affairs, 1987.

Gal-Or, Naomi. *International Cooperation to Suppress Terrorism.* London: Croom Helm, 1985.

Gaucher, Roland. *The Terrorists: From Tsarist Russia to the OAS,* translated by Paula Spurlin. London: Secker and Warburg, 1965.

Gordon, David C. *Lebanon: The Fragmented Nation.* London: Croom Helm, 1980.

Gillespie, Richard. *Soldiers of Peron: Argentina's Monteneros.* Oxford: Oxford University Press, 1982.

Grosscup, Beau. *The Explosion of Terrorism.* Far Hills, N.J.: New Horizon Press, 1987.

Guillen, Abraham. *Philosophy of the Urban Guerrilla,* Donald C. Hodges, ed. New York: William Morrow, 1973.

Gutteridge, William, ed. *The New Terrorism.* London: Mansell Publishing Ltd., 1986.

Hans, Rogger, and Eugen Weber. *The European Right.* Berkeley: University of California Press, 1966.

Henze, Paul. *The Plot to Kill the Pope.* New York: Charles Scribner's Sons, 1985.

Hoffman, Bruce. *Terrorism in the United States and the Potential Threat to Nuclear Facilities.* Santa Monica, Calif.: Rand, 1986.

Hussian, Asaf. *Islamic Iran.* London: Frances Pinter Publishers, 1985.

Hyams, Edward. *Terrorists and Terrorism.* New York: St. Martin's Press, 1974.

Jenkins, Brian Michael. *The Lessons of Beirut.* Santa Monica, Calif.: Rand, 1984.

Jennings, Peter. *An End to Terrorism.* Herts, U.K.: Lion Publishing, 1984.

Khalidi, Rashid. *Under Siege: PLO Decisionmaking During the 1982 War.* New York: Columbia University Press, 1986.

Klare, Michael T., and Peter Kornblush, eds. *Low Intensity Warfare: Counterinsurgency, Proinsurgency, and Antiterrorism in the Eighties.* New York: Pantheon, 1988.

Kohl, J., and J. Litt, eds. *Urban Guerrilla Warfare in Latin America.* Cambridge, Mass.: MIT Press, 1974.

Kurz, Anat, ed. *Contemporary Trends in World Terrorism.* New York: Praeger, 1987.

Laqueur, Walter. *The Age of Terrorism.* Boston: Little, Brown & Co., 1987.

——. *Terrorism.* Boston: Little, Brown & Co., 1977.

——. *The Terrorism Reader.* New York: New American Library, 1978.

Lee, Alfred McClung. *Terrorism in Northern Ireland.* Bayside, N.Y.: General Hall Inc., 1988.

Lentz, Harris M., III. *Assassinations and Executions: An Encyclopedia of Political Violence, 1865–1986.* Jefferson, N.C.: McFarland & Co., Inc. Publishers, 1988.

Levitt, Geoffrey M. *Democracies Against Terror.* New York: Praeger, 1988.

Livingston, Marins H. ed. *International Terrorism in the Contemporary World.* Westport, Conn.: Greenwood Press, 1978.

Livingstone, Neil C. *The War Against Terrorism.* Lexington, Mass.: Lexington Books, 1982.

Martin, David, and John Walcott. *Best Laid Plans: The Inside Story of America's War Against Terrorism.* New York: Harper & Row, 1988.

McForan, Desmond. *The World Held Hostage.* London: Oak-Tree Books, 1986.

Merkl, Peter H. *Political Violence and Terror: Motifs and Motivations.* Berkeley: University of California Press, 1986.

Mickolus, Edward F. *Transnational Terrorism: A Chronology of Events, 1968–1979.* Westport, Conn.: Greenwood Press, 1980.

Mickolus, Edward F., Todd Sandler, and Jean M. Murdock. *International Terrorism in the 1980's: A Chronology of Events, 1980–1987,* 2 vols. Ames: Iowa University Press, 1989.

Netanyahu, Benjamin, ed. *Terrorism: How the West Can Win.* New York: Farrar, Strauss, Giroux, 1986.

O'Ballance, Edgar. *Language of Violence: The Blood Politics of Terrorism.* San Rafael, Calif.: Presidio Press, 1979.

O'Brien, Conor Cruise. *Passion and Cunning.* New York: Simon and Schuster, 1985.

O'Neil, Brad, *et al.,* eds. *Insurgency in the Modern World.* Boulder, Colo.: Westview Press, 1980.

O'Sullivan, Noel, ed. *Terrorism, Ideology and Revolution.* Brighton, U.K.: Wheatsheaf Books Ltd., 1986.

Poland, James M. *Understanding Terrorism: Groups, Strategies, and Responses.* Englewood Cliffs, N.J.: Prentice Hall, 1988.

Porter, Jack Nusan, ed. *Genocide and Human Rights.* Washington, D.C.: University Press of America, 1982.

Porzecanski, Arturo. *Uruguay Tupamaros.* New York: Praeger Publishers, 1973.

Rapoport, David C., ed. *Inside Terrorist Organizations.* New York: Columbia University Press, 1988.

Rosie, George. *The Dictionary of International Terrorism.* Edinburgh: Mainstream Publishing, 1986.

Rubenstein, Richard. *Alchemists of Revolution: Terrorism in the Modern World.* New York: Basic Books, 1987.

Schaerf, Carlo, and David Carlton, eds. *Contemporary Terror.* New York: St. Martin's Press, 1978.

Schid, Alex P. *Political Terrorism.* Amsterdam: SWIDOC, 1983.

Schlagheck, Donna. *International Terrorism.* Lexington, Mass.: Lexington Books, 1988.

Seale, Patrick. *Asad of Syria: The Struggle for the Middle East.* Berkeley: University of California Press, 1989.

Segaller, Stephen. *Invisible Armies: Terrorism into the 1990s.* London: Michael Joseph, 1986.

Shafer, D. Michael. *Deadly Paradigms: The Failure of U.S. Counterinsurgency Policy.* Princeton: Princeton University Press, 1988.

Sick, Gary. *All Fall Down: America's Tragic Encounter With Iran.* New York: Random House, 1985.

Simpson, John, and Jana Bennett. *The Disappeared.* London: Robson Books, 1985.

Slann, Martin and Bernard Schectermann, eds. *Multidimensional Terrorism.* Boulder, Colo. Lynne Rienner, 1987.

Smith, Colin. *Carlos: Portrait of a Terrorist.* New York: Holt, Rinehart and Winston, 1976.

Sterling, Claire. *The Terror Network.* New York: Holt, Rinehart and Winston, 1981.

Stohl, Michael. *Terrible Beyond Endurance? The Foreign Policy of State Terrorism.* New York: Greenwood Press, 1988.

Taheri, Amir. *Holy Terror: The Inside Story of Islamic Terrorism.* London: Hutchinson, 1987.

———. *The Spirit of Allah: Khomeini and the Islamic Revolution.* London: Hutchinson, 1985.

Thackrah, John Richard. *Encyclopedia of Terrorism and Political Violence.* London: Routledge and Kegan Paul, 1987.

Theroux, Peter. *The Strange Disappearance of Iman Moussa Sadr.* London: Weidenfeld and Nicolson, 1987.

Watson, Francis M. *Political Terrorism: The Threat and Response.* Washington, D.C.: Robert B. Luce Co., Inc., 1976.

Weinberg, Leonard, and Paul Davis. *Introduction to Political Terrorism.* New York: McGraw-Hill, 1989.

Weinberg, Leonard, and William Lee Eubank. *The Rise and Fall of Italian Terrorism.* Boulder, Colo.: Westview Press, 1987.

Wilkinson, Paul, ed. *British Perspectives on Terrorism.* London: George, Allen & Unwin, 1981.

Wilkinson, Paul, and Alasdair M. Stewart, eds. *Contemporary Research on Terrorism.* Aberdeen: Aberdeen University Press, 1987.

Wright, Robin. *Sacred Rage.* New York: Simon & Schuster, 1985.

MONOGRAPHS AND ARTICLES:

Aston, Clive C. "Political Hostage Taking in Western Europe." *Conflict Studies* 157 (1984).

Austen, Dennis, and Anirudha Gupta. "Lions and Tigers: The Crisis in Sri Lanka." *Conflict Studies* 211 (1988).

Bagley, Bruce M. "Colombia and the War on Drugs." *Foreign Affairs* 67 (Fall 1988): 70–92.

———. "Colombia: The Wrong Strategy." *Foreign Policy* 77 (Winter 1989–90): 154–71.

Baratta, Robert Thomas. "Political Violence in Ecuador and the AVC." *Terrorism* 10 (1987): 165–74.

Bell, J. Bowyer. "Assassination in International Politics: Lord Moyne, Count Bernadotte, and the Lehi." *International Studies Quarterly* 1 (1972): 59–82.

Bernstein, Alvin H. "Iran's Low Intensity War with the United States." *Orbis* 30 (Spring 1986): 149–67.

Brenchley, Frank. "Diplomatic Immunities and State-sponsored Terrorism." *Conflict Studies* 164 (1984).

——. "Living With Terrorism: The Problem of Air Piracy." *Conflict Studies* 184 (1986).

Brock, David. "The World of Narcoterrorism." *American Spectator* 22 (June 1989): 24–28.

Browning, David. "Conflicts in El Salvador." *Conflict Studies* 168 (1984).

Clawson, Patrick. "Coping with Terrorism in the United States." *Orbis* 33 (Summer 1989): 341–56.

Clissold, Stephen. "Croat Separatism: Nationalism, Dissidence, and Terrorism." *Conflict Studies* 103 (1979).

Crenshaw, Martha. "The Causes of Terrorism." *Comparative Politics,* 13 (1981): 379–97.

Garfincle, Adam "Sources of the Al-Fatah Mutiny." *Orbis* 27 (1983).

Green, L. C. "Terrorism and its Responses." *Terrorism* 8 (1985): 33–77.

Gunter, Michael. "The Armenian Terrorist Campaign Against Turkey." *Orbis* 27 (Summer 1983): 447–77.

——. "Contemporary Armenian Terrorism." *Terrorism* 8 (1986): 213–52.

Gutteridge, William, ed. "Libya: Still a Threat to Western Interests?" *Conflict Studies* 160 (1984).

Halperin, Ernst. "Terrorist in Latin America." *The Washington Papers* 33, The Center for Strategic and International Studies, Georgetown University, 1976.

Horchem, Hans Josef. "Terrorism in West Germany." *Conflict Studies* 186 (1986).

Hunter, Shireen T. "Terrorism: A Balance Sheet." *The Washington Quarterly* 12 (Summer 1989): 17–32.

Institute for the Study of Conflict. "Northern Ireland: An Anglo-Irish Dilemma?" *Conflict Studies* 185 (1986).

James, Alan. "Interminable Interim: The UN Force in Lebanon." *Conflict Studies* 210 (1988).

Jenkins, Brian. "New Modes of Conflict." *Orbis* 28 (Spring 1984): 5–16.

Kerr, Donald M. "Coping With Terrorism." *Terrorism* 8 (1985): 113–26.

Kidder, Rushworth. "State-Sponsored Terrorism." *The Christian Science Monitor* (May 14, 1986): 11–24.

Kim, Jae Taik. "North Korean Terrorism: Trends, Characteristics and Deferrence." *Terrorism* 11 (1988): 309–22.

Laqueur, Walter. "The Origins of Guerrilla Doctrine." *Journal of Contemporary History* 10 (July 1975).

——. "Reflections on Terrorism." *Foreign Affairs* 65 (Fall 1986): 86–100.

LeMoyne, James. "El Salvador's Forgotten War." *Foreign Affairs* 68 (Summer 1989): 105–25.

Livingstone, Neil C. "Death Squads." *World Affairs* 146 (1983–84).

Merari, Ariel. "Classification of Terrorist Groups." *Terrorism* 1 (1978): 331–46.

Moxon-Browne, Edward. "Spain and the ETA: The Bid for Basque Autonomy." *Conflict Studies* 201 (1987).

New York State Policy Group on Terrorism, Report on the Brinks Incident. *Terrorism* 9 (1987): 169–206.

Nice, David C. "Abortion Clinic Bombings as Political Violence." *American Journal of Political Science* 32 (February 1988): 178–95.

Oakley, Robert. "International Terrorism." *Foreign Affairs* 65 (Summer 1987): 611–29.

Peretz, Don. "Intifadeh: The Palestinian Uprising." *Foreign Affairs* 66 (Summer 1988): 964–80.

Rapoport, David C. "Fear and Trembling: Terrorism in Three Religious Traditions." *The American Political Science Review* 78 (1984): 658–77.

——. "Messianic Sanctions for Terror." *Comparative Politics* 20 (January 1988): 195–213.

Reinares, Fernando. "Nationalism and Violence in Basque Politics." *Conflict* 8: 141–55.

Ross, Jeffery Ian. "Attributes of Domestic Political Terrorism in Canada." *Terrorism* 11 (1988): 213–33.

Russell, Charles A., and Bowman H. Miller. "Profile of a Terrorist." *Terrorism* 1 (1977): 17–34.

Scherer, John L. "The Plot to Kill the Pope." *Terrorism* 7 (1985): 351–66.

Stohl, Michael. "National Interests and State Terrorism in International Affairs." *Political Science* 36 (July 1984).

Suall, Irwin, and David Lowe. "The Hate Movement Today: A Chronicle of Violence and Disarray." *Terrorism.* 10 (1987): 345–64.

Vice President's Task Force on Combatting Terrorism. *Public Report of the Vice President's Task Force on Combatting Terrorism.* Washington, D.C.: Government Printing Office, 1986.

Villalobos, Joaquin. "A Democratic Revolution For El Salvador." *Foreign Policy* 74 (Spring 1989): 103–22.

Wardlaw, Grant. "Linkages Between Illegal Drugs Traffic and Terrorism." *Conflict* 8 (Summer 1988): 5–26.

Wilson, Michele, and John Lynxwiler. "Abortion Clinic Violence as Terrorism." *Terrorism* 11 (1988): 263–74.

INDEX